New Perspectives on Kristallnacht: After 80 Years, The Nazi Pogrom in Global Comparison

The Jewish Role in American Life

An Annual Review of the Casden Institute for the Study of the Jewish Role in American Life

New Perspectives on Kristallnacht: After 80 Years, the Nazi Pogrom in Global Comparison

The Jewish Role in American Life

An Annual Review of the Casden Institute for the Study of the Jewish Role in American Life

Volume 17

Steven J. Ross, *Editor*
Wolf Gruner, *Guest Editor*
Lisa Ansell, *Associate Editor*

Published by the Purdue University Press for the USC Casden Institute for the Study of the Jewish Role in American Life

© 2019
University of Southern California
Casden Institute for the
Study of the Jewish Role in American Life.
All rights reserved.

Production Editor, Marilyn Lundberg

Cover photo supplied by the Private Archive Elisheva Avital Family, New Jersey.
Attack on a Jewish home by SA men, probably Nuremberg, November 9–10, 1938.
Back cover photo supplied by the Jewish Federation Council of Greater Los Angeles, Community Relations Committee Collection, Part 2, Special Collections and Archives, Oviatt Library, California State University, Northridge.
Anti-Nazi Protest Outside Deutsches Haus, Los Angeles, August 1938.

Paperback ISBN: 978-1-55753-870-3
ePDF ISBN: 978-1-61249-617-7
ePUB ISBN: 978-1-61249-616-0

Published by Purdue University Press
West Lafayette, Indiana
www.press.purdue.edu
pupress@purdue.edu

Printed in the United States of America.

For subscription information,
call 1-800-247-6553

Contents

FOREWORD vii

EDITORIAL INTRODUCTION ix

CHAPTER 1
Ulrich Baumann and François Guesnet 1
Kristallnacht—Pogrom—State Terror: A Terminological Reflection

CHAPTER 2
Wolf Gruner 25
"Worse Than Vandals." The Mass Destruction of Jewish Homes
and Jewish Responses during the 1938 Pogrom

CHAPTER 3
Maximilian Strnad 51
A Question of Gender! Spaces of Violence and Reactions to
Kristallnacht in Jewish-Gentile Families

CHAPTER 4
Mary Fulbrook 69
Social Relations and Bystander Responses to Violence:
Kristallnacht November 1938

CHAPTER 5
Norman Domeier 91
A Scream, Then Silence. Kristallnacht and the American
Journalists in Nazi Germany: The "Night of Broken Glass"
as an Unwanted Transnational Media Event

CHAPTER 6
Anne-Christin Klotz 115
Journalism as a Weapon: Jewish Journalists from Warsaw
and the Production of Knowledge during Hitler's Rise to
Power in 1933 and the November Pogroms in 1938

CHAPTER 7
Jeffrey Koerber 149
What Did Soviet Jews Make of Kristallnacht?
The Nazi Threat in the Soviet Press

CHAPTER 8
Stephanie Seul 171
The Absence of "Kristallnacht" and Its Aftermath in
BBC German-language Broadcasts during 1938–1939

CHAPTER 9
Gershon Greenberg   195
Orthodox Jewish Reflective Responses to Kristallnacht

CHAPTER 10
Hasia Diner   215
1938: American Jews Respond to a Very Bad Year

CHAPTER 11
Steven J. Ross   237
The Ambiguous Legacy of Kristallnacht: Nazis,
Jewish Resistors, and Anti-Semitism in Los Angeles

CHAPTER 12
Alexander Walther   259
Jewish Anti-Fascism? "Kristallnacht" Remembrance
in the GDR between Propaganda and Jewish Self-Assertion

CHAPTER 13
Liat Steir-Livny   283
"Kristallnacht in Tel Aviv": Nazi Associations in the
Contemporary Israeli Socio-Political Debate

CHAPTER 14
Nathalie Ségeral   311
The Kristallnacht Paradigm in Narratives by
Survivors of the Rwandan and Rohingya Genocides

CHAPTER 15
Baijayanti Roy   333
The Long Shadow of the "Kristallnacht" on the
"Gujarat Pogrom" in India? A Comparative Analysis

ABOUT THE CONTRIBUTORS   359

ABOUT THE USC CASDEN INSTITUTE   365

Foreword

The idea for a volume reassessing Kristallnacht came together at the Association of Jewish Studies Conference in December 2016. At the time, I was writing about the impact of Kristallnacht in Los Angeles, while my colleague Wolf Gruner, the Shapell-Guerin Chair in Jewish Studies and History and founding director of the USC Shoah Foundation Center for Advanced Genocide Research, was researching the mass destruction of private homes and Jewish reactions toward violence during the November 1938 pogroms.

The historical works I consulted suggested that the horrors of Kristallnacht turned American—and much of world—public opinion against the Hitler regime. Yet, what I discovered was that despite worldwide condemnations, very little changed for Jews in the United States. Although American anti-Nazi groups became more forceful in their attacks on Nazi Germany after the November 1938 massacres, so, too, did members of the German-American Bund grow more militant. Inspired by the lack of western opposition to Hitler, Bundists began preparing in earnest for *Der Tag*, the day Nazis would seize control of the American government.

If the American response to Kristallnacht was more complicated than historians had suggested, I wondered how much more complex European responses must have been. With the 80th anniversary of Kristallnacht only two years away, Wolf Gruner—who was far more expert in the period—and I agreed to organize an international conference that would reassess the worldwide impact of the horrible events of November 9–10, 1938. With the help of outside funders and the staff from our two institutes—the USC Casden Institute and the Center for Advanced Genocide Research—we succeeded in bringing twenty-two scholars from six countries to the University of Southern California on November 5–7, 2018 to reassess the events surrounding Kristallnacht and its lasting legacy.

Volume 17 of the *Casden Annual* includes fifteen of the articles presented at our conference "New Perspectives on Kristallnacht: After 80 Years, the Nazi

Pogrom in Global Comparison." Examining events eighty years after the violent pogrom of 1938, contributors to this volume offer new cutting-edge scholarship on the event and its repercussions. We hope the essays will inspire further research into one of the most important tragedies of the twentieth century.

I wish to thank my co-editor, Wolf Gruner, for helping to make the conference and this volume a reality. I also wish to thank Marilyn Lundberg Melzian for her wonderful work as our volume's production editor.

Steven J. Ross
Myron and Marian Casden Director
Professor of History

Editorial Introduction

by Wolf Gruner and Steven J. Ross

On November 9 and 10, 1938, under the pretext of revenge for the assassination of a Nazi diplomat by a young Polish Jew, SS, SA, and citizens in Germany, Austria, and the Sudetenland, acting on orders of the Nazi leadership, launched the deadliest violence in the region's history. Armed with axes and sledgehammers, with gasoline and pistols, groups of perpetrators systematically demolished Jewish synagogues, schools, businesses and other properties while looting, beating, raping, and murdering innocent Jews. By the time Joseph Goebbels stopped the violence, the soon-dubbed "Kristallnacht" pogrom left an unknown number of Jewish men and women dead (estimates are as high as several hundred), more than ten thousand Jewish businesses destroyed, and over two thousand synagogues burned to the ground; thirty thousand male Jews were arrested and sent to Nazi concentration camps, where several hundred more died from beatings, starvation, and cold.[1]

The reasons for the violence went back to the end of 1937, when the Nazi leadership began to realize that strategies developed since 1933 to expel the Jews from Germany stalled because of the growing pauperization of the Jewish population and the unwillingness of countries abroad to accept Jewish refugees and emigrants. After Germany annexed Austria in March 1938, previous efforts at expulsion evaporated, as greater numbers of Jews lived under Nazi rule.[2] Moreover, a war seemed increasingly imminent as the political crisis over the Sudeten Germans in Czechoslovakia heated up. The Nazi leadership, however, was determined to drive all Jews out of the country before the outbreak of a potential war. In August 1938, the Nazi state decided to dedicate all its hard currency to prepare for war instead of financing mass emigration. This created a fundamental dilemma: on the one hand, the Nazis wanted all Jews to leave as soon as possible; on the other hand, they did not want Jewish emigration to cost the Nazi regime any money. To cut this Gordian knot of the expulsion policy, which the government itself had tied, the Nazi leadership proceeded with violence and brutality. On the evening of November 9, 1938 in Munich, after learning about the passing of the German diplomat vom Rath in Paris, Hitler decided that the Jews should now "feel the force of the people's rage," and Goebbels gave later instructions on how this "upsurge" of popular anger should be organized.[3]

However, even with the launch of previously unprecedented, organized nationwide anti-Jewish violence, the National Socialist leadership did not succeed in their main goal: to expel all Jews from the German Reich. Blaming the victims for instigating the violence, the Nazi government imposed a $400 million (1 Billion Reichmark) fine upon the German Jewish community. Yet, the lack of money prevented many Jews from leaving. The Nazi leadership, thus, developed a new double strategy: to force emigration by all means, while separating the remaining Jews from the rest of society.[4]

This volume offers new and innovative scholarly research that changes our traditional views of the course of and the reactions to the violent anti-Jewish event. The selected essays originate from an international conference, "New Perspectives on Kristallnacht: After 80 Years, the Nazi Pogrom in Global Comparison," held on November 5–7, 2018 at the University of Southern California in Los Angeles and Villa Aurora in Pacific Palisades. This was the only international academic conference to mark the 80th anniversary of the fateful events of November 1938.

The event was co-organized by the USC Shoah Foundation Center for Advanced Genocide Research and the USC Casden Institute for the Study of the Jewish Role in American Life, and presented in cooperation with the Jack, Joseph and Morton Mandel Center for Advanced Holocaust Studies at the US Holocaust Memorial Museum, Washington DC, and the Center for Research on Antisemitism at the Technical University Berlin, Germany. Our gathering featured twenty-two junior and senior scholars from six countries (the United States, Germany, Israel, Canada, the United Kingdom and India), who represented multiple disciplines, including history, literature, philosophy, religion, political science, film and cultural studies, and French and Jewish studies. The conference aimed to resituate the anti-Jewish pogrom in its historical context as well as its place in world history.

NEW RESEARCH ON THE VIOLENT EVENTS

Kristallnacht is often thought of as one of the most well researched events in the history of the Third Reich. The essays in this volume challenge a variety of traditional perceptions of the pogrom of November 1938 and explore facets of the two days of carnage throughout Greater Germany that have not received significant scholarly attention. Our authors offer insights into new aspects of the violence, including the impact of violence on gender, the mass participation of citizens in rioting, the destruction of homes, and the wide variety of Jewish reactions—from the Yiddish press in Eastern Europe to orthodox rabbis throughout the world to Jewish organizations in the United States. The volume's concluding essays examine the lingering global legacy of Kristallnacht by exploring violent events in Rwanda, India, and Israel.

In the opening chapter, Francois Guesnet (London) and Ulrich Baumann (Berlin) trace historical shifts in terminology regarding the events of November 9–10, 1938—shifts that carry enormous political implications. At the time it occurred, the November violence was widely referred to as a pogrom, while soon after 1945 politicians and scholars referred to it as *Kristallnacht* or *Reichskristallnacht*, a term that had emerged before the war ended. However, over the past several decades, historians and citizens—especially in Germany—started using the term pogrom or November pogrom, since they found the former too euphemistic for the violent event. The authors make us aware that these terms and their use deserve further scrutiny. For the authors, pogrom generally refers to unplanned eruptions of anti-Semitic violence by local groups, yet the events in November 1938 need to be understood as state-sponsored violence. To label them as pogroms, they argue, is to minimize the scope of violence by simply attributing it to disgruntled local anti-Semites rather than to a clear government policy. Thus, both authors advocate using "state terror"—not pogrom—as a term that better captures the centrally organized dimensions of Kristallnacht.

Wolf Gruner's research provides surprising insights into two greatly overlooked aspects of Kristallnacht: the mass destruction of private homes, and, Jewish reactions toward violence. Using examples drawn from large cities and small towns throughout Greater Germany, he reveals how the demolition and vandalizing of Jewish homes was systematic and of an astonishing scale and intensity. The widespread destruction of home furnishings was accompanied by beatings, sexual violence and murder. This rampant violation of privacy had enormous impact on families and on the Jewish population as a whole. Gruner also shows how Jews reacted in unexpected ways to the violent event:

Jews petitioned the Gestapo to stop violence and arrests; they documented the destruction of synagogues and shops; they protested in public or with anonymous letters; and they physically defended themselves from attacks.

Examining the gendered nature of violence against married Jewish-Christian couples, Maximilian Strnad argues that mixed religious households headed by Jewish men experienced far more death and destruction during Kristallnacht than those headed by Christian husbands and their Jewish wives. Jewish-headed mixed households also had higher rates of family separations and divorces following the November violence. For intermarried Jews, Strnad concludes, the feeling of being responsible for the misery their families experienced often lasted for decades.

Mary Fulbrook turns our attention to the less well-understood role of ordinary citizens in "bystander" violence, passivity, complicity, and courage during the November terror. She explores five categories of what she calls "bystander" reaction: active intervention on behalf of victims; demonstrative sympathy for victims; neutral, inactive, impassive eyewitnesses; support for acts of perpetrators; and, active participatory complicity on the side of perpetrators.

ON MEDIA AND OTHER REACTIONS

The extraordinary violence unleashed during Kristallnacht was reported in newspapers, radios, and newsreels throughout the world. Various essays in this volume explode the myth that people around the world did not know what was happening in Germany. Norman Domeier examines media coverage of Kristallnacht by American journalists based in Berlin. Drawing from a wide variety of sources, Domeier details the experiences, reports, and reflections of four journalists who wrote for the *New York Times,* the *New York Herald Tribune* and the Associated Press. His chapter shows how quick and thorough the event was covered in the American press. Domeier argues that until December 1941, the American public was the best-informed public in the world about Nazi Germany.[5]

Chapters by Anne-Christin Klotz and Jeffrey Koerber dealing with press coverage of Kristallnacht in Poland and the Soviet Union deepen our understanding of what was known and shared among Jewish and non-Jewish citizens in both countries at the time. Klotz examines the ways in which Polish-Jewish journalists and the Yiddish press in Warsaw reported on events in Germany from 1933 to 1938. She recounts the extent to which reporters actively tried to help Jewish compatriots suffering inside the Nazi regime. Journalists found the boundaries between "objective" reportage and activism continually blurred during times of crisis. Likewise, Koerber looks at the ways in which Soviet Yiddish- and Russian-language newspapers covered growing anti-Semitism in Germany—coverage that allowed Jewish readers to follow developments in Nazi Germany long before the onset of World War II. He explores the similarities and differences between the coverage of events by the Soviet Yiddish- and Russian-language newspapers.

Turning to Great Britain, Stephanie Seul describes how Kristallnacht caused an outcry from the British press and Parliament but not from the BBC—which acted as an unofficial wing of the Foreign Office. Both the government and the BBC's German-language broadcasts refrained from criticizing the event or the Hitler regime. Seul argues they did this for three reasons: Whitehall feared that any public condemnation of Germany would worsen the situation for its Jewish residents; the British government viewed anti-Jewish policy as a purely German internal affair; and, finally, Prime Minister Neville Chamberlain believed his nation was not militarily prepared for war and therefore did not want to risk aggravating already tense relations with Nazi Germany.

The media was not the only source of information about Kristallnacht or the only ones to analyze the event and the causes of rising anti-Semitism in Germany. Jewish thinkers and organizations throughout the world tried to make sense of the difficult situation unfolding before their eyes. Gershon Greenberg looks at how Orthodox Jewish rabbis and commentators in Eastern Europe, Palestine, and the United States responded to the violent events of Kristallnacht. Many Orthodox writers (predominantly rabbis), he argues, blamed the events of November 1938 on German Jews who were supposedly being punished by God for abandoning Torah in favor of assimilation.

Looking beyond the usual government and public responses in the United States, Hasia Diner sees 1938 as a turning point for Jews in America.[6] Rejecting the idea of American Jewish passivity, she argues that following Hitler's rise to power many groups and individuals discussed the best ways to respond to growing repression and anti-Semitism in Germany. The events of 1938, culminating in Kristallnacht, motivated American Jews to act, organize, and speak out. Diner details the range of communal reactions and responses, including raising funds for refugees, greater public and political advocacy, forming Jewish community councils, and reorganizing Jewish organizations to respond more quickly to escalating dangers and needs both abroad and in the United States.

Steven J. Ross argues that Kristallnacht had a major impact in the United States, but not in the way we usually think. Focusing on Los Angeles, he shows how Nazi aggression abroad was accompanied by Nazi aggression at home as local Bundists secretly began preparing for *Der Tag*, "the day" when Nazis and their supporters would seize control of the American government. Yet, the knowledge of the Kristallnacht violence also produced an increase in local Jewish resistance. Leon Lewis, who had run a local spy ring against pro-Nazi activities in Los Angeles since the summer of 1933, stepped up his efforts at infiltration and surveillance after November 1938, and passed on information gleaned from his undercover operatives to the FBI, and Naval and Army Intelligence that helped foil a series of Nazi and fascist plots aimed at murder and sabotage in California.

AFTERMATH AND LEGACY

The legacy of Kristallnacht lasted for decades well beyond the November terror and in places well beyond Greater Germany. Alexander Walther challenges the supposed absence of commemorations in East Germany. Kristallnacht and the Shoah, he argues, were memorialized throughout the GDR's existence. Yet, for most of that time, East German authorities used November 9 commemorations to celebrate communist resistance to Nazism and to criticize capitalist West Germany, while—as an overlooked aspect—the East German Jewish communities used the days of commemoration for their political agenda and internal audience. Not until the 1970s, and especially after the collapse of the GDR, was East Germany's Jewish minority (especially its survivors) able to highlight the experiences and sufferings of the state-sponsored November pogrom's Jewish victims to a broader public.

Turning to Israel, Liat Steir-Livny shows how left and right public figures have used the memory of Kristallnacht and the Holocaust in varied ways to boost their political agendas. Her essay examines a violent demonstration against African immigrants orchestrated by right-wing activists in South Tel Aviv on May 23, 2012, which was immediately dubbed and condemned by left-leaning political groups as "Kristallnacht in Tel Aviv." Israelis on both sides of the ideological spectrum used social media to exploit the original histori-

Editorial Introduction

cal event by turning references to Kristallnacht into a series of symbols and memes, while newspapers in Europe, Russia, and the United States referred to the Tel Aviv riots as the "Israeli Kristallnacht." By so doing, Steir-Livny argues, Israelis and media coverage deprived the 1938 event of its profound historical context and meaning and turned Kristallnacht into a simple metaphor for shattered property and violence toward "others."

Associations of racial violence and Kristallnacht also made their way into literary narratives written by survivors of the Rwandan genocide and the mass violence in Myanmar. Focusing on works by Rwandan Scholastique Mukasonga and Rohingyan Habiburahamn, Nathalie Ségeral describes how these authors used the terms Kristallnacht, pogrom, and Holocaust when referring to the waves of massacres perpetrated by the Hutu against the Tutsi from the late 1950s to the culmination of violence during the 1994 genocide, and to the persecution of the Burmese Rohingyas that lasted until 2018. In both instances, she concludes, the Kristallnacht paradigm is employed as highly relevant to contemporary "minority" histories and as the lasting symbol of a turning point in genocidal violence.

The volume's concluding chapter brings our discussion back to the opening essay's concern with terminology. Baijayanti Roy compares the German pogrom of November 1938 with the "Gujarat pogrom" perpetrated by members of the majority Hindu community against the minority Muslims in the Indian federal state of Gujarat between February 28 and March 1, 2002. Although often referred to in the press as a pogrom, Roy—like Baumann and Guesnet—argues that the violence was not spontaneous (as were most pogroms) but was comprised of a series of premeditated, carefully orchestrated attacks on Muslims instigated by today's Indian prime minister and back-then chief minister of Gujarat Narendra Modi and right-wing Hindu nationalist groups with the aim of ethnic cleansing. The deadly state-sponsored violence that left one thousand to two thousand dead (mostly Muslims) and 150,000 rendered homeless, she argues, had more in common with the Nazi state sponsored "Kristallnacht" than it did with more spontaneous communal oriented pogroms of Eastern Europe.

This volume marks the beginning of what we hope will be a major re-examination of Kristallnacht, an event that many perceive as a turning point leading to the Holocaust. Our authors demonstrate how important new knowledge can be gained by re-approaching a well-known event and challenging traditional assumptions. Yet, there is so much more to explore about Kristallnacht that goes beyond the themes raised in this volume. In particular, we need to know more about the reactions and responses, the defiance and resistance of the individual Jews and their organizations and communities. Likewise, we need a fuller exploration of the participation of ordinary Germans and Austrians in the destruction and plunder, the sexual violence and murders, which seemed to have been more widespread than previously assumed. Finally, we need to understand the context and lasting legacy of the state sponsored terror of November 1938. We hope that scholars will use this volume as a launching point for exploring new avenues and interdisciplinary perspectives on one of the crucial events of the twentieth century.

Notes

1. For histories of Kristallnacht, see Lionel Kochan, *Pogrom: November 10, 1938* (London: Andre Deutsch, 1957); Rita Thalmann and Emmanuel Feinermann, *Crystal Night: 9–10 November 1938* (New York: Holocaust Library, 1974); John Mendelsohn, *The Holocaust: The Crystal Night Pogrom*, vol. 3 (New York: Garland, 1982); *Kristallnacht: November 9–10, 1938: A Resource Book and Program Guide* (Los Angeles: Simon Wiesenthal Center, 1988); Kurt Pätzold and Irene Runge, *Pogromnacht 1938* (Berlin: Dietz, 1988); Wolf-Arno Kropat, *"Reichskristallnacht." Der Judenpogrom vom 7. bis 10. November 1938. Urheber, Täter, Hintergründe. Mit ausgewählten Dokumenten* (Wiesbaden: Kommission für die Geschichte der Juden in Hessen, 1988); Dieter Obst, *"Reichskristallnacht." Ursachen und Verlauf des antisemitischen Pogroms vom November 1938* (Frankfurt am Main: Peter Lang, 1991); Anthony Read and David Fisher, *Kristallnacht: The Nazi Night of Terror* (New York: Crown, 1990); Walter H. Pehle, ed., *November 1938: From "Reichskristallnacht" to Genocide* (New York: Berg, 1991); Andreas Heusler and Tobias Weger, *"Kristallnacht." Gewalt gegen die Münchner Juden im November 1938* (Munich: Buchendorfer, 1998); Martin Gilbert, *Kristallnacht: Prelude to Destruction* (New York: HarperCollins, 2006); Mitchell G. Bard, *48 Hours of Kristallnacht: Night of Destruction/Dawn of the Holocaust* (n.p.: Lyons Press, 2008); Bastian Fleermann and Angela Genger, eds., *Novemberpogrom 1938 in Düsseldorf* (Essen: Klartext Verlag, 2008); Alan Steinweis, *Kristallnacht 1938* (Cambridge, MA: Belknap Press, 2009); Andreas Nachama, Uwe Neumärker, and Hermann Simon, eds., *Fire! Anti-Jewish Terror on "Kristallnacht" in November 1938* (Berlin: Topography of Terror, 2009); Uta Gerhardt and Thomas Karlauf, *The Night of Broken Glass: Eyewitness Accounts of Kristallnacht* (Malden, MA: Polity, 2012); Siegfried Breuer, *Kristallnacht—The Night of Broken Glass* (Amazon Digital Services, 2015); Wolfgang Benz, *Gewalt im November 1938. Die "Reichskristallnacht." Initial zum Holocaust* (Berlin: Metropol Verlag, 2018); Daniel Ristau, *Bruch|Stücke. Die Novemberpogrome in Sachsen 1938* (Berlin: Hentrich und Hentrich Verlag, 2018).
2. For this and the following, see Wolf Gruner, "Vertreibungen, Annexionen, Massenauswanderung. Die NS-Judenpolitik und Èvian im Jahre 1938," in *Jahrbuch für Antisemitismusforschung*, 2019 (Berlin: Metropol, forthcoming).
3. On Hitler's instructions, see Goebbels diary entry, November 10, 1938: Elke Fröhlich, ed., *Die Tagebücher des Joseph Goebbels*, Teil I: *Aufzeichnungen 1923–1941*, Band 6: August 1938—Juni 1939 (Munich: de Gruyter Saur, 1998), 180.
4. Friedländer, *Nazi Germany*, 310.
5. Deborah Lipstadt, *Beyond Belief: The American Press and the Coming of the Holocaust, 1933–1945* (New York: Free Press, 1986); Barry Trachtenberg, *The United States and the Nazi Holocaust: Race, Refuge, and Remembrance* (New York: Bloomsbury, 2018).

6. For American reactions to Kristallnacht, see Arthur D. Morse, *While Six Million Died: A Chronicle of American Apathy* (New York: Random House, 1968); Haskel Lookstein, *Were We Our Brothers' Keepers? The Public Response of American Jews to the Holocaust* (New York: Hartmore House, 1985); Maria Mazzenga, ed., *American Religious Responses to Kristallnacht* (New York: Palgrave Macmillan, 2009); Trachtenberg, *The United States and the Nazi Holocaust*.

Bibliography

Bard, Mitchell G. *48 Hours of Kristallnacht: Night of Destruction/Dawn of the Holocaust.* N.p.: Lyons Press, 2008.

Benz, Wolfgang. *Gewalt im November 1938. Die "Reichskristallnacht." Initial zum Holocaust.* Berlin: Metropol Verlag, 2018.

Breuer, Siegfried. *Kristallnacht—The Night of Broken Glass.* Amazon Digital Services, 2015.

Fleermann, Bastian, and Angela Genger, eds. *Novemberpogrom 1938 in Düsseldorf.* Essen: Klartext Verlag, 2008.

Fröhlich, Elke, ed. *Die Tagebücher des Joseph Goebbels,* Teil I: *Aufzeichnungen 1923–1941,* Band 6: August 1938—Juni 1939. Munich: de Gruyter Saur, 1998.

Gerhardt, Uta, and Thomas Karlauf. *The Night of Broken Glass: Eyewitness Accounts of Kristallnacht.* Malden, MA: Polity, 2012.

Gilbert, Martin. *Kristallnacht: Prelude to Destruction.* New York: HarperCollins, 2006.

Gruner, Wolf. "Vertreibungen, Annexionen, Massenauswanderung. Die NS-Judenpolitik und Èvian im Jahre 1938." In *Jahrbuch für Antisemitismusforschung,* 2019. Berlin: Metropol, forthcoming.

Heusler, Andreas, and Tobias Weger. *"Kristallnacht." Gewalt gegen die Münchner Juden im November 1938.* Munich: Buchendorfer, 1998.

Kochan, Lionel. *Pogrom: November 10, 1938.* London: Andre Deutsch, 1957.

Kristallnacht: November 9–10, 1938: A Resource Book and Program Guide. Los Angeles: Simon Wiesenthal Center, 1988.

Kropat, Wolf-Arno. *"Reichskristallnacht." Der Judenpogrom vom 7. bis 10. November 1938. Urheber, Täter, Hintergründe. Mit ausgewählten Dokumenten.* Wiesbaden: Kommission für die Geschichte der Juden in Hessen, 1988.

Lipstadt, Deborah. *Beyond Belief: The American Press and the Coming of the Holocaust, 1933–1945.* New York: Free Press, 1986.

Lookstein, Haskel. *Were We Our Brothers' Keepers? The Public Response of American Jews to the Holocaust.* New York: Hartmore House, 1985.

Mazzenga, Maria, ed. *American Religious Responses to Kristallnacht.* New York: Palgrave Macmillan, 2009.

Mendelsohn, John. *The Holocaust: The Crystal Night Pogrom.* Vol. 3. New York: Garland, 1982.

Morse, Arthur D. *While Six Million Died: A Chronicle of American Apathy.* New York: Random House, 1968.

Nachama, Andreas, Uwe Neumärker, and Hermann Simon, eds. *Fire! Anti-Jewish Terror on "Kristallnacht" in November 1938.* Berlin: Topography of Terror, 2009.

Obst, Dieter. *"Reichskristallnacht." Ursachen und Verlauf des antisemitischen Pogroms vom November 1938.* Frankfurt am Main: Peter Lang, 1991.

Pätzold, Kurt, and Irene Runge. *Pogromnacht 1938*. Berlin: Dietz, 1988.

Pehle, Walter H., ed. *November 1938: From "Reichskristallnacht" to Genocide*. New York: Berg, 1991.

Read, Anthony, and David Fisher. *Kristallnacht: The Nazi Night of Terror*. New York: Crown, 1990.

Ristau, Daniel. *Bruch|Stücke. Die Novemberpogrome in Sachsen 1938*. Berlin: Hentrich und Hentrich Verlag, 2018.

Steinweis, Alan. *Kristallnacht 1938*. Cambridge, MA: Belknap Press, 2009.

Thalmann, Rita, and Emmanuel Feinermann. *Crystal Night: 9–10 November 1938*. New York: Holocaust Library, 1974.

Trachtenberg, Barry. *The United States and the Nazi Holocaust: Race, Refuge, and Remembrance*. New York: Bloomsbury, 2018.

CHAPTER 1

Kristallnacht—Pogrom—State Terror: A Terminological Reflection

by Ulrich Baumann and François Guesnet

INTRODUCTION

The past several decades have witnessed a major shift in terminology concerning the events of November 9 and 10, 1938 in Nazi Germany and Austria, namely from "Kristallnacht" to "Pogrom." Given that the attacks against the Jewish population represented a major stepping stone from discrimination and exclusion of German and Austrian Jews to persecution and violence, it seems remarkable that this shift in terminology—its context and motivations—has not been investigated by historians more carefully. This chapter questions and challenges in particular the motives for the ubiquitous use of the term "pogrom," both in academic and non-academic parlance, for this terror attack on the Jewish population under Nazi control in November 1938. "Pogrom" seems to reflect an urge for an expression commensurate to the horror with which we view such a case of organized violence upon a defenseless minority. It furthermore avoids the risk in using a euphemism, such as "Kristallnacht," a term which was apparently coined shortly after the events. For these good reasons, the term "Kristallnacht" has somewhat faded to the background.

This chapter posits that the term "pogrom" is equally misleading, if only for a different set of reasons. As we will demonstrate, it refers in its original eastern European setting to interethnic violence in consequence of a breakdown in the complex social and cultural interaction between majority and minority groups. The inaction or ambivalence in the attitude of state actors is of crucial relevance in these occurrences, very much in contrast to the events in 1938, when the Nazi regime unleashed its destructive potential on the already diminished Jewish community under its control. Not in the least because of the centrality of the events in November 1938, it is more than appropriate to use more adequate terminology, as will be suggested in the conclusion of this chapter.

In the immediate context of the events, a variety of terms were used. The perpetrators—various agencies of the Nazi regime—called the attack on German and Austrian Jewries an "Aktion," the "Judenaktion," "Vergeltungsaktion" (revenge action) or "Rath-Aktion," after Ernst vom Rath, the murdered German diplomat. At that time, the oddly sarcastic and inappropriate term "Reichskristallnacht" emerged. It is first recorded in June 1939, in a speech by the NSDAP speaker Wilhelm Börger (1896–1962), at a party convention in Lüneburg about the policies of the regime towards the Jews.[1] In it, he referred to the term "Reichskristallnacht" as having "elevated [the attack on the Jews] through humour":[2]

> After the Reichskristallnacht last year, November 11, for instance—look, this matter enters history as Reichskristallnacht [*applause, laughter*]. You see, this has thus been elevated by humour, well. One might have asked, is this economically viable? One has to import the window panes from Belgium, for foreign currency. One can have different views on this. One thing however is for sure: they [the Jews] now know perfectly well: when one pushes the button, the bell rings, everywhere [*laughter*].

The most likely origin of the term "Reichskristallnacht" is Berlin popular parlance mocking the pomposity of Nazi vocabulary adding "Reich" to whichever project the regime undertook. Both the reaction of the audience—made up of Nazi functionaries—as well as the flattered appropriation by Börger illustrates the ambiguities of the term. The speech also reflects with great clarity the further reaching objectives in the Nazi hierarchy: "There has not been enough kicking [during *Kristallnacht*], they should have beaten the heads much more [*laughter*], and we would have been done by now [*applause*]."[3] These quotes demonstrate that the term "Reichskristallnacht" resonated in ambiguous ways, on the one hand as expression of a distant attitude towards dictatorship (ironic enough not to be persecuted by the Gestapo), and on the other hand taken up and willingly misinterpreted, by a high-ranking Nazi.

This article first reflects on the term *pogrom* as it emerged in the eastern European context and how it has been discussed in recent scholarship. Additionally, we would like to shed light on the trajectory of the terminology used in the German and English languages. To that end, this article discusses how after the war, both Reichskristallnacht and Kristallnacht, the short version of the term, gained common currency in public as well as academic discourse, in both East and West Germany, Austria, and beyond German speaking countries. Over time, however, it has been supplanted by the term "pogrom," which has become almost ubiquitous in a range of variations, both in common parlance as well as in academic language. The use of terms like *Pogromnacht* (pogrom night), *Reichspogromnacht*, *Novemberpogrom* or *Novemberpogrome*, was motivated by the hope, especially from the 1970s onwards, that such a terminology allowed one to avoid seemingly euphemistic terminology such as Kristallnacht, which was perceived as highly inadequate. The final part of the chapter will focus on the emphatic use of the term pogrom outside of Germany, and mostly by Jewish authors after 1938.

"WHAT IS A POGROM?" THE TERMINOLOGY ON ANTI-JEWISH VIOLENCE IN EASTERN EUROPE

Over the past generation, historians have broadened our understanding of anti-Jewish violence in eastern Europe and the history of the term "pogrom." The Russian term originally referred to widespread devastation, particularly in the context of wars. It was first used to identify anti-Jewish violence after the attack on the Jewish community in Odessa in 1871. The mass occurrence of anti-Jewish violence in 1881–82 led to a narrowing of its meaning in the Russian language to mark interethnic violence against Jews.[4] In his recent analysis of the pogrom in Kishinev in 1903, Steven Zipperstein presents convincing evidence that the term pogrom did not gain common currency beyond Russia before the early years of the twentieth century.[5]

Interethnic violence, including anti-Jewish violence, was a recurrent phenomenon across Europe since time immemorial. Both Jewish and non-Jewish contemporaries, however, considered the more than four hundred anti-Jewish riots in 1881–82 in Eastern Europe as a new phenomenon, for which the relatively recent term "pogrom" seemed appropriate. John D. Klier (1944–2007) argued that these incidents represented a major shift in anti-Jewish violence.⁶ Their novel character resided in the fact that they would take place in urban settings and that they were triggered by more recent developments of infrastructure like railways and telegraphs, and the wider dissemination of the press, which established the *idea* of the anti-Jewish pogrom in the popular mind, as Klier wrote.⁷

In their studies, Hans Rogger (1923–2002), I. Michael Aronson, and John D. Klier have rejected the hypothesis that the pogroms of 1881–82 had been ordered, inspired or triggered by the Tsar or higher echelons of the Russian imperial administration.⁸ They have emphasized the contrast between the very high number of incidents (four hundred between April 1881 and May 1882, in three major waves of violence) and the relatively low intensity of the violence itself: among the nearly forty fatalities, half were pogromists. Klier⁹ has also emphasized the virtual absence of religious framing in this instance, citing the example of Orekhov, Tauride province, where the synagogue was the only Jewish building that was not touched during the pogrom.

The violence occurred in the southern provinces, which did not have a long history of Jewish residence and experienced considerable in-migration occasioned by rapid economic change.¹⁰ It was also in these southern provinces of the Empire that in 1903 the pogrom of Kishinev would mark the transition to a much more lethal pattern of pogrom violence: with forty-five Jewish victims, twice as many people were murdered in the three-day Kishinev pogrom of 1903 than during the hundreds of incidents of 1881–82. The pogroms of 1898 in Galicia, recently analyzed in depth by Tim Buchen, featured patterns very similar to those in Russia 1881–82: local residents turning against their Jewish neighbors after a period of intense political mobilization and the targeted spreading of rumors.¹¹ A similar picture emerges from Darius Staliunas' investigation of the infrequent cases of anti-Jewish violence in Lithuanian provinces around the turn of the twentieth century.¹² He follows the definition of pogrom violence of German sociologist Werner Bergmann, who describes a pogrom as "a one-sided, non-governmental form of social control." Pogrom violence can be mobilized in situations when one group feels legitimated to get down to "self-help" against another group because it does not expect any support by the state.¹³ This definition reflects the significant impact of the competitive ethnicity model proposed by Roberta Senechal de la Roche. Among the ingredients for the triggering of interethnic violence, Senechal de la Roche identified the perception among a majority or hegemonic community of a perceived upward shift in the position of a minority or marginal community, combined with a perception of state authorities to be weak and/or not taking action against this upward shift.¹⁴ Prejudice and stereotypes about the minority or marginalized community are a further prerequisite in the transition to physical violence, as it contributes to polarization and thus lowers the threshold of using force against a group of people one has cohabited with for extended periods of time.

The relative deprivation theory at the basis of this model describes the violence as "culturally constructed, discursively mediated, symbolically saturated, and ritually regulated."¹⁵ As Buchen and Staliunas emphasize, anti-Jewish violence in Eastern Europe of this period was considered to "redress" or "rectify" the injustice of Jews occupying space and status they did not, in the eyes of the pogromists, deserve. One key feature of this attitude was the expectation that Jews were "enemies for one day," though part of the social fabric after being "put in their place" by the attacks.

A perspective which both the competitive ethnicity model as well as the analysis of the "deadly ethnic riot" by Donald Horowitz share is that each outbreak of violence lessens social constraints and taboos against this form of violence in the future.¹⁶ This undoubtedly applies to mass violence against the Jews in eastern Europe in the late nineteenth and early twentieth centuries, with specific places and towns being again the site of such attacks in 1905.¹⁷

While scholarship has by now established that the authorities did not order or authorize the anti-Jewish riots of this period, they were by no means neutral. The empathy expressed by officers, ministers, or monarchs after violence had occurred, encouraged a significant shift in perception of anti-Jewish violence around 1900. Initially, in 1881, pogroms were seen as misguided and undesirable, but nonetheless understandable acts directed *against* Jewish exploitation. In the early twentieth century, as Jews were collectively viewed as an unreliable political element, pogroms came to be viewed as action *in support of* the government. Thus, Nicholas II, in grateful disbelief, interpreted the pogroms embedded in the revolutionary disorders of 1905 as a form of political mobilization in support of the autocracy.¹⁸ The instances of eastern European anti-Jewish riots that gave a certain type of interethnic violence their name— pogrom—were neither ordered nor authorized by the government or the authorities. Leading officials, members of governments or heads of state would come to condone such riots, but their fear of loss of control would prevent them from making the incitement to mass violence, or its implementation, a tool of governance.¹⁹ Instead, these riots were the result of strong intercommunal tensions, anti-Jewish resentment, and targeted incitement by anti-Semitic authors, agitators, and movements.²⁰ In his recent book on pogroms in the Russian Empire, Stefan Wiese has argued that to comprehend the violence we need to study the opportunity structures of the riots (including even weather conditions) and the leeway for negotiations between potential victims and attackers.[21]

The difference between these pogroms and the Nazi terror on the Jews of Germany and Austria in November 1938 is that the former was locally instigated, often slowly developing, while the latter was orchestrated by the state and carried out area-wide within a few days. As historians have now documented, the attacks in November 1938 originated in an order by Hitler to Goebbels. Formulated in indirect terms by Hitler, the decision to embark on violence all over the country was conveyed by phone from the Old City Hall in Munich to the Nazi leadership on the level of the provinces (or *Gaue*) and further down the chain of command to district and local branches of the party. Uniformed members of the SA and SS, gathered for the celebrations commemorating the fifteenth anniversary of the *Hitlerputsch* in 1923, started the attack while it was still night. In the course of a few hours, Jewish individuals, shops and dwellings, as well as places of worship, were attacked and often destroyed. The attacks encompassed the entirety of the Jewish communities in Nazi Germany and Austria, from Ostfriesland to the Burgenland, from Baden to Eastern Prussia, and mark a major transition from discrimination, expropriation, harassment

Hof (Saale), November 10, 1938, destruction of the synagogue by the I. Sturmbann of the 41st SS Brigade. The photos were taken by the firm Foto Eckart and were presumably placed in the town archive before 1945. The series is part of the exhibition "'Kristallnacht'—Anti-Jewish Terror in 1938. History and Remembrance," curated by Foundations Memorial to the Murdered Jews of Europe and Topography of Terror; Stadtarchiv Hof.

and persecution to mass arrests and targeted violence against broad segments of the remaining Jewish leadership, and to the physical destruction of property and buildings. After this terror attack, Jews in the reach of the Nazi regime ceased to be (second class) citizens worthy of political or moral consideration, but had become mere objects of police and Gestapo measures.[22]

POSTWAR GERMANY, *DEUTSCHER HERBST* AND THE "POGROM TURN" IN THE FEDERAL REPUBLIC OF GERMANY

In the postwar period, commemorations of the November events were, it seems, limited to Germany, and revolved around the round or "half round" anniversaries.[23] In 1948, commemorative events referred to the November 1938 attacks exclusively as "Kristallnacht." They were organized by the VVN (Vereinigung der Verfolgten des Naziregimes, an association of those persecuted by the Nazi regime), with the most prominent ceremony taking place in the Deutsches Theater in Soviet occupied zone of Berlin.[24]

In hindsight, the 1953 commemorations on the occasion of the fifteenth anniversary of the events seem a turning point leading to what Schmid identifies as a process of "pluralization" and "growing routine" (*Habitualisierung*) of historical memory at least in the Federal Republic of Germany. At this point in time, the German Democratic Republic followed the template of Stalin's Soviet Union and adopted anti-Semitic policies. The regime accused Jewish citizens of being "Zionists." In consequence, one third of East Germany's Jews fled to West Berlin in February 1953. Prominent displays commemorating Jewish victims of National Socialism were held in the GDR until 1963. They started again on a modest level, as a nervous, Cold War reaction of the East German leadership to the increasingly flourishing "culture of commemoration" in western Germany. Indeed, in the Federal Republic a broad range of institutions, parties, movements, and religious communities made the November events an often-marked reference for the memory of the Nazi terror.[25] Commemoration ceremonies often took place at the sites of former synagogues, and commemorative plaques and monuments often framed the persecution in 1938 as an attack on German and Austrian Jews exclusively in religious terms. In this period (1950s to 1970s), these increased activities for commemoration in western Germany were accompanied only by limited public interest in getting to know details about how the crime took place locally.

This would change during the next decades. Early on, there had been a growing discomfort with the designation of the events. The late 1970s and 1980s saw a tendency in the Federal Republic of Germany to avoid the term of "(Reichs-) Kristallnacht" in public and academic discourse when speaking of the events of November 9–10, 1938. "Reichskristallnacht" became a synonym for a trivialization of the crimes in 1938. It euphemized smashed glass as "crystal" and it left aside any reference to the perpetrators—it neither spoke of the state's or the Nazi party's role, nor about local perpetrators. Hence using the term was seen as a cynical obfuscation of what happened.[26] Over the years, this led to a complete avoidance of the word in public discourse.

We find a paradigmatic expression of the motives for this shift in an article by one of the pioneers of western German Holocaust research, Wolfgang Scheffler (1929–2008). It was published in 1978 in "*aus politik und zeitgeschichte*," a high-impact supplement to the weekly *Das Parlament* with wide distribution to schools, the media, and the political world and worth quoting at length:[27]

> Pogrom—this Russian term means 'annihilation, destruction, riot,' and, as the Brockhaus explains, "a persecution specifically of the Jews, combined with plunder and violence." History offers many examples of this. The events beginning in the night from 9–10 November, commonly known as "Reichskristallnacht," was an exemplary case of a pogrom. One should therefore identify these events as such, and restrict the generally used "Kristallnacht," which expresses only one aspect, namely the smashing of windows, only in passing/as a footnote.[28]

This quote demonstrates the attempt to distance scholarship from the use of the term "Reichskristallnacht." As historiography would turn to the question of how to define anti-Jewish violence in Russia and eastern Europe only in the following ten years, it is no surprise that Scheffler had to refer to a general encyclopedia in order to define a pogrom, and not expert scholarship.[29]

Scheffler's article was part of a massive expansion and broadening of commemoration referring to November 1938 in West Germany. "It is like the floodgates have opened," wrote the New York magazine *Aufbau* in December 1978 in an article on the Federal Republic's commemoration of the fortieth anniversary of the wave of terror in November 1938. There were at least 380 events, held in 101 towns. For the first time, a German Chancellor delivered a speech on this anniversary and it was the first time that the Federal President attended such an event. The ceremony in Cologne Roonstraße Synagogue was broadcast live on television.

The shift in terminology—from "Reichkristallnacht" to "Pogrom," "Novemberpogrom" or "Reichspogromnacht"—was part of the increased interest in the events of 1938. It reflects both a renewed interest in history in general and more specifically, in the history of National Socialism. The reasons are manifold. Western German society experienced an increased interest in history, triggered in part by doubts about the sustainability of economic development and a growing general apprehension about future environmental issues. Consequently, history became more politicized, partially as a consequence of the youth and student movements of 1968 and the increased emphasis on understanding the history of everyday life and ordinary people.[30] This new sense of urgency in engaging with local and regional history would lead to the founding of initiatives like the *Geschichtswerkstätten* (historical workshops), a development influenced not in the least by the turn to social history in English language historiography: "Grabe wo du stehst" ("Dig where you are") became the leitmotiv of this new historical sensitivity.

Furthermore, the so-called Hitler craze ("Hitler-Welle") after 1973, with glorifying references to National Socialism and attempts to commercialize this interest by marketing memoirs, illustrated volumes and records, demonstrated that Germany had not fully turned its back on the Nazi past.[31] Jewish communities were alarmed. The Central Council of Jews in Germany hosted a "2nd Youth- and Culture Conference" in Dortmund on November 10, 1978, dedicated to investigate "Nationalsozialismus und die jüdische Gegenwart" (National Socialism and the Jewish Present). Among younger politicians in attendance was the head of the Jusos, the youth organisation of the Social Democratic Party (SPD), the later chancellor Gerhard Schröder. They faced critical questions from young members of the Jewish community (including Micha Brumlik and Henryk M. Broder, who would later become well known public intellectuals) concerning impending time limitations for accusations for murder, including crimes committed during Nazi rule and World War Two. Such restrictions would have significantly curtailed any persecution of Nazi crimes.[32] This statute of limitations was permanently lifted by the German parliament only in 1979.

The reluctance to use the term "Reichkristallnacht" occurred simultaneously with the introduction of the term "Reichspogromnacht." Its first use dates back to November 9, 1977, when two social-democratic members of parliament, Klaus Thüsing (b. 1940) and Karl-Heinz Hansen (1927–2014) fitted a commemorative plaque onto the walls of an ancient fortress, Wewelsburg, which had served as an SS-"Ordensburg," located close to the former Niederhagen concentration camp (not far from the district town of Paderborn).³³ These left-wing members of the SPD wanted to ensure that the lessons of the catastrophe of National Socialism were not forgotten. It is by no means accidental that the term "Reichspogromnacht" emerged in this context. The term was used for the first time in one of the speeches during the fitting of the plaque. In his autobiography, Karl-Heinz Hansen described the general ambiance of the moment as follows:³⁴

> The year is 1977. Deutscher Herbst [German autumn], 9. November, 39th anniversary of the pogrom. (...). The papers in Düsseldorf write about expressions of sympathy for the SS murderers accused in the Majdanek trial, and about insults against concentration camp witnesses (...). The head of the Christian Democrats in Bremen asks for the burning of Erich Fried poetry.³⁵

Hansen thus clearly situates the commemorative plaque in the context of debates and events of 1977. Looking back in his memoirs and probably overstating the ferocity of the political confrontations at the time, he blends different aspects: the climate of political panic in the context of far-left terrorism ("German Autumn"), and the perception of persisting right-wing attitudes.

The western German Left undoubtedly was on the defensive. The legislation restricting professional activities of those suspected of having a critical view of the constitution, the "Radikalenerlass," led to 3.5 million checks of political reliability, mostly targeting individuals on the left. Terrorist attacks of the RAF (Rote Armee Fraktion) and the abduction and murder of Hans-Martin Schleyer, president of the employers' federation, were branded as a left-wing continuation of national-socialist crimes by conservative media. In this difficult context, one exit strategy for the left was empathy with the victims of National Socialism and an identification with them—not in the least in contrast to the students' movement of the 1960s, which was still largely indifferent to their fate.

This identification—for which the term "Reichspogromnacht" stands as a code—allowed them to bridge this gap. The term pogrom offered a stronger sense of immediacy of the danger emanating from the political right, and thus compared the situation of the political left to the one of Jews during the terror attacks of November 1938. Thus the advent of the term "Reichspogromnacht" cannot be explained by referring to a single development (like the "Hitler craze"), but is a reaction to complex changes within left and liberal segments of the western German public.

A number of scholars and activists criticized this change in terms. In the words of the well-known author, Barbara Noack:[36]

> Does Reichspogromnacht offer a more adequate description of these horrors? Pogroms are unfortunately frequent phenomena. Do we [the Germans] want to hide by blending into the mass of rioters? and pretend we're actually the same? By the same token, we will help let fade into the background the uniqueness of the Nazi crimes, the dimensions and the unheard-of systematic character of how we Germans proceeded gets lost.[37]

This was the year when both terms, "Reichskristallnacht" and "Reichspogromnacht," were listed by the Society for German Language as candidate terms for the "Word of the Year."[38] Thus, political context and motivations need to be taken into consideration when attempting to historicize the history of the term. However, to identify one's own embattled situation with the one of the persecuted Jews in Germany and Austria, as significant segments of the liberal and left-wing public in the Federal Republic of Germany did, represented a historical short-cut of considerable dimensions. The ambiguous term "Kristallnacht" or "Reichskristallnacht" was replaced by the equally problematic neologism "Pogromnacht."

"POGROM" AS AN EMPHATIC TERM USED BY JEWISH AUTHORS

In his recent assessment of the 1903 pogrom in Kishinev—which marked the transition from incidents of anti-Jewish riots in east central and eastern Europe with a comparatively low degree of physical violence to massacres with high numbers of Jewish fatalities—Zipperstein observes that the term "pogrom" is "sturdily portable" and "was believed to capture accurately centuries of Jewish vulnerability, the deep well of Jewish misery." Zipperstein sees a complete contrast to the Holocaust, since "pogroms would never—despite their Russian origins—be tethered to a particular time, place, or dictator."[39]

It thus does not come as a surprise that immediate reactions by Jewish observers outside Nazi Germany would frame the events as a pogrom.[40] Press outlets frequently used this term in headlines while stressing in the actual analysis that the events had been carefully masterminded and orchestrated by the Nazi regime. Thus, the headline of the November 11, 1938 issue of *Nasz Przegląd*, the flagship paper of the Polish-Jewish intelligentsia, "Terrible Pogrom of the Jews in Germany," emphasized that despite the fact that Goebbels referred to the violence as an outbreak of popular wrath, "thousands of proofs demonstrate that the entire anti-Jewish campaign (in the Polish original: *akcja*) was 'inspired by Nazi forces.'"[41] One of the earliest treatises assessing the catastrophic impact of the attack on Jews in Germany and Austria was published under the title *Die Novemberpogrome in Deutschland* by the "Centre de Documentation" in Strasbourg still in 1938. Rejecting the collective responsibility forced upon the victims of the attack, it described the propaganda strategy of the Nazi regime:

> In Germany, however, the press undertook it to bring the public mood to boiling point in order to have a "psychological" explanation at hand for the terrible outbreaks of hate which erupted between 9 to 11 November and which were carefully prepared and reminded everyone of the Russian pogroms of the Tsarist period, and to pretend, that they were the result of an all-too-well understandable anger (Erregung) of the entire German population, that they were, as Mr Göbbels [sic] formulated, a "reaction of healthy instinct" of the German people.[42]

There are indications that the publishers of this treatise belonged to the circles of exiled Social Democrats and Communists in Strasbourg, probably around Ernst Roth (1901–51, SPD, later member of the German Bundestag) and Robert Klausmann (1896–1972, KPD).[43] The *Germany Reports* (*Deutschlandberichte*) of the Social Democrat Party leadership in exile stressed the same points as the Strasbourg publishers: the violence had been executed by the Nazi party suborganizations; it was part of a general and persistent "terror against the Jews" which had already developed into a "permanent pogrom" (in the original: *Dauerpogrom*).[44] Publications within the proletarian resistance movement in Nazi Germany used the term "pogrom" as well.[45] One can surmise that this emphatic term was used in these contexts in order to stress the violence of the attacks and to frame them as reminiscent of anti-Jewish violence in the Middle Ages or in nineteenth-century Russia.

American correspondents in Nazi Germany witnessing the events of November 9–12 often used the term "terror" to describe the events, and emphasized the coordinated character of the attack and its obvious function in stepping up the oppression of the Jewish population. As of November 15, 1938 ("A New Phase in Germany") *New York Times* op-ed noted:[46]

It is evident now that last week's day of terror in Germany signified something more than the unleashing of Nazi ferocity. It marked an important stage in the development of the National Socialist revolution. For it is now clear that the outbreak of violence was a prologue to a performance previously prepared and rehearsed. The punitive decrees which have followed in quick succession are too drastic and comprehensive to be improvised on the spur of the moment.

An undated British typescript drafted undoubtedly very close to the events and preserved in the Wiener Library equally referred to the attack as "German pogroms."[47] This item, which probably has been redacted in Alfred Wiener's office or in Amsterdam or in London explains that

November 10, 1938 meant the eruption of "popular fury." It was, like everything in the Third Reich, by order—no further proof being required since the facts in themselves are plain enough evidence.

The explicit reference to "German" pogroms in the title of this collection of short reports obviously invites the association of the term "pogrom" with the more familiar "Russian pogroms," thus integrating the atrocities of Nazi Germany into the grand narrative of anti-Jewish violence, or the "deep well of Jewish misery," as Zipperstein put it. It seems, however, noteworthy that by referring to the violence as "pogrom," these authors reiterated Goebbels' deceitful reference to the events as the result of "popular wrath" or "vengeance" and not as coordinated state-sanctioned violence.

In the postwar period, the religious framing of the attack appeared in texts dedicated to the November events outside Germany, and resonated with the development of the early commemorative culture in western Germany.

Lionel Kochan (1922–2005) wrote in 1957 that the term "pogrom" integrated the events into the long history of Christian anti-Judaism and that for religious reasons, "Jew and European stand at opposing poles."[48] In a 1959 publication commemorating the twentieth anniversary of the event, Eva Reichmann (1897–1998), a central figure in the Jewish support and rescue organization within Nazi Germany until 1938, pleaded to avoid the term "Kristallnacht" as it evoked ideas of youthful tricks or at the most of laddish pranks, thus trivializing the horrors of the events: "What happened in reality was the crime of sacrilege," referring to the events later in the lecture as "Pogromnacht."[49] Like Reichmann, other Jewish authors qualified the enormity of the devastation of the November attacks by using the term "pogrom" and integrating it into a history of religious prejudice. By so doing, the core dynamic of the terror as an instance of state-directed violence exacted on the Jews of Germany and Austria got lost.

CONCLUSION: 1938—A POGROM?

In the night from November 9–10 and on November 10, 1938, Jewish places of worship in Nazi Germany were destroyed, Jewish property vandalized or robbed, thousands of Jews were arrested or hurt, and hundreds killed. While the details of the terror attack only became apparent over days and weeks after the events, their enormity was perceived immediately. This is reflected in both the neologism of Kristallnacht or Reichskristallnacht, which sought to encapsulate the unheard-of character of what had happened, as well as in the term "pogrom," integrating devastation, persecution, and murder, into a terminological framework shaped by the Jewish historical experience in eastern Europe.

It is also a reflection of the inability of "polite society"—of Jews and non-Jews—to comprehend that the institutions at the very foundations of civil society—the police, uniformed people, political representatives—would be at the very core of this violence inflicted on the Jews of Germany and Austria, or contribute, as, for instance, fire departments, to its devastating effect.

In contrast to the anti-Jewish riots as they unfolded in eastern Europe in the nineteenth and early twentieth centuries, the violence directed against Jews, Jewish property, and Jewish places of worship on the night of November 9–10, 1938 appears of a very different character: coordinated, centrally organized, and executed by armed and uniformed units directly depending on the central agencies of the Nazi regime. It was a systematic, comprehensive and coordinated terror attack, as the simple exercise of overlaying the maps of Jewish communities in 1933 and of the location of the attacks in November 1938 demonstrates: with the exception of those territories appropriated by Nazi Germany since 1933, these maps are congruent.

Indeed, spontaneous and popular violence occurred in the context of this state-sponsored terror attack. But it was clearly a phenomenon that accompanied the centrally organized attacks. Those responsible for spontaneous acts of violence have not yet been the objects of sufficient systematic research, although the brutality of their actions did equal the one of the terror attacks involving the SA, the SS and members of other branches of the NS hierarchy.[50]

So far, we only have preliminary research by Edith Raim, who surveyed postwar trials in the French, British and American zones of occupation (as well as a smaller number of trials that took place in the Federal Republic of Germany).[51] Further research could be based on a comparative analysis of reports and testimonies of these 2,468 investigations and 1,174 trials. Among these 17,700 individuals were members of both groups: perpetrators involved in the terror attack orchestrated by the Nazi hierarchy, as well as those involved in spontaneous attacks, which in part undoubtedly qualify as pogroms.

To use the identical term for these two sides of the November events is historically misleading. It would be problematic not in the least because it would fail to call out Goebbels' deceit of the "spontaneous people's wrath." To avoid the term pogrom does not exclude the events of November 9–12, 1938 from the long history of anti-Jewish violence. The advantage of an increased terminological precision would, however, help distinguish the dynamic which unfolded in the case of the unique dynamic towards the catastrophe of the genocide and make it much more tangible.[52] These events were planned, organized, centrally triggered and executed, to the most devastating of effects. A variety of designations would reflect this dimension of a state-sponsored terror attack on a minority population, such as "November terror," "anti-Jewish terror" or "state terror," which would all identify the events of November 1938 more adequately as a coordinated and systematic attack of a depraved regime on a defenseless minority.

Notes

1. Harald Schmid, *Erinnern an den "Tag der Schuld." Das Novemberpogrom von 1938 in der deutschen Geschichtspolitik* (Hamburg: Ergebnisse, 201), 82; Gerhard Hirschfeld, ed., *Judenverfolgung und jüdisches Leben unter den Bedingungen der nationalsozialistischen Gewaltherrschaft* (Berlin: Verlag für Berlin-Brandenburg, 1996), 154.
2. Wilhelm Börger gave his speech on June 24, 1939. Börger had been a member of parliament for the NSDAP since 1930 and since 1938 a high level official in the Reich Department for Labor (*Reichsarbeitsministerium*). In the original: "Nach der Reichskristallnacht voriges Jahr, am 11. November, sehen Sie, also die Sache geht als Reichskristallnacht in die Geschichte ein (*Beifall, Gelächter*). Sie sehn, das ist humoristisch erhoben, nicht wahr, schön. Man hätte sagen können, ist das wirtschaftlich richtig? Die Scheiben müssen wir aus Belgien holen, das kostet Devisen. Kann man zweierlei Meinung darüber sein. Eins aber steht fest, die wissen jetzt ganz genau, wird auf'n Knopf gedrückt, hat es jeklingelt, überall (*Gelächter*)."
3. In the original: "Es ist zuwenig getreten worden, die hätten noch mehr auf die Birne hauen müssen (Gelächter), dann wären wir fertig damit (Beifall)."
4. John D. Klier, "The Pogrom Paradigm in Russian History," in *Pogroms: Anti-Jewish Violence in Modern Jewish History*, ed. John D. Klier and Shlomo Lambroza (Cambridge: Cambridge University Press, 1992), 34–35.
5. Steven Zipperstein, *Pogrom: Kishinev and the Tilt of History* (New York: Liveright Publishing, 2018), 5.
6. John D. Klier, *Jews, Russians, and the Pogroms of 1881–82* (Cambridge: Cambridge University Press, 2010), 59.
7. [The press] provided the newspapers, official broadsides, and printed decrees that expedited the spread of the misinformation and rumor that played such an important role in sparking pogroms. Most importantly, these factors established the *idea* of the anti-Jewish pogrom in the popular mind, creating a precedent, and a model, for future riots. Klier, *Jews, Russians, and the Pogroms*, 59.
8. Hans Rogger, *Jewish Policies and Right Wing Politics in Imperial Russia* (Berkeley: University of California Press, 1986); I. Michael Aronson, *Troubled Waters: The Origins of the 1881 Anti-Jewish Pogroms in Russia* (Pittsburgh: University of Pittsburgh Press, 1990); Klier, *Jews, Russians, and the Pogroms*, 58–88.
9. Klier, *Jews, Russians, and the Pogroms*, 70.
10. Heinz-Dietrich Löwe, "Pogroms in Russia: Explanations, Comparisons, Suggestions," *Jewish Social Studies* 11, no. 1 (2004), 20–21.
11. Tim Buchen, *Antisemitismus in Galizien. Agitation, Gewalt und Politik gegen Juden in der Habsburgermonarchie um 1900* (Berlin: Metropol Verlag, 2012). Buchen does not undertake a systematic group analysis of the "pogrom specialists" in Galicia, although his thick description would have allowed for that. In contrast, see the

chapter on Pavel Krushevan, a key instigator of the Kishinev pogrom in Zipperstein, *Pogrom*, 145–84.
12. Darius Staliunas, *Enemies for a Day: Antisemitism and Anti-Jewish Violence in Lithuania under the Tsars* (Budapest: Central European University Press, 2015).
13. "I define pogroms as a one-sided and non-governmental form of social control, as 'self-help by a group' that occurs when no remedy from the state against the threat which another ethnic group poses can be expected. The pogrom is different from other forms of control, such as lynching, terrorism, and vigilantism, in that the participants in such a pogrom hold the entire out-group responsible and therefore act against the group as a whole, and also in that it usually displays a low degree of organization," in Werner Bergmann, "Ethnic Riots in Situations of Loss of Control: Revolution, Civil War, and Regime Change as Opportunity Structures for Anti-Jewish Violence in Nineteenth- and Twentieth-Century Europe," in *Control of Violence: Historical and International Perspectives on Violence in Modern Societies*, ed. Wilhelm Heitmeyer, Heinz-Gerhard Haupt, Stefan Malthaner, and Andrea Kirschner (New York: Springer, 2011), 488.
14. Roberta Senechal de la Roche, "Collective Violence as Social Control," *Sociological Forum* 11, no. 1 (1996): 116.
15. Roger Brubaker and David D. Laitin, "Ethnic and Nationalist Violence," *Annual Review of Sociology* 24 (1998), 441.
16. David Horowitz, *The Deadly Ethnic Riot* (Berkeley: University of California Press, 2001). Horowitz identifies the following core elements of the deadly ethnic riot: (1) a growing focus on the hated group, to the neglect of others; (2) a belief that the hated group possesses fixed characteristics and dispositions to action; (3) a compression of intragroup differences attributed to members of the hated group; and (4) a sense of repulsion toward the group and its members" (543).
17. *Die Judenpogrome in Russland. Herausgegeben im Auftrag des Zionistischen Hilfsfonds in London von der zur Erforschung der Pogrome eingesetzten Kommission(Allgmeiner Teil)* (Frankfurt am Main: Jüdischer Verlag, 1910), 1:189–91. This was the case among others for Balta, Elisavetgrad, Kiev, Kishinev, Konotop, Odessa, Pereiaslav, and Smela.
18. Nicholas II reportedly stated that "a whole mass of loyal people suddenly made their power felt. Because nine-tenths of the troublemakers are Jews, the People's whole anger turned against them. That's how the pogroms happened," cited in Klier, *Russians, Jews, and the Pogroms*, 88.
19. The impact of strong policing in Prussia 1882–84 and in Galicia 1898, and its absence/impossibility in underpoliced Russia, seems one of the most relevant differences in coping with xenophobic incitement—a difference which seems to have lost nothing of its pertinence in twenty-first century Central Europe.
20. David Engel, "What's in a Pogrom? European Jews in the Age of Violence," in *Anti-Jewish Violence: Rethinking the Pogrom in East European History*, ed. Jonathan

Dekel-Chen, David Gaunt, Natan M. Meir, and Israel Bartal (Bloomington: Indiana University Press, 2011), 23–25.
21. Stefan Wiese, *Pogrome im Zarenreich. Dynamiken kollektiver Gewalt* (Hamburg: Hamburger Edition HIS Verlagsgesellschaft, 2016), 52–55.
22. Ulrich Herbert, "Von der 'Reichskristallnacht' zum Holocaust. Der 9. November und das Ende des 'Radau-Antisemitismus,'" in *Arbeit, Volkstum, Weltanschauung: über Fremde und Deutsche im 20. Jahrhundert*, ed. Ulrich Herbert (Frankfurt am Main: Fischer Taschenbuch-Verlag, 1995), 75.
23. Schmid, *Erinnern*, 166–79.
24. Andreas Nachama and Uwe Neumärker, *"Kristallnacht." Antijüdischer Terror 1938. Ereignisse und Erinnerung* (Berlin: Stiftung Denkmal für die ermordeten Juden Europas, Stiftung Topographie des Terrors, 2018), 176.
25. Hermann Graml, *Der 9. November 1938. "Reichskristallnacht"* (Bonn: Bundeszentrale f. Heimatdienst, 1953) reflects this shift in the historical imagery of the events of November 1938.
26. Schmid, *Erinnern*, 330.
27. Wolfgang Scheffler, "Ausgewählte Dokumente zur Geschichte des Novemberpogroms 1938," *Aus Politik und Zeitgeschichte* (November 4, 1978): B44.
28. In the original: "Pogrom—das aus dem Russischen stammende Wort bedeutet 'Verwüstung, Zerstörung, Krawall,' vor allem die, wie im Brockhaus [a standard encyclopedia] formuliert wird, 'mit Plünderung und Gewalttaten verbundene Hetze, besonders gegen die Juden.' Beispiele hierfür bot die Geschichte in reichem Maße. Die in der Nacht vom 9. zum 10. November einsetzenden Ereignisse, im allgemeinen als 'Reichskristallnacht' bezeichnet, waren das Musterbeispiel eines Pogrom. Man sollte daher diesen Vorgang auch als einen solchen bezeichnen und die oft übliche Kennzeichnung als 'Kristallnacht,' die lediglich die eine Seite, nämlich das Zerschlagen der Fensterscheiben, versinnbildlicht, nur als Fußnote verwenden."
29. It is more surprising in more recent scholarship concerning the November events. Thus, the editors of contemporary witness accounts argue in favor of the term pogrom with a reference to the *Oxford English Dictionary*, hardly an expert source on the history of anti-Jewish violence, see Ruth Levitt, ed., *Pogrom November 1938: Testimonies from "Kristallnacht"* (London: Souvenir Press, 2015), XIV. For a criticism of the use of inadequate reference works in order to justify problematic historical terminology in the context of anti-Jewish violence and pogroms see Sam Johnson, "'Pogrom' in the Anglo-American Imagination, 1881–1919," in *Jews in the Eastern European Borderlands: Essays in Honor of John D. Klier*, ed. Eugene M. Avrutin and Harriet Murav (Boston: Academic Studies Press, 2012), 149–50.
30. Harald Schmid, "Die 'Stunde der Wahrheit' und ihre Voraussetzungen. Zum geschichtskulturellen Wirkungskontext von 'Holocaust,'" *Zeitgeschichte-online*,

March 2004, 6, accessed October 4, 2018, https://zeitgeschichte-online.de/thema/die-stunde-der-wahrheit-und-ihre-voraussetzungen.
31. Bernd Weber, "'Hitlerwelle' und historisch-politischer Unterricht. Phänomene-Ursachen-Konsequenzen," *Frankfurter Hefte. Zeitschrift für Politik und Kultur* 34, no. 3 (1979), 21–30; Anneliese Manzmann, ed., *Hitlerwelle und historische Fakten* (Königstein: Scriptor, 1979).
32. Alexander Ginsburg, "Pressestimmen zur 2. Jugend- und Kulturtagung. Ein Beitrag zur Vergangenheitsbewältigung," *Jüdischer Pressedienst* 7/8 (1978): 31.
33. Oral communication given by Klaus Thüsing to Ulrich Baumann, 2018. Thüsing misdated the event to the year 1978. 1978 was in fact the year when Thüsing used the term "Reichspogromnacht" in an article in the SPD press service. Klaus Thüsing, "Wie steht es mit unserer Glaubwürdigkeit? 'Reichskristallnacht'—nicht nur ein historisches Datum," in *Sozialdemokratischer Pressedienst* 218 (1978): 3. See also Thorsten Eitz and Georg Stötzel, *Wörterbuch der "Vergangenheitsbewältigung." Die NS-Vergangenheit im öffentlichen Sprachgebrauch* (Hildesheim: Georg Olms Verlag, 2007), 526.
34. Karl-Heinz Hansen, *"Es ist nicht alles schlecht, was scheitert": Ein politischer Lebenslauf* (Hamburg: KVV Konkret Verlag, 2014), 92.
35. Erich Fried (1921–88), born to a Viennese-Jewish family, was a poet and politically involved author of considerable popularity especially in the 1970s and 1980s. After his father had been killed by the Gestapo, he had fled Nazi Germany in 1938. Fried was identified with the Left and more specifically with the disarmament and peace movement. The mentioned politician was Bernd Neumann (CDU), later Federal Government Commissioner for Culture and the Media in the cabinet of Chancellor Angela Merkel. He indeed expressed the wish of burning a poem of Erich Fried during a heated debate with the deputy Henning Scherf (chairman of the Bremen branch of SPD). Neumann later met Fried.
36. Barbara Noack, "'Reichskristallnacht'—ein Euphemismus," *taz. die tageszeitung* no. 2656 (November 7, 1988): 18.
37. In the original: "Kann 'Reichspogromnacht' dieses Grauen noch adäquater beschreiben? Pogrome gab es und gibt es (leider) vielerorts. Wollen wir uns einreihen in die Schar derer, die Minderheiten verfolgten und verfolgen, um weniger aufzufallen? Sind wir auch nicht anders als andere? Damit lassen wir die Einzigartigkeit der Nazi-Verbrechen zurücktreten, es verschwindet das besondere Ausmaß und die unvergleichliche Systematik, mit der wir Deutschen vorgegangen sind."
38. Erika Ising, "Kristallnacht—Pogromnacht: Schlusspunkt oder neue Fragezeichen?" *Der Sprachdienst* 33, no. 6 (1989): 171; Detlev Claussen and Harald Martenstein, *Vor aller Augen. Verfolgung, Vertreibung und Vernichtung der Juden in Deutschland* (Berlin: Pressestiftung des Tagesspiegels, 1988). Other terms listed were *Robbensterben* (the mass phenomenon of seals perishing in the North Sea), *Kälbermastskandal* (a scandal involving the cramming of veals) and *Europäischer*

Binnenmarkt (the European single market, introduced then). The term selected by a search committee was "Gesundheitsreform" (the reform of the German health care provision system).

39. Zipperstein, *Pogrom*, 3.
40. Michael Berkowitz, "Kristallnacht in Context: Jewish War Veterans in America and Britain and the Crisis of German Jewry," in *American Religious Responses to Kristallnacht*, ed. Maria Mazzenga (New York: Palgrave McMillan, 2009); Gershon Greenberg, "The American Ultra-Orthodox Jewish Theological Response," in Mazzenga, *American Religious Responses*.
41. Ingo Loose, "Das war einmal [. . .] die jüdische Glanzepoche in Deutschland. Reaktionen auf den Novemberpogrom in der jüdischen Presse in Polen 1938/39," in *"Es brennt!" Antijüdischer Terror im November 1938*, ed. Andreas Nachama, Uwe Neumärker, and Hermann Simon (Stiftung Denkmal für die ermordeten Juden Europas; Stiftung Topographie des Terrors; Berlin: Stiftung Topographie des Terrors, 2008), 131.
42. *Die Novemberpogrome in Deutschland*, ed. the Centre de documentation, Strasbourg, 1938, Wiener Library microfilm 88038/K211. In the original: "In Deutschland aber versuchte man, durch die Presse die Volkserregung bis zur Siedehitze aufzupeitschen, um für die sorgsam vorbereiteten an die russischen Pogrome zur Zeit der Zarenregierungen erinnernden entsetzlichen Hassausbrüche, wie sie sich zwischen dem 9. und 11. November ereigneten, eine 'psychologische' Erklärung bei der Hand zu haben, *um vorzutäuschen, dass sie 'spontan' aus der 'allzubegreiflichen tiefen Erregung des gesamten deutschen Volkes' herzuleiten seien, dass sie, wie sich Herr Göbbels ausdrückte, noch 'eine Reaktion des gesunden Instinkts' des deutschen Volkes'* gewesen wären" [no page numbers, emphasis in original].
43. The unkown publishers of the pamphlet refer to information given by a "Service d'information in Strassburg." A report written by the Gestapo (Staatspolizeistelle Neustadt an der Weinstraße) from September 1939 does link Roth and Klausmann to a *Service d'information*, see a report to the Gestapo/Berlin, from the Staatspolizeistelle Neustadt a. d. Weinstraße (September 28, 1939), Landesarchiv Speyer, Inventory: Geheime Staatspolizei Neustadt/Ermittlungsakten (H 91), Nr. 566. The authors express their indebtedness to Jens Späth (Universität des Saarlands) for sharing these details.
44. *Deutschland-Berichte*, 1181.
45. Schmid, *Erinnern*, 82; Detlev Peukert, *Der deutsche Arbeiterwiderstand gegen das Dritte Reich* (Berlin: Gedenkstätte Deutscher Widerstand, 1990), 32.
46. We are grateful to Norman Domeier for sharing his insights into the history of American reporting about *Kristallnacht*, focusing specifically on the reporting of Otto Tolischus and Ralph Barnes. The latter defined the attack as "Police-controlled reign of terror planned by Nazis" already in his first despatch of November 9, 1938 (*New York Herald Tribune*, November 10, 1938). For further details see Norman

Domeier, "A Scream, Then Silence. Kristallnacht and the American Journalists in Nazi Germany," in this volume.
47. *The German Pogrom. November 1938. An Account of Facts,* Wiener Library WL/JMB MF 88036, unpaginated.
48. Lionel Kochan, *Pogrom: 10 November 1938* (London: Andre Deutsch, 1957), 13. He continues: "There was nothing spontaneous about the pogrom. But nor was it wholly contrived and organized. Of necessity, a great deal had to be left to local initiative. The result was a horrible combination of anti-Semitic passion set in motion, and sometimes reinforced, by every kind of technical resource. The lower links in the chain of command were still animated by the same crude mentality as had been their precursors in, for example, Eastern Europe. But technical advance made it possible to replay them on an unprecedented scale."
49. Eva Reichmann, "Die Lage der Juden in der Weimarer Republik," in *Die Reichskristallnacht. Der Antisemitismus in der deutschen Geschichte* (Bonn: Friedrich-Ebert-Stiftung, 1959), 19, 30. Later in the lecture Reichmann would refer to the events as "Pogromnacht" (30).
50. See the observations by Mary Fulbrook, "Social Relations and Bystander Responses to Violence: Kristallnacht November 1938," in this volume, on the considerable role of young people already socialised in Nazi Germany.
51. Edith Raim, *Justiz zwischen Diktatur und Demokratie. Wiederaufbau und Ahndung von NS-Verbrechen in Westdeutschland 1945–1949,* Quellen und Darstellungen zur Zeitgeschichte, 96 (Munich: Oldenbourg-Verlag, 2013), 918–19.
52. It is not the task of this contribution to propose yet another term for the events. Describing it as an act of state terror would, however, undoubtedly add to a more adequate contextualization.

Bibliography

"A New Phase in Germany." *New York Times*, November 15, 1938. Accessed March 1, 2019 through Proquest Historical Newspapers.

Aronson, I. Michael. *Troubled Waters: The Origins of the 1881 Anti-Jewish Pogroms in Russia*. Pittsburgh: University of Pittsburgh Press, 1990.

Bergmann, Werner. "Ethnic Riots in Situations of Loss of Control: Revolution, Civil War, and Regime Change as Opportunity Structures for Anti-Jewish Violence in Nineteenth- and Twentieth-Century Europe." In *Control of Violence: Historical and International Perspectives on Violence in Modern Societies*, edited by Wilhelm Heitmeyer, Heinz-Gerhard Haupt, Stefan Malthaner, and Andrea Kirschner, 487–516. New York: Springer, 2011.

———. "Pogroms." In *International Handbook of Violence Research*, edited by Wilhelm Heitmeyer and John Hagan, 351–67. Dordrecht: Kluwer Academic Publishers, 2003.

Berkowitz, Michael. "Kristallnacht in Context: Jewish War Veterans in America and Britain and the Crisis of German Jewry." In *American Religious Responses to Kristallnacht*, edited by Maria Mazzenga, 57–84. London: Palgrave McMillan, 2009.

Brass, Paul R. "Introduction: Discourses of Ethnicity, Communalism, and Violence." In *Riots and Pogroms*, edited by Paul R. Brass, 1–55. London: Palgrave Macmillan, 1996.

Brubaker, Roger, and David D. Laitin. "Ethnic and Nationalist Violence." *Annual Review of Sociology* 24 (1998): 423–52.

Buchen, Tim. *Antisemitismus in Galizien. Agitation, Gewalt und Politik gegen Juden in der Habsburgermonarchie um 1900*. Berlin: Metropol Verlag, 2012.

Claussen, Detlev, and Harald Martenstein. *Vor aller Augen. Verfolgung, Vertreibung und Vernichtung der Juden in Deutschland*. Berlin: Pressestiftung des Tagesspiegels, 1988.

Deutschland-Berichte der Sozialdemokratischen Partei Deutschlands, 1938. Vol. 5. Edited by Exilvorstand der Sozialdemokratischen Partei Deutschlands (Sopade). Petra Nettelbeck, 1980.

Eitz, Thorsten, and Stötzel, Georg. *Wörterbuch der "Vergangenheitsbewältigung" Die NS-Vergangenheit im öffentlichen Sprachgebrauch*. Hildesheim: Georg Olms Verlag, 2007.

Engel, David. "What's in a Pogrom? European Jews in the Age of Violence." In *Anti-Jewish Violence. Rethinking the Pogrom in East European History*, edited by Jonathan Dekel-Chen, David Gaunt, Natan M. Meir, and Israel Bartal, 19–37. Bloomington: Indiana University Press, 2011.

The German Pogrom. November 1938. An Account of Facts. Wiener Library WL/JMB MF 88036, unpaginated.

Geschichte der deutschen Arbeiterbewegung. Vol. 5. Institut für Marxismus-Leninismus beim ZK der SED, 1966.

Ginsburg, Alexander. "Pressestimmen zur 2. Jugend- und Kulturtagung. Ein Beitrag zur Vergangenheitsbewältigung." *Jüdischer Pressedienst* 7/8 (1978): 31–34.

Graml, Hermann. *Der 9. November 1938. "Reichskristallnacht."* Bonn: Bundeszentrale f. Heimatdienst, 1953.

Greenberg, Gershon. "The American Ultra-Orthodox Jewish Theological Response." In *American Religious Responses to Kristallnacht*, edited by Maria Mazzenga, 145–82. New York: Palgrave McMillan, 2009.

Hansen, Karl-Heinz. *"Es ist nicht alles schlecht, was scheitert": Ein politischer Lebenslauf.* Hamburg: KVV Konkret Verlag, 2014.

Herbert, Ulrich. "Von der 'Reichskristallnacht' zum Holocaust. Der 9. November und das Ende des 'Radau-Antisemitismus.'" In *Arbeit, Volkstum, Weltanschauung: Über Fremde und Deutsche im 20. Jahrhundert*, edited by Ulrich Herbert, 59–77. Frankfurt am Main: Fischer Taschenbuch-Verlag, 1995.

Hirschfeld, Gerhard, ed., *Judenverfolgung und jüdisches Leben unter den Bedingungen der nationalsozialistischen Gewaltherrschaft.* Berlin: Verlag für Berlin-Brandenburg, 1996.

Horowitz, Donald. *The Deadly Ethnic Riot.* Berkeley: University of California Press, 2001.

Ising, Erika. "Kristallnacht—Pogromnacht: Schlusspunkt oder neue Fragezeichen?" *Der Sprachdienst* 33, no. 6 (1989): 169–72.

Johnson, Sam. "'Pogrom' in the Anglo-American Imagination, 1881–1919." In *Jews in the Eastern European Borderlands: Essays in Honor of John D. Klier*, edited by Eugene M. Avrutin and Harriet Murav, 147–66. Boston: Academic Studies Press, 2012.

Die Judenpogrome in Russland. Herausgegeben im Auftrag des Zionistischen Hilfsfonds in London von der zur Erforschung der Pogrome eingesetzten Kommission. Vol. 1 (*Allgmeiner Teil*). Frankfurt am Main: Jüdischer Verlag, 1910.

Kishinev, Yakov Mikhailovich et al., eds. *Kishinevskii pogrom. Sbornik dokumentov i materialov.* Kishinev: Ruxanda, 2000.

Klier, John D. *Jews, Russians, and the Pogroms of 1881–82.* Cambridge: Cambridge University Press, 2010.

———. "The Pogrom Paradigma in Russian History." In *Pogroms: Anti-Jewish Violence in Modern Jewish History*, edited by John D. Klier and Shlomo Lambroza, 13–38. Cambridge: Cambridge University Press, 1992.

Kochan, Lionel. *Pogrom: 10 November 1938.* London: Andre Deutsch, 1957.

Levitt, Ruth, ed. *Pogrom November 1938: Testimonies from "Kristallnacht."* London: Souvenir Press, 2015.

Löwe, Heinz-Dietrich. "Pogroms in Russia: Explanations, Comparisons, Suggestions." *Jewish Social Studies* 11, no. 1 (2004): 16–24.

Loose, Ingo. "Das war einmal [...] die jüdische Glanzepoche in Deutschland. Reaktionen auf den Novemberpogrom in der jüdischen Presse in Polen 1938/39." In *"Es brennt!" Antijüdischer Terror im November 1938*, edited by Andreas Nachama, Uwe Neumärker, and Hermann Simon, 128–35. Stiftung Denkmal für die ermordeten Juden Europas; Stiftung Topographie des Terrors. Berlin: Stiftung Topographie des Terrors, 2008.

Manzmann, Anneliese, ed. *Hitlerwelle und historische Fakten*. Königstein: Scriptor, 1979.

Mazzenga, Maria, ed. *American Religious Responses to Kristallnacht*. London: Palgrave McMillan, 2009.

Nachama, Andreas, and Uwe Neumärker. "*Kristallnacht.*" *Antijüdischer Terror 1938. Ereignisse und Erinnerung*. Stiftung Denkmal für die ermordeten Juden Europas; Stiftung Topographie des Terrors. Berlin: Stiftung Topographie des Terrors, 2018.

Noack, Barbara. "'Reichskristallnacht'—ein Euphemismus." *taz. die tageszeitung* no. 2656 (November 7, 1988).

Die Novemberpogrome in Deutschland, edited by the Centre de documentation. Wiener Library microfilm 88038/K211. Centre de documentation. Strasbourg, 1938.

Peukert, Detlev. *Der deutsche Arbeiterwiderstand gegen das Dritte Reich*. Berlin: Gedenkstätte Deutscher Widerstand, 1990.

Raim, Edith. *Justiz zwischen Diktatur und Demokratie. Wiederaufbau und Ahndung von NS-Verbrechen in Westdeutschland 1945-1949*. Quellen und Darstellungen zur Zeitgeschichte, 96. Munich: Oldenbourg-Verlag, 2013.

Reichmann, Eva. "Die Lage der Juden in der Weimarer Republik." In *Die Reichskristallnacht. Der Antisemitismus in der deutschen Geschichte*, 19-32. Bonn: Friedrich-Ebert-Stiftung, 1959.

Rogger, Hans. *Jewish Policies and Right Wing Politics in Imperial Russia*. Berkeley: University of California Press, 1986.

Scheffler, Wolfgang. "Ausgewählte Dokumente zur Geschichte des Novemberpogroms 1938." *Aus Politik und Zeitgeschichte* (November 4, 1978): B 41-45.

Schmid, Harald. *Erinnern an den "Tag der Schuld." Das Novemberpogrom von 1938 in der deutschen Geschichtspolitik*. Hamburg: Ergebnisse Verlag, 2001.

———. "Die 'Stunde der Wahrheit' und ihre Voraussetzungen. Zum geschichtskulturellen Wirkungskontext von 'Holocaust.'" *Zeitgeschichte-online*, March 2005, 6. Accessed October 4, 2018. https://zeitgeschichte-online.de/thema/die-stunde-der-wahrheit-und-ihre-voraussetzungen.

Senechal de la Roche, Roberta. "Collective Violence as Social Control." *Sociological Forum* 11, no. 1 (1996): 97-128.

Staliunas, Darius. *Enemies for a Day: Antisemitism and Anti-Jewish Violence in Lithuania under the Tsars*. Budapest: Central European University Press, 2015.

Thüsing, Klaus. "Wie steht es mit unserer Glaubwürdigkeit? 'Reichskristallnacht'—nicht nur ein historisches Datum." *Sozialdemokratischer Pressedienst* 218 (1978): S. 3-4.

Weber, Bernd. "'Hitlerwelle' und historisch-politischer Unterricht. Phänomene-Ursachen-Konsequenzen." *Frankfurter Hefte. Zeitschrift für Politik und Kultur* 34 no. 3 (1979): 21-30.

Wiese, Stefan. *Pogrome im Zarenreich. Dynamiken kollektiver Gewalt*. Hamburg: Hamburger Edition HIS Verlagsgesellschaft, 2016.

Zipperstein, Steven. *Pogrom: Kishinev and the Tilt of History*. New York: Liveright Publishing, 2018.

CHAPTER 2

"Worse Than Vandals."
The Mass Destruction of Jewish Homes and Jewish Responses during the 1938 Pogrom[1]

by Wolf Gruner

For many decades, scholars have perceived the November pogrom as the best investigated event in the Third Reich.[2] Yet, our view and understanding seem still quite limited. When the pogrom is discussed, most literature as well as public media solely emphasize the attacks on synagogues and shops across Germany. A few accounts mention the destruction of other Jewish institutions, such as schools and offices, yet almost no attention is paid to the attacks on private homes.[3] During the last decade, books on the pogrom occasionally described the destruction of houses and apartments in more detail based on testimonies written during the war, postwar trials and re-compensation claim records.[4] Yet, the scale and intensity of the violation of privacy during the brutal November attacks has never been thoroughly analyzed, nor has its impact on the Jewish population and their responses.

REPORTS AND NUMBERS

The most commonly cited numbers about the extent of the Kristallnacht violence do not include private homes. Two days after the pogrom, Reinhard Heydrich told high-ranking Nazi leaders that 177 synagogues and 7,500 stores in the Reich had been demolished as well as thirty-five Jews murdered.[5] Later, these numbers were raised to 276 destroyed synagogues, 7,500 damaged stores and ninety-one killed Jews.[6]

While these widely cited figures failed to mention damage of Jewish houses or apartments, the same Reinhard Heydrich, writing to Hermann Göring on November 11, 1938, listed as destroyed: 815 stores, twenty-nine department stores, 169 synagogues, and eleven Jewish community buildings; he also mentioned 171 burned or demolished private Jewish houses. Heydrich suggested that the actual number of destroyed dwellings was far greater than given in his report.[7] Although the Nazis never produced a final assessment of the violence, new research suggests that the number of demolished synagogues surpassed 2,000, and destroyed shops over 10,000; in Berlin alone, at least 3,000 Jewish stores were damaged.[8] Yet, scholars made little effort to obtain any estimates for the loss of private homes.

Closer research, however, quickly yields astonishing results. In a preliminary report on December 2, 1938, the president of the administrative district Schneidemühl noted that sixteen synagogues had been subjected to arson, sixty-three shops destroyed, and 231 homes demolished.[9] Sources for the city of Nuremberg point to equally surprising numbers. The day after the pogrom, Franconian Nazi party Gauleiter Julius Streicher told a mass party meeting that the "demonstrations" in his district had been "generally disciplined, clear and far-sighted." Yet, the police reported that attackers had burned down several synagogues and badly damaged seventy Jewish businesses as well as 236 Jewish homes in Nuremberg.[10] For the region around Nuremberg and Fürth, reports revealed that forty-two synagogues and 115 Jewish businesses had been destroyed, and 594 dwellings vandalized.[11]

The number of destroyed homes in both cases was four to five times the number of demolished stores, which is not surprising when we take into account that the number of private homes was much higher than the number of shops owned by Jews.

In Düsseldorf, more than four hundred private houses as well as rental apartments were demolished.[12] A contemporary report about the attacks in fourteen small towns in Mainz county talked about the destruction of five stores and fifty-three Jewish homes. Yet, from other sources we know that in one of these towns the mayor reported only four instead of nine demolished houses.¹³ Thus, underreporting by mayors, police officers or local SS complicates our assessment. Numbers might have been deliberately deflated, although in villages and small towns the demolished houses were locally known. By contrast, in big cities, the actual scale of the destruction might have been overlooked. While ruins of smoldering synagogues and smashed store windows caught everybody's eyes, most Jews lived in rental apartments in three- or four-story buildings. If no furniture had been thrown out the windows, demolition could easily have gone unnoticed by passers-byes.

In Leipzig, the police district Mitte reported that seven synagogues, 193 stores and thirty-four private homes had been destroyed during the "revenge action" (*Vergeltungsaktion*).¹⁴ For district West, the police recorded the destruction of four synagogues, one orphanage and one elderly home, seventeen stores and sixteen apartments, for district South, fifty stores and five flats as damaged.¹⁵ While the reported amount in Leipzig was smaller than in Nuremberg, the attacks still left dozens and dozens of homes demolished in the Saxon city. Moreover, eyewitnesses emphasized the "mindless destruction of furnishings," beatings and furniture thrown out of windows.¹⁶

For Breslau, an early SS-report mentioned the destruction of three synagogues, three Jewish facilities, ten Jewish inns, thirty-five businesses and over five hundred shops.¹⁷ After looking at other cities, the absence of homes in the list seems peculiar. And indeed, Walter Tausk trusted his diary with a very different account, noting that in Breslau the attacks extended to "apartment storms, strangulations, lynchings and men slaughtered."¹⁸ Another report, issued a day later by the Breslau SS, admitted that all Jewish shops and most Jewish homes and flats had been destroyed, as well as twenty-eight synagogues and two-dozen Jewish facilities.¹⁹

The Munich criminal police did not mention apartments in their first official report, just forty-two destroyed stores, the arsoning of one synagogue and the killing of one Jewish man.²⁰ In reality, the attackers had set ablaze the two remaining main synagogues and destroyed Jewish elderly homes, schools, shops, department stores and dwellings, including by fire the villa of the industrialist Karl Bach.²¹

Attacks on Jewish homes frequently went unnoticed because apartments were often located in the back of stores or on the upper floor of the same building, especially in smaller towns and villages. In Silixen (North-Rhine Westphalia), a report mentioned the destruction of three stores and the attached flats.²² Of the four hundred destroyed homes in Düsseldorf, around sixty had been located at the same premises as shops and practices.²³ In Kaiserslautern, a devastated Anna Bluethe recalled how the perpetrators came with iron rods. First, she thought they wanted to beat the family to death, but they asked for the offices. There they cut the telephone line, destroyed the desks and smashed the windows. Later, others appeared, again with iron rods, brought down a heavy bronze lamp and now smashed her whole place, including living room and kitchen. No cup was left unbroken, no window left intact, she recalled: "We were outlawed."²⁴

Other destroyed or burned apartments were attached to or located inside assaulted synagogues, Jewish community buildings, orphanages, retraining camps, schools and mourning halls at Jewish cemeteries—as was the case in Krefeld, Königsberg, Erfurt, Leipzig, and Vienna.²⁵

It is clear that the destruction of Jewish homes was more widespread than administrative reports acknowledged. In Rostock, Nuremberg, and Mannheim virtually all Jewish homes, in Düsseldorf three quarters of the apartments and stores were destroyed.²⁶ These numbers indicate that the actual figure of destroyed flats across Germany and Austria must have been in the thousands, if not tens of thousands. How is it possible that this mass assault on Jewish homes has been overlooked by media and academia, despite the fact that many survivors addressed such attacks in horrendous detail in their testimonies?

THE INTENSITY OF THE DESTRUCTION

In Hanover, the police president reported after the pogrom that a synagogue, a Jewish cemetery, ninety-four stores and twenty-seven apartments had been demolished. He downplayed the damages by emphasizing that in a number of apartments destruction was limited to the breaking of a few furniture items or windows and mirrors.²⁷ By contrast, survivors from Hanover recalled that furniture "had been methodically hacked to pieces," and household property was burned "in the presence of a cheering crowd" at a public square.²⁸

Hence, it was not just the scale, but also the systematic nature and the intensity of the destruction that is astonishing. We do not know exactly what Goebbels told the Nazi party leadership that night in Munich, other than what he wrote in his diary: that Hitler ordered demonstrations to proceed and that Goebbels informed the Nazi leaders accordingly that night at a gathering.²⁹ The Vienna Gauleiter, Odilo Globocnik, who attended the meeting in city hall, noted that Goebbels requested drastic actions with free range for anybody aiming at the destruction of Jewish property.[30] Later, at the Nazi party office in Munich, Goebbels drafted a circular, probably to the Gau leadership, in which he detailed a radical course of action. The document has not yet been unearthed by researchers.[31]

However, in Vienna, an order from the Reich propaganda office (*Reichspropagandaamt*) which demanded drastic action arrived by telegraph at 3:00 am at the Gau leadership.[32] In Koblenz, the Gau leader ordered the destruction of synagogues and furnishings in private Jewish homes.[33] In Heilsberg (East Prussia), the local NSDAP leader read a written order to the SA men to burn synagogues, destroy business papers and demolish the interior furnishings of Jewish homes.[34]

Thus, it seems very likely that Goebbels gave concrete instructions to attack and fully destroy Jewish homes. During the night of the pogrom, members of Nazi organizations as well as neighbors stormed houses everywhere and systematically destroyed them. In Beuthen (Silesia), the merchant Martin Fröhlich came home in the afternoon of the fateful day. The door was broken, a fallen wardrobe blocked the entrance. He had to wade through knee-deep shards and rags. Everything was smashed to pieces: glass, china, clocks, the piano, his violin, furniture, chairs, lamps and paintings. Realizing that his home was now uninhabitable, Fröhlich started crying like a child. As he wrote to his daughter, the Nazis had acted "worse than Vandals."[35]

In Kamp near Boppard (Rhine), attackers broke in from the backside of the house of the Kaufmann family, destroyed furniture and lamps on the ground floor, ripped stove pipes and doors out and broke walls. When parts of the ceiling on the first floor collapsed, the family escaped and sought shelter in a nearby monastery. In Groß-Auheim (Hesse), two Jewish homes were vandalized after a speech of the local Nazi party leader. The perpetrators used sledge hammers to destroy everything, including lamps, radios, clocks and furniture, they spilled ink on paintings, rugs and tablecloths, and cut blankets with glass shards, etc. After the war, glass and china splinters could still be seen impressed in the wooden floor.[36]

The Swiss merchant René Juvet, who was on a business trip through Bavaria, wanted to visit Jewish friends in Nuremberg. When he entered the premises, he found the door unhinged, furniture thrown in the garden, water everywhere, the railing at the stairs and all doors hacked to pieces with axes, valuable paintings cut with knives, and the piano broken. His hosts had both been terribly beaten, and the man died the next day in the hospital.[37]

Attack on a Jewish home by SA men, probably Nuremberg, November 9–10, 1938 (Private Archive Elisheva Avital Family, New Jersey).

Jewish home after an attack by SA men, probably Nuremberg, November 9–10, 1938 (Private Archive Elisheva Avital Family, New Jersey).

"Worse than Vandals." The Mass Destruction of Jewish Homes 31

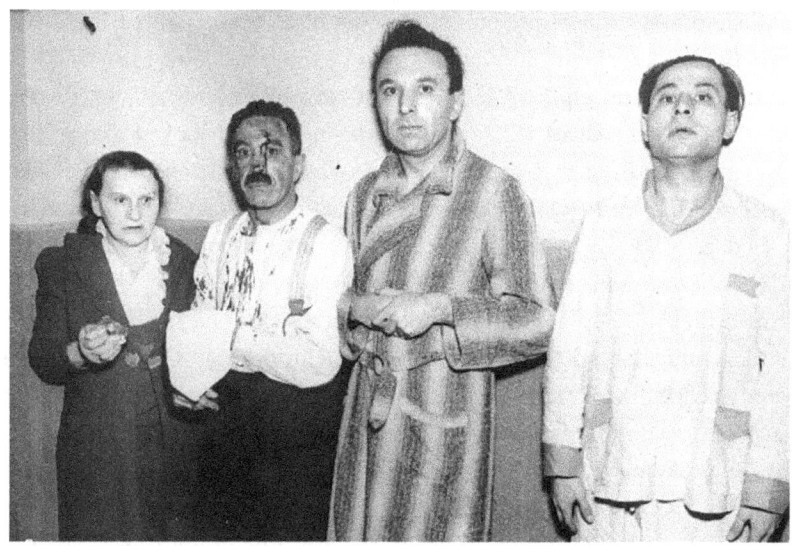

Jews after the attack on their home and beatings by SA men, probably Nuremberg, November 9–10, 1938 (Private Archive Elisheva Avital Family, New Jersey).

PLUNDER, SEXUAL ASSAULT, BEATINGS, AND MURDER

The extreme gravity of home destruction was accompanied by the massive plunder of Jewish goods. In villages and small towns, like Mechernich, Badenweiler, Heidenheim, Emden, or Bad Kreuznach, perpetrators, among them many women, exploited the general mayhem and stole rugs, valuables of all sorts, paintings, money, vacuum cleaners, clothing, table cloths, silverware, wine, and food.[38]

The massive invasion of private homes also explains the growing evidence for sexual humiliation, sexual assault and rape during the pogrom. In Rimbach (Hesse), storm troopers broke into the home of the Weichsel family, dragged the couple out of their bed, physically abused the husband and beat his wife, who was just wearing a night gown, with sticks between the legs and touched her breasts.[39] In Linz, SA men forced a Jewish woman to take off her clothes and to pose for them naked; later, two Storm troopers sexually assaulted her. The SA leader from Rheinhausen raped a thirteen-year-old Jewish girl in Duisburg after abducting the unsuspecting child.[40] Women were not the only ones to suffer sexual assaults. In Düsseldorf, a female leader of the Nazi women's organization, humiliated a seventy-year old Jewish man by driving him onto the street just wearing a night shirt, and then lifting his shirt in front of the staring crowd.[41]

The destruction of private homes was often accompanied by frequent beatings of their residents. In Vienna, over one thousand Jews, including women and children, were hurt.[42] In a letter of November 20th, a Jewish woman from Vienna told a relative: "You can't imagine, how it looked like at home. Papa with a head injury, bandaged, I with severe attacks in bed, everything ravaged and shattered. [...] Since all glassware, windows and mirrors had been smashed, as had been my psyche, there were so many shards and splinters that we did not know how to help ourselves."[43]

Murder was also common.[44] In Bremen, SA stormed the home of Selma Zwienicki and shot her to death in her own bedroom.[45] In Cologne, two men entered the apartment and hair salon of Moritz Spiro. When Spiro tried to stop them from destroying his furniture, one of the intruders beat him over the head and broke his skull. He died several days later in the Jewish hospital.[46] In Berlin, two SA-Men followed Willy Wurceldorf to his apartment in the district Friedrichshain and beat him to death in the morning of the 10th.[47] In Hilden near Düsseldorf, SA and SS gangs broke into the apartment of the Willner family, vandalized the premises and shot the sixty-eight-year-old mother. Then, they went to another apartment and killed Karl Herz with a knife. Later, they returned to the Willner flat and killed the son Ernst, who had hidden, with a shot to the head.[48]

ATTACKS AND CONSEQUENCES ACROSS GREATER GERMANY

SA and SS targeted private Jewish homes across the country. The western and central parts of Berlin saw massive destruction and looting of Jewish shops; Jewish apartments were also demolished in Berlin-Charlottenburg.[49] More homes were attacked in the Northern and Eastern city districts, where young uniformed men burglarized many apartments.[50] A Jewish woman noted in a letter that "the beasts" pushed their way "into apartments, threw the furniture out the windows a[nd] slit open the beds."[51]

In the Austrian capital, raids on seventy percent of the Jewish houses and apartments resulted in the destruction of furniture, looting of valuables, and setting off fires.[52] In 1946, Malka Johles talked about her experience in Vienna: "On November 10th, they invaded our [apartment] maybe twenty Gestapo-men, they took everything, all jewelry, all silverware, everything they took from me!"⁵³ In Ruth Birnholz's parents apartment, intruders smashed furniture, broke all the mirrors and stole her mother's jewelry.⁵⁴

Across the Greater German Reich, large groups of perpetrators roamed villages and small towns. At 6:00 am in the morning of the 10th, eighty to one hundred people, some in uniform, others in civilian clothes, formed several groups which demolished homes and the synagogue in Sobernheim (Rhineland-Palatinate). In Neustadt-Aich (Bavaria), approximately one hundred SA-men split into smaller groups and vandalized the homes of the five remaining Jewish families. In many cases, they had lists with addresses, which they either received from Nazi party organizations or, as in Trier, from the municipality.⁵⁵

Chava Rechnitz, who fled the devastation in Berlin by taking a train, found her home in Ratibor (Silesia) deserted and "five of the rooms totally destroyed, broken windows, broken furniture, even my mother's beloved grand piano, a Bechstein, was in pieces."⁵⁶ In Weisswasser and Bad Muskau (both Saxonia), SA men broke into several Jewish apartments, hacked their home furnishings into pieces with axes, and threw furniture out of windows.⁵⁷ In Geldern, near the Dutch border, SS first burned the synagogues, then destroyed the two shops as well as all homes of the twelve Jewish families.⁵⁸ Homes were not just damaged, but in some cases burned to the ground, as in Euskirchen (Rhineland) the house of the Horn family.⁵⁹

The nationwide attacks on private homes received some international attention. Although most foreign diplomats wrote appalled reports about the attacks on synagogues and shops as well the mass arrest of Jewish men, only a few mentioned the destruction of homes. The consul general of Italy reported on November 12 that in Innsbruck bands of thugs armed with knives and steel clubs had intruded the homes of the few remaining Jewish families, destroyed furniture and china and knifed down several people. Five Jews were murdered and many more suffered severe injuries.⁶⁰ On November 15, the US consul general in Stuttgart, Samuel Honaker, wrote to the US-ambassador in Berlin: "Of all the places in this section of Germany, the Jews in Rastatt, which is situated near Baden-Baden, have apparently been subjected to the most ruthless treatment. Many Jews in this section were cruelly attacked and beaten and the furnishings of their homes almost totally destroyed."⁶¹ The Swiss consul in Cologne informed his ambassador in Berlin that "organized patrols" had been going from one flat to another, where they smashed the place and threw belongings out of the windows: gramophones, sewing machines, typewriters. Three days after the violence, bed feathers could still be seen on bushes and trees.⁶²

Countless Jews had to abandon homes without windows and doors in the cold November weather. Seeking shelter elsewhere, some stayed with non-Jewish neighbors, some at Jewish institutions, others with relatives in town or beyond city limits, and some with friends.[63] In Vienna, fifty people found shelter at the Jewish apprentice hostel and fifteen in the flat of the head of the Jewish community.[64] In Guntersblum, most Jews left to stay with relatives in neighboring cities such as Frankfurt. Several months after the pogrom, only four of the original fifty-four Jews still lived in Guntersblum.[65] The Holzers, who were driven out of their home in the small town Traunstein, moved to Munich to live with their relative Anna Neuburger.[66] To a letter, which Anna Neuburger wrote to her children in the United States, they added: "My loved ones, as you can see we are still with your mom. Don't worry she's doing well considering the circumstances. We'll remain here until we can return home. Of course the best thing would be to go to America right away."[67]

These accounts make it clear that the demolition of private homes and rented apartments was a mass phenomenon during the November pogrom that demands further investigation. The destruction of the last refuge, their homes, and the loss of security and privacy for so many families, must have taken a severe emotional, material and psychological toll on the Jewish population. The brutality of attacks that rendered thousands of Jews homeless, beaten or sexually assaulted, helps us understand the reasoning for the high number of Jewish suicides and decisions to flee. In addition to underestimating the scope and intensity of these attacks, scholars have also underestimated the widespread occurrence of non-Jewish and even Jewish protests against the pogrom.

JEWISH RESPONSES DURING AND AFTER THE VIOLENCE

A day after the pogrom, the county commissioner in Herford, a small town near Bielefeld, reported that after everything had calmed down, most "party and people's comrades" perceived the action as absolutely necessary, because "lately the attitude of the Jews had been fresh and impudent bordering hubris [*Überheblichkeit*]. The Jews would think nothing could happen to them. For this very reason, everybody who is in favor of the fatherland appreciated the air clearing thunderstorm as liberating."[68] Yet, the district president in Upper Bavaria saw the effects of the violence differently. He reported that the population perceived the protest action as organized and had criticized the violence.[69]

During the last decade, new research has suggested there was more criticism of the pogroms by non-Jewish Germans than we previously assumed. These concerns were motivated less by economical concerns as emphasized by older literature, than by humanistic and moral ones.[70] Even the SS acknowledged this fact. While the SD-Main office report for November 1938 highlighted the economic motives behind most of the critique, it also admitted that in various places the population had publicly expressed sympathy with the persecuted Jews. Ironically, some even smashed the windows of the homes of party officials who were seen as responsible for the violent actions.[71] The SD in Hannover summarized later that "the protest action had been perceived differently in the German population. While most people's comrades, with exception of catholic circles, supposedly agreed with the demolition of the synagogue, the destruction of shops and private homes have been rejected."[72]

Even more astonishing than the critique among non-Jewish Germans is the fact that the brutal nationwide pogrom did not deter Jewish Germans from protesting the violence.[73] After more than twenty-seven people died in Vienna, the Jewish community petitioned Adolf Eichmann's Central office to stop the violence, the mass arrests of Jewish males and the demolition of private homes. The representatives criticized that so many apartments had been raided and destroyed, among them the home of an emigration councilor working for the Jewish community. At his home, the assailants destroyed important papers, including fifteen affidavits for immigration to the United States.[74]

Across Germany, SA had also raided many re-training camps where Jewish youths prepared for emigration by receiving agricultural training. Students and instructors were arrested at many camps, including Ellguth/Silesia, Freienstein/Pomerania, Gehringsdorf near Fulda, and Neuendorf near Fürstenwalde.[75] On November 19, the German umbrella organization of the Jewish communities (the *Reichsvertretung*) intervened at Gestapo headquarters against the destruction of retraining facilities and the internment of students and teachers in concentration camps. At the end of the month, managers and teachers were released to resume the emigration training.[76]

Jewish individuals responded in a variety of ways. Some saved religious objects or private goods, others documented the crimes and the destruction, either by creating lists or taking pictures of damaged businesses.[77] Andreas Kirschbaum was arrested photographing damaged Jewish stores in Berlin. Although he was released and got his camera back, he never received the film.[78]

Some Jews openly denounced the pogrom as a barbaric act.[79] In Frankfurt/Main, Mrs. Henriette Schäfer entered her neighbor's shop after the pogrom and asked, "What are you saying about the fact that everything is being destroyed and the synagogues are being set on fire?" After the shop keeper responded along official lines that people had been outraged by the murder of a German diplomat by a Jew, Schäfer replied, "This is not the people, but the government. They are all blackguards, scamps, and criminals. Hitler is the biggest bandit. If I could, I would poison them all." For this comment, the special court punished her with six months in prison under the treacherous attacks law of 1934.[80]

In a small Bavarian place Krumbach, on November 19, 1938, Minna Klopfer told the owner of a milk shop in front of half a dozen witnesses that once things have calmed down, the Catholics will be next. They will suffer the same fate as we did. Since this was not the first time Klopfer had criticized the Nazis, she received six months in prison.[81] The tanner Ernst Nachmann was one of the thirty thousand men arrested during the pogrom. After his release from Buchenwald concentration camp, he openly talked about his experiences: how SS guards abused rabbis and beat and murdered prisoners. In front of witnesses in Frankfurt, he called Hitler a *Kelef*, which was Hebrew for dog, a cruel guy and a tramp.[82]

Edith Wolff of Berlin mailed postcards calling National Socialism the biggest cultural outrage, and signed them, "The Eternal Jew." In Hamburg, Walter G. wrote, copied, and distributed a fourteen-page protest letter with the title "J'accuse," which projected the doom of 500,000 Jews.[83] The Vienna Gestapo, as they wrote in a report, received a number of anonymous letters disparaging "with genuine Jewish impudence the Führer and the party." One such letter read: "Dear sweet Gestapo. We will soon beat your ass. Until the German mutt race will arrive in our ghetto alley, Hosanna to our Greenshpan, the hero boy from Paris. Where now the murder frenzy unfolds, there you will soon come into a big fuss. Gun down the dog, the Hitler! . . ."[84]

During the pogrom, a few Jews even resisted physically. In Peine (Lower Saxony), located between Hanover and Brunswick, a group of SS men invaded and destroyed twenty family homes. When the SS broke into the Marburger family apartment and started beating his father, Hans, a seventeen-year-old boy, tried to fight them off. However, the three SS men overwhelmed him, brought him to the synagogue, and shot the Jewish teenager to death. Then, they set ablaze the synagogue using gasoline.[85] In Urfeld, storm troopers raided the agricultural campsite where teenagers trained for the emigration to Palestine. First the intruders beat up the boys, then the girls. When it was sixteen-year-old Daisy Gronowsky's turn, an SA-man approached her with a knife. Without warning,

Daisy head-butted him in the stomach, a Jiu Jitsu self-defense she had learned at her Zionist youth group Hashomer Hatzair in Berlin. Exploiting his surprise, she twisted the knife out of his hand and stabbed him in his stomach. Leaving him unconscious, she and some friends were able to escape into the fields.[86]

CONCLUSION

Jews reacted in various ways to the devastating violence launched by SS, storm troopers and Hitler youth members and neighbors: they documented the crimes, secured goods, helped other Jews, protested via official channels, sent leaflets and publicly spoke out against the crimes. Recently photos from two cities surfaced that confirm the enormous destruction of private homes during the pogrom of November 1938. These photos were taken by Jewish victims to document the crimes and expose the extraordinary levels of violence.[87]

Given the preliminary accounts of violence presented here, which are based on a study of administrative reports, trial documents and testimonies, the pogrom dubbed Kristallnacht deserved the name not only because of the shattered shop windows, but because of the countless broken windows, mirrors and china in Jewish homes. Although the attacks on and destruction of private homes were not as visible to contemporaries as burning synagogues or looted shops, they were severe and widespread as testimonies of survivors reveal in great detail. Yet, these attacks were often not acknowledged or were consciously downplayed in official administrative reports authored by the SS, SA or mayors; and they were equally overlooked in contemporary media and diplomatic reports.

The systematic vandalism of Kristallnacht rendered countless Jewish homes uninhabitable across Greater Germany. The evidence presented here offers a preliminary account of the scale and intensity of the mass demolishment of private homes and apartments of German and Austrian Jews. We can only begin to fathom the enormous psychological and material toll the violence took on the Jewish families and individuals. Many Jews were devastated, having witnessed the intrusion of their homes and the violent demolition of furniture, musical instruments, paintings, clothing, china and food. They also experienced humiliations, beatings, sexual violence, murder, and last, but not least, the loss of treasured personal belongings and memories.

After the violent attacks, many Jews in Nazi Germany and annexed Austria found themselves deprived of their last refuge.[88] The violent attacks on their homes seems to be an important overlooked factor to understand the motivation of the masses of Jewish individuals who now decided that there was no future in Nazi Germany anymore—men and women who either committed suicide or fled their homeland leaving everything behind.

Notes

1. This chapter is a preliminary account of a larger book project on this topic. Thanks to Marion Kaplan (New York University) who gave generous feedback on an early version of this chapter. I also thank the conference discussants and my coeditor Steve Ross for helpful comments.
2. Wolfgang Benz, "Erziehung zur Unmenschlichkeit. Der 9. November 1938," in *Der 9. November. Fünf Essays zur deutschen Geschichte*, ed. Johannes Willms (Munich: C. H. Beck, 1994), S. 50. Cited by Daniel Ristau, "Der 9. November 1938: Die Novemberpogrome in Sachsen im Spannungsfeld zwischen Geschichtsforschung, Gedenkkultur und persönlicher Erinnerung," *Medaon* 12 (2018), 23, p. 2, http://www.medaon.de/pdf/medaon_23_ristau_artikel.pdf.
3. Some exceptions need to be mentioned: Kurt Pätzold, "Der Pogrom und sein Platz in der Geschichte der Vertreibung der jüdischen Deutschen," in *Pogromnacht 1938*, ed. Kurt Pätzold and Irene Runge (Berlin: Dietz, 1988), 63, and photo with caption (between 96 and 97); Marion Kaplan, *Between Dignity and Despair: Jewish life in Nazi Germany* (New York: Oxford University Press, 1998), 119. Stefanie Schüler-Springorum pointed to its importance as an experience of violence: *Geschlecht und Differenz* (Paderborn: Schöningh, 2014), 126–27. By contrast Friedländer mentions it by citing a consul report, but does not go further: Saul Friedländer, *Nazi Germany and the Jews*, vol. I, *The Years of Persecution, 1933–1939* (New York: HarperCollins, 1996), 277; similarly Alexander Korb, *Reaktionen der deutschen Bevölkerung auf die Novemberpogrome* (Saarbrücken: VDM, 2008), 2–3.
4. Raphael Gross mentions the destruction of flats just once in passing in his introduction, yet the testimonies in the collection often describe it in detail: Ben Barkow, Raphael Gross, and Michael Lenarz, eds., *Novemberpogrom 1938. Die Augenzeugenberichte der Wiener Library* (London: Jüdischer Verlag im Suhrkamp Verlag, 2008), 22. For the destruction, see for example: 155–67, 173. By contrast, Alan Steinweis mentions it several times in his important book, but provides no further detail or analysis, Alan Steinweis, *Kristallnacht 1938* (Cambridge, MA: Belknap Press of Harvard University Press, 2009), 1, 69, 75, 80, 83–86; Michael Wildt's account is similar, but he provides vivid detail: Michael Wildt, *Volksgemeinschaft als Selbstermächtigung. Gewalt gegen Juden in der deutschen Provinz 1919 bis 1939* (Hamburg: Hamburger Edition, 2007), 325–35. Bastian Fleermann dedicates a small subchapter focusing on the plunder in his account on the destruction of the Jewish homes in Düsseldorf: Bastian Fleermann, "Nach dem Pogrom. Bilanz der Ausschreitungen in Düsseldorf," in *Novemberpogrom 1938 in Düsseldorf*, ed. Mahn-und Gedenkstätte Düsseldorf (Düsseldorf: 2017), 375–80.
5. Conference, 12 November 1938, protocol printed in Susanne Heim, ed., *Verfolgung und Ermordung der europäischen Juden [VEJ]*, vol. 2 (Munich: R. Oldenbourg Verlag, 2009), Doc. 146, pp. 415 and 422.

6. Friedländer, *Nazi Germany and the Jews*, 276.
7. Reinhard Heydrich to Hermann Göring, November 11, 1938, in Pätzold/Runge, *Pogromnacht 1938*, 136, Doc. 22.
8. "Liste der im Deutschen Reich von 1933 bis 1945 zerstörten Synagogen," *Wikipedia*, accessed January 17, 2019, https://de.wikipedia.org/wiki/Liste_der_im_Deutschen_Reich_von_1933_bis_1945_zerst%C3%B6rten_Synagogen; Christoph Kreutzmüller, *Ausverkauf: Die Vernichtung der jüdischen Gewerbetätigkeit in Berlin 1930–1945* (Berlin: Metropol, 2012), 172 (in English as *Final Sale in Berlin: The Destruction of Jewish Commercial Activity 1930–1945* (New York: Berghahn, 2015).
9. Bogdan Frankiewicz and Wolfgang Wilhelmus, "Selbstachtung wahren und Solidarität üben. Pommerns Juden während des Nationalsozialismus," in *"Halte fern dem ganzen Lande jedes Verderben . . ." Geschichte und Kultur der Juden in Pommern. Ein Sammelband*, ed. Margret Heitmann, Julius H. Schoeps, and Bernhard Vogt (Hildesheim: Olms, 1995), 464.
10. Donald McKale, "A Case of Nazi 'Justice': The Punishment of Party Members Involved in the Kristallnacht 1938," *Jewish Social Studies* 35, no. 3–4 (July–October, 1973): 231. See also for some individual cases: Edith Raim, *Justiz zwischen Diktatur und Demokratie. Wiederaufbau und Ahndung von NS-Verbrechen in Westdeutschland 1945–1949* (Munich: Oldenbourg Verlag, 2013), 833–35.
11. Edith Raim, "Die Verfolgung und Vernichtung der fränkischen Juden in der NS-Zeit," in *Die Juden in Franken*, ed. Michael Brenner and Daniela F. Eisenstein (Munich: Oldenbourg, 2011), 208.
12. Account of the author based on Barbara Suchy, "Überfallen in Düsseldorf. Der Novemberpogrom in Selbstzeugnissen und Dokumenten," in *Novemberpogrom 1938 in Düsseldorf*, ed. Bastian Fleermann and Angela Genger (Essen: Klartext Verlag, 2008), 125–265.
13. Sven Felix Kellerhoff, *Ein ganz normales Pogrom. November 1938 in einem deutschen Dorf* (Stuttgart: Klett-Cotta, 2018), 132 and 137.
14. StA Leipzig, Polizeipräsidium, PP_V 4965, fol. 210: Report for November 1938, police, district Leipzig-Mitte, November 29, 2018.
15. StA Leipzig, Polizeipräsidium, PP_V 4965, fol. 211RS: Report for November 1938, police, district Leipzig-West, November 30, 2018; ibid., fol. 212: Report for November 1938, police, district Leipzig-Süd, November 29, 2018.
16. See testimony (January 1939), in Barkow, Gross, and Lenarz, eds., *Novemberpogrom 1938*, 304; and testimonies in Martin Gilbert, *Kristallnacht: Prelude to Destruction* (New York: Harper Perennial, 2006), 87–88.
17. Pätzold and Runge, *Pogromnacht 1938*, 118, Doc 8. Cited by Abraham Ascher, *A Community under Siege: The Jews of Breslau under Nazism* (Stanford, CA: Stanford University Press, 2007), 170.
18. Entry, November 15, 1938, in Walter Tausk, *Breslauer Tagebuch 1933–1940* (Berlin: Rütten und Loening, 1975), 193.

19. Report SS Breslau, November 11, 1938, in Pätzold and Runge, *Pogromnacht 1938*, 134, Doc 20. See also testimony in Barkow, Gross, and Lenarz, eds., *Novemberpogrom 1938*, 264.
20. Report, November 10, 1938 (Facsimile), in Andreas Heusler and Tobias Weger, *"Kristallnacht." Gewalt gegen die Münchner Juden im November 1938* (Munich: Buchendorfer, 1998), 51.
21. Thirty-three Jews committed suicide in Munich in 1938; Heusler and Weger, "Kristallnacht," 37, 52–64, 74–75, 78–80, 115–116, 144; Barkow, Gross, and Lenarz, eds., *Novemberpogrom 1938*, 480–81.
22. Otto Dov Kulka and Eberhard Jäckel, eds., *The Jews in the Secret Nazi Reports on Popular Opinion in Germany, 1933–1945* (New Haven: Yale University Press, 2010), CD-No. 2633: NSDAP Kreisleitung Detmold report, November 12, 1938. More examples in Raim, *Justiz*, 811–14.
23. Account of the author based on Suchy, "Überfallen in Düsseldorf," 125–265. See for Berlin: Klaus Behnken, ed., *Sopade: Deutschland-Berichte der Sozialdemokratischen Partei Deutschlands 1934–1940* (Salzhausen, Germany: Nettelbeck, 1980), vol. 5 (December 1938), A II, 1340.
24. Anna and Leo Bluethe Letters, Kristallnacht in Kaiserslautern: Letter, April 26, 1939, 1–3, RG 02 099, USHMM Washington, DC.
25. *VEJ*, vol. 2, Docs. 128 and 131, pp. 371–71, 378–79; Barkow, Gross, and Lenarz, eds., *Novemberpogrom 1938*, 302; Raim, *Justiz*, 808, 841; Jutta Hoschek, *Der Novemberpogrom 1938 in Erfurt. Aus Dokumenten und Erinnerungen*, ed. Landeshauptstadt Erfurt, Stadtverwaltung und das Netzwerk "Jüdisches Leben Erfurt" (Jena: Vopelius 2018), 30; *Novemberpogrome 1938 in Niedersachsen Peine*, accessed January 19, 2019, https://pogrome1938-niedersachsen.de/peine/; "'Kristallnacht'—Als im 'Reich' die Synagogen brannten," accessed January 19, 2019, https://www.myheimat.de/peine/kultur/kristallnacht-als-im-reich-die-synagogen-brannten-d2723453.html; USHMM Washington, DC, RG 02.092.01, Victor Gans Memoir, Shanghai, February 14, 1939 (later English translation), 40.
26. Joint memorandum, November 30, 1938, in *VEJ*, Vol. 2, Doc. 185, pp. 518–21; Fleermann and Genger, *Novemberpogrom 1938 in Düsseldorf*, 14.
27. Police President, Letter, December 3, 1938, facsimile in John Mendelsohn, ed., *The Holocaust*, vol. 3, *The Crystal Night Pogrom* (New York: Garland Publishing, 1982), 63–64.
28. Gilbert, *Kristallnacht*, 90, 102.
29. Joseph Goebbels, diary entry, November 10, 1938, in Elke Frölich, ed., *Die Tagebücher von Joseph Goebbels*, Teil I, Bd. 6 (Munich: de Gruyter, 1998), 179–81. Printed in *VEJ*, vol. 2, Doc. 124, p. 364.
30. Odilo Globocnik, Report about the "Jew action" on November 10 and 11 (no date), in *VEJ*, vol. 2, Doc. 133, p. 385.
31. Joseph Goebbels, diary entry, November 10, 1938.

32. Odilo Globocnik, Report about the "Jew action."
33. Franz-Josef Schmit, *Novemberpogrom in Wittlich 1938. Ablauf-Hintergründe-offene Fragen-juristische Aufarbeitung* (Butzweiler: Trier-Verlag: 2013), 65.
34. USHMM Washington, DC., RG-68.083M, Selected Records of the Supreme Tribunal of the Nazi Party (BA Berlin, NS 36/13, fol. 23): Judgement, Supreme Tribunal of the Nazi Party, December 20, 1938, 5.
35. *VEJ*, vol. 2, Doc. 163, 470–71.
36. Raim, *Justiz*, 805.
37. René Juvet, Excerpt published in 1944, in Oliver Lubrich, ed., *Reisen ins Reich. 1933–1945 Ausländische Autoren berichten aus Deutschland* (Munich: Eichborn, 2009), 197–98.
38. Raim, *Justiz*, 806–14, 851–56.
39. Wolfgang Benz, "Pogrom und Volksgemeinschaft. Zwischen Abscheu und Beteiligung: Die Öffentlichkeit des 9. November 1938," in *Die Novemberpogrome. Versuch einer Bilanz*, ed. Claudia Steur (Berlin: Stiftung Topographie des Terrors, 2009), 15.
40. USHMM Washington, DC., RG-68.083M Selected Records of the Supreme Tribunal of the Nazi Party (BA Berlin, NS 36/13); McKale, "A Case of Nazi 'Justice,'" 233–34; Steinweis, *Kristallnacht*, 117–18.
41. Raim, *Justiz*, 819–20.
42. Barkow, Gross, and Lenarz, eds., *Novemberpogrom 1938*, 753–57, 772–809.
43. Hans Witek and Hans Safrian, *Und keiner war dabei: Dokumente des alltäglichen Antisemitismus in Wien 1938* (Vienna: Picus Verlag, 2008), 177.
44. For example in Lesum, Lünen, Chemnitz, Neidenburg, Heilsburg, Lichtenfels, Aschaffenburg and Munich; *VEJ*, vol. 2, Doc. 134, pp. 388–91; McKale, "A Case of Nazi 'Justice,'" 234–36; Steinweis, *Kristallnacht 1938*, 69–70, 83; USHMM Washington, DC., RG-68.083M Selected Records of the Supreme Tribunal of the Nazi Party (BA Berlin, NS 36/13); Report Siegfried Rose (Borna) cited by Ristau, "Der 9. November 1938: Die Novemberpogrome in Sachsen," 11–12.
45. Senator für Justiz und Verfassung der Freien Hansestadt Bremen, *"Reichskristallnacht" in Bremen. Vorgeschichte, Hergang und gerichtliche Bewältigung des Pogroms vom 9./10. November 1938* (Bremen: Steintor, 1988), 44–59.
46. Horst Matzerath, ed., *Jüdisches Schicksal in Köln 1918–1945: Ausstellung des Historischen Archivs der Stadt Köln/NS-Dokumentationszentrum vom 8. November 1988 bis 22. Januar 1989* (Köln: Stadt Köln, 1988), 275 and 357–62.
47. Christoph Kreutzmüller and Theresa Polley, "Geplündert und gelistet. Eine Fallstudie zum Novemberpogrom in Berlin," *Zeitschrift für Geschichtswissenschaft* 66, no. 11 (2018): 935–36.
48. Holger Berschel, "Die Gestapo Düsseldorf und der Pogrom," in *Novemberpogrom 1938 in Düsseldorf*, ed. Bastian Fleermann and Angela Genger (Essen: Klartext Verlag, 2008), 95.

49. Raim, *Justiz*, 903.
50. Joint report, November 30, 2018, in *VEJ*, vol. 2, Doc. 185, p. 525; *Sopade-Berichte* 5 (December 1938): A II, 1340.
51. Cited by Wolf Gruner, *The Persecution of the Jews in Berlin 1933–1945: A Chronology of Measures by the Authorities in the German Capital* (Berlin: Stiftung Topographie, 2014), 34. See also Kreutzmüller and Polley, "Geplündert und gelistet," 931.
52. Jewish community Vienna to Zentralstelle für jüdische Auswanderung, Vienna, November 11, 1938, in *VEJ*, vol. 2, Doc. 135, pp. 393–96. See also Barkow, Gross, and Lenarz, eds., *Novemberpogrom 1938*, 753–57, 772–809.
53. Malka Johles, interview by David Boder, August 28, 1946, in Geneva. Thanks go to Todd Pressner, Los Angeles, for providing me with a searchable digital version of the English transcripts of the more than hundred audio interviews of the David Boder collection at the Illinois Institute of Technology. For the transcript with the original German see: http://voices.iit.edu/interview?doc=johlesM&display=johlesM_de, accessed May 24, 2019.
54. Gilbert, *Kristallnacht*, 56.
55. Raim, *Justiz*, 866, 876, 879.
56. Cited by Gilbert, *Kristallnacht*, 112.
57. Hans Brenner et al., eds., *NS-Terror und Verfolgung in Sachsen. Von den frühen Konzentrationslagern bis zu den Todesmärschen* (Dresden: Sächsische Landeszentrale für politische Bildung, 2018), 190.
58. Yad Vashem Jerusalem, O2/1160.3, fol. 303: Report, SS-Sturm 10/25, November 15, 1938.
59. Letter, December 19, 1938, in Hans-Dieter Arntz, ed., *Isidors Briefe. Über die Korrespondenz eines Juden aus Euskirchen* (Aachen: Helios, 2009), 34.
60. Christian Dirks and Hermann Simon, eds., *Von Innen nach Aussen. Die Novemberpogrome 1938 in Diplomatenberichten aus Deutschland* [From the Inside to the Outside. The 1938 November Pogroms in Diplomatic Reports from Germany] (Berlin: Metropol Verlag, 2014), 60–61.
61. Samuel Honaker to Messersmith, November 15, 1938, Facsimile, in ibid, 157. See also document facsimile in Mendelsohn, *The Holocaust*, vol. 3, 176–80, here 176.
62. *Diplomatic Documents of Switzerland* (*Dodis*), 1019–20: Doc. 445 E 2001 (D) 3/163 Le Consul de Suisse à Cologne, F. von Weiss, au Ministre de Suisse à Berlin, H. Frôlicher, Cologne, November 12–13, 1938. Parts of the document are cited by Friedländer, *Nazi Germany and the Jews*, 276.
63. *VEJ*, vol. 2, Doc. 163, 470.
64. Jewish community Vienna, letter to Zentralstelle für jüdische Auswanderung, Vienna, November 11, 1938, in *VEJ*, vol. 2, Doc. 135, 395.
65. Kellerhoff, *Ein ganz normales Pogrom*, 155–59. For Frankfurt see Gilbert, *Kristallnacht*, 100–01.
66. "Die Vertreibung der jüdischen Familie Holzer. 'Reichskristallnacht' in Traunstein

vor 70 Jahren," Traunsteiner Tageblatt, 45/2008, Nr. 45, accessed April 23, 2018, https://www.traunsteiner-tagblatt.de/das-traunsteiner-tagblatt/chiemgau-blaetter/chiemgau-blaetter-2018_ausgabe,-die-vertreibung-der-juedischen-familie-holzer-_chid,752.html (thanks for the information goes to Bruce Neuburger, San Francisco).

67. Anna Neuburger and Hedi Holzer, Munich, to Johanna and Fritz Neuburger, November 12, 1938, Private Archive Bruce Neuburger, San Francisco (thanks to Bruce Neuburger for providing me with a copy).
68. Landrat Herford, report November 10, 1938, November 21, 1938, in Kulka and Jäckel, *The Jews*, CD-No. 2669.
69. Heusler/Weger, *Kristallnacht*, 156–57.
70. Peter Longerich, *"Davon haben wir nichts gewusst!" Die Deutschen und die Judenverfolgung, 1933-1945* (Munich: Siedler Verlag, 2006), 129–35; Korb, *Reaktionen*; Wolf Gruner, "Indifference? Participation and Protest as Individual Responses to the Persecution of the Jews as Revealed in Berlin Police Logs and Trial Records, 1933-45," in *The Germans and the Holocaust. Popular Responses to the Persecution and Murder of the Jews*, ed. Alan Steinweis and Susanna Schrafstetter (New York: Berghahn, 2016), 67–68.
71. SD-Hauptamt II 112, report for November 1938, December 7, 1938, in Kulka and Jäckel, *The Jews*, CD-No. 2550.
72. SD-Oberabschnitt Nord-West II 112, Bericht für 1938, Hannover, o. D. in Kulka and Jäckel, *The Jews*, CD. 2772; cited by Korb, *Reaktionen*, 56.
73. In general on Jewish individual Resistance and for the following see: Wolf Gruner, "'The Germans Should Expel the Foreigner Hitler': Open Protest and Other Forms of Jewish Defiance in Nazi Germany," *Yad Vashem Studies* 39, no. 2 (2011): 13–53; idem, "Defiance and Protest: A Comparative Micro-Historical Re-evaluation of Individual Jewish Responses towards Nazi Persecution," in *Microhistories of the Holocaust*, ed. Claire Zalc and Tal Bruttmann (New York: Berghahn Books, 2017), 209–26.
74. Bundesarchiv Berlin, ZB 7050, A. 17, in *VEJ*, vol. 2, 393–96.
75. Yad Vashem Jerusalem 051/OSOBI, Nr. 92 (Moskau 500/1/387), fol. 64–67: Reichsvertretung-List, December 9, 1938.
76. Yad Vashem Jerusalem, O.51/OSOBI, Nr. 92 (Moskau 500/1/387), fol. 43: Note SD-Ref. II 112, November 19, 1938; ibid., fol. 58: Cable, Sicherheitshauptamt to SD-OA, December 1, 1938. See also Wolf Gruner, *Jewish Forced Labor under the Nazis: Economic Needs and Racial Aims (1938–1944)* (New York: Cambridge University Press, 2006), 45.
77. University of Southern California, Shoah Foundation/Visual History Archive, Elena Marx, tape 1, min. 25; ibid., Lea Aronson, tape 1 min. 27–31; Gruner, "Defiance and Protest," 215–16; Landesarchiv Berlin, B Rep. 020 Acc 1201, Nr. 6949, fol. 441: Police Journal, Berlin-Schöneberg, entry No. 331.

78. Landesarchiv Berlin, B Rep 020 Acc 1201, Nr. 6949 Polizeitagebücher Schöneberg, unfol.: 174. Police precinct Berlin-Schöneberg, Entry No. 330, November 10, 1938.
79. Cited by Gruner, "The Germans Should Expel the Foreigner Hitler," 38.
80. Cited by Gruner, "Defiance and Protest," 216.
81. Yad Vashem Jerusalem, M55, JM 27135 Staatsarchiv München, Staatsanwaltschaften, No. 9261, fol. 1: Gendarmerie Krumbach to Bezirksamt Krumbach, November 23, 1938; ibid, fol. 17–18: Judgement Special court München, March 15, 1939.
82. Hessisches Hauptstaatsarchiv Wiesbaden, Abt. 461 Staatsanwaltschaft Frankfurt/Main, No. 7878 Ernst Nachmann, fol. 3: Gestapo note, December 8, 1938; see also ibid, Abt. 409/6 Haftanstalten, Nr. 59.
83. Gruner, "The Germans Should Expel the Foreigner Hitler," 38–39.
84. "Süsse holde Gestapo. Dir klopfen wir noch den Po. Bis die deutsche Köterrasse kommt in unsere Ghettogasse, Hosiannah unser Grünschpan, Heldenjüngel von Paris. Wo entfesselt nun der Mordwahn ist, kommt ihr auch bald ins Geschiss. Nieder knallt den Hund, den Hitler!"; Dokumentationsarchiv des Österreichischen Widerstandes Wien, Gestapo-leitstelle Wien Tagesrapport, Nr. 11, 24.–25.11.1938, fol. 39789.
85. Solomon Perel, *Europa, Europa* (New York: John Wiley, 1997), 69–70; *Novemberpogrome 1938 in Niedersachsen Peine*; "'Kristallnacht'—Als im 'Reich' die Synagogen brannten"; "Der Mord in der Peiner Kristallnacht," *Hannoversche Presse*, July 6, 1950 (thanks to Monica Simpson, San Diego, a relative of Hans Marburger, for bringing his case to my attention).
86. For more details see the chapter, "Daisy Gronowsky from Berlin," in Wolf Gruner, "This Thug Hitler! Forgotten Stories of Individual Jewish Protest and Defiance in Nazi Germany" (in preparation).
87. Christoph Kreutzmüller, "Bilder der Bedrohung. Von Juden aufgenommene Fotos der Verfolgung," in *Medaon—Magazin für jüdisches Leben in Forschung und Bildung* 12, no. 23 (2018), 1–6, http://www.medaon.de/pdf/medaon_23_kreutzmueller.pdf.
88. Guy Miron, "'Lately, Almost Constantly, Everything Seems Small to Me': The Lived Space of German Jews under the Nazi Regime," *Jewish Social Studies* 20, no. 1 (2013): 137. Miron does not mention these effects of the pogrom, since he relies on a few diaries of prominent authors who had not been affected.

Bibliography

Archives

Bundesarchiv Berlin.
Diplomatic Documents of Switzerland (Dodis).
Dokumentationsarchiv des österreichischen Widerstandes.
Hessisches Hauptstaatsarchiv Wiesbaden.
Landesarchiv Berlin.
Private Archive Bruce Neuburger, San Francisco.
Staatsarchiv Leipzig.
USC Shoah Foundation/Visual History Archive.
United States Holocaust Memorial Museum. Washington, DC.
Yad Vashem Archives. Jerusalem, Israel.

Publications

Arntz, Hans-Dieter, ed. *Isidors Briefe. Über die Korrespondenz eines Juden aus Euskirchen*. Aachen: Helios, 2009.
Ascher, Abraham. *A Community under Siege: The Jews of Breslau under Nazism*. Stanford, CA: Stanford University Press, 2007.
Barkow, Ben, Raphael Gross, and Michael Lenarz, eds. *Novemberpogrom 1938. Die Augenzeugenberichte der Wiener Library*. London: Jüdischer Verlag im Suhrkamp Verlag, 2008.
Behnken, Klaus, ed. *Sopade: Deutschland-Berichte der Sozialdemokratischen Partei Deutschlands 1934–1940*. Vol. 5. Reprint. Salzhausen, Germany: Nettelbeck, 1980.
Benz, Wolfgang. "Erziehung zur Unmenschlichkeit. Der 9. November 1938." In *Der 9. November. Fünf Essays zur deutschen Geschichte*, edited by Johannes Willms, S. 49–65. München: C. H. Beck, 1994.
———. "Pogrom und Volksgemeinschaft. Zwischen Abscheu und Beteiligung: Die Öffentlichkeit des 9. November 1938." In *Die Novemberpogrome. Versuch einer Bilanz*, edited by Claudia Steur, 8–19. Berlin: Stiftung Topographie des Terrors, 2009.
Berschel, Holger. "Die Gestapo Düsseldorf und der Pogrom." In *Novemberpogrom 1938 in Düsseldorf*, edited by Bastian Fleermann and Angela Genger, 67–106. Essen: Klartext Verlag, 2008.
Brenner, Hans, et al., eds. *NS-Terror und Verfolgung in Sachsen. Von den frühen Konzentrationslagern bis zu den Todesmärschen*. Dresden: Sächsische Landeszentrale für politische Bildung, 2018.
"Der Mord in der Peiner Kristallnacht." *Hannoversche Presse*, July 6, 1950.
"Die Vertreibung der jüdischen Familie Holzer. 'Reichskristallnacht' in Traunstein

vor 70 Jahren." In *Traunsteiner Tageblatt*, 45/2008, Nr. 45. Accessed April 23, 2018. https://www.traunsteiner-tagblatt.de/das-traunsteiner-tagblatt/chiemgau-blaetter/chiemgau-blaetter-2018_ausgabe,-die-vertreibung-der-juedischen-familie-holzer-_chid,752.html.

Dirks, Christian, and Hermann Simon, eds. *Von Innen nach Aussen. Die Novemberpogrome 1938 in Diplomatenberichten aus Deutschland* [From the Inside to the Outside. The 1938 November Pogroms in Diplomatic Reports from Germany]. Berlin: Metropol Verlag, 2014.

Fleerman, Bastian. "Nach dem Pogrom. Bilanz der Ausschreitungen in Düsseldorf." In *Novemberpogrom in Düsseldorf*, edited by Mahn-und Gedenkstätte Düsseldorf, 359–412. Düsseldorf, 2017.

Fleermann, Bastian, and Angela Genger. *Novemberpogrom 1938 in Düsseldorf*. Essen: Klartext Verlag, 2008.

Frankiewicz, Bogdan, and Wolfgang Wilhelmus. "Selbstachtung wahren und Solidarität üben. Pommerns Juden während des Nationalsozialismus." In *"Halte fern dem ganzen Lande jedes Verderben . . ." Geschichte und Kultur der Juden in Pommern. Ein Sammelband*, edited by Margret Heitmann, Julius H. Schoeps, and Bernhard Vogt, 453–71. Hildesheim: Olms, 1995.

Friedländer, Saul. *Nazi Germany and the Jews*. Vol. I, *The Years of Persecution, 1933–1939*. New York: HarperCollins, 1996.

Gilbert, Martin. *Kristallnacht: Prelude to Destruction*. New York: Harper Perennial, 2006.

Globocnik, Odilo. Report about the "Jew action" on November 10 and 11 (no date). In *Verfolgung und Ermordung der europäischen Juden*. Vol. 2, edited by Susanne Heim, Doc. 133, 385. Munich: R. Oldenbourg Verlag, 2009.

Goebbels, Joseph. *Die Tagebücher von Joseph Goebbels*, Teil I, Bd. 6, edited by Elke Frölich. Munich: de Gruyter, 1998.

Gruner, Wolf. "Daisy Gronowsky from Berlin." In "This Thug Hitler! Forgotten Stories of Individual Jewish Protest and Defiance in Nazi Germany," Wolf Gruner. In preparation.

———. "Defiance and Protest: A Comparative Micro-Historical Re-evaluation of Individual Jewish Responses towards Nazi Persecution." In *Microhistories of the Holocaust*, edited by Claire Zalc and Tal Bruttmann, 209–26. New York: Berghahn Books, 2017.

———. "'The Germans Should Expel the Foreigner Hitler'. Open Protest and Other Forms of Jewish Defiance in Nazi Germany." *Yad Vashem Studies* 39, no. 2 (2011): 13–53.

———. "Indifference? Participation and Protest as Individual Responses to the Persecution of the Jews as Revealed in Berlin Police Logs and Trial Records, 1933-45." In *The Germans and the Holocaust: Popular Responses to the Persecution and Murder of the Jews*, edited by Alan Steinweis and Susanna Schrafstetter, 59–83. New York: Berghahn, 2016.

———. *Jewish Forced Labor under the Nazis: Economic Needs and Racial Aims (1938–1944)*. New York: Cambridge University Press, 2006.

———. *The Persecution of the Jews in Berlin 1933–1945: A Chronology of Measures by the Authorities in the German Capital*. Berlin: Stiftung Topographie, 2014.

Heim, Susanne, ed. *Verfolgung und Ermordung der europäischen Juden*. Vol. 2. Munich: R. Oldenbourg Verlag, 2009.

Heusler, Andreas, and Tobias Weger. *"Kristallnacht." Gewalt gegen die Münchner Juden im November 1938*. Munich: Buchendorfer, 1998.

Hoschek, Jutta. *Der Novemberpogrom 1938 in Erfurt. Aus Dokumenten und Erinnerungen*. Edited by Landeshauptstadt Erfurt, Stadtverwaltung und das Netzwerk "Jüdisches Leben Erfurt." Jena: Vopelius, 2018.

Johles, Malka. Interview by David Boder. August 28, 1946, in Geneva. In digital copy of the English transcripts (provided by Todd Pressner, Los Angeles).

Kaplan, Marion. *Between Dignity and Despair: Jewish life in Nazi Germany*. New York, Oxford: Oxford University Press, 1998.

Kellerhoff, Sven Felix. *Ein ganz normales Pogrom. November 1938 in einem deutschen Dorf*. Stuttgart: Klett-Cotta, 2018.

Korb, Alexander. *Reaktionen der deutschen Bevölkerung auf die Novemberpogrome*. Saarbrücken: VDM, 2008.

Kreutzmüller, Christoph. *Ausverkauf: Die Vernichtung der jüdischen Gewerbetätigkeit in Berlin 1930-1945*. Berlin: Metropol, 2012; English version: *Final Sale in Berlin: The Destruction of Jewish Commercial Activity 1930–1945*. New York: Berghahn, 2015.

———. "Bilder der Bedrohung. Von Juden aufgenommene Fotos der Verfolgung." In *Medaon—Magazin für jüdisches Leben in Forschung und Bildung* 12, no. 23 (2018): 1–6. http://www.medaon.de/pdf/medaon_23_kreutzmueller.pdf.

"'Kristallnacht'—Als im 'Reich' die Synagogen brannten." Accessed January 19, 2019. https://www.myheimat.de/peine/kultur/kristallnacht-als-im-reich-die-synagogen-brannten-d2723453.html.

Kulka, Otto Dov, and Eberhard Jäckel, eds. *The Jews in the Secret Nazi Reports on Popular Opinion in Germany, 1933–1945*. New Haven: Yale University Press, 2010.

"Liste der im Deutschen Reich von 1933 bis 1945 zerstörten Synagogen." Wikipedia. Accessed January 17, 2019. https://de.wikipedia.org/wiki/Liste_der_im_Deutschen_Reich_von_1933_bis_1945_zerst%C3%B6rten_Synagogen.

Longerich, Peter. *"Davon haben wir nichts gewusst!" Die Deutschen und die Judenverfolgung, 1933–1945*. Munich: Siedler Verlag, 2006.

Lubrich, Oliver, ed. *Reisen ins Reich. 1933–1945 Ausländische Autoren berichten aus Deutschland*. Munich: Eichborn, 2009.

Matzerath, Horst, ed. *Jüdisches Schicksal in Köln 1918–1945: Ausstellung des Historischen Archivs der Stadt Köln-NS-Dokumentationszentrum: 8. November 1988 bis 22. Januar, 1989*. Köln: Stadt Köln, 1988.

McKale, Donald. "A Case of Nazi 'Justice': The Punishment of Party Members Involved in the Kristallnacht 1938." *Jewish Social Studies* 35, no. 3-4 (July– October, 1973): 228–38.

Mendelsohn, John, ed. *The Holocaust*. Vol. 3, *The Crystal Night Pogrom*. New York: Garland Publishing, 1982.

Miron, Guy. "'Lately, Almost Constantly, Everything Seems Small to Me': The Lived Space of German Jews under the Nazi Regime." *Jewish Social Studies* 20, no. 1 (2013): 121–49.

Novemberpogrome 1938 in Niedersachsen Peine. Accessed January 19, 2019. https://pogrome1938-niedersachsen.de/peine/.

Pätzold, Kurt. "Der Pogrom und sein Platz in der Geschichte der Vertreibung der jüdischen Deutschen." In *Pogromnacht 1938*, edited by Kurt Pätzold and Irene Runge, 39–110. Berlin: Dietz, 1988.

Pätzold, Kurt, and Irene Runge, eds. *Pogromnacht 1938*. Berlin: Dietz, 1988.

Perel, Solomon. *Europa, Europa*. New York: John Wiley, 1997.

Raim, Edith. "Die Verfolgung und Vernichtung der fränkischen Juden in der NS-Zeit." In *Die Juden in Franken*, edited by Michael Brenner and Daniela F. Eisenstein, 199–218. Munich: Oldenbourg, 2011.

———. *Justiz zwischen Diktatur und Demokratie. Wiederaufbau und Ahndung von NS-Verbrechen in Westdeutschland 1945–1949*. Munich: Oldenbourg Verlag, 2013.

Ristau, Daniel. "Der 9. November 1938: Die Novemberpogrome in Sachsen im Spannungsfeld zwischen Geschichtsforschung, Gedenkkultur und persönlicher Erinnerung." *Medaon* 12 (2018): 23, pp. 1–20. http://www.medaon.de/pdf/medaon_23_ristau_artikel.pdf.

Schmit, Franz-Josef. *Novemberpogrom in Wittlich 1938. Ablauf-Hintergründe-offene Fragen-juristische Aufarbeitung*. Butzweiler: Trier-Verlag: 2013.

Senator für Justiz und Verfassung der Freien Hansestadt Bremen. *"Reichskristallnacht" in Bremen. Vorgeschichte, Hergang und gerichtliche Bewältigung des Pogroms vom 9./10. November 1938*. Bremen: Steintor, 1988.

Schüler-Springorum, Stefanie. *Geschlecht und Differenz*. Paderborn: Schöningh, 2014.

Steinweis, Alan. *Kristallnacht 1938*. Cambridge, MA: Belknap Press of Harvard University Press, 2009.

Suchy, Barbara. "Überfallen in Düsseldorf. Der Novemberpogrom in Selbstzeugnissen und Dokumenten." In *Novemberpogrom 1938 in Düsseldorf*, edited by Bastian Fleermann and Angela Genger, 125–265. Essen: Klartext Verlag, 2008.

Tausk, Walter. *Breslauer Tagebuch 1933–1940*. Berlin: Rütten und Loening, 1975.

Wildt, Michael. *Volksgemeinschaft als Selbstermächtigung. Gewalt gegen Juden in der deutschen Provinz 1919 bis 1939*. Hamburg: Hamburger Edition, 2007.

Witek, Hans, and Hans Safrian. *Und keiner war dabei: Dokumente des alltäglichen Antisemitismus in Wien 1938*. Vienna: Picus Verlag, 2008.

CHAPTER 3

A Question of Gender! Spaces of Violence and Reactions to Kristallnacht in Jewish-Gentile Families

by Maximilian Strnad

INTRODUCTION

Memoirs, diaries and correspondence from Jewish and Non-Jewish members of mixed marriages offer the striking impression that families with Jewish husbands reported experiencing excessive violence during Kristallnacht, while families with Jewish wives generally talked more about violence happening to other Jewish relatives and friends rather than about self-experienced violence. Certainly, this assessment does not apply to every single source, but reading some dozen documents written by intermarried Jews and looking into at least one hundred of their compensation files from all over Germany, this rule seems to be evident.[1]

To demonstrate why the experience of violence in mixed marriages during Kristallnacht was highly gendered, this article begins by taking a close look at the spaces where violence was directed on November 9 and on subsequent days. Depending on the gender of its Jewish part, intermarried couples had different access to social spheres and spaces. For a better understanding, why persecution in general and Kristallnacht violence in particular had a more severe impact on mixed marriages with Jewish men, the general situation of intermarried Jews under Nazi-rule will briefly be outlined in the beginning of this chapter. Thereafter the text focuses on gender and shows how members of mixed marriages reacted to Kristallnacht and how this experience affected their agency. The last section deals with the aftermath of Kristallnacht and demonstrates how the experience influenced the family situation of mixed marriage couples. In doing so, the information drawn from memoires and testimonies will be contrasted with statistics focusing on Munich.[2]

With the enactment of the Nuremberg Laws in 1935, the Nazi-regime prohibited weddings between Jews and non-Jews. Existing mixed marriages were not dissolved by force, but Nazi officials increased pressure to get such couples to divorce. From 1933 on, while Jewish spouses were subjected to all anti-Jewish measures of the regime, their gentile partners also had to accept restrictions at work or even lose their positions because of being related to a Jew. Public servants married to Jews were systematically demoted, retired or dismissed.[3] With the introduction of the so-called *Arierparagraph* in 1933, gentiles married to Jews were excluded from most professional institutions and from becoming civil servants. In addition to the loss of economic security, many intermarried couples lost their social networks as more and more of their gentile friends and family members turned their backs on them. Gestapo and party officials openly blackmailed gentiles to leave their Jewish spouses in order to free themselves from persecution.[4]

All mixed marriages suffered persecution, but anti-Jewish measures had far greater effect on families with Jewish breadwinners, who were mainly male. These families were hit by economic sanctions with full force and gentile spouses had little chance to compensate for the loss of income and security. Jewish men/gentile women couples were also attacked for ideological reasons. German women, especially German mothers, were considered as preservers of the German race. Children of such liaisons, the so-called *Mischlinge*, had in Nazi ideology no value to the "Volksgemeinschaft." This is why the regime placed extraordinary pressure on intermarried gentile women and their families. A significant number of mixed marriages did not stand up to this pressure, yet as late as mid-1938 the majority remained intact.[5] In Munich, e.g., less than five percent were dissolved before Kristallnacht.[6]

SPACES OF VIOLENCE AND THE IMPACT OF KRISTALLNACHT ON MIXED MARRIAGES

In 1933 close to 500,000 Jews lived in Germany, and about 35,000 lived in a mixed marriage.[7] Up to that moment intermarriage was a rising phenomenon. One year earlier, just before this development was ended abruptly with the Nazi takeover, twenty-three percent of all Jews who got married, chose a non-Jewish partner. As the social environment in metropoles was far more liberal than in rural regions and smaller towns, the proportion was even higher in cities like Berlin—which had by far the largest Jewish population—Breslau, Hamburg and Frankfurt. A total of almost fifteen thousand Jews lived in Munich during 1933–45; approximately one thousand of them were intermarried.

How did the events on November 9 and November 10 affect those intermarried families? As far as we know, there were no official instructions on how to treat intermarried Jews that night. They were neither exempted nor treated in a special way.[8] The reason why intermarried Jewish men and their families were hit comparatively harder than families with gentile men can be found by observing the general line of attack during Kristallnacht. Indeed, by examining the spaces under attack, the gender-specific impact of Kristallnacht on mixed marriages becomes more obvious.

The violence unleashed by Nazi perpetrators during those nights was not solely directed against Jewish men; large numbers of women were also affected. Brutal force even was often explicitly directed against Jewish women.[9] Nevertheless, most attacks were directed against Jewish property and against its mainly male owners. This was done in order to destroy the livelihood of Jews in Germany and to force them and their families to emigrate. Subsequent to the brutal attacks on companies, shops and houses—not to mention the burning of synagogues and demolition of Jewish institutions—the Gestapo arrested vast numbers of Jewish men and brought them to concentration camps to pressure them to abandon their businesses, sell their assets, and leave Germany immediately. The thirty thousand persons rounded up included many intermarried men.[10] Women were only arrested as an exception and promptly released.[11]

In regard to the mixed marriages, these preconditions were of central relevance. It determined who was affected by Kristallnacht and who predominately was spared. Of course, there are exceptions to this general rule. Some shops owned by intermarried non-Jews were destroyed and looted on November 9 too and had to close for a short time afterwards,[12] but most were spared even if they were situated in a Jewish neighborhood.[13] There is also no indication in the available sources, that gentile intermarried men were arrested in their homes during the raids.

Still, intermarried Jewish woman and their families became victims of violence during the events in the night from November 9 to November 10. In Frankfurt, for example, rioters threw the furniture of the Lehr family out the windows of their flat.[14] This was especially true in rural communities and small towns where violence was directed against all remaining Jews. In Immenhausen near Kassel, for example, some drunken SA-men threw a brick through the window of the Jahn family's home.[15] In Solingen, once the local SA leader and his brigade finished their bloody work against all Jews, they extended the nightly hunt for Jews to include intermarried women. They even demolished the house of a physician who was divorced from a Jewess and threatened him in order to get a hold of his ex-wife, who they assumed was hiding in his place. They only left after one hour of unsuccessful interrogation and upon destroying the furniture and windows in his medical practice and living quarters situated above.[16] But the general line of attack was against Jewish men.

Before Kristallnacht, many Jews found shelter from growing Nazi hostility in the private spaces of individual households. As violence reached their homes, their illusion of security was destroyed.[17] In his contribution to this volume, Wolf Gruner points to the fact that violence in private homes—which was an integral part of Kristallnacht—has been overlooked by historians, especially when compared to the widely known demolition of shops and synagogues that was taking place under public scrutiny. This statement is even more surprising, as the violence to their homes, the destruction of their furniture and the physical assaults during the attacks often are essential elements in victims' recollections of Kristallnacht shortly after the war and are well documented in their claims for compensation. Until recently, oral history interviews and compensation files only played second fiddle in historiography. Focusing on these sources will contribute to shifting our perception of violence in Kristallnacht from public to private spaces.

In addition to Gruner's observation, the impact of another element of Kristallnacht has largely been neglected in historiography. As mentioned earlier, immediately after the attacks during Kristallnacht on synagogues, shops, houses and flats, the Gestapo conducted a well-known raid against Jewish men. With this raid a second wave of violence was brought directly into their homes. When police officers, often accompanied by SS- and SA-men, were knocking on their doors to arrest all Jewish men between the age of sixteen and sixty, not only the Jewish head of the household, but the entire family was in great danger. The perpetrators used the opportunity to extend their actions against the Jews, even after most violence ended on the morning of November 10.[18] A large percentage of the violence against Jews conducted in private space occurred during these raids. With regard to intermarried couples, this fact is of important significance, because only families with Jewish men were affected.

The following examples show the serious consequences such mixed-marriage couples had to face. In Memmingen, a small town in southern Germany, the order to attack the Jews did not reach Nazi-officials in time during the night from the 9th to the 10th of November. The next morning, a horde of local SA-men and police officers destroyed and looted Jewish property, and forcibly entered the house of the Guggenheimer family in Herrenstrasse 7. They arrested Alfred Guggenheimer, smashed his furniture, windows and the flatware, slashed the sofas and blankets, and even cut the family's underwear in pieces.[19] Such intrusions often introduced life-threatening situations. Many intermarried Jewish men were badly injured and some even murdered. In Berlin, Friedrich Wilhelm Block was shot when members of the SA came to arrest him on November 11. After his non-Jewish wife Lotte returned home, the murderers told her that he committed suicide. These situations also were very dangerous for the gentile family members. Lotte Block was immediately arrested and put in Gestapo prison for several months. We do not know if she was mistreated, because her statement does not shed light on this question.[20]

In other cases severe attacks on gentile wives are well documented. In a home next to Alfred Guggenheimer, Hugo Günzburger's wife was beaten by the SA men when they came to arrest him.[21] In Munich a group of unknown men assaulted Heinrich Obermayer and his non-Jewish wife on November 10 in their apartment. They were both brutally beaten with a cudgel and Mrs. Obermayer lost her left eye as a result of the attack.[22] In Kleinmachnow near Berlin, a *Mischling* was arrested and detained in custody for several days because the policemen could not lay their hands on his Jewish father, who had gone into hiding after a non-Jewish colleague warned him of the forthcoming arrests. Several hours earlier, the SA had smashed all windows of the house where Harry Loewenberg and his family lived.[23]

We do not know how many intermarried Jews were arrested nationwide on Kristallnacht and the following days. Since Jewish men more often married gentile women than the other way around, and younger men in particular tended towards mixed marriages, one can expect that their number among all arrested Jews aged sixteen to sixty during Kristallnacht was significant. According to the Database on Jews of Munich from 1933–45, every sixth Jew from the Bavarian capital who was arrested and detained in the Dachau concentration camp after Kristallnacht was intermarried.[24]

Many of those who were beaten to death or who perished due to the catastrophic conditions in the crowded special sections in the camps for Jews were intermarried too. One of them was the thirty-seven-year-old type setter Theodor Oppenheimer from Frankfurt, who died in the Buchenwald concentration camp.[25] Others died immediately after their release—a release often informed by the desire to make sure these deaths could not officially be linked to their imprisonment. Sixty-five-year-old Georg Kalischer died on November 27, 1938 only three days after he was discharged from Buchenwald. Pastor Otto Haas, who held the funeral, later recalled that Kalischer, who was a well-known chemist at I. G. Farben in Frankfurt, had to be entombed "like a criminal." The Gestapo banned all former colleagues, friends and relatives from attending the funeral and forbade them to express their condolences in public. Only his wife Marie was allowed to take part in the funeral, but she was not allowed to speak a word.[26]

From the end of November on, the remaining prisoners were released. Harry Stein argued in his publications that intermarried Jews were among the first group of prisoners to be set free by the SS.[27] However, there is no evidence for this argument. Actually, veterans of World War I were released first[28]—many of them were intermarried. Maybe this is why fellow prisoners got the impression that intermarried Jews were privileged. Statistics for Munich reveal that most detained intermarried Jews were released from mid-December on, along with the majority of all other Kristallnacht-prisoners from Dachau Concentration Camp.[29]

REACTIONS OF INTERMARRIED FAMILIES TO KRISTALLNACHT

The impact of violence during Kristallnacht was generally much higher in mixed marriages with a Jewish male householder. The reactions of intermarried families to the events significantly depended on gender too. This section will discuss how intermarried Jews responded to the violence of Kristallnacht.

Like Harry Loewenberg, many Jewish men avoided arrest by going underground. For several weeks the Gestapo searched the streets for hidden Jews and frequently went back to their homes. We know that many men found shelter in the homes of elderly Jews, who were not affected by the raid and in the homes of families whose husbands had already been arrested and where the police probably would not return. Sometimes non-Jewish friends offered shelter. Intermarried Jewish men more often had opportunities to access gentile spaces in order to wait for the end of the raid, because they could call upon gentile family members.[30] Harry Loewenherz found shelter at the home of a former colleague, an elderly Jew himself, and then with non-Jewish family members in a nearby town. Eduard Meyer and his gentile wife and newborn baby left Düsseldorf straight after SA-men invaded the family's flat and brutally beat him with steel rods. Meyer was seriously injured and endured a serious concussion when they traveled to the Munich hinterland where his gentile sister-in-law gave them asylum.[31]

The shocking experience of Kristallnacht resulted in a wave of mass emigration. Ten thousand Jews sought to leave the country immediately after November 9. While only a few intermarried Jewish wives emigrated, a large number of intermarried Jewish men left Germany. In Munich 255 out of 1,094 intermarried Jews emigrated, 140 after Kristallnacht. While every second Jew of Munich left Germany to live abroad between 1933–41, only twenty-three percent of the intermarried ones did.[32] Looking into the details helps to explain this gap. Indeed, the quota of emigration for intermarried couples was generally lower, but with a distinct discrepancy regarding gender. While thirty-two percent of all intermarried men of Munich emigrated, only 9.5 percent of intermarried Jewish woman did.[33] This fact becomes even more obvious when examining the exact numbers of intermarried refugees fleeing Munich: 215 of the 255 intermarried Jews were men (eighty-five percent), only forty were women.

Jewish men and their families were not only affected to a much higher degree by the violence during Kristallnacht, but also responded to it more directly. The economic impact of persecution was more severe for them than for mixed marriages with non-Jewish men. The latter still had much to lose. Some maintained businesses or were employed, others did not want to lose their non-Jewish relatives or their heritage. They rather accepted persecution, hoping that it wouldn't be that bad and National Socialism would be over soon. The price of losing their social status, of leaving their homeland, and of maybe not finding an equivalent position in a foreign country with a foreign language was too much to cope with, so they often remained in Germany, reluctant to pay more than a quarter of their fortune as the Reich flight tax, which they would need to pay to obtain the right to leave, or in other cases unable to pay the high visa and transit costs for emigration.[34] Additionally, non-Jewish husbands and half-Jewish sons could not legally emigrate if they were of military age.³⁵ Only very few women, such as Frida Kraus of Augsburg, choose to emigrate on their own, leaving husbands and children behind.³⁶

Kristallnacht had two dramatic effects on the integrity of mixed marriages. Due to the imminent threat of being detained in a concentration camp, many Jewish men, intermarried or not, had to leave the country immediately. Since it often proved impossible to get all the visas and collect enough money for all family members within a short period of time, some couples sent the jeopardized men first, because as the Aub family of Augsburg recounted after the war, "the Aryan woman and half-Aryan children, did not have to fear serious danger at the time being."³⁷ For non-Jewish wives who had to manage all necessary arrangements for their imprisoned men, this often meant saying farewell for a very long time. It often proved impossible for them to rejoin their husbands before the borders closed at the beginning of the war; since reunion was impossible directly after the war, these separations often lasted until 1946 or longer—as was the case of the Aub family.

Sometimes this spatial segregation led to breakup and divorce. For gentile wives, divorce was the only opportunity to avoid further ostracism and persecution. The Gestapo pressured these solitary women to divorce and to return to "Volksgemeinschaft."³⁸ Many women decided against divorce, but some decided in favor in order to protect their children. Others did it for their own convenience.

Pressure on mixed marriages to split up increased after 1933. Statistics for the city of Munich reveal that Kristallnacht had a major effect on the integrity of those marriages. In the Bavarian capital, the divorce rate of intermarried couples reached its climax after November 9, 1938. Half of all 117 divorces were submitted between Kristallnacht and the end of 1940. Several factors were responsible for this. The Nazi-regime, for example, had eased legal conditions for gentiles to divorce Jewish partners in the summer of 1938.³⁹ Nevertheless, the experience of personal threat during the violent events in November 1938, together with the fear of losing economic security during the forthcoming Aryanisation process had a major impact on this development. Mathilde Edelstein chose to divorce her Jewish husband Ludwig in December 1938, after party officials threatened to take their draper's shop in Munich away from her because she was married to a Jew.⁴⁰ The greatest number of divorces occurred in mixed marriage households headed by Jewish men. In Munich this figure reached nearly seventy-five percent; in other cities, such as Hamburg, it was even higher.⁴¹

AFTERMATH

Kristallnacht fundamentally disrupted the life of German Jews. Immediately after the event, Nazi-leadership implemented a number of new laws and decrees in order to increase pressure on the Jews. At the same time, they offered gradual exceptions from persecution to some specific types of mixed marriages. In late December 1938, Hermann Goering, with Hitler's approval, created the category of privileged mixed marriages. Families with gentile husbands and families with children raised as non-Jews, were exempted from some key persecution measures because of their supposedly closer ties to the German "Volksgemeinschaft" and spared from being ghettoized. With the onset of war, those female Jewish spouses were not subjected to food restrictions and did not have to wear the yellow badge required of all Jews after September 1941.[42] Intermarried Jews were generally exempted from deportation, which started on the eastern and western boarders of Germany in 1939–40, followed by hundreds of mass-transports from all over the German Reich from October 1941 on.[43] Divorced intermarried Jews were deported in a nationwide action in January 1944 to the ghetto of Theresienstadt. After some time, many were transferred to Auschwitz and killed. One year later in February 1945 the Gestapo finally decided to lay hands on intermarried Jews too. At that time, approximately 12,500 of them still remained in the territory of the so-called Old-Reich (without Austria and the annexed countries). Due to the turbulences in the final stage of the war a majority of those affected managed to avoid deportation by going underground or with the help of others, often informed by the desire to gather credit for the time after the imminent collapse of the regime. Nevertheless 1,901 persons were sent to Theresienstadt. Most of them fortunately survived the last weeks of Nazi-rule.[44] Due to their exceptional status, intermarried Jews were by far the biggest group (twelve to thirteen thousand) among German holocaust survivors after the war. Two to three thousand other German Jews survived in hiding, some six thousand returned from the camps and ghettos.[45]

Their high survival rate is also the reason why many intermarried Jews testified in trials against perpetrators and applied for compensation. Many of those testimonies are related to Kristallnacht. They give an impression not only of the extent of violence towards mixed marriages but also on how these experiences strongly influenced those Jews in their feeling of self-worth within their own family.

When the Nazi-hordes attacked his house in Kleinmachnow, Harry Loewenberg, who had converted to Christianity many years earlier, attributed his predicament and that of his family to his Jewish descent. "It was through me, that they had been drawn into this. (...) I felt, they all were looking at me full of reproach—which was not the case—reproach that I, with my existence and my origin as a member of the 'vilest of all races,' had brought on this calamity." Loewenberg's first reaction was to withdraw from his family in order to protect them. "I went downstairs, put on my old, grey overcoat, and wanted to leave the house. I felt that my personal existence was now completely worthless as I was not only unable to be of any use to my family and take care of them, but was actually putting them in personal jeopardy by my presence." Only after a hard struggle, was his family able to persuade him to stay.[46]

For intermarried Jews, this feeling of being responsible for the misery of their family often lasted for decades. Ludwig Edelstein, who was hardly disappointed with his wife for divorcing him after Kristallnacht, and who wanted to receive compensation for losing the family's draper's shop, in 1971 still felt guilty for his spouse's situation in 1938, when he declared before compensation authorities: "nevertheless, I do not want my ex-wife to pay me compensation. I know exactly what it was like by the time for an Aryan woman to be married to a Jew."[47]

CONCLUSION

The impact of Kristallnacht on mixed marriages was gendered to a high degree. In contrast to Jewish families, in intermarried couples only one spouse was Jewish. Focusing on the spaces where violence was mainly committed on November 9, 1938 and on the following days, reveals that the assaults were most prominent in the households of Jewish men, while households of non-Jewish men often were lucky to escape violence. This statement is not only true for the looting of their businesses and shops, but also for the destruction of their homes. Historiography has overlooked for a long time the fact, that a significant number of the assaults on Jewish homes were not only conducted in the nightly events from November 9–10 but also during the following raids against Jewish men, when police, SS- and SA members together with local NSDAP-officials invaded their homes. Often the intruders did not content themselves with arresting the Jewish men. They demolished their furniture and even brutally attacked them. Many were killed or even murdered during these raids, which also degenerated into attacks on non-Jewish members of the family. This experience of helplessness affected the self-esteem of many intermarried men. Their feeling of guilt sometimes lasted for decades.

Consequently, intermarried Jewish men and their families not only were hit harder by but also reacted more directly to Kristallnacht. Their emigration rate after Kristallnacht increased dramatically. In mixed marriages more than three quarter of all refugees were men. Often, they had to flee the country immediately, leaving their families behind. The divorce rate among intermarried couples also increased significantly after Kristallnacht. Again, far more marriages with Jewish men were split up than the other way around.

This was not a random development. In Nazi-ideology Jewish men were a direct threat to the "purity of the race" and thereby to the "Volksgemeinschaft."[48] By targeting Jewish men National Socialists intended to weaken especially those mixed marriages in order to get the non-Jewish wives to abandon their husbands. After the divorce, the regime promised the women a return into "Volksgemeinschaft."[49] This leitmotif of the Nazi-policy towards mixed marriages becomes once more evident, when taking a close look at the spaces where violence affected intermarried couples most during Kristallnacht.

Notes

1. Parts of this essay refer to the chapter on Kristallnacht in my unpublished dissertation "Privileg Mischehe? Handlungsräume sogenannter 'jüdisch versippter' Familien 1933–1949" (PhD diss., University of Munich, 2016).
2. The Database *Biographisches Gedenkbuch der Münchner Juden 1933–1945* contains close to fifteen thousand datasets of Jews from Munich. It is the biggest and most sophisticated collection of information on Jews in Nazi-Germany. For this article, the Database was systematically evaluated for several questions related to Kristallnacht. All following statistical information on Munich are drawn out of it (as of December 31, 2016).
3. Circular of the Reichs Ministry of Finance, January 11, 1937, Bundesarchiv (BArch), RH 26-7 Nr. 386. See Christiane Kuller, *Finanzverwaltung und Judenverfolgung. Die Entziehung jüdischen Vermögens in Bayern während der NS-Zeit* (Munich: Beck, 2008), 40; Lothar Gruchmann, *Justiz im Dritten Reich 1933–1940. Anpassung und Unterwerfung in der Ära Gürtner* (Munich: Oldenbourg, 1988), 172–73.
4. Strnad, "Privileg Mischehe?" 93–96.
5. Ursula Büttner, "Bollwerk Familie. Die Rettung der Juden in 'Mischehe,'" in *Mut zur Menschlichkeit. Hilfe für Verfolgte während der NS-Zeit*, ed. Günther B. Ginzel (Cologne, Rheinland-Verlag, 1993), 68.
6. Stadtarchiv München (StadtAM), Biographisches Gedenkbuch der Münchner Juden 1933–1945, Database.
7. Herbert A. Strauss, "Jewish Emigration from Germany: Nazi Policies and the Jewish Responses (I)," *Leo Baeck Institution Yearbook*, no. 25 (1980): 317.
8. Ursula Büttner, "An Unknown Case of Resistance. The Rescue of Jews in Christian-Jewish Mixed Marriages," in *The Moral Imperative. New Essays on the Ethics of Resistance in National Socialist Germany 1933–1945*, ed. Andrew Chandler (Boulder, Westview Press, 1998), 111.
9. Stefanie Schüler-Springorum, *Geschlecht und Differenz* (Paderborn: Schöningh, 2014), 110–37; Marion Kaplan, "Changing Roles in Jewish Families," in *Jewish Life in Nazi Germany: Dilemmas and Responses*, ed. Francis R. Nicosia and David Scrase (New York: Berghan Books, 2010), 43–44; Alan Steinweis, *Kristallnacht 1938* (Cambridge, Belknap Press of Harvard University Press, 2009), 72–78.
10. Hans-Jürgen Döscher, *Reichskristallnacht. Die Novemberpogrome 1938* (Frankfurt am Main: Ullstein, 1988) 110–12.
11. Harry Stein, "Das Sonderlager im Konzentrationslager Buchenwald nach den Pogromen 1938," in *"Nach der Kristallnacht." Jüdisches Leben und antijüdische Politik in Frankfurt am Main 1938–1945*, ed. Monica Kingreen (Frankfurt am Main: Campus-Verlag, 1999), 26. See also *Die Nacht als die Synagogen brannten. Texte und Materialien zum 9. November 1938*, ed. Landeszentrale für politische Bildung

Baden-Württemberg (Stuttgart, self-published, 1998), 28, accessed January 29, 2019, http://www.lpb-bw.de/publikationen/pogrom/Pogrom.pdf.

12. Wolfram Selig, *Leben unterm Rassenwahn. Vom Antisemitismus in der "Hauptstadt der Bewegung"* (Berlin: Metropol, 2001), 226.
13. Sibylle Krause-Burger, *Herr Wolle lässt noch einmal grüßen. Geschichte meiner deutsch-jüdischen Familie* (Munich: Deutsche Verlags-Anstalt, 2007), 149.
14. See Material on the Lehr family, in Zentralarchiv der Evangelischen Kirche in Hessen, Nassau und Frankfurt am Main (EKHN), 160, Vol. 5.
15. Martin Doerry, *"Mein verwundetes Herz." Das Leben der Lilli Jahn 1900–1944* (Stuttgart and Munich: Deutsche Verlags-Anstalt, 2002), 120–21.
16. Judgement of the court, June 12, 1948, Hauptstaatsarchiv Düsseldorf, 191/72, cited in Institut für Zeitgeschichte (IfZ), NSG-Database, record 7046.
17. Schüler-Springorum, *Geschlecht und Differenz*, 126.
18. Stein, "Das Sonderlager," 25; Wolf-Arno Kropat, *"Reichskristallnacht." Der Judenpogrom vom 7. bis 10. November 1938. Urheber, Täter, Hintergründe. Mit ausgewählten Dokumenten* (Wiesbaden: Kommission für die Geschichte der Juden in Hessen, self-published, 1997), 138.
19. Susanne Beer, Johannes Schwartz, and Maximilian Strnad, "Anti-Semitism," in *Ruptures in the Everyday: Views of Modern Germany from the Ground*, ed. Andrew Bergerson and Leonard Schmieding (New York, Berghan Books, 2017), 176; Maximilian Strnad, "Manchen Spuren menschlicher Existenz verblassen schneller als andere. Die Geschichte einer 'privilegierten Mischehe' in Memmingen," in *Allgäuerinnen. Ein Lesebuch*, ed. Barbara Lochbihler (Berlin: Edition Ebersbach, 2013), 174.
20. Lotte Block to Kath. Hilfswerk Berlin, March 15, 1946, Diözesanarchiv Berlin (DAB), I/1-72.
21. Application for compensation of Hugo Günzburger, March 27, 1950, Bayerisches Hauptstaatsarchiv (BayHStA), Landesentschädigungsamt (LEA) 1369.
22. Application for compensation of Käthe Obermayer, March 27, 1950, BayHStA, LEA 27255.
23. Peter C. Loewenberg, *Requiem of a B-Man* (Great Falls, self-published, 1998), 79–81. A copy of the manuscript is located at the Library of the United States Holocaust Memorial Museum (USHMM), Washington DC.
24. Fifty-one out of the 301 registered cases. After Kristallnacht a total of one thousand Jews of Munich had been arrested. See Andreas Heusler and Tobias Weger, eds., *"Kristallnacht": Gewalt gegen die Münchner Juden im November 1938* (Munich: Buchendorfer Verlag, 1998), 122. Not all of the cases have been added to the database yet.
25. Cf. EKHN, 160 Vol. 7, see also death notice Abt. III Schutzhaftlager of the KZ Buchenwald, 9.12.1938, International Tracing Service (ITS), ID 6748032.
26. Statement of Otto Haas, May 7, 1945, EKHN, 160, Bd. 4; Prisoner card of Georg

Kalischer KZ Buchenwald, ITS, ID 6222427. See also: Volker Mahnkopp, "Georg Kalischer: Einsame Bestattung für IG-Farben-Direktor," in *Getauft, ausgestoßen— und vergessen? Zum Umgang der evangelischen Kirchen in Hessen mit den Christen jüdischer Herkunft im Nationalsozialismus*, ed. Heinz Daume (Hanau, CoCon, 2013), 196–200.

27. Harry Stein, "Juden im Konzentrationslager Buchenwald 1938–1942. Pogromnacht und Holocaust. Frankfurt, Weimar, Buchenwald," in *Die schwierige Erinnerung an die Stationen der Vernichtung*, ed. Thomas Hofmann, Hanno Loewy, and Harry Stein (Weimar: Böhlau, 1994), 111.

28. Paul Sauer, *Dokumente über die Verfolgung der jüdischen Bürger in Baden-Württemberg durch das nationalsozialistische Regime 1933–1945* (Stuttgart: Kohlhammer, 1966), 2:50; Heinz Keil, *Dokumentation über die Verfolgungen der jüdischen Bürger von Ulm/Donau* (Ulm: self-published, 1961), 184.

29. See, for example, BayHStA, 222 (Berthold Lehmann, released December 27, 1938), 10246 (Heinrich-Carl Emmerich, released December 20, 1938), 12046 (Adolf Freitag, released December 19, 1938), 18451 (Edmund Jonas, released December 15, 1938), etc.

30. Hubert Schneider, *Leben nach dem Überleben: Juden in Bochum nach 1945* (Berlin: Lit Verlag, 2014), 399. See also Memoir of Horst Hartwich, Leo Baeck Institute (LBI), ME 1362, 19–20.

31. Eduard Meyer to Adolf Brochhausen and Marlene, April 28, 1954, Stadtarchiv München (StadtAM), Judaica-Varia 157/15.

32. A total of 6,394 (45%) of all 14,286 persons registered in the Database emigrated. See StadtAM, Biographisches Gedenkbuch der Münchner Juden 1933–1945, Database.

33. 670 out of 1094 intermarried were men (61%), 424 were women (39%), ibid.

34. For general information on Reichsfluchtsteuer see Dorothee Mußgnug, *Die Reichsfluchtsteuer 1931–1953* (Berlin: Duncker & Humblot, 1993).

35. Maria von der Heydt, "Möglichkeiten und Grenzen der Auswanderung von 'jüdischen Mischlingen' 1938–1941," in *"Wer bleibt, opfert seine Jahre, vielleicht sein Leben." Deutsche Juden 1938–1941*, ed. Susanne Heim, Beate Meyer, and Francis R. Nicosia (Göttingen: Wallstein, 2010), 90–91.

36. Benigna Schönhagen, *"Getrennt von allem, was uns geblieben. . . ." Der Weg der Familie Kraus aus Augsburg* (Augsburg: Jüdisches Kulturmuseum Augsburg-Schwaben, self-published, 2008), 22. See also the case of Robert Breusch, Harvard University Library, MS Ger 91 (38), 57–58.

37. Rudolf Aub, "Handlanger in Sierra Leone. Amtsarzt in Jamaika," in *Das Exil der kleinen Leute. Alltagserfahrung deutscher Juden in der Emigration*, ed. Wolfgang Benz (Munich, Beck, 1994), 105. On the history of the Aub family, see Benigna Schönhagen, *"Glücklich wieder vereint." Der Weg der Familie Hartmann aus Augsburg* (Augsburg: Jüdisches Kulturmuseum Augsburg-Schwaben, self-published, 2014).

38. Beate Meyer, *"Jüdische Mischlinge."* Rassenpolitik und Verfolgungserfahrung 1933–1945 (Hamburg: Dölling und Galitz, 1999), 80.
39. Gesetz zur Vereinheitlichung des Rechts der Eheschließung und der Ehescheidung im Lande Österreich und im übrigen Reichsgebiet, July 6, 1938, in *Reichsgesetzblatt* (*RGBl*) I 1938, 808–22. Meyer, *"Jüdische Mischlinge,"* 73.
40. Simon Goeke, Martin Rühlemann, and Maximilian Strnad, *Sendling arisiert. Enteignung und Vertreibung jüdischer Nachbarn im Nationalsozialismus* (Munich: Franz Schiermeier Verlag, 2016), 26–29.
41. Beate Meyer, "The Mixed Marriage—A Guarantee of Survival or a Reflection of German Society during the Nazi Regime?" in *Probing the Depths of German Antisemitism: German Society and the Persecution of the Jews 1933–1941*, ed. David Bankier (New York: Berghahn Books, 2000), 76–77.
42. Decree of the Reichs Ministry of Alimentation and Agriculture, March 11, 1940, Nürnberger Dokumente (Institut für Zeitgeschichte), NI 14581; Police regulations on the mandatory identification of Jews, September 1, 1941, in *Reichsgesetzblatt* (*RGBl*) I 1941, 547.
43. Alfred Gottwaldt and Diana Schulle, *Die "Judendeportationen" aus dem Deutschen Reich 1941–1945. Eine kommentierte Chronologie* (Wiesbaden: Marixverlag, 2005).
44. Maximilian Strnad, "The Fortune of Survival—Intermarried German Jews in the Dying Breath of the 'Thousand-Year Reich.'" *Dapim* 29, no. 3 (2015): 185–93.
45. Strnad, "Privileg Mischehe," 279.
46. Loewenberg, *Requiem of a B-Man*, 79–81.
47. Ludwig Edelstein to Bayerisches Landesentschädigungsamt, June 18, 1971, BayHStA, LEA 9789.
48. Cornelia Essner, *Die "Nürnberger Gesetze" oder die Verwaltung des Rassenwahns 1933–1945* (Paderborn: Schöningh, 2002), 55–75.
49. Express letter of Hermann Göring, December 28, 1938, cited in Paul Sauer, *Die Schicksale der jüdischen Bürger Baden-Württembergs während der nationalsozialistischen Verfolgungszeit 1933–1945* (Stuttgart: Kohlhammer, 1969), 2:83f.

Bibliography

Archives

Bayerisches Hauptstaatsarchiv.
Bundesarchiv Berlin.
Diözesanarchiv Berlin.
Harvard University Library.
Institut für Zeitgeschichte.
International Tracing Service.
Leo Baeck Institute, New York.
Reichsgesetzblatt (RGBl).
Stadtarchiv München.
Zentralarchiv der Evangelische Kirche in Hessen, Nassau und Frankfurt am Main.

Secondary Sources

Aub, Rudolf. "Handlanger in Sierra Leone. Amtsarzt in Jamaika." In *Das Exil der kleinen Leute. Alltagserfahrung deutscher Juden in der Emigration*, edited by Wolfgang Benz, 101–22. Munich, Beck, 1994.

Beer, Susanne, Johannes Schwartz, and Maximilian Strnad. "Anti-Semitism." In *Ruptures in the Everyday: Views of Modern Germany from the Ground*, edited by Andrew Bergerson and Leonard Schmieding, 168–200. New York, Berghan Books, 2017.

Büttner, Ursula. "An Unknown Case of Resistance. The Rescue of Jews in Christian-Jewish Mixed Marriages." In *The Moral Imperative. New Essays on the Ethics of Resistance in National Socialist Germany 1933–1945*, edited by Andrew Chandler, 105–17. Boulder, Westview Press, 1998.

Büttner, Ursula. "Bollwerk Familie. Die Rettung der Juden in 'Mischehe.'" In *Mut zur Menschlichkeit. Hilfe für Verfolgte während der NS-Zeit*, edited by Günther B. Ginzel, 59–77. Cologne, Rheinland-Verlag, 1993.

Die Nacht als die Synagogen brannten. Texte und Materialien zum 9. November 1938. Stuttgart: Landeszentrale für politische Bildung Baden-Württemberg, self-published, 1998. Accessed January 29, 2019. http://www.lpb-bw.de/publikationen/pogrom/Pogrom.pdf.

Döscher, Hans-Jürgen. *Reichskristallnacht. Die Novemberpogrome 1938*. Frankfurt am Main: Ullstein, 1988.

Doerry, Martin. *"Mein verwundetes Herz." Das Leben der Lilli Jahn 1900–1944*. Stuttgart and Munich: Deutsche Verlags-Anstalt, 2002.

Essner, Cornelia. *Die "Nürnberger Gesetze" oder die Verwaltung des Rassenwahns 1933–1945*. Paderborn: Schöningh, 2002.

Goeke, Simon, Martin Rühlemann, and Maximilian Strnad. *Sendling arisiert. Enteignung und Vertreibung jüdischer Nachbarn im Nationalsozialismus.* Munich: Franz Schiermeier Verlag, 2016.

Gottwaldt, Alfred and Diana Schulle. *Die "Judendeportationen" aus dem Deutschen Reich 1941–1945. Eine kommentierte Chronologie.* Wiesbaden: Marixverlag, 2005.

Gruchmann, Lothar. *Justiz im Dritten Reich 1933–1940. Anpassung und Unterwerfung in der Ära Gürtner.* Munich: Oldenbourg, 1988.

Heusler, Andreas, and Tobias Weger, eds. *"Kristallnacht": Gewalt gegen die Münchner Juden im November 1938.* Munich: Buchendorfer Verlag, 1998.

Heydt, Maria von der. "Möglichkeiten und Grenzen der Auswanderung von 'jüdischen Mischlingen' 1938–1941." In *"Wer bleibt, opfert seine Jahre, vielleicht sein Leben." Deutsche Juden 1938–1941*, edited by Susanne Heim, Beate Meyer, and Francis R. Nicosia, 77–95. Göttingen: Wallstein, 2010.

Kaplan, Marion. "Changing Roles in Jewish Families." In *Jewish Life in Nazi Germany: Dilemmas and Responses*, edited by Francis R. Nicosia and David Scrase, 15–45. New York: Berghan Books, 2010.

Keil, Heinz. *Dokumentation über die Verfolgungen der jüdischen Bürger von Ulm/Donau.* Ulm: Self-published, 1961.

Krause-Burger, Sibylle. *Herr Wolle lässt noch einmal grüßen. Geschichte meiner deutschjüdischen Familie.* Munich: Deutsche Verlags-Anstalt, 2007.

Kropat, Wolf-Arno. *"Reichskristallnacht." Der Judenpogrom vom 7. bis 10. November 1938. Urheber, Täter, Hintergründe. Mit ausgewählten Dokumenten.* Wiesbaden: Kommission für die Geschichte der Juden in Hessen, self-published, 1997.

Kuller, Christiane. *Finanzverwaltung und Judenverfolgung. Die Entziehung jüdischen Vermögens in Bayern während der NS-Zeit.* Munich: Beck, 2008.

Loewenberg, Peter C. *Requiem of a B-Man.* Great Falls, self-published, 1998.

Mahnkopp, Volker. "Georg Kalischer: Einsame Bestattung für IG-Farben-Direktor." In *Getauft, ausgestoßen—und vergessen? Zum Umgang der evangelischen Kirchen in Hessen mit den Christen jüdischer Herkunft im Nationalsozialismus*, edited by Heinz Daume, 196–200. Hanau, CoCon, 2013.

Meyer, Beate. *"Jüdische Mischlinge." Rassenpolitik und Verfolgungserfahrung 1933–1945.* Hamburg: Dölling und Galitz, 1999.

Meyer, Beate. "The Mixed Marriage—a Guarantee of Survival or a Reflection of German Society during the Nazi Regime?" In *Probing the Depths of German Antisemitism: German Society and the Persecution of the Jews 1933–1941*, edited by David Bankier, 54–77. New York: Berghahn Books, 2000.

Mußgnug, Dorothee. *Die Reichsfluchtsteuer 1931–1953.* Berlin: Duncker & Humblot, 1993.

Sauer, Paul. *Dokumente über die Verfolgung der jüdischen Bürger in Baden-Württemberg durch das nationalsozialistische Regime 1933–1945.* Stuttgart: Kohlhammer, 1966.

Schneider, Hubert. *Leben nach dem Überleben: Juden in Bochum nach 1945*. Berlin: Lit Verlag, 2014.

Schönhagen, Benigna. *"Getrennt von allem, was uns geblieben. . . ." Der Weg der Familie Kraus aus Augsburg*. Augsburg: Jüdisches Kulturmuseum Augsburg-Schwaben, self-published, 2008.

Schönhagen, Benigna. *"Glücklich wieder vereint." Der Weg der Familie Hartmann aus Augsburg*. Augsburg: Jüdisches Kulturmuseum Augsburg-Schwaben, self-published, 2014.

Schüler-Springorum, Stefanie. *Geschlecht und Differenz*. Paderborn: Schöningh, 2014.

Selig, Wolfram. *Leben unterm Rassenwahn. Vom Antisemitismus in der "Hauptstadt der Bewegung."* Berlin: Metropol, 2001.

Stein, Harry. "Juden im Konzentrationslager Buchenwald 1938–1942. Pogromnacht und Holocaust. Frankfurt, Weimar, Buchenwald." In *Die schwierige Erinnerung an die Stationen der Vernichtung*, edited by Thomas Hofmann, Hanno Loewy, and Harry Stein, 81–171. Weimar: Böhlau, 1994.

———. "Das Sonderlager im Konzentrationslager Buchenwald nach den Pogromen 1938." In *"Nach der Kristallnacht." Jüdisches Leben und antijüdische Politik in Frankfurt am Main 1938–1945*, edited by Monica Kingreen, 19–54. Frankfurt am Main: Campus-Verlag, 1999.

Steinweis, Alan. *Kristallnacht 1938*. Cambridge, Belknap Press of Harvard University Press, 2009.

Strauss, Herbert A. "Jewish Emigration from Germany: Nazi Policies and the Jewish Responses (I)." *Leo Baeck Institution Yearbook*, no. 25 (1980): 313–61.

Strnad, Maximilian. "The Fortune of Survival—Intermarried German Jews in the Dying Breath of the 'Thousand-Year Reich.'" *Dapim* 29, no. 3 (2015): 173–96.

———. "Manchen Spuren menschlicher Existenz verblassen schneller als andere. Die Geschichte einer 'privilegierten Mischehe' in Memmingen." In *Allgäuerinnen. Ein Lesebuch*, edited by Barbara Lochbihler, 171–90. Berlin: Edition Ebersbach, 2013.

———. "Privileg Mischehe? Handlungsräume sogenannter 'jüdisch versippter' Familien 1933–1949." PhD diss., University of Munich, 2016.

CHAPTER 4

Social Relations and Bystander Responses to Violence: Kristallnacht November 1938[1]

by Mary Fulbrook

The organized violence against Jews across Germany on the night of November 9–10, 1938, often termed "Reichskristallnacht" or "Kristallnacht," and which continued in different forms over the following days and weeks, constituted a major turning point for Jewish victims of Nazi persecution.[2] The burning of synagogues, destruction of sacred objects including Torah scrolls, physical violence and public humiliations, violation of domestic spaces, smashing of shop windows and looting of goods, and the arrests and incarceration of some thirty thousand adult male Jews in Dachau, Buchenwald and Sachsenhausen—all this, in the context of ongoing pauperization, "aryanization" of property, exclusion from public spaces and loss of social status, dramatically signified the unmistakable end of any viable life in the Third Reich for people of Jewish descent. For hundreds of Jews, the November events were fatal, whether immediately or in the weeks that followed. For individuals who had the necessary financial means and personal support, the events were the final precipitant for emigration, in face of by now almost insurmountable challenges. Those left behind struggled on for three or four more years before being subjected to radical policies of deportation and murder.

Much attention has focused on decision-making at the top, the coordination of violence by the Nazi leadership, and on the experiences of Jews. Less well understood to date are the roles played by "bystanders" to this nation-wide explosion of state-sponsored violence, with debates over popular reactions from participation and plundering to expressions of sympathy and shame. In relation to bystander passivity, the question has been raised as to whether the widely noted apparent "indifference" of ordinary Germans in November 1938 in fact amounted to a form of "moral complicity," paving the way for genocide. Following a brief review of historical debates, I argue that bystander behaviors were not only a result of opinions on specific issues at the time of the event, but were also rooted in a distinctive combination of complicity and constraint in preceding years.

Bystander behaviors may be plotted along a spectrum of possible responses to specific incidents of violence, depending on both sympathies and actions.[3] Those who are initially neither direct perpetrators nor immediate victims cannot stay neutral for very long. Let us call this apparently "neutral" position 3, and place it in the middle of a theoretical five-point scale, as below:

Bystander Responses				
1	2	3	4	5
Active intervention on behalf of victims	Demonstrative sympathy for victims	"Neutral": Inactive, impassive eyewitnesses	Demonstrative support for acts of perpetration	Participatory complicity: active on the side of perpetrators

Time is crucial in this scenario. Depending on circumstances, bystanders may try to remain impassive and inactive for as long as possible. But, having sized up what is going on, they may eventually express sympathy for victims (position 2) or even intervene actively on their behalf (position 1). Moving in the other direction, by contrast, they may express solidarity with the perpetrator side, perhaps jeering at victims or egging on the perpetrators (4), or they may themselves participate in or profit from the fruits of violence (5 on the scale). Inaction, position 3, is only at the beginning neutral. In a persisting system of state-sustained collective violence, it is difficult for people to remain neutral. They may try not to register what is going on, seeking "not to see" and "not to know," precisely in order not to feel the discomfort occasioned by facing the question: "Whose side are you on?" But by not acting, bystanders effectively condone violence, allowing perpetrators to proceed unhindered, uncensored, unreported, and failing to give even symbolic succor to those on the receiving end of violence.

I draw on autobiographical accounts written between August 1939 and April 1940 to explore the development of what I call a "bystander society" that, through widespread passivity, effectively permitted violence. These essays, under the title "My Life in Germany before and after 1933," were composed for a competition announced by three Harvard professors and advertised in the German-language exile press and American newspapers.[4] Some 230 individuals entered the competition; they came from across the Reich and at the time of writing were mostly well beyond its borders, in the United States, the United Kingdom, Palestine, Shanghai, Australia, with a few still in Europe. As well as Jews, writers include Protestants, Catholics, people of no religion, in mixed relationships or mixed marriages, as well as the offspring of such liaisons. They represent views across the political spectrum, with even a few Nazi sympathizers, and a wide range of ages and occupations, with a predictable preponderance of professionals. Precisely because memories were not as yet overshadowed by knowledge of the organized mass extermination yet to come, these essays give vivid and detailed descriptions of everyday life, and provide illuminating insights into changing social relations in Nazi Germany during the peacetime years.

HISTORICAL INTERPRETATIONS OF NOVEMBER 1938

Despite the relative richness of sources—official state and party reports, critical commentaries by regime opponents, snippets gathered for the exiled social democratic party (Sopade), eye-witness accounts from varying perspectives—scholars disagree on how best to characterize popular reactions to Kristallnacht.[5]

Many highlight widespread disapproval of specific aspects. Ian Kershaw and others comment on shock at the wanton destruction of property; David Bankier vividly describes people registering that they were "ashamed to be German," and points to egoistic concerns about business being adversely affected by how Germany might be viewed in the wider world.[6] Wolf-Arno Kropat points out that people were critical not only of the destruction of material goods, but also of the inhumanity of the rabble, and were shocked that the state engaged in open terror in this way; even those who supported the regime, and approved of Nazi social and economic measures, including party members, saw this violence as "unworthy" of the German "cultural nation" (*Kulturnation*), amounting to a "break with culture and a national scandal."[7] Dieter Obst paints a picture in which large numbers helped individuals in distress; both neighbors and people who did not personally know the victims gave short-term assistance in the form of shelter, food, or loans of household objects to replace those that had been damaged or stolen.[8] This picture of individual assistance is confirmed by Wolf Gruner's detailed work on Berlin.[9]

A recent tendency among other historians, by contrast, has been to highlight popular support for and indeed participation in the violence, which was by no means restricted to party activists. Alan Steinweis uses the records of postwar trials to emphasize widespread involvement in public humiliations and looting, including by women and children, some of whom came on organized school class trips.[10] Wolfgang Benz notes that, particularly in rural areas, "adults encouraged children and young people to participate in the pogrom" which "suggests the enthusiasm with which the aims of the regime were, for the most part, shared by the inhabitants."[11]

Not merely attitudes towards material goods and cultural values, but also the social dynamics of local situations and particular personalities played a role in shaping responses.[12] While the pogrom was instigated from above and organized on a nation-wide basis, research on specific areas and communities is contributing to a multifaceted picture of regional variations. The big cities—Berlin, Hamburg, Frankfurt—were more secularized, the sizeable Jewish communities more assimilated, than was the case in the countryside. Close-knit communities in provincial towns and villages enacted rituals of public humiliation and violence against Jews in a manner not so evident in large cosmopolitan environments. Religious differences between predominantly Catholic or predominantly Protestant areas, as well as prior voting patterns—areas with high support for Nazism compared with those previously more resistant—also played a role. Bystanders seem more likely to have intervened on the side of Nazi activists in small communities and rural areas—even when victims and perpetrators knew each other personally—than in large towns and cities, where crowds of onlookers seemed more likely to remain silently disapproving at the time of violence, and some even offered assistance on an individual basis.[13] Benz suggests that "a silent majority in large cities expressed solidarity with the discriminated and humiliated minority" whereas in smaller towns "bystanders were caught in the whirlwind of the vandalistic avant-garde: curious onlookers mixed with raving fanatics, forming a marauding, hooting, violent mob charging through the streets"; driven by a "desire for excitement," people went onto the streets, where "neighbors had turned into plundering intruders, and individual citizens had become part of a collective frenzy."[14] In small communities, it would seem, peer group pressure to go along with Nazi violence counteracted inhibitions rooted in personal acquaintance with the victims. Despite a growth of local studies since the 1980s, however, there remains much to be done to explore patterns and variations.[15]

For all the differences of emphasis, it would nevertheless appear that in 1938 a majority of non-Jewish Germans remained passive onlookers. Even those who disapproved of violence were generally not prepared to intervene on behalf of victims. It is the passivity of bystanders on which I wish to concentrate.

Passivity or *inaction* is sometimes interpreted as "indifference," arguably helping to make genocide possible. Ian Kershaw has indeed notably suggested that while the "road to Auschwitz was built by hate" it was "paved with indifference."[16] Kershaw's pithy assertion, appealing though it may be, is not uncontentious.

A debate has arisen about apparent "indifference." Does it mean simply "lack of interest," as Kershaw intended, or, more strongly, can it be interpreted as a "lack of moral concern," amounting in effect to "passive complicity," as Otto Dov Kulka and Aron Rodrigue argue?[17] Was it rather, as Frank Bajohr suggested, an "embarrassed distance"?[18]

Kershaw prefers "indifference" as a supposedly neutral, descriptive term, and considers "moral complicity" to be a normative term. But "indifference" is a substantive description of attitudes, which may be more or less apposite. And "complicity" too can be used as an analytic category: it is both a legal and an everyday concept to indicate morally compromised proximity to wrongdoing: being an accomplice or accessory to a crime, facilitating a crime; knowing about a crime, but not seeking to prevent or report it. (Reporting, of course, could hardly apply where the authorities themselves instigated or condoned the violence.) In these senses, a considerable degree of complicity was arguably prior to and underlay apparent indifference. People were aware of the inhumanity of Nazi exclusionary policies yet continued to comply with and actively perform the precepts underlying the "people's community" (*Volksgemeinschaft*), as well as to benefit from the consequences.

Conversely, could inaction be largely explained not by indifference or complicity but rather by apprehension and fear? Terror certainly played a role for some. Choosing not to intervene resulted from considerations about personal risks, as well as possible rewards and benefits. Actions were also affected by assumptions about the likely behaviors of others, and how one might oneself be perceived. Importantly, too, inaction might result from a sense of lack of agency or frustrated impotence. Even those who felt strong sympathy for victims, and were by no means indifferent to their fate, thought there was little they could do to help.

Could the inaction that Kershaw interprets as indifference be better understood, then, as behavioral conformity born of a complex set of uneasy compromises, where sympathy with victims might be combined with concern for more immediate personal interests, including fear of retribution? In this case, it would be changing circumstances that account for variations in behaviors, as people weighed up potential risks and benefits around participation on one side or the other in any given situation. Particular historical constellations foster conditions in which people are more likely to be wary of intervention, rather than willing to stand up for victims. Considerations about the wider situation are, then, just as important as specific opinions or attitudes towards particular aspects of violence.

It is important therefore to refocus attention on the underlying social processes, experiences and contexts accounting for bystander *behaviors*—which were, of course, what made a difference to those who were targets of violence. This context-based instability and fluctuation is why it is not possible to provide estimates of the proportions of the population falling into one category or another: the typology of positions relates to *behaviors*, not *people*, and any individual might move right across the spectrum depending on circumstances.

But it was not only circumstances that changed, in the sense of, for example, the changing risks of intervention in an expanding system of terror and repression. People's relationships with one another also changed over time. In Germany, people who were not excluded from the *Volksgemeinschaft* changed both emotionally and socially in accommodating themselves to the new regime over time. Responses to violence in 1938 were not just a matter of specific opinions, but were also a product of distinctive social processes. Where there was indeed indifference, a declining sense of empathy might be based not only on pre-existing antisemitism or newly learned prejudices, but also on changing relations between "Aryans" and those who were ousted from the *Volksgemeinschaft*. Where there was rather a declining sense of personal agency, irrespective of sympathy with victims, it might be rooted in growing apathy reinforced by repeated experiences over the years, or in pangs of a bad conscience and related emotional strategies for covering up moral compromises that had been entered into along the way.

There are different aspects of significance in understanding passivity in face of violence and inhumanity: not caring (indifference); not feeling able to do anything about it effectively, rendering it not worth taking the risk of intervention (impotence); and there is a further layer of complexity, in that behaviors were often at odds with emotions, sometimes making it easier simply to look away, disregard, not know (ignorance). To understand bystander responses in November 1938, we have to bear in mind the ways in which not only politics but also social relations had changed since Hitler's accession to power.

THE SOCIAL PRODUCTION OF INDIFFERENCE, IMPOTENCE, AND IGNORANCE

Ideological antisemitism clearly played a significant role among Nazi activists; debates and disagreements were primarily about the means, manner and timing of policies to "cleanse" Germany of Jews. A less virulent, everyday form of antisemitism, in the sense of implicit assumptions about invidious distinctions between Jews and non-Jews, was more widely prevalent. But among a significant proportion of the population, particularly in cities with assimilated Jewish communities and high numbers of conversions, the salience of religious differences had been decreasing in the early twentieth century. Furthermore, with rising rates of intermarriage there were growing numbers of so-called *Mischlinge*, children or grandchildren of marriages between Jews and Christians.[19] Despite the fact that they formed only a tiny percentage of the German population, their experiences point up markedly what was involved in the severing of emotional bonds with the imposition of racial categories.[20]

Nazi policies set in motion significant shifts in ways in which Germans thought about their identity. People increasingly began to talk in the racialized terminology of "Aryans" and "non-Aryans," rather than referring to themselves and others as "Gentiles" or "Christians" and "Jews." This is evident in unwitting slides from one vocabulary of distinction to another. Along with official stigmatization and legal discrimination went informal processes of social isolation, including the dropping of friendships and loss of social status.[21] Overall, people began to identify more with others in a similar situation. Many "non-Aryan" Germans now began to address what a "Jewish" identity might mean, and to spend more time with Jews, even while rejecting the supposed distinction between "German" and "Jew." The Nuremberg Laws of 1935 also set in motion processes of legal and physical segregation, with "non-Aryans" having to dismiss any non-Jewish household servants under the age of forty-five, or having to change their lodgings if they were renting in a property with "Aryan" servants.

Those not excluded from the *Volksgemeinschaft* were in many ways complicit in enacting a new "aryanized" society through multiple tiny acts in everyday life. Many engaged in social performances of conformity out of peer group pressure, fear of humiliation or loss of personal advantages, and dislike of being on the receiving end of epithets such as "Jewish lackey" (*Judenknecht*). Only a few stood out against the rising tide.

These experiences have been well documented from the perspective of Germans of Jewish descent.[22] Less well explored, however, is the question of what this meant for members of the "majority society." For "Aryan" Germans it became easier to ignore what was happening to those with whom one had anyway dropped contact. "Learned indifference" and "learned ignorance" were in this way added to pre-existing or newly acquired antisemitism. Under the influence of schools, the Hitler Youth and related social activities, there was growing enthusiasm for Nazism among younger Germans (although with notable exceptions and misfits). A generational split became widely evident, posing significant strains between parents and children and adding to pressures to conform, as evidenced in many accounts at the time, even from as early as 1933.

When looking at changes in social relations up to 1938, it becomes clear that people repeatedly took little steps to enact segregation and discrimination in everyday life, not wanting to be cognizant of the consequences for the ousted other. They did in some sense "know" what was going on, because they were actually "doing" it themselves. But they could also claim they did not "know" the fate of these ousted others, since "non-Aryans" were increasingly physically as well as socially isolated.

In November 1938 violence against Jews was no longer in any way masked as "legal" discrimination, as in the Nuremberg Laws, but was brutally visible across the Reich, no longer something that could be "not seen." Violence had of course been evident from the early months of the regime, against political opponents and against Jews (including both the boycott and the legislation of April 1933), and was sporadically and repeatedly evident in the following years, including on the part of radical activists in the summer of 1935. Yet with the promulgation of the Nuremberg Laws in 1935 there had been a sense, among those not directly affected, that matters had been "regularized"; they could more easily turn a blind eye to the consequences for those now officially ousted from the community.

But in November 1938 the possibility of "not knowing" diminished massively: it was virtually impossible to ignore what was happening to the victims of state-sponsored antisemitism. Yet many ordinary Germans did not step in on behalf of the persecuted. This was not only a result of indifference; it was also a consequence of decreasing willingness to act—or at least to be seen to be acting in support of the victims.

By 1938 perceptions of what actions might be possible had changed. Right from Hitler's accession to power those who actively opposed the regime had been brutally maltreated and political opposition repressed. The majority of Germans had neither the will and courage nor the organizational links to stand up against Nazism, and popular responses covered a broad spectrum. Some were swept up by a sense of national renewal; others found it easiest just to go along with the new tide; many felt that their material circumstances were improving even if there remained much to grumble about; careerism, opportunism, and fear of the consequences of not "falling into line" also played a crucial role; there was also a hope, in more critical quarters, that the Hitler regime would be as short-lived as most of its Weimar predecessors, and the storm clouds might well blow over soon. As the regime became more deeply entrenched, however, and particularly from the mid-1930s, many became increasingly apathetic, resigned, feeling they were unable to stand out against the prevailing tide. Denunciations might result in significant penalties for expressing opinions that did not conform to Nazi views, and there was a corresponding growth of mutual mistrust; it was safest to mutter only muted jokes or critical comments among friends. Personal experiences or second-hand knowledge of regime brutality also acted as a significant deterrent in some quarters. Many simply conformed through their external behavior, enacting what was required of them; and some even, since this was easier to live with, persuaded themselves that they had genuinely changed their convictions.

Debates about the extent to which the Third Reich was primarily based on terror or was a "consensual dictatorship" miss the psychological complexities of these processes at a personal level.[23] All of these approaches were daily rehearsed and repeatedly practised, establishing a repertoire of responses that became "second nature." By 1938 few, in short, were in a place where they were willing to act on behalf of victims. Even so, the eruption of physical violence across the Reich came as a shock.

EMOTIONAL REACTIONS AND BEHAVIORAL CHOICES IN NOVEMBER 1938

During the night of November 9–10 and the following days, young people were readily mobilised to engage in violence. These were members of a generation that had by now been particularly steeped in Nazi propaganda and actively involved in the organizational life of Nazi Germany. They were mobilized by people in positions of authority, including not only the obvious groups—SS, SA, HJ—but also by schoolteachers, and there are indications that there were additional pecuniary inducements for their involvement.[24] Everywhere, too, there were adults who were willing to engage in acts of self-enrichment, looting and plundering, as well as onlookers who appear to have been laughing at the humiliated victims of violence.

In terms of a spectrum of bystander involvement, there was far more apparent popular support for the perpetrator side—positions 4 and 5 on my scale—than there had been at the time of the April 1933 boycott.[25] This can in part be accounted for first, by the mobilization of youth; and secondly, by the pursuit of personal advantage, which was in a sense the opposite of the situation in April 1933, when the boycott of Jewish shops had disrupted consumers' habits. There was also apparently less willingness to intervene on the part of victims than there had been in 1933 (positions 1 and 2 on the scale), though even then the passivity of most onlookers had been notable.

Most prevalent in 1938, arguably, was a position of unhappy passivity. Rudolf Bing, for example, summarizes reactions in Nuremberg, as "a feeling of deep depression and shame" spread among the population; "for the first time, some circles were prepared to express their sympathy," saying they were "ashamed to be German"—a point now noted by innumerable historians.[26] Erna Albersheim, a half-Jewish widow and businesswoman, commented after her shop was smashed in and she herself beaten up: "For the first time I heard open criticism [of the regime]. The people were shocked and disgusted. Before that if they had no contact with Jews, they thought that they were being treated well; they saw them on the streets, in their stores. Some even thought that they were being treated with too much consideration. Now, their eyes were opened. If they made a remark, in public, they were arrested. You could hear more whispering than formerly."[27]

There are some patterns of intervention on behalf of victims that are worth brief consideration here. Reading through accounts written close to the events of November 1938, it is clear that there were several categories of people prepared to register sympathy, assist or intervene on behalf of victims of violence.

Least surprisingly, those with personal connections or emotional links with victims of persecution were more likely to intervene on their behalf. Many accounts mention how the intervention of good friends assisted them, whether through prior warnings or providing refuge in order to evade arrest and imprisonment. Alfred Oppler was first warned by a friend of impending arrests, and later managed to stay overnight with other friends.[28] Several remark on the interventions not only of close friends but even of known Nazis related through marriage to Jewish families. Erna Albersheim repeatedly "heard of Aryans helping their former Jewish friends during this terrible time," and also recounts the story of a Nazi party member helping his Jewish brother-in-law whom his sister had married.[29] "Aralk" comments extensively on how her faithful household servant Anna helped to save her life by her reactions during Kristallnacht.[30]

The relationship could simply be one of supportive neighborliness. Maria Kahle, an "Aryan" housewife, recounts how she and her sons attempted to assist local Jewish businesses where they knew the shopkeepers. This assistance had severe consequences for her family: her husband was dismissed from his university professorship, one of her sons lost his place as a student, the family was ostracised by former friends and colleagues, and she herself was offered the deadly Veronal by a friendly doctor, who advised her to commit suicide, saying that this was the only way to save her family. In the end, the Kahle family succeeded in escaping to England.[31]

Rather more surprisingly, however, a remarkable number mention the friendly assistance of officials—civil servants and police officers, people in positions of authority. They make distinctions between the really bad individuals, the brutal thugs, and those who evidenced a degree of sympathy with their plight, by making it a little easier to deal with bureaucratic hurdles, treating them with some civility, almost apologising for what it was they had to do. Oppler remarks that the police officers with whom he came into contact seemed to dislike the task of arresting Jews, and treated people relatively decently, in contrast to the Gestapo and SS.[32] Eugen Altmann comments in a similar vein, speaking of how police officials, "particularly those of the old school, were friendlier than one was used to even in normal times." He speaks of the feeling, shared by others, that the "polite and obliging behaviour" of many police officers might be an expression of their "dislike of their rivals, the Gestapo."[33] Even more surprisingly, it was a young man in SS uniform who assisted Altmann to avoid being sent to a concentration camp on November 10, 1938, by "placing words into his mouth" that would provide the appropriate answers to questions, providing the written basis for his release.[34] Altmann says further that he had heard of many similar stories from others. Albert Dreyfuss was saved from the general arrest of all Jewish adult males by a hair's breadth—a decent officer in charge of a troop of four SA men looked at his WWI papers and medals and obtained the authorisation not to arrest him. In the following days Dreyfuss discovered how lucky he had been.[35] These people in official positions of responsibility were clearly uncomfortable with the violence they were tasked with administering. Even some young people, as Erna Albersheim noted, sought to evade their duties: "Hitler youth was forced to help in this work. I know of boys who pretended to be sick so that they did not have to join the mob. One S.S. man was foolish enough to openly voice his disgust. On the following day his parents were informed that he had accidently shot himself while cleaning his rifle."[36]

Particularly interesting is the question of bystander reactions when these were people who did not know the victims personally. For them, action on behalf of victims was both without obvious reward and evidently risky; spontaneous intervention on behalf of victims at scenes of violence was likely to bring about severe penalties. Altmann recalled that many "Aryans" who even showed their sympathy were "arrested on the spot"; twelve factory workers who had organized a protest on behalf of the Jews were shot dead, while some four hundred others were deported to a concentration camp.[37] Whether or not a protest of this magnitude can be independently verified (Altmann does not provide details of the location), it is significant that Jewish contemporaries perceived that there was such strong sympathy among "Aryan" compatriots; and there are numerous examples of incidents when an individual intervened only to be severely harmed, sometimes fatally, or arrested, while others got into trouble simply for criticizing the events at a distance.[38]

In the light of such experiences, it is scarcely surprising that probably most Germans opted for passivity. Alfred Oppler noted that the events "unleashed a wave of sympathy for the Jews" but that "in fear and trembling, most did not dare to speak of this."[39] But from these accounts, it would appear that passivity was not always or entirely rooted in indifference, in the sense of not caring, being uninterested in the fate of the Jews. For many it was based rather in a well-grounded fear of the likely consequences of intervention, sometimes accompanied by admiration for those who had dared to act. Maria Kahle received an anonymous letter of support on November 20, 1938, stating that "all decent human beings would like to have done the same, but we lacked the courage."[40] Others, as summarized by Miriam Arrington in Vienna, were simply overwhelmed by a sense of "apathy," or "exhaustion of the spirit."[41]

The situation was clearly complex, and perceptions of the likely reactions of others played a role in expressions of emotion or otherwise. Ernst Schwartzert summarized his experiences of November 10 in Berlin in terms of the general unwillingness of members of the population to express any reaction at all, remaining silent and retaining their distance from each other. Even the police who were placed near sites of destruction simply "stared into the air" without meeting anyone's eyes; no-one dared to put a question.[42] Non-Jewish diary-writers made similar comments about the perceived responses of other Berliners, emphasizing that there were widespread indications of sympathy despite an inability to act or intervene effectively on behalf of victims.[43]

When not observed by others, however, some individuals were prepared to indicate sympathy with victims of violence who were preparing to emigrate, saying that they too would like to get out if they had the chance. Others tried to deal with the potential distress occasioned by witnessing such events simply by pushing them out of consciousness. Alfred Oppler comments on a "deadening of the soul: one gradually got used to the fact that the Jews were being persecuted and had to suffer."[44]

Ernst Rathgeber's response was unusual. Having helped his Jewish friends to emigrate, this committed Christian now felt he too could no longer remain in Germany:

> As long as such vandalism is carried out, without facing any opposition, by a regime that styles itself as the standard-bearer of the "moral sensitivity of the Germanic race," then my own humanity forbids me to continue any longer to consider myself a member of this state. And should the German people, as its current leaders claim, really affirm and approve of such barbarism, then I am no longer a German![45]

The majority remained part of a radically changed national community and one, moreover, that was on the brink of war.

Although these considerations are somewhat speculative, the autobiographical essays collected by the Harvard professors provide hints as to the kinds of social psychological processes involved. Only in November 1938 were those who had been complicit in the ousting of Jews from German society clearly confronted with the consequences, and forced to realize where this complicity had led. While some "onlookers" now preferred to "look away" and accept the justifications of the regime, others may have engaged in expressions of being "ashamed to be German" in part because this displaced the shame they felt about themselves and their own complicity in isolating Jews and making the violence of activists possible. In order to restore a degree of inner emotional equilibrium and make themselves feel better, many engaged in expressions of shame or moral outrage amongst each other when they felt it was safe to do so. Mutual expressions of shame also helped to make people feel part of a wider collective of those who were "inwardly opposed" but felt helpless, lacking in agency, unable to do anything about it. The circumstances in which it was felt safe to express one's feelings were highly restricted, and might only be momentary, fleeting, within intimate settings—among just a couple of friends, or within the relative privacy of one's home. It is remarkable that in November 1938 such settings were also, on occasion, among anonymous strangers in public places, on a bus or tram, as noted by some contemporaries.[46]

CONCLUSION

On the basis of his reading of the Harvard essays, historian Leonidas E. Hill suggests the pogrom revealed that "large numbers of Germans disapproved, but their resistance was minimal. The war itself would prove that 'ordinary men' not only would fight dependably but could be relied upon to murder innocent civilians of all ages who were designated as the enemy."[47] This is true, as far as such a brief summary goes, but it does not do justice to the sheer extent of changes in both interpersonal relations and an associated sense of self among "Aryan" Germans over the course of the preceding years.

Put simply: the Nazi regime had from 1933 introduced a hostile environment and initiated practical measures, from violence through legislation, to establish the desired "people's community"; and by being largely compliant with this environment, for whatever reasons, the majority of those included in the "people's community" had further transformed themselves, in the process creating an even more hostile environment—one in which it was possible to carry out terror in broad daylight without significant unrest or intervention on behalf of the persecuted.

Living within the Third Reich was not only a matter of "reacting" to policies according to different values or interests; it was also a process of "enacting" the Nazi community over a period of time, to such an extent that many people gradually became able to believe in their own performances, while for others there was a continuing, underlying sense of discomfort about compromises that had been entered into, and unease about the outcome, while at the same time being too fearful to act in any way other than conforming while expressing shame. These experiences and emotions would feed into the decades of unease about the Nazi past in postwar discourses.

An analysis of bystander behaviors is crucial to understanding the dynamics of collective violence more generally. "Bystanding" can make all the difference, tipping the balance of historical outcomes; it is all the more important to clarify the different aspects involved. In the case of the run-up to Kristallnacht, it can be argued that the social production of indifference, through complying with the injunction to separate "Aryans" from "non-Aryans," was indeed a form of complicity. But it can also be suggested that the fear of doing more than express sentiments of shock and shame was in large measure a product of constraint and fear, and indeed a sense of impotence. The ensuing emotional imbalance for many was soon subsumed by the far more immediate and life-threatening demands of a nation at war. But the reactions of both engagement and self-distancing would be rehearsed once again, in the ultimately more fateful radicalization of antisemitic policies on the road to genocide.

Notes

1. This paper is based in a research project on "Compromised identities? Reflections on perpetration and complicity under Nazism," sponsored by the Arts and Humanities Research Council, and on the related book that I am currently writing, entitled *On the Brink of Genocide: Bystander Society in Nazi Germany*. I am very grateful to the AHRC for its support.
2. There are debates over terminology, and difficulties with the terms "pogrom" and "Reichskristallnacht"—the latter having a slightly ironic flavor, mocking the Nazi predilection for the prefix "Reichs-." Irrespective of the relative merits of different positions, I shall continue to use "Kristallnacht" as well as "pogrom" to refer to these events. For these discussions see the chapter by Ulrich Baumann and François Guesnet in this volume.
3. Mary Fulbrook, *Bystanders to Nazi Violence: The Transformation of German Society in the 1930s*, Search and Research 29 (Jerusalem: Yad Vashem, 2018); Mary Fulbrook, "Bystanders: Catchall Concept, Alluring Alibi, or Crucial Clue?" in *Bystanders in Holocaust History*, ed. Christina Morina and Krijn Thijs (New York: Berghahn, 2018), ch. 1, 15–35.
4. Harry Liebersohn and Dorothee Schneider, "*My Life in Germany before and after January 30, 1933.*" *A Guide to a Manuscript Collection at Houghton Library, Harvard University* (Philadelphia: American Philosophical Society, 2001) (hereafter HHL).
5. Published collections of sources include not only the Sopade and SD reports, long used by historians, but also, notably, Otto Dov Kulka and Eberhard Jäckel, eds., *Die Juden in den geheimen NS-Stimmungsberichten 1933–1945* (Düsseldorf: Droste Verlag, 2004); and Ben Barkow, Raphael Gross, and Michael Lenarz, eds., *Novemberpogrom 1938. Die Augenzeugenberichte der Wiener Library, London* (Frankfurt: Jüdischer Verlag im Suhrkamp Verlag, 2008).
6. Ian Kershaw, *Popular Opinion and Political Dissent. Bavaria 1933–1945* (Oxford: Oxford University Press, 1983); David Bankier, *The Germans and the Final Solution: Public Opinion under Nazism* (Oxford: Blackwell, 1992).
7. Wolf-Arno Kropat,"*Reichskristallnacht.*" *Der Judenpogrom vom 7. bis 10. November 1938—Urheber, Täter, Hintergründe* (Wiesbaden: Kommission für die Geschichte der Juden in Hessen, 1997), 168.
8. Dieter Obst, *"Reichskristallnacht." Ursachen und Verlauf des antisemitischen Pogroms vom November 1938* (Frankfurt am Main: Peter Lang, 1991).
9. Wolf Gruner, "Indifference? Participation and Protest as Individual Responses to the Persecution of the Jews as Revealed in Berlin Police Logs and Trial Records, 1933–45," in *The Germans and the Holocaust: Popular Responses to the Persecution and Murder of the Jews*, ed. Susanna Schrafstetter and Alan E. Steinweis (New York: Berghahn, 2016), 59–83.
10. Alan Steinweis, *Kristallnacht 1938* (Cambridge: Harvard University, 2009).

11. Wolfgang Benz, "The November Pogrom of 1938: Participation, Applause, Disapproval," in *Exclusionary Violence: Antisemitic Riots in Modern German History*, ed. Christoph Hoffmann, Werner Bergmann, and Helmut Walser Smith (Ann Arbor: University of Michigan Press, 2002), 152.
12. Andrea Löw and Frank Bajohr, eds., *The Holocaust and European Societies: Social Processes and Social Dynamics* (London: Palgrave Macmillan, 2016); Obst, "Reichskristallnacht," 319–48; Sven Felix Kellerhoff, *Ein ganz normales Pogrom. November 1938 in einem deutschen Dorf* (Stuttgart: Klett-Cotta, 2018); Herbert Schultheis, *Die Reichskristallnacht in Deutschland nach Augenzeugenberichten* (Bad Neustadt: Rötter, 1985).
13. Ruth Andreas-Friedrich, *Der Schattenmann* (Berlin: Suhrkamp, 2000; orig. 1947 and 1984); Gruner, "Indifference?"
14. Benz, "November Pogrom," 149.
15. An attempt at popular synthesis by renowned historian Martin Gilbert unfortunately evidences sloppy scholarship, as when he claims that in three southern German villages there was significant resistance to the pogrom, even "preventing" it: Martin Gilbert, *Kristallnacht: Prelude to Destruction* (New York: Harper Perennial, 2007), 39, mis-citing a book by Anthony Read and David Fisher (with inaccuracies relating to the name of one of the villages, the title of the book footnoted, and even the page reference), whose discussion appears in fact to be based an analysis of these three villages by E. N. Peterson, *The Limits of Hitler's Power* (Princeton: Princeton University, 1969), 404–27.
16. Kershaw, *Popular Opinion*, 277.
17. Ian Kershaw, "Preface to the Second Edition," *Popular Opinion and Political Dissent* (2nd ed.; Oxford: Clarendon Press, 2002), xxv; Otto Dov Kulka and Aron Rodrigue, "The German Population and the Jews in the Third Reich," *Yad Vashem Studies* 16 (1984): 421–35; Ian Kershaw, "German Popular Opinion and the 'Jewish Question,' 1939–1943: Some Further Reflections," in *Die Juden im nationalsozialistischen Deutschland 1933–1943*, ed. Arnold Paucker (Tübingen: Mohr Siebeck, 1986), 365–86.
18. Frank Bajohr, "Über die Entwicklung eines schlechten Gewissens. Die deutsche Bevölkerung und die Deportationen 1941–1945," in *Die Deportation der Juden aus Deutschland: Pläne—Praxis—Reaktionen 1938-1945*, ed. Birthe Kundrus (Göttingen: Wallstein Verlag, 2004), 180–95; cf. also Peter Longerich, *"Davon haben wir nichts gewusst." Die Deutschen und die Judenverfolgung 1933–1945* (Munich: Pantheon Verlag, 2007), 7–21.
19. Beate Meyer, *"Jüdische Mischlinge." Rassenpolitik und Verfolgungserfahrung 1933–1945* (Munich: Dölling und Galitz, 1989).
20. Mary Fulbrook, *On the Brink of Genocide: Bystander Society in Nazi Germany* (forthcoming).
21. Mary Fulbrook, "Subjectivity and History: Approaches to Twentieth-century

German Society" (*German Historical Institute London Annual Lecture 2016*, November 4, 2016); Mary Fulbrook, "Private Lives, Public Faces: On the Social Self in Nazi Germany," in *Private Life and Privacy in Nazi Germany*, ed. Elizabeth Harvey, Johannes Hürter, and Maiken Umbach (Cambridge: Cambridge University, 2019), 55–80; Anna Ullrich, "Fading Friendships and the 'Decent German': Reflecting, Explaining and Enduring Estrangement in Nazi Germany, 1933–1938," in *The Holocaust and European Societies*, ed. Andrea Löw and Frank Bajohr (London: Palgrave Macmillan, 2016), ch. 2, 17–31.

22. Marion Kaplan, *Between Dignity and Despair: Jewish Life in Nazi Germany* (Oxford: Oxford University Press, 1998).
23. For an overview, cf. Richard Evans, *The Third Reich in Power* (New York: Penguin Books, 2006), 113–18.
24. Barkow, Gross, and Lenarz, eds., *Novemberpogrom 1938*, 141.
25. Cf. Benz, "November Pogrom of 1938," 142.
26. HHL, b MS Ger 91 (28), Rudolf Bing, 44.
27. HHL, b MS Ger 91 (3), Erna Albersheim, 61.
28. HHL, b MS Ger 91 (172), Alfred Christian Oppler, 71–72.
29. HHL, b MS Ger 91 (3), Erna Albersheim, 64–65.
30. HHL, b MS Ger 91 (8), "Aralk."
31. HHL, b MS Ger 91 (101), Maria Kahle; Mary Fulbrook, *Dissonant Lives: Generations and Violence through the German Dictatorships* (Oxford: Oxford University Press, 2011).
32. HHL, b MS Ger 91 (172), Alfred Christian Oppler, 75–76.
33. HHL, b MS Ger 91 (5), Eugen Altmann, 52.
34. HHL, b MS Ger 91 (5), Eugen Altmann, 42.
35. HHL, b MS Ger 91 (54), Albert Dreyfuss, 38–39.
36. HHL, b MS Ger 91 (3), Erna Albersheim, 67.
37. HHL, b MS Ger 91 (5), Eugen Altmann, 43.
38. E.g., HHL, b MS Ger 91 (172), Alfred Christian Oppler, 72; HHL, b MS Ger 91 (3), Erna Albersheim, 61; HHL, b MS Ger 91 (217) Karl (Charles) Sorkin, 68–69; HHL, b MS Ger 91 (54), Albert Dreyfuss, 39; Willy Cohn, *Kein Recht, Nirgends. Tagebuch vom Untergang des Breslauer Judentums 1933–41*, ed. Norbert Conrads, 2 vols. (Köln: Böhlau Verlag, 2006), 2:541.
39. HHL, b MS Ger 91 (172), Alfred Christian Oppler, 79.
40. HHL, b MS Ger 91 (101), Maria Kahle, "Anhang," 3.
41. HHL, b MS Ger 91 (9), Miriam Arrington, 77.
42. HHL, b MS Ger 91 (209), Ernst Schwartzert, 75–76.
43. E.g., Andreas-Friedrich, *Der Schattenmann*, 26ff.; Jochen Klepper, *Unter dem Schatten deiner Flügel. Aus den Tagebüchern der Jahre 1932–1942* (Stuttgart: Deutsche Verlags-Anstalt, 1956, repr. 1983), 676, 679.
44. HHL, b MS Ger 91 (172), Alfred Christian Oppler, 79.

45. HHL, b MS Ger 91 (181), Ernst Rathgeber, 17.
46. Cf., e.g., Andreas-Friedrich, *Der Schattenmann*, 26–35.
47. Leonidas E. Hill, "The Pogrom of November 9–10, 1938 in Germany," in *Riots and Pogroms*, ed. Paul Brass (London: Macmillan, 1996), ch. 3, 108.

Bibliography

Archives

Houghton Library, Harvard University.

Secondary Sources

Andreas-Friedrich, Ruth. *Der Schattenmann*. Berlin: Suhrkamp, 2000; orig. 1947 and 1984.

Bajohr, Frank. "Über die Entwicklung eines schlechten Gewissens. Die deutsche Bevölkerung und die Deportationen 1941–1945." In *Die Deportation der Juden aus Deutschland: Pläne—Praxis—Reaktionen 1938–1945*, edited by Birthe Kundrus, 180–95. Göttingen: Wallstein Verlag, 2004.

Bankier, David. *The Germans and the Final Solution: Public Opinion under Nazism*. Oxford: Blackwell, 1992.

Barkow, Ben, Raphael Gross, and Michael Lenarz, eds. *Novemberpogrom 1938, Die Augenzeugenberichte der Wiener Library, London*. Frankfurt: Jüdischer Verlag im Suhrkamp Verlag, 2008.

Benz, Wolfgang. "The November Pogrom of 1938: Participation, Applause, Disapproval." In *Exclusionary Violence: Antisemitic Riots in Modern German History*, edited by Christoph Hoffmann, Werner Bergmann, and Helmut Walser Smith, 141–59. Ann Arbor: University of Michigan Press, 2002.

———. *Gewalt im November 1938. Die "Reichskristallnacht." Initial zum Holocaust*. Berlin: Metropol Verlag, 2018.

Cohn, Willy. *Kein Recht, Nirgends. Tagebuch vom Untergang des Breslauer Judentums 1933–41*, edited by Norbert Conrads. 2 vols. Köln: Böhlau Verlag, 2006.

Evans, Richard. *The Third Reich in Power*. New York: Penguin, 2006.

Fulbrook, Mary. "Bystanders: Catchall Concept, Alluring Alibi, or Crucial Clue?" In *Bystanders in Holocaust History*, edited by Christina Morina and Krijn Thijs, ch. 1, 15–35. New York: Berghahn, 2018.

———. *Bystanders to Nazi Violence: The Transformation of German Society in the 1930s*. Search and Research 29. Jerusalem: Yad Vashem, 2018.

———. *Dissonant Lives: Generations and Violence through the German Dictatorships*. Oxford: Oxford University Press, 2011.

———. *On the Brink of Genocide: Bystander Society in Nazi Germany*. Forthcoming.

———. "Private Lives, Public Faces: On the Social Self in Nazi Germany." In *Private Life and Privacy in Nazi Germany*, edited by Elizabeth Harvey, Johannes Hürter, and Maiken Umbach, 55–80. Cambridge: Cambridge University, 2019.

———. "Subjectivity and History: Approaches to Twentieth-century German Society." Lecture for *German Historical Institute London Annual Lecture 2016*, November 4, 2016.

Gilbert, Martin. *Kristallnacht: Prelude to Destruction*. New York: Harper Perennial, 2007.
Gruner, Wolf. "Indifference? Participation and Protest as Individual Responses to the Persecution of the Jews as Revealed in Berlin Police Logs and Trial Records, 1933–45." In *The Germans and the Holocaust: Popular Responses to the Persecution and Murder of the Jews*, edited by Susanna Schrafstetter and Alan E. Steinweis, 59–83. New York: Berghahn, 2016.
Hill, Leonidas E. "The Pogrom of November 9–10, 1938 in Germany." In *Riots and Pogroms*, edited by Paul Brass, ch. 3, 108. London: Macmillan, 1996.
Kaplan, Marion. *Between Dignity and Despair: Jewish Life in Nazi Germany*. Oxford: Oxford University Press, 1998.
Karlauf, Thomas. "Introduction: 'Thus Ended My Life in Germany.'" In *The Night of Broken Glass: Eyewitness Accounts of Kristallnacht*, edited by Uta Gerhardt and Thomas Karlauf, 1–16. Translated by Robert Simmons and Nick Somers. Cambridge: Polity Press, 2012.
Kellerhoff, Sven Felix. *Ein ganz normales Pogrom. November 1938 in einem deutschen Dorf*. Stuttgart: Klett-Cotta, 2018.
Kershaw, Ian. "German Popular Opinion and the 'Jewish Question,' 1939–1943: Some Further Reflections." In *Die Juden im nationalsozialistischen Deutschland 1933–1943*, edited by Arnold Paucker, 365–86. Tübingen: Mohr Siebeck, 1986.
———. *Popular Opinion and Political Dissent: Bavaria 1933–1945*. Oxford: Oxford University Press, 1983.
———. "Preface to the Second Edition." *Popular Opinion and Political Dissent*. 2nd ed. Oxford: Clarendon Press, 2002.
Klepper, Jochen. *Unter dem Schatten deiner Flügel. Aus den Tagebüchern der Jahre 1932–1942*. Stuttgart: Deutsche Verlags-Anstalt, 1956, repr. 1983.
Kropat, Wolf-Arno. *"Reichskristallnacht." Der Judenpogrom vom 7. bis 10. November 1938–Urheber, Täter, Hintergründe*. Wiesbaden: Kommission für die Geschichte der Juden in Hessen, 1997.
Kulka, Otto Dov, and Eberhard Jäckel, eds. *Die Juden in den geheimen NS-Stimmungsberichten 1933–1945*. Düsseldorf: Droste Verlag, 2004.
Kulka, Otto Dov, and Aron Rodrigue. "The German Population and the Jews in the Third Reich." *Yad Vashem Studies* 16 (1984): 421–35.
Liebersohn, Harry, and Dorothee Schneider. *"My Life in Germany before and after January 30, 1933." A Guide to a Manuscript Collection at Houghton Library, Harvard University*. Philadelphia: American Philosophical Society, 2001.
Löw, Andrea, and Frank Bajohr, eds. *The Holocaust and European Societies: Social Processes and Social Dynamics*. London: Palgrave Macmillan, 2016.
Longerich, Peter. *"Davon haben wir nichts gewusst." Die Deutschen und die Judenverfolgung 1933–1945*. Munich: Pantheon Verlag, 2007.
Meyer, Beate. *"Jüdische Mischlinge." Rassenpolitik und Verfolgungserfahrung 1933–1945*. Munich: Dölling und Galitz, 1989.

Obst, Dieter. *"Reichskristallnacht." Ursachen und Verlauf des antisemitischen Pogroms vom November 1938*. Frankfurt am Main: Peter Lang, 1991.

Peterson, E. N. *The Limits of Hitler's Power*. Princeton: Princeton University Press, 1969.

Schultheis, Herbert. *Die Reichskristallnacht in Deutschland nach Augenzeugenberichten*. Bad Neustadt: Rötter, 1985.

Steinweis, Alan. *Kristallnacht 1938*. Cambridge: Harvard University Press, 2009.

Ullrich, Anna. "Fading Friendships and the 'Decent German.' Reflecting, Explaining and Enduring Estrangement in Nazi Germany, 1933–1938." *The Holocaust and European Societies*, edited by Andrea Löw and Frank Bajohr, ch. 2, 17–31. London: Palgrave Macmillan, 2016.

CHAPTER 5

A Scream, Then Silence. Kristallnacht and the American Journalists in Nazi Germany: The "Night of Broken Glass" as an Unwanted Transnational Media Event

by Norman Domeier

If things had gone according to the intent of the propaganda in the "Third Reich," the November Pogrom of 1938—the "Night of Broken Glass"—would not have been a full-scale media event. The decision-makers among the Nazi leaders—Hitler and Goebbels—did want the excesses of violence, as they occurred, and perhaps even in a more radical form. The world public, they initially believed, might accept crimes against a defenceless minority, perhaps even condone it, as was the case with many coups of Nazi policy since 1933. In the German press that had been forced into line, the National Socialist regime could reframe and minimise the events of the pogrom from November 7–14, 1938.

The international press, however, especially the American press, which had a strong presence in Berlin, would not be controlled, as this article will show. Quite the contrary: the events in question were reported quickly and truthfully to the United States (and thus to a global audience), and criticised in a manner devastating for the prestige of Hitler's Germany, which had reached its zenith with the Munich Agreement. Even National Socialist sympathisers in the foreign press, such as George Ward Price, turned away from the regime.[1]

The enormous loss of prestige and social capital, in Bourdieu's sense, was caused not necessarily because the foreign journalists were offended by the persecution of the Jews—the beginning of what we call the "Holocaust" today.[2] No, most of the foreign sympathisers of the regime now realised, that they would soon have to choose sides in a coming European war.[3] Hitler's government left no doubt in two respects: a war was looming, and it would bring with it the destruction of the European Jews. In Hitler's infamous speech on January 30, 1939, he declared a nexus of the dynamic of war and genocide. This became gruesome reality until the last days of National Socialist rule in spring 1945. This speech by Hitler was the mental conclusion, derived from Nazi ideology, of the November Pogrom of 1938, and the start of the phase of European global expansion and genocide.[4]

Looking at secondary literature on the persecution of Jews in the Third Reich, which also takes news coverage into account, the November Pogrom of 1938 is remarkably underexposed. Hence, this chapter is an attempt to reconstruct the coverage of the pogrom by the leading American foreign correspondents. Hitherto, scholars emphasized that American journalism provided highly selective, ideologically biased, partially anti-Semitic and, in general, inaccurate articles on the persecution of Jews in Hitler's Germany, both by the standards of the time and of today.[5]

This perspective is closely connected with a key problem in the history of media and journalism regarding the Holocaust: the striking silence in the American press on the murder of the European Jews. Especially after America entered the war in December 1941, there could have been numerous occasions for large-scale coverage on front pages, even for press campaigns against the murder of the Jews. But until the liberation of the first concentration camps by Allied troops, there were only scattered references to massacres and pogroms somewhere in the East. "Buried," as Laurel Leff fittingly put it, in the daily mass of newspaper information, also-ran features on the last pages of the quality papers.[6] This phase of silence also included a lack of images. During 1942 until 1944, not one picture in the Allied mass media is known that depicted the Holocaust.

By contrast, the "Night of Broken Glass," from November 9–10, 1938, was an event reported in great detail in the international media. The focus is on four American journalists, who held long-term accreditations in Nazi Germany, and who each received Pulitzer Prizes between 1934 and 1940 for their reports from the "Third Reich": Otto Tolischus and Frederick Birchall from the *New York Times*, their direct competitor Ralph Barnes from the *New*

York Herald Tribune, and one of the most well-known and influential foreign correspondents in Germany, Louis P. Lochner, Chief Correspondent of the New York news agency *Associated Press* (AP). As the largest news agency in the world, AP supplied hundreds of newspapers in the United States and worldwide with their reports.

QUICK AND DETAILED PRESS COVERAGE AFTER THE ASSASSINATION IN PARIS

> Here and there, windows were smashed, synagogues had caught fire or went up in flames some other way. The reports should [not] be made up too big, no headlines on the front page. For now, no pictures. No collective reports from the whole Reich, but it may be reported that similar actions were conducted throughout the country. No individual case studies. Local events can be reported in detail. All of this only on the second or third page. If comments are considered necessary, they must be short and say, for instance, that the understandable outrage of the population found its expression in this spontaneous answer to the murder of the attaché.[7]

This press directive from the Ministry of Propaganda reflects how the Nazi regime wanted to see "Crystal Night" portrayed in the media, in other words, which "truth" it intended to impose on the people under its rule. The German press, which was no longer edited by journalists, but by "editors" (*Schriftleiter*) and thus by National Socialist functionaries, was forced to execute.[8] Deviations, mistakes and editorial errors, especially in regional papers, were punished, sometimes with draconic measures. The system of press directives had already been in place for several years, and worked to perfection by 1938.[9]

The problem was the foreign correspondents in Berlin, most notably those from the United States and Great Britain, who were not only major powers in military, but also in media terms. American foreign correspondents generally had something close to an allergic reaction when they had the feeling they were being duped by an official National Socialist interpretation of events. By 1938, they hardly had anything in common anymore with their German "colleagues." Speed and exclusiveness of the news item counted: the "scoop" was the fuel for the American journalists. Already on the 8th of November, one day after the assassination of the German diplomat Ernst vom Rath in

Paris, the American public knew everything about the events. Vom Rath was still alive when, on November 8, the news agency United Press (UP) reported from Berlin that leading National Socialists declared: "The Jewish Question will now find its own solution."[10] And the American press was everywhere, not only in Berlin. Its resources were considerable, with unrestricted mobility in the German Reich, but also in Europe. Every means of transport was used, including the expensive and exclusive airplane routes of the time, in order to beat the competition. The major competitor of UP, Associated Press (AP), had their own journalists at the celebration of the fifteenth anniversary of the attempted Putsch in Munich, on the evening of November 9, 1938. Hitler's commemorative speech was recorded and analysed minutely. The American newspapers that had subscribed to AP reported on November 9, that the "Führer" had attacked the Jews in general, and blamed them for the catastrophe after the First World War. The first indications of anti-Semitic action were mentioned in the AP report, such as the Berlin Head of Police Count Helldorf having all Jews disarmed, and attacks on the synagogues of Kassel and Dessau.[11]

Two correspondents based in Berlin, and competing directly for readers in New York, Otto Tolischus (*New York Times*) and Ralph Barnes (*New York Herald Tribune*), were also admirably well-informed. Already on November 8, Tolischus pointed out to his readers the plans of revenge of a regime, which interpreted the deed of seventeen-year-old Herschel Grynszpan as a "new plot of the Jewish world conspiracy against National Socialist Germany." Tolischus indicated that the entire commercial activity of the Jews in Germany would probably be brought to an end.[12]

But the scoop of having reported about the "Night of Broken Glass" before anyone else goes to Frederick Birchall, Tolischus' boss in the office of the *New York Times* in Berlin. "The correspondent going off late watch in the *New York Times* bureau in Berlin," Birchall writes of himself in his memoirs, "saw some sort of racket in progress in the Leipzigerstrasse at three o'clock in the morning of Thursday, November 10, 1938. After a quick look, he hurried to a telephone and called a colleague out of bed. Between them they told a sensational story in the same morning's paper in New York. It was the story of Berlin's Anti-Semitic terror."[13] Already in 1934, Birchall had won the Pulitzer Prize in "Correspondence" for his reports on the National Socialist "revolution" of 1933. In his articles after 1933, Birchall concentrated on the persecution of political enemies and disliked minorities such as the Jews.[14] As the press critic George Seldes granted in 1937: "None but Nazis have found fault with a single word or line in the Birchall dispatches."[15]

The report of Ralph Barnes, printed on November 10th in the *New York Herald Tribune*, illustrates how chaotic things were in the Berlin offices of the American press from November 9–10, 1938. This included a wireless report from UP, which was probably added in New York, to support the second heading: "Police-Controlled Reign of Terror Is Planned." It also mentioned the fact that "half a million Jews in Germany lived through a night of a police-controlled regime of ruthless persecution."[16] The report was compiled hastily, with two levels of narrative time, but it was nonetheless accurate and, above all, it arrived fast. The German public, on the other hand, was informed of vom Rath's state of health, but could read nothing about the excesses of violence against the Jews directed from above.

What was not known at the time was the individual behaviour of many American foreign correspondents, who offered shelter to persecuted Jews. Years later, in 1943, AP Chief Correspondent Louis Lochner wrote in his book, *What About Germany?*, that for him, Crystal Night is always connected with a sense of pride of being American: "During that hideous night, when no Jew dared remain in his home for fear he might be tortured or murdered, there was not an American house in Berlin which did not offer shelter to some Jewish fugitive from Nazi terror." His opposite number at UP, Frederick C. Oechsner and his wife, also took in Jews too frightened to return home. "A later check-up revealed," Lochner wrote, "that Americans generally regarded it as their self-evident duty to shield the Jews."[17]

THE CRUSHING CRITICISM IN THE AMERICAN PRESS AND THE PROPAGANDA STRATEGY OF THE NAZI LEADERSHIP

The American correspondents enjoyed reporting openly, which had continued to be a thorn in the side of the Nazi Leadership since 1933. But now the pipe burst. Otto Tolischus' article in the *New York Times*, dated November 10, 1938, may be considered one of the most depressing descriptions of the "Night of Broken Glass," and one of the most severe journalistic reckonings with the "Third Reich." The headline, "Reich Swept by Anti-Jew Terrorism," left no doubt as to what Tolischus thought of the German authorities. In a wide historical arc, he termed the excesses of the last few hours a "wave of destruction, looting and incendiarism, unparalleled in Germany since the Thirty Years' War and in Europe generally since the bolshevist revolution." Tolischus also included moving episodes in his account of the larger events: "Foreign embassies in Berlin and consulates throughout the country were besieged by frantic telephone calls and by persons, particularly weeping women and children, begging help that could not be given them."[18]

Ralph Barnes, Tolischus' competitor on the New York media market, kept this pace in his articles for the *New York Herald Tribune*. "An Anti-Semitic terror, unprecedented in civilized countries since the Middle Ages, was sweeping the Greater Reich today as Nazi authorities, ably supported by mobs, dealt blow upon blow against the panic-stricken 500,000 persons who now compose German Jewry."[19] And on the next day, November 12: "Hence the terror may be said to have passed from its gangster orgy-stage, marked by man hunts, pillage and destruction of Jewish property—including the burning, bombing and defiling of synagogues—to what might be termed a 'legal stage.'"[20]

Also on the side of the National Socialist propaganda apparatus, this was an exceptional situation. No foreign correspondent was threatened with serious consequences for newspaper articles, which in more peaceful times had led to immediate expulsion from the Reich. But this concern remained. "There are rumors of impending expulsions of American correspondents," noted Wallace Deuel on November 22, 1938. The regime was still "much annoyed with the reporting of the 'action of punishment and education.'"[21]

In light of the "rampage" in the foreign newspapers, as Goebbels called the international press war on the November Pogrom, small measures such as individual expulsion would hardly have any effect.[22] Instead, Goebbels, as the head of the Reich propaganda ministry, spoke himself before foreign correspondents on November 11, 1938, where he did not apologise, but went over to the offensive. One of the crucial and most intelligent arguments of National Socialist propaganda in a crisis was to place the excesses in a global context, and thus relativize them. Many foreign correspondents drew historic comparisons, and complementary to this, the German press ran week-long stories on the British Empire in Palestine. The aim of putting the crimes committed in Germany into perspective succeeded to a certain extent. "Is it humane to fight Arab nationalism with wholesale executions and the dynamiting of entire blocks of houses in the name of British civilisation?" This was an argument given from the National Socialist propaganda authorities, which even the *Manchester Guardian*, critical of colonialism, was receptive to.[23] Since this argument was reproduced almost identically by the entire German press, however,[24] many foreign correspondents in Berlin criticised the evident "orchestration" of German newspapers by a "higher source," which meant, of course, Goebbels.[25] In the course of November 11, Goebbels prepared an article justifying the events for the next day's edition of the *Völkischer Beobachter*, which was also circulated among the foreign correspondents. The author did not intend to calm the outrage in newspapers abroad, but provoked even further by outright blackmail, stating that the Jews in the United States should better keep quiet, if they did not want to cause harm to their co-religionists in Germany. Ralph Barnes filled the title page of the *New York Herald Tribune* on November 12, 1938 with the inflammatory words of the German Minister of Propaganda.

Title page of the New York Herald Tribune, November 12, 1938.

The British press also seized on Goebbel's open threat, that the Jewish Question would now be solved systematically. "The hatred in the foreign press does not worry us. Germany is safe, and no one will be permitted to protest if we fight these troublesome parasites."[26] In Goebbels' diary, he reflected on the situation: "My appeal worked wonders. The Jews can even be grateful to me. The foreign press is very negative. Especially in the US. I receive the Berlin foreign correspondents and explain the whole question to them. That impresses them. Then, I dictate a spirited essay for the German press. Here, the problem is described and explained for our own public."[27]

The German press tried to hush the pogrom up, and only to provide the barest information necessary.[28] German newspapers were banned, "until further notice," from publishing photographs of the events.[29] But the Berlin

AP office would not be intimidated. AP was able to use its technologically advanced radio-photo-system, and send its own pictures, which had been transported by airplane from Berlin to Copenhagen, from there via London and New York with their transmitters to its subscribers all over the world.[30] In a 1983 interview with photo historians, the head of the photography section of AP Germany in the 1930's, Günter Beukert, remembered that AP had its four best photographers out in the streets of Berlin to document the riots.[31]

The (attempted) photo ban on behalf of the National Socialists was discussed in *Life* on November 26, 1938. The journal was proud to be able to show the few photos, which had made it out of the Reich, including one of the New Jewish Synagogue in the Prinzregentenstraße in flames. Smugly, the magazine contrasted the images of destruction and suffering with pictures of the baptism of Göring's daughter Edda, which showed "Germany's two head men," Hitler and Göring, playing with the child.[32]

AP Chief Correspondent Louis Lochner commented on the "liberal" position of the National Socialist propaganda system towards foreign press

Life *magazine, November 26, 1938. Left: the New Jewish Synagogue in the Prinzregentenstraße in flames; right: German citizens outside a Jewish-owned shop.*

reporting on Jewish topics. "So blind were the Nazis in their hatred of the Jew that they had less objection to truthful reporting on anti-Semitic measures and action than on almost any other manifestation of Nazi-regimented German life." Perhaps this explains why there were no post-factum sanctions against the precipitate photo-sending by AP, or why no American or British foreign correspondent faced consequences for their coverage of the November Pogrom. Lochner reported regularly about the persecution of Jews in Germany, just like the entire American press corps in Berlin. "American correspondents in Germany were unceasing in their vigilance concerning new manifestations of anti-Semitism."[33]

By contrast, in the auto-suggestive style typical for his diaries, Joseph Goebbels drew an interim balance on November 13, 1938: "My explanations to the foreign press are published as big news in the whole world. They bring all of our arguments together. We are in the offensive again. The chief correspondent of Reuter flies to Berlin especially for an interview. I enlighten him without reserve and complain about the position of the British press, listing a vast number of examples. He is disconcerted. I believe he will write something accordingly. Makes a good impression."[34]

In fact, the criticism of the pogrom in the foreign press was so devastating, that the National Socialist regime instigated one of their most extreme measures in dealing with the non-German press: it ordered the Gestapo to confiscate the London *Times* and most other foreign newspapers when they were delivered to Berlin, on November 11 and 12, 1938 (Friday and Saturday). As had become customary in recent years, no reason for this was given. The *Times* explained, however, that the cause was openly critical journalism and numerous negative letters to the editor.[35] In this case, it was especially dangerous for the regime if sceptical German citizens read foreign newspapers, which were still available in Germany, and noticed the striking discrepancy to the domestic news coverage.

UNANIMOUS PRESS VERDICT WITHOUT POLITICAL CONSEQUENCES

The opinions voiced in the American press were catastrophic for the "Third Reich." In various press reviews quality newspapers cited each other and backed each other up with regard to content. The main argument ran thus:

it was a breach with civilisation, and an act of barbarism to blame an entire segment of the population for the deed of one man.[36] The British press was also unanimously damning, including the *Times*, which distanced itself now from supporting the Appeasement policy of Chamberlain's government, and even Lord Beaverbrook's *Daily Express*, which, for years, had reported with sympathy for National Socialism.[37] "No foreign propagandist, bent upon blackening Germany before the world, could outdo the tale of burnings and beatings, of black-guardly assaults upon defenseless innocent people which disgraced that country," ran the verdict in the *Times*. The *Daily Express* called upon its readers, that "at such a moment as this we in Britain have got to reiterate the virtue of tolerance and must dedicate ourselves anew to worship at that shrine."[38]

Five days after Kristallnacht, President Roosevelt instituted an unusual sanction against Nazi Germany. He recalled Ambassador Hugh Robert Wilson from Berlin, and this post remained vacant until the entry of the United States into the Second World War in December 1941. Roosevelt gave a press conference, at which he proclaimed it repulsive, "that such things could occur in a twentieth-century civilization." After the first indignation had died down, however, the main part of the American press still opposed "European entanglements" and giving up neutrality. Perhaps not the majority of foreign correspondents, but the majority of American journalists back home, who set the tone of the commentary, stood firm against all initiatives to let more refugees into the country, or to change immigration laws. Gallup surveys revealed similar tendencies in the general population. Even after the pogrom, most Americans did not want to open the gates to more refugees.[39]

Public opinion and the political reactions in the United States were taken seriously by the National Socialist leadership and influenced the policy of the regime. This underlines the political causalities, which a media event can unleash: the political event "Crystal Night" impinged upon international coverage, particularly in the American and British press. This coverage, in a performative circle, affected the political actions of the Nazi regime in turn, and so, again, the (media) event "Crystal Night." No source reveals this more convincingly than the entries Goebbels made in his diary. On November 10, 1938: "All morning long a hail of new reports. The Führer and I think about appropriate measures. Allow them to carry on with the violence or call it off? That is the question."[40] One day later, he writes: "His (Hitler's) ideas are very radical and aggressive. (. . .) We are waiting now for reactions from abroad. At the moment, just silence. But the thunder will come."[41]

The early and staunchly critical reporting in the American press probably contributed to the end of violence, proclaimed officially by Goebbels in the afternoon on November 10, 1938. The news was passed on immediately to North America, citing Goebbels order: "The justified and understandable anger of the German people over the cowardly Jewish murder of a German diplomat in Paris found extensive expression during last night. In numerous cities and towns of the Reich, retaliatory action has been undertaken against Jewish buildings and businesses. Now, a strict request is issued to the entire population to cease immediately all further demonstrations and actions against Jewry, no matter of what kind. The final answer to the Jewish assassination in Paris will be given Jewry by way of legislation and ordinance."[42]

By "letting the anger of the people loose," Goebbels had gone too far, also for rivals such as Göring and Himmler. They were afraid the events would develop their own dynamic, which would move beyond the unconditional control from above that many leading National Socialists considered imperative. Aside from this, Goebbels was reproached for besmirching the German name abroad. Himmler's SS saw its plans disturbed to arrange for the emigration of the German Jews to other nations in the world.[43] By announcing the persecution and deprivation of rights of the Jews on a gigantic, but "legal" scale, Goebbels managed to end the friction within the National Socialist leadership. Once more, Goebbels was satisfied with himself: "The press and public opinion are entirely preoccupied with the latest laws on the Jews. The German people are fully in agreement. The other countries only take provisional notice. Fuming commentaries will probably follow. The German press offers invaluable help. Our journalists know what is at stake."[44]

In the global public, the National Socialist regime could not redeem itself. Even his exclusive Reuters interview did not do Goebbels any good, as he had to concede—which rarely happened—the limits of his propaganda capacities: "Reuter is presenting my interview on a big scale. The whole English press is publishing it. I release it to the German press, as well. The foreign newspapers continue to foam at the mouth. But we cannot do anything about that now. I let the German papers beat this down."[45]

Goebbels meant not only the disastrous articles and reports, but also the extremely negative comments in the American press, which almost never came from foreign correspondents accredited in Germany. The correspondents concentrated on news which would not offer the regime an excuse for restrictions and extraditions. The real arguments against the "Third Reich," and subsequent discussions, were carried out in the commentary, which included strong judgments from which the foreign correspondents could distance themselves out of self-preservation. They had to do this in order to keep their daily work in Nazi Germany running, by referring to the necessary journalistic division of labour. Under the heading "Great Germany," the *New York Times* commented on November 11: "Thus does a great Government take revenge for the act of a maddened boy, a Government which exercises supreme and unquestioned power over 80.000.000 people, boasts of the order it maintains and aspires to spread this order over all of Central Europe. Recently, this Government has extended its domain with the consent of the Western Powers who acquiesced in its bloodless victories as the prelude to European appeasement. Instead they were the prelude to the scenes witnessed yesterday, scenes which no man can look upon without shame for the degradation of his species."[46]

Many correspondents and commentators stressed the religious element. In a similar vein, apart from the articles on the pogrom, on November 13, 1938 the American and British press reported about smashed windows in the palace of the Munich cardinal Faulhaber. This took place after Gauleiter Adolf Wagner had ranted against Catholics as allies of the Jews two days earlier.[47] Ralph Barnes stressed the anti-Jewish, anti-Christian ideology of Hitler's regime in general. "It is interesting to note that Chancellor Adolf Hitler's organ, the Voelkischer Beobachter, published an editorial commenting on today's decrees under the sacrilegious heading: 'Jehova's Bankruptcy.'"[48] Already before the November Pogrom, the National Socialist regime had prepared anti-Jewish measures, as Sonia Tomara emphasised in the *New York Herald Tribune* under the heading "Jews Knew the Nazis Awaited 'Incident' to Loose New Terror." The Jews she had spoken to on her recent trip through Germany all, without exception, expected the establishment of ghettos and "special concentration camps for Jews." The assassination of vom Rath by Grynszpan provided the government with a welcome excuse to intensify the persecution.[49]

THE "NIGHT OF BROKEN GLASS" AND THE AMERICAN PRESS ON THE HOLOCAUST 1942–44

Even at the high point of the British policy of Appeasement, it is not clear why there were no serious consequences on an international level for Hitler's Germany after the November Pogrom and the following disenfranchisement of the German Jews. The anti-Jewish decrees by Hermann Göring as commissioner of the four-year plan had been cited by the American press word for word on November 13.⁵⁰

The Austrian journalist in exile, Anton Kuh, offered one of the best explanations in the magazine of exile, *Aufbau*. For Kuh, it was clear that "the demolished memory is one of the principle columns of support for Nazi rule." For without remembering and memory, Kuh argues, there is no justice. He states that most remarkable in the relationship between the "Third Reich" and a world audience is the enormous pace: "The ruling principle is: increasing speed. The new rulers hope that the memory of the other countries will not be able to keep up with the increased pace of their lies and misdeeds."⁵¹

Some American foreign correspondents were aware of the correlation between the pace of Nazi misdeeds and the lack of public memory. In a title story in the *New York Times* on November 23, 1938, Otto Tolischus warned the Americans not to forget what had just occurred in Germany. He cites the SS journal *Das schwarze Korps* (also to pre-empt any allegations of "atrocity propaganda"), which demanded that all Jews should leave Greater Germany as soon as possible, otherwise they would be "exterminated with 'fire and sword.'"⁵² It was for such explicitly anti-National Socialist articles that Tolischus received the Pulitzer Prize for "Correspondence" one year after Lochner, in 1940. After this, the German Foreign Ministry let his visa expire. Even though he had fallen into disgrace, and his days in Berlin were numbered, Tolischus still had the courage to accompany the Wehrmacht troops marching into Denmark and Norway. From Oslo, he sent a confidential memorandum to the editors of the *New York Times* in April 1940, specifying what he knew about the persecution of the Jews: "The Poles, like the Jews, are marked for extermination—physical extermination for the Jews and for those Poles who cannot reconcile themselves to German rule. . ." Arthur Hays Sulzberger, owner of the *New York Times*, considered Tolischus' note so timely, that he sent it to Henry Morgenthau, who passed it on to President Roosevelt.⁵³ But still a year and a half had to pass before the United States entered the Second World War in December 1941.

What Barnet Nover had already predicted on November 15, 1938 came to pass late, but not too late: "In the long run, their savagery is certain to prove a boomerang. The fact that they have so repeatedly flouted world opinion and suffered no penalties does not mean that they can continue to do so indefinitely. No nation can put itself outside the pale of decent opinion as Nazi Germany has done without courting ultimate retribution. No nation ever benefits by failing to exhibit that 'decent respect for the opinions of mankind' displayed by the founding fathers of our nation."⁵⁴

There is nothing to criticise in the American press coverage of the November Pogrom of 1938 with respect to journalistic standards, neither of the period nor today. Quite the contrary, articles, reports (usually sent directly from Berlin) and comments (written mostly by the editors in the United States) were exemplary concerning speed, correctness and apt interpretation. This is also true for the further reporting until December 1941—as long as American foreign correspondents were present in Berlin.

Thanks to the daily "checks and balances" among the foreign correspondents in Berlin, and among the newspapers and magazines in the United States, journalistic reporting was far superior to that in the diplomatic sector. There, governments were sometimes offered quite bizarre interpretations of the November Pogrom, such as by the British Consul General, Robert Smallbones, with his theory of a specifically German brand of homosexuality.[55] Although Smallbones behaved without reproach in political practice, helping thousands of Jews to emigrate to Great Britain after the pogrom, and thus forming an exception amongst the high-ranking diplomats of the period, he felt the need to explain the riots in terms of sexual pathology: "The explanation of this outbreak of sadistic cruelty may be that sexual perversion, and in particular homo-sexuality, are very prevalent in Germany. It seems to me that mass sexual perversity may offer an explanation for this otherwise inexplicable outbreak."[56]

On behalf of American diplomacy, no real help was offered during the pogrom, even if many American correspondents used their quasi-diplomatic status to hide Jews. Also after the pogrom, the United States refused to accept more refugees from territories controlled by Nazi Germany than their quotas allowed. For Germany, this quota was not even fulfilled, so restrictive was the American visa policy.[57] One of the favourite arguments of Hitler and Goebbels, that the Western democracies should follow up their philo-Semitic proclamations with words and take in Jewish émigrés, footed on the sad reality of the international rejection of refugees. At most, as in Great Britain, there were neo-colonial pseudo-debates on potential, remote safe havens in the British Empire.

Provided they read the papers regularly, until December 1941, Americans could learn much of what went on in Nazi Germany, decidedly more than the German public, which after 1938 only had the one-line National Socialist press to refer to.[58] Indeed, the American public consisted of the best-informed readers in the world, thanks to the global network of their foreign correspondents and the strong competition among these journalists, among different media and media companies for scoops. Then as today, readers may have rejected articles as "fake news" (the Allied propaganda lies of the First World War had a horrible impact). Or decided to accept them as true but without relevance for their everyday lives.

In his notorious speech of January 30, 1939, Hitler announced the elimination of the European Jews, should it come to another world war. This message, crucial to us looking back today, was indeed registered by the foreign press. But other aspects of this several-hour harangue overlaid the announcement of genocide, and were considered more significant at the time. Some journals understood Hitler's speech, once more, as the expression of his will for peace, if only justified German demands, such as the return of its former colonies, were fulfilled.[59] For British weeklies, which had an influence on the foreign policy of the British Empire, "Crystal Night" and the heightened persecution of the Jews were regarded as irrelevant for the Western democracies,[60] who had to look on while their "last bastions" on the European continent fell away, as described by the senior foreign correspondent in Vienna and Prague, George Gedye.[61] On November 16, 1941, only weeks before the American entry into the war, Joseph Goebbels presented in an article in "Das Reich" under the title "The Jews are to blame!," "ten points" against the Jews. The article made public and legitimized that the Nazi regime was in the process of murdering the Jews of Europe: "We are experiencing the fulfilment of this prophecy [in Hitler's speech from January 30, 1939] and Jewry is meeting a destiny which is harsh, but more than deserved. Sympathy or compassion is entirely inappropriate. World Jewry completely misjudged the forces at its disposal in the war it unleashed, and is now suffering the gradual process of annihilation, which it had intended for us, and would see through without a doubt, if it possessed the power to do so. It is now being destroyed by its own law: 'An eye for an eye, a tooth for a tooth!'" Even in this legitimation of genocide, Goebbels did not forget to point out the power of the American and British press: "It is characteristic that every measure we take against the Jews is printed in the English and United States papers the next day. So still today, the Jews have secret connections to enemy powers, and use these not only to their own ends, but in all matters important to the war effort of the Reich. The enemy is therefore in our midst. [...] The Jews are to blame for the war. The way we treat them is no injustice. They have more than deserved it. To finish up with them once and for all is the business of the government."[62] The American press reported this from Berlin already on November 14, 1941, two days before the original Goebbels article appeared in "Das Reich."[63]

The American press could not report on the murder of European Jews in the field, however, for with the declaration of war in December 1941, all

American foreign correspondents were interned and exchanged, in spring 1942, against German diplomats and journalists in Lisbon.[64] But AP stayed on, as I recently discovered. Well camouflaged, the largest news agency in the world was embedded into the structures of the "Third Reich" and embarked on a daily photographic exchange with the National Socialist regime, through the neutral capitals Lisbon and Stockholm, until April 1945.[65] This secret deal, sanctioned by the White House, may serve to explain the "phase of silence" of the American press, or at least AP, on the Holocaust between 1942 and 1944. For if one invests enormous resources into keeping contact with an enemy power, one is certainly quite satisfied with the exclusive material one receives in the trade-off. Even the harshest reporting in the American press on the National Socialist persecution of the Jews had no political consequences—this was the lesson learnt from Kristallnacht by the American media. Why should one have risked a perfectly working secret arrangement during the Second World War, which yielded countless spectacular events worth reporting in articles and—exclusive—photos, to probe such an inconceivable phenomenon as the disappearance of the European Jews?

Notes

1. On Ward Price, see Norman Domeier, "Staatsgeheimnis und Auslandspresse im Dritten Reich. Spielraum für Aushandlungen zwischen Regime und ausländischen Journalisten," in *Kampf um Wissen. Spionage, Geheimhaltung und Öffentlichkeit zwischen Nationalstaat und Globalisierung (1870-1940)*, ed. Lisa Medrow, Daniel Münzner, and Robert Radu (Paderborn: Universität Rostock, 2015), 159-175. On the November Pogrom 1938 as turning point for many until-then Nazi friendly British papers see Franklin Reid Gannon, *The British Press and Germany 1936-1939* (Oxford: Clarendon, 1971), 226-28.
2. Walter H. Pehle, ed., *Der Judenpogrom 1938. Von der "Reichskristallnacht" zum Völkermord* (Frankfurt: Fischer Taschenbuch, 1988).
3. Richard Griffiths, *Fellow Travellers of the Right: British Enthusiasts for Nazi Germany, 1933-39* (London: Faber & Faber, 1980).
4. Reproduced and commented in London: "Herr Hitler's Forecast: 'Long Period of Peace'. The Case for the Colonies," *The Times*, January 31, 1939, 12, 14.
5. Deborah E. Lipstadt, *Beyond Belief. The American Press and the Coming of the Holocaust 1933-1945* (New York: Free Press, 1993), 100-07. Cf. the edited volume: Robert M. Shapiro, ed., *Why Didn't the Press Shout? American and International Journalism during the Holocaust* (Jersey City: Ktav Publishing House, 2002). A brief overview in Christoph Kreutzmüller, "Augen im Sturm. Britische und amerikanische Zeitungsberichte über die Judenverfolgung in Berlin 1918-1938," *Zeitschrift für Geschichtswissenschaft* 62 (2014): 25-48, esp. 42-44.
6. Laurel Leff, *Buried by the Times: The Holocaust and America's Most Important Newspaper* (Cambridge: Cambridge University Press, 2005).
7. Press instruction No. 3209, 10 November 1938, in *NS-Presseanweisungen der Vorkriegszeit: Edition und Dokumentation, Vols. 1933-1939*, ed. Hans Bohrmann and Gabriele Toepser-Ziegert (Munich/Berlin: K. G. Saur, 1984-2001), 1060-61.
8. Dieter Obst, *Reichskristallnacht: Ursachen und Verlauf des antisemitischen Pogroms vom November 1938* (Frankfurt: Peter Lang, 1991), 65-78.
9. On the system of press instructions for the nazified German press see Jürgen Hagemann, *Die Presselenkung im Dritten Reich* (Bonn: Bouvier Verlag, 1970).
10. *New York Herald Tribune*, November 9, 1938, 19.
11. *Boston Daily Globe*, November 9, 1938, 9. On the first local riots see, e.g., Ulrich Popplow, "Der Novemberpogrom 1938 in Münden und Göttingen," *Göttinger Jahrbuch* 28 (1980): 177-92.
12. Otto Tolischus, *The Globe and Mail* (Toronto), November 9, 1938, 3. *New York Times*, November 9, 1938, 24.
13. Frederick T. Birchall, *The Storm Breaks. A Panorama of Europe and the Forces That Have Wrecked Its Peace* (London: Viking 1940), 297-98.

14. Heinz-Dietrich Fischer, ed., *Outstanding International Press Reporting. Pulitzer Prize Winning Articles in Foreign Correspondence*. Vol. 1, *1928–1945* (Berlin/New York: de Gruyter, 1984), 123–39.
15. George Seldes, *Freedom of the Press* (New York: Bobs-Merrill Company, 1937), 207.
16. "German Jews Face Reprisals in Rath's Death," *New York Herald Tribune*, November 10, 1938, 6.
17. Louis P. Lochner, *What about Germany?* (New York: Dodd, Mead & Company 1943), 178.
18. "Reich Swept by Anti-Jew Terrorism," *The Globe and Mail* (Toronto), November 11, 1938, 1.
19. "Nazis Vent Rage on Jews. Riots All Over Germany. Mobs Kill, Loot and Burn," *New York Herald Tribune*, November 11, 1938, 1.
20. "Nazis Herd Jews in Camps, Plan Ghettos, Warn Those in America to Keep Quiet," *New York Herald Tribune*, November 12, 1938, 1.
21. Wallace Deuel to Carroll Binder, November 22, 1938, The Papers of Wallace R. Deuel, Box 6, Manuscript Division, Library of Congress.
22. On the modern phenomenon of press war, see Dominik Geppert, *Pressekriege. Öffentlichkeit und Diplomatie in den deutsch-britischen Beziehungen 1896–1912* (Munich: Oldenbourg Wissenschaftsverlag, 2007).
23. "Commons and the Riots. The Nazi Reply," *Manchester Guardian*, November 12, 1938, 15.
24. Press instruction 3247, November 14, 1938, in *NS-Presseanweisungen*, 1071.
25. "Commons and the Riots," 15.
26. "'Peace' disturbed by Murder," *Manchester Guardian*, November 14, 1938, 12.
27. Joseph Goebbels, diary entry from November 12, 1938, in *The Diary of Joseph Goebbels*, ed. Elke Fröhlich on behalf of the Institut für Zeitgeschichte. Part I: Aufzeichnungen 1923–1941. Vol. 6: August 1938–June 1939 (Munich: K. G. Saur), 183–85.
28. Christoph Kreutzmüller, *Ausverkauf. Die Vernichtung der jüdischen Gewerbetätigkeit in Berlin 1930–1945* (Berlin: Metropol, 2012), 173.
29. Press instruction 3209, November 10, 1938, in *NS-Presseanweisungen*, 1060–61.
30. As published in "Jewish Shop and Synagogue Wrecked by Nazis," *New York Times*, November 11, 1938, 3.
31. Günter Beukert, "Als Bildjournalist in der 'Reichskristallnacht,'" in *Die Gleichschaltung der Bilder. Pressefotografie 1930–1936*, ed. Diethart Kerbs, Walter Uka, and Brigitte Walz-Richter (Berlin: Verlag Frölich & Kaufmann, 1983), 191–93. One of them was Gerd Baatz. He later joined the Waffen-SS and took the famous pictures of Hitler and Mussolini meeting after the assassination attempt of July 20, 1944. Baatz continued his career with AP after 1945 without a hitch, working for *Life*, *Look*, and in the 1970s for the *Stern* in Hamburg; *Der Journalist* 1 (1962): 22; *Der Journalist* 3 (1984): 6.

32. "Brutal Nazi Wrecking Gangs Leave Path of Destruction," *Life*, November 26, 1938, 14–16.
33. Lochner, *What About Germany?* 238.
34. Joseph Goebbels, diary entry, November 13, 1938, vol. 6, 185–86.
35. "The Times Confiscated in Berlin," [London] *Times*, November 15, 1938, 14. Goebbels in his diary: "I order the Times to be confiscated. Its agitating is outrageous. All English newspapers are gone for now." Joseph Goebbels, diary entry from November 17, 1938, vol. 6, 188–90.
36. "American Press Comments on Nazi Riots," *New York Times*, November 12, 1938, 4. "American Press Indignant over Nazi 'Outrages,'" *New York Herald Tribune*, November 13, 1938, 2.
37. Andrew Sharf, *The British Press and the Jews under Nazi Rule* (Oxford: Oxford University Press, 1984), 14.
38. "Nazis Complicate Chamberlain Task," *New York Times*, November 11, 1938, 2. See also the British press review: "British Indignant at Nazi Terrorism," *New York Times*, November 12, 1938, 1. For the uniformly critical view of the French press, see: "Rites Set in Paris for Slain German," *New York Times*, November 12, 1938, 5.
39. Lipstadt, *Beyond Belief*, 104–09.
40. Joseph Goebbels, diary entry from November 10, 1938, vol. 6, 179–81. On the chains of command of the Nazi elite assembled, for the most part, in Munich, and the sequence of events after the death of vom Rath, see Kreutzmüller, *Ausverkauf,* 167–74.
41. Joseph Goebbels, diary entry from November 11, 1938, vol. 6, 182–83.
42. "Reich Swept by Anti-Jew Terrorism," 1.
43. Heinz Lauber, *Judenpogrom. "Reichskristallnacht" November 1938 in Großdeutschland. Daten, Fakten, Dokumente, Quellentexte, Thesen und Bewertungen* (Gerlingen: Bleicher Verlag, 1981), 152–53, 177–78.
44. Joseph Goebbels, diary entry from November 14, 1938, vol. 6, 186–87.
45. Joseph Goebbels, diary entry from November 15, 1938, vol. 6, 187–88.
46. "Great Germany," *New York Times*, November 11, 1938, 24.
47. "Nazis Fine Jews $400.000.000, Evict from All Business; Munich Cardinal's Palace Stoned," *New York Herald Tribune*, November 13, 1938, 1.
48. Ibid.
49. "Jews Knew the Nazis Awaited 'Incident' to Loose New Terror," *New York Herald Tribune*, November 13, 1938, A1.
50. "Texts of Anti-Jewish Decrees," *New York Herald Tribune*, November 13, 1938, 2.
51. Anton Kuh, "Geschichte und Gedächtnis," *Aufbau* 5, no. 1 (January 1, 1939): 7–8. The text is taken from a speech by Kuh as "critic of the times" in the radio hour of the GJC on November 26, 1938.
52. *New York Times*, November 23, 1938, 1, 8. The article by Tolischus was also published in the *Houston Post* on November 23, 1938 with the heading "Nazi Germany Threatens to Exterminate the Jews."

53. The memorandum is just marked with "Berlin correspondent." According to Laurel Leff (*Buried by the Times*, 75–76), only Tolischus was in Oslo at that time. Henry Morgenthau to Franklin D. Roosevelt, April 20, 1940, Morgenthau Correspondence, Box 277, Franklin D. Roosevelt Presidential Library and Museum.
54. "Can Hitler's Hand Be Stayed?" *Washington Post*, November 15, 1938, 11.
55. On the drawing on homosexuality in international politics, see Norman Domeier, *The Eulenburg Affair: A Cultural History of Politics in Imperial Germany* (Rochester/New York: Camden House, 2015).
56. Frank Bajohr, ed., *Fremde Blicke auf das "Dritte Reich." Berichte ausländischer Diplomaten über Herrschaft und Gesellschaft in Deutschland 1933–1945* (Göttingen: Wallstein, 2011), 29.
57. Ibid.
58. William Sheridan Allen, "Die deutsche Öffentlichkeit und die 'Reichskristallnacht,'" in *Die Reihen fast geschlossen. Beiträge zur Geschichte des Alltags unterm Nationalsozialismus*, ed. Detlev Peukert and Jürgen Reulecke (Wuppertal: Peter Hammer Verlag, 1981), 397–412.
59. "Herr Hitler's Forecast," 12.
60. Morris argues that in most of the weeklies, "it [Crystal Night] was dismissed as irrelevant to the international situation." Benny Morris, *The Roots of Appeasement: The British Weekly Press and Nazi Germany in the 1930s* (London: Routledge, 1991), 153.
61. George E. R. Gedye, *Fallen Bastions: The Central European Tragedy* (London: Victor Gollancz, 1939).
62. "Die Juden sind schuld!" *Das Reich*, November 16, 1941, 1–2.
63. "Goebbels Spurs Abuse for Jews," *New York Times*, November 14, 1938, 11. The *Times* (London) reproduced a part of Goebbels' article from *Das Reich* with his ten points against the Jews on November 17, 1941 on page 3 with the heading "Jews Are to Blame. Goebbels Venom in Das Reich. Ten Articles of Hate." Delivered from the "German Frontier" "From Our Special Correspondent." See also Leff, *Buried by the Times*, 75–76.
64. A number of experienced American journalists left Nazi Germany already before December 1941, or were extradited like Otto Tolischus. In the Berlin office of the *New York Times*, only the pro-German senior correspondent Guido Enderis stayed on, supported by two young assistants (Leff, *Buried by the Times*, 62). On the internment in Bad Nauheim only a small study exists: Charles B. Burdick, *An American Island in Hitler's Reich: The Bad Nauheim Internment* (Menlo Park: Markgraf Publications Group, 1987).
65. Norman Domeier, "Geheime Fotos. Die Kollaboration von Associated Press und NS-Regime 1942–1945," *Zeithistorische Forschungen/Studies in Contemporary History* 2 (2017): 199–230, http://www.zeithistorische-forschungen.de/2-2017/id=5484.

Bibliography

Newspaper Articles

"American Press Comments on Nazi Riots." *New York Times*, November 12, 1938, 4.
"American Press Indignant over Nazi 'Outrages.'" *New York Herald Tribune*, November 13, 1938, 2.
Boston Daily Globe, November 9, 1938, 9.
"British Indignant at Nazi Terrorism." *New York Times*, November 12, 1938, 1.
"Brutal Nazi Wrecking Gangs Leave Path of Destruction." *Life*, November 26, 1938, 14–16.
"Can Hitler's Hand Be Stayed?" *Washington Post*, November 15, 1938, 11.
"Commons and the Riots. The Nazi Reply." *Manchester Guardian*, November 12, 1938, 15.
Der Journalist 1 (1962): 22.
Der Journalist 3 (1984): 6.
"Die Juden sind schuld!" *Das Reich*, November 16, 1941, 1–2.
"German Jews Face Reprisals in Rath's Death." *New York Herald Tribune*, November 10, 1938, 6.
"Goebbels Spurs Abuse for Jews." *New York Times*, November 14, 1938, 11.
"Great Germany." *New York Times*, November 11, 1938, 24.
"Herr Hitler's Forecast: 'Long Period of Peace'. The Case for the Colonies." *The Times*, January 31, 1939, 12, 14.
"Jewish Shop and Synagogue Wrecked by Nazis." *New York Times*, November 11, 1938, 3.
"Jews Knew the Nazis Awaited 'Incident' to Loose New Terror." *New York Herald Tribune*, November 13, 1938, A1.
"Nazis Complicate Chamberlain Task." *New York Times*, November 11, 1938, 2.
"Nazis Fine Jews $400.000.000, Evict from All Business; Munich Cardinal's Palace Stoned." *New York Herald Tribune*, November 13, 1938, 1.
"Nazis Herd Jews in Camps, Plan Ghettos, Warn Those in America to Keep Quiet." *New York Herald Tribune*, November 12, 1938, 1.
"Nazis Vent Rage on Jews. Riots All Over Germany. Mobs Kill, Loot and Burn." *New York Herald Tribune*, November 11, 1938, 1.
New York Herald Tribune, November 9, 1938, 19.
New York Times, November 9, 1938, 24.
"'Peace' disturbed by Murder." *Manchester Guardian*, November 14, 1938, 12.
"Reich Swept by Anti-Jew Terrorism." *The Globe and Mail* (Toronto), November 11, 1938, 1.
"Rites Set in Paris for Slain German." *New York Times*, November 12, 1938, 5.
"Texts of Anti-Jewish Decrees." *New York Herald Tribune*, November 13, 1938, 2.
"The Times Confiscated in Berlin." [London] *Times*, November 15, 1938, 14.
Tolischus, Otto. *The Globe and Mail* (Toronto), November 9, 1938, 3.

———. "Nazi Germany Threatens to Exterminate the Jews." *Houston Post*, November 23, 1938.
———. *New York Times*, November 23, 1938, 1, 8.

Secondary Sources

Allen, William Sheridan. "Die deutsche Öffentlichkeit und die 'Reichskristallnacht.'" In *Die Reihen fast geschlossen. Beiträge zur Geschichte des Alltags unterm Nationalsozialismus*, edited by Detlev Peukert and Jürgen Reulecke, 397–412. Wuppertal: Peter Hammer Verlag, 1981.
Bajohr, Frank, ed. *Fremde Blicke auf das "Dritte Reich." Berichte ausländischer Diplomaten über Herrschaft und Gesellschaft in Deutschland 1933–1945*. Göttingen: Wallstein, 2011.
Beukert, Günter. "Als Bildjournalist in der 'Reichskristallnacht.'" In *Die Gleichschaltung der Bilder. Pressefotografie 1930–1936*, edited by Diethart Kerbs, Walter Uka, and Brigitte Walz-Richter, 191–93. Berlin: Verlag Frölich & Kaufmann, 1983.
Birchall, Frederick T. *The Storm Breaks. A Panorama of Europe and the Forces That Have Wrecked Its Peace*. London: Viking, 1940.
Bohrmann, Hans, and Gabriele Toepser-Ziegert, eds. *NS-Presseanweisungen der Vorkriegszeit: Edition und Dokumentation*, Vols. 1933–1939. Munich: K. G. Saur, 1984–2001.
Burdick, Charles B. *An American Island in Hitler's Reich: The Bad Nauheim Internment*. Menlo Park: Markgraf Publications Group, 1987.
Deuel, Wallace R. Papers. The Library of Congress, Manuscript Division.
Domeier, Norman. *The Eulenburg Affair: A Cultural History of Politics in Imperial Germany*. Rochester: Camden House, 2015.
———. "Geheime Fotos. Die Kollaboration von Associated Press und NS-Regime 1942–1945." *Zeithistorische Forschungen/Studies in Contemporary History* 2 (2017): 199–230. http://www.zeithistorische-forschungen.de/2-2017/id=5484.
———. "Staatsgeheimnis und Auslandspresse im Dritten Reich. Spielraum für Aushandlungen zwischen Regime und ausländischen Journalisten." In *Kampf um Wissen. Spionage, Geheimhaltung und Öffentlichkeit zwischen Nationalstaat und Globalisierung (1870–1940)*, edited by Lisa Medrow, Daniel Münzner, and Robert Radu, 159–75. Paderborn: Universität Rostock, 2015.
Fischer, Heinz-Dietrich, ed. *Outstanding International Press Reporting. Pulitzer Prize Winning Articles in Foreign Correspondence*. Vol. 1, *1928–1945* (Berlin: de Gruyter, 1984).
Gannon, Franklin Reid. *The British Press and Germany 1936–1939*. Oxford: Clarendon, 1971.
Gedye, George E. R. *Fallen Bastions: The Central European Tragedy*. London: Victor Gollancz, 1939.
Geppert, Dominik. *Pressekriege. Öffentlichkeit und Diplomatie in den deutsch-britischen Beziehungen 1896–1912*. Munich: Oldenbourg Wissenschaftsverlag, 2007.

Goebbels, Joseph. *The Diary of Joseph Goebbels*, edited by Elke Fröhlich on behalf of the Institut für Zeitgeschichte. Part I: Aufzeichnungen 1923–1941. Munich: K. G. Saur.

Griffiths, Richard. *Fellow Travellers of the Right: British Enthusiasts for Nazi Germany, 1933–39.* London: Faber & Faber, 1980.

Hagemann, Jürgen. *Die Presselenkung im Dritten Reich.* Bonn: Bouvier Verlag, 1970.

Kreutzmüller, Christoph. "Augen im Sturm. Britische und amerikanische Zeitungsberichte über die Judenverfolgung in Berlin 1918-1938." *Zeitschrift für Geschichtswissenschaft* 62 (2014): 25–48.

———. *Ausverkauf. Die Vernichtung der jüdischen Gewerbetätigkeit in Berlin 1930–1945.* Berlin: Metropol, 2012.

Kuh, Anton. "Geschichte und Gedächtnis." *Aufbau* 5, no. 1 (January 1, 1939): 7–8.

Lauber, Heinz. *Judenpogrom. "Reichskristallnacht" November 1938 in Großdeutschland. Daten, Fakten, Dokumente, Quellentexte, Thesen und Bewertungen.* Gerlingen: Bleicher Verlag, 1981.

Leff, Laurel. *Buried by the Times: The Holocaust and America's Most Important Newspaper.* Cambridge: Cambridge University Press, 2005.

Lipstadt, Deborah E. *Beyond Belief. The American Press and the Coming of the Holocaust 1933–1945.* New York: Free Press, 1993.

Lochner, Louis P. *What about Germany?* New York: Dodd, Mead & Company, 1943.

Morgenthau Correspondence, Box 277, Franklin D. Roosevelt Presidential Library and Museum.

Morris, Benny. *The Roots of Appeasement: The British Weekly Press and Nazi Germany in the 1930s.* London: Routledge, 1991.

Obst, Dieter. *Reichskristallnacht: Ursachen und Verlauf des antisemitischen Pogroms vom November 1938.* Frankfurt: Peter Lang, 1991.

Pehle, Walter H., ed. *Der Judenpogrom 1938. Von der "Reichskristallnacht" zum Völkermord.* Frankfurt: Fischer Taschenbuch, 1988.

Popplow, Ulrich. "Der Novemberpogrom 1938 in Münden und Göttingen." *Göttinger Jahrbuch* 28 (1980): 177–92.

Sharf, Andrew. *The British Press and the Jews under Nazi Rule.* Oxford: Oxford University Press, 1984.

Seldes, George. *Freedom of the Press.* New York: Bobs-Merrill Company, 1937.

Shapiro, Robert M., ed. *Why Didn't the Press Shout? American and International Journalism during the Holocaust.* Jersey City: Ktav Publishing House, 2002.

CHAPTER 6

Journalism as a Weapon: Jewish Journalists from Warsaw and the Production of Knowledge during Hitler's Rise to Power in 1933 and the November Pogroms in 1938.[1]

by Anne-Christin Klotz

In autumn 1938, an anonymous report from Poland reached the press agency of the Union of Jewish Communities in Switzerland, a report that described how Polish Jews had reacted on a recent and unprecedented event, which the Nazis simply called *Polenaktion*.[2] It reads:

> Polish Jewry immediately made arrangements to help the unfortunate and enabled them to live their lives at least to some extent. In Warsaw a non-party committee was organized on Thursday, November 4th, consisting of 15 gentlemen, presided by University professor and senator, Rabbi Dr. M. Schorr. The most important Jewish personalities belong to the committee (. . .). In Warsaw the displaced were accommodated in private houses, (. . .) Zionist organizations offered in some towns their localities as an emergency shelter. Immediately blankets, soaps, towels and medicine were brought to a camp in Zbąszyń. Furthermore, doctors and nurses made themselves available. The Jewish Writers and Journalists Association in Warsaw has imposed a tax on itself and the Warsaw rabbinate decided to take two percent of the earnings of its members in favor of the persecuted.[3]

The anonymous writer described in detail the immediate actions Polish-Jewish politicians, merchants, social workers as well as journalists and writers took, when in October 1938 Nazi Germany expelled thousands of Polish Jews from Germany by pushing them across the Polish border. Within a few days, a central aid committee for Jewish refugees in Poland was set up in Warsaw. Its task was to coordinate the work on site in the refugee camp in Zbąszyń, a small town right on the Polish side of the border as well as the work of other local committees throughout Poland.

The report is a good example for the involvement of Polish-Jewish public leaders regardless of their respective political affiliation within the political struggle against the persecution of Jews in Nazi Germany in 1938. However, their support did not emerge out of a vacuum in 1938. Ever since Hitler was appointed chancellor in January 1933, Polish Jews were deeply engaged in protesting Nazi policies on different levels, as well as in organizing material and financial help for Jewish refugees from Germany, who reached Poland from early 1933 on. Among the group who actively engaged in the protest were a notable number of journalists, who worked for the most important Jewish daily newspapers in Warsaw, namely the Zionist leaning newspapers *Haynt*, *Der Moment* and *Nasz Przegląd* as well as the Bundist *Naye Folkstsaytung* and the orthodox *Dos Yudishe Togblot*.[4] Throughout the 1930s they had become experts on Nazi Germany by gathering first-hand, non-official information as well as by observing, analyzing and interpreting the events the anti-Semitic and fascist policies the National Socialists had implied. This knowledge, which they had accumulated over time and their interpretations of the political developments in Nazi Germany permanently shaped the images of Nazi Germany and German Jews on the one hand, as well as the self-images of Polish Jews on the other during the 1930s and beyond.

International intellectual, political and journalistic responses to the crucial events of 1938 like the so-called *Polenaktion* and the November pogroms are important and often discussed topics within the research community.[5] Nevertheless, in comparison with the rich literature about the reception of the West as well as of Western European Jews,[6] there is a shortage of theoretically informed and empirically detailed studies on how Central and Eastern European Jewish intellectuals, and here especially Yiddish speaking intellectuals and journalists, responded to events between 1933 and 1939.[7] In addition to that, questions of "what they knew, when they knew it, and in what ways that knowledge translated into thought, discussion, expression and action" are open questions.[8]

In combining archival material and memoirs with various articles from different Polish-Jewish newspapers from Warsaw,[9] this chapter discusses, how Polish-Jewish journalists and editors gathered and processed information on the persecution of Jews in Nazi Germany between Hitler's coming to power in January 1933, the *Polenaktion* and the November pogroms in 1938. Following the assumptions of Susanne Marten-Finnis that the Jewish press in Eastern Europe wanted to enlighten, to modernize and to mobilize their Jewish readers, I consider them as active agents of history with their own political mission and as journalists who wanted more than just to provide news.[10] In times of crisis, they used their professional skills to respond practically to anti-Semitism and persecution. Through their journalistic work, they also possessed the necessary capabilities and contacts to gather, interpret and spread information on Nazi Germany on to the "Jewish street" in Poland. As journalists, they had the power to influence and encourage their Jewish readers to participate in the protest movement.[11] But as their own perspectives for a future in Poland for themselves and their offspring started to look rather dark as they experienced anti-Semitic violence and institutional discrimination on an everyday basis,[12] it affected not only their press coverage but also their own perception of the year 1938—as a personal and political struggle between activism, optimism and despair.

SPRING 1933: PRELUDE

With Hitler's coming to power, in January 1933 the Polish-Jewish press reported extensively about the persecution of Jews and political dissidents in Nazi Germany. Before 1933, they closely monitored the political developments in the final years of the Weimar Republic, covering in detail anti-Semitic outbursts as well as political fights between social democrats, communists and members of the National Socialist party.[13]

Their reasons for covering news from Germany in such detail were numerous. With the end of the first World War and the proclamation of the Weimar Republic on November 9, 1918, Germany, and especially Berlin, became one of the most important places within Europe for the international Jewish and non-Jewish press.[14] Already in the early years of the Weimar Republic political power struggles, the strength of the German Social Democracy and finally, the rise of the of the National Socialist party made it worth covering news from Germany. In addition, Germany had served for centuries as a role model and object of comparison for intellectual Jews in Eastern Europe.[15] Polish Jews spoke with admiration of German high culture, and for some, Goethe and Schiller meant more than Poland's most famous writer Adam Mickiewicz.[16] When the National Socialists came to power, Jewish public leaders from Warsaw mourned the destruction of German and German-Jewish culture.[17] Many Jewish journalists from Warsaw had personal ties to their neighboring country. More than a few had studied in Germany or shared otherwise friendly contacts to Jewish and non-Jewish German intellectuals.[18] Melekh Ravitsh (1893–1976), journalist and president of the local journalist's union the *Farayn fun yidishe literatn un zhurnalistn* (Association of Jewish Writers and Journalists), kept in his address books from the 1920s the private contacts of Else Lasker-Schüler, Salomon Adler-Rudel, Simon Dubnow, Frank Leonhard and others.[19] From time to time, Jewish journalists traveled from Poland to Germany or the other way around for business trips or other political matters.[20]

The detailed press coverage was possible when after the First World War Berlin emerged as a new center of migration for Jews from Eastern Europe and "numerous and not very well-known journalists, who were writing for the Yiddish press" found their way to the German capital.[21] Through their assignment, the Polish-Jewish press was very well informed. Two of these correspondents, Yeshayahu Klinov (1890–1963), who wrote for the *Haynt*, and Hermann Swet (1893–1968), who was the correspondent for *Der Moment*, were working in Berlin for a Yiddish daily in Warsaw. Both journalists moved from Odessa to Berlin in 1922,[22] where they joined several professional clubs, making their way into the city's German and Jewish society. Both held a standing press accreditation for the German *Reichstag*[23] and had a profound professional network, reaching deep into the highest German and Jewish political circles. At the annual ball of the *Verein der Auswärtigen Presse zu Berlin* (Association of the Foreign Press to Berlin),[24] they met with high ranking German politicians. In 1931, for instance, they dined with German chancellor Heinrich Brüning and foreign minister Julius Curtius.[25]

After January 1933, when it became increasingly more difficult to get verified information and German Jews refused to speak to journalists, Jewish correspondents used private sources and informants.[26] Often journalists talked to someone from the Polish embassy or met with Jews in private in order to incorporate their experiences into articles anonymously.[27] The journalists possessed not only profound professional and informal networks, they also spoke all the required languages and could understand political matters which directly affected the German-Jewish or Eastern-European Jewish community in Berlin. Hence, they served the high expectations of their employers in Warsaw as well as the needs of their mostly Eastern European-Jewish readership quite perfectly.[28]

These correspondents were not the only source of information. To get first-hand knowledge out of Germany, the editors of Warsaw's Jewish newspapers used their transnational contacts and invited Jewish and non-Jewish writers to contribute guest columns on specific aspects of the situation in Germany. Among them were well-known journalists and intellectuals like American journalist Dorothy Thompson and the German-Jewish journalists and politicians Dr. Paul Arnsberg and Esriel Carlebach.[29] Polish-Jewish journalists from Warsaw also began traveling to Nazi Germany to see everything with their own eyes and especially during the first months of the Nazi regime, Polish-Jewish newspapers featured countless travelogues on Nazi Germany.[30] Sometimes Jewish newspapers would even send a journalist to Germany for several weeks, as was the case with Mark Turkow (1904–83) of *Der Moment* and Bernard Singer (1893–1966) of *Nasz Przegląd*.[31]

In spring 1933, Polish-Jewish coverage of Nazi Germany intensified. The front pages of newspapers featured analyses, travelogues, poems, caricatures, articles and reports sent by the correspondents in Berlin.[32] As they themselves became enemies of the Nazi regime, journalists increasingly wrote about their own fate in Nazi Germany, intermingling their personal experiences into articles. In March 1933, Yeshayahu Klinov sent a report to the office of the *Haynt* explaining that one of their colleagues, the famous economist and correspondent of the New Yorker *Forverts* Jacob Lestschinsky (1876–1966), had been arrested by the Gestapo. The arrest gave the impulse for the group of Jewish correspondents to gather for a meeting in order to discuss their current situation.[33] Already before January 1933 a widespread net of different German ministries and newly formed National Socialist organizations tried to control, intimidate, arrest and finally force Jewish as well as socialist and communist correspondents to leave the country.[34] The repression had tremendous effects on the life of Jewish correspondents and their families, which is why most of them had left Berlin willingly or unwillingly until summer 1933.[35]

In the following years as knowledge of Nazi Germany circulated around the offices of the Warsaw Jewish newspapers, editors and journalists used their expertise to support and organize a cultural and economic protest movement against the persecution of Jews in Nazi Germany. In March 1933, the

Farayn fun yidishe literaten un zhurnalisten (Association of Jewish Writers and Journalists) published a protest note condemning the Nazi policies and "calling upon all free-thinking and working elements around the world to unite in protest and to gather all forces to oppose the dark reaction, which threatens us all."[36] When on March 27, 1933, the first public protest meeting took place in Warsaw, politically active journalists like Abraham Goldberg (*Haynt*), Yoshua Gottlieb (*Der Moment*) and Moshe Kleinbaum (*Der Moment*) gave public speeches in the *Nowości* theater.[37] Only a few weeks later the Journalists' Association gave away a part of their clubrooms in the ulica Tłomackie 13 to the newly formed *Faraynigter yidisher komitet tsu bekemfen di drifes oyf yidn in Daytshland* (United Jewish Protest Committee against the persecution of Jews in Germany), which served as the nationwide central committee and which established there their first provisory office.[38] The journalist Mark Turkow remembered that even the whole idea for an organized protest came up at a meeting in the rooms of the journalist association in order to prevent a fragmentation of the protest.[39] The protest movement in Warsaw later consisted of three independent committees, splitting up their work in order to focus equally on the political protest, the economic boycott, and furnishing the material and financial help for incoming Jewish refugees on-site.[40] Numerous journalists like Esriel Carlebach, Mark Turkow, Yosef Kruk, Barukh Shefner and Bernard Singer gave talks on their travels through Nazi Germany or political and literary lectures in Warsaw and other Polish towns to promote the protest.[41] The close connection between the protest movement and the Warsaw daily newspapers meant that the journalists could easily meet with Jewish refugees in order to gather interviews or stories, which they could feature in their articles.[42]

In June 1935, the protest movement ground to a halt due to severe interference by the Polish authorities, as the Warsaw police searched the rooms in the *Centrala Związek Kupców w Polsce* (Central Buyer's Association in Poland)[43] in the ulica Senatorska 22, which is where the central committee, which was responsible for organizing the boycott of German products, had its seat.[44] While the Polish government initially supported the boycott movement, they changed their attitude to the opposite over time. This shift was mainly the result of the new and improved German-Polish relations, which manifested themselves in January 1934, when the Polish-German Non-Aggression declaration was signed.[45]

SUMMER 1935: THE WIND OF CHANGE

Although the appearance and the rise of the National Democrats (*Endecja*) and other extreme rightwing groups in Poland as well as daily anti-Semitic discrimination and violence had hit the Jewish community of Poland since the early 1930s, it was after the death of Józef Piłsudski in 1935, when the political landscape in Poland changed once more drastically, as did the general situation of Polish Jewry. In addition to their already precarious economic status, the "toxic legacy" of the first half of the 1930s, made Polish Jews cope with a spreading and intensifying anti-Jewish economic boycott, multiple pogroms, and increasing anti-Semitic discrimination in public universities and administrations.[46] In 1936 the journalist Yikhezkl Moyshe Nayman (1893–1956), who worked for the *Haynt,* wrote a guest contribution for an American Jewish journal about his serious concerns regarding a positive prospect for Jews in Poland and the permanent danger Jews had to face: "[t]he terror of the present situation cannot be exaggerated. All former descriptions—such as 'discrimination', 'political disfranchisement', 'economic oppression'—are obsolete. It is war, active war. Every day bombs are thrown at synagogues, Jewish communal buildings, Jewish business establishments, and harmless individuals."[47] In the memoirs of journalists or political leaders who survived the Shoah, they remembered in detail anti-Semitic attacks, which were directed against Jewish newspapers offices or individual journalists throughout the 1930s in Poland.[48]

At the same time, the Jewish press had to deal with an intensifying censorship and repression through the Polish government, which affected their work on a daily basis.[49] Sometimes Polish and German spies lingered around the Journalists' Association and from time to time single articles or even whole newspapers would be confiscated.[50] Usually, the censors tried to put pressure on the journalists beforehand in order to prevent critical articles. This was the case when Joseph Goebbels visited Warsaw in June 1934 as well as Herman Göring in January 1935.[51] Pinkhas Shvarts, who worked for the *Naye Folkstsaytung* remembered, that

> the government confiscated during these days the edition of the "Folkstsaytung" two times. At this day [when Goebbles visited Warsaw, AK] the censor spoke for a long time into the phone of the editorial office, asking why one is "making him troubles" and why one is printing stuff, which is embarrassing for the government with special regard to his neighbor (Nazi Germany). Finally, the talk ended with one of the sharper forewarnings, which was directed to the address of the editors, stating that it could end with more than just

a simple confiscate. This was a direct hint towards the possibility of shutting down the whole newspaper and to send the editor into prison, to Bereza Kartuska....[52]

Moreover, journalists had to cope with the constant fear of losing their jobs (or finding one in the first place), as the number of the newspapers dropped dramatically. A document prepared by Warsaw's Government Commissariat shows that the *Haynt* in November 1938 had a daily circulation of 34,900 newspapers compared to its peak of around 100,000 during the early 1920s. Other newspapers fell even more behind like the *Naye Folkstsaytung* with a number of 21,000 newspapers per day and *Der Moment* with a circulation of only 19,000.[53] In trying to prevent bankruptcy some of the newspapers remodeled themselves and founded cooperatives.[54] They also applied quite frequently for financial support from international Jewish organizations. In December 1937, the *Joint Distribution Committee* (JDC) gave the Journalists Association 5,000 Zlotys, the *Haynt* cooperative 30,000 Zlotys and provided funds to other newspapers.[55]

A letter from the journalist Barukh Shefner (1896–1977) to his friend the popular writer Melekh Ravitsh, summarizes the situation in which most of the public intellectuals were trapped towards the end of the 1930s. Ravitsh had held the position of executive secretary of the Journalists association for over ten years before leaving Poland in 1934 and was replaced by Shefner. Nevertheless, Ravitsh kept his ties to Warsaw and often contributed to the *Naye Folkstsaytung* for which Shefner worked as an editor. On January 1, 1938 Shefner wrote to Ravtish:

> My dearest Ravitsh, (...) You probably already know about my happiness concerning my daughters. Both could not make themselves feel homely in Warsaw, which is why even I began to think about to part with Poland. But in the last minute Merushe was accepted by the Polytechnic and she considered herself lucky. Over there she is the only Jewish girl. She drinks the cup, but she is stubborn. It is the stubbornness of the youth: "No other than out of spite."... Now I have no right to leave and even if I maybe would already have the permit, they [the Bund; AK] would under no circumstances allow it and without the permission from the party, I will not "run away." It is against my nature. And by the way, where to go?... You already know Buenos Aires a little, do you know, how the possibilities to fit in for someone like me are looking over there?

It's not only about "Putchero,"⁵⁶ I also occupy quite a position here in Warsaw.⁵⁷

In Shefner's letter, his inner conflict between leaving Poland for the sake of his family's future and his willingness to fulfill his duty as a journalist and public figure of the Warsaw Jewish community became visible. Like Shefner, most intellectuals believed in their role as spokespeople and educators of the Jewish community, a role that became even more important over time.⁵⁸

AUTUMN 1938: BETWEEN ACTIVISM, HOPE, AND DESPAIR
When in October 1938 Nazi Germany expelled thousands of Polish Jews from Germany and shortly after an uncountable number of Jewish shops, houses and synagogues were destroyed by the Nazis on the 9th and 10th of November 1938, a desperate situation had arisen. A secret report prepared by Warsaw's Government Commissariat noted that the Jewish community in Warsaw was caught off guard, when the first train with expelled Jews from Germany reached the city.⁵⁹ The report claimed, that "[t]he entire Jewish opinion in Warsaw was emotionally affected by the arrival of the first transport of Jewish refugees, who had been displaced by the Germans." The first reactions were dominated by "an utter astonishment, because despite the incoming news about the deportation, no one suspected such a rapid arrival of a transport in Warsaw" itself.⁶⁰ Yet, it soon became clear to Jewish intellectuals in Warsaw how deeply intertwined their fate was with that of Jews living in Germany. The journalist and writer Zusman Segalovitsh (1884–1949) remembered how he experienced the *Polenaktion*:

> I remember those days when the Germans deported in a cruel way thousands of Jews to the Polish territory, to Zbąszyń. Under the bayonet, they pushed them at night over the Polish border. (. . .) During that time Jews were also beaten up in Warsaw. In the Ogród Saski [Saxson Garden; AK] hired thugs turned over strollers with children in it. When the mothers tried to defend their children, they spat on them. I understood then that there was a connection between Zbąszyń and the Ogród Saski.⁶¹

The connection between the brutal expulsion organized by the Nazis and anti-Semitic attacks in Warsaw that Segalovitsh felt is one reason why Jewish intellectuals in Warsaw and other Polish cities reacted without hesitation and set up new aid committees for incoming refugees. On November 14, 1938, the president of the Warsaw lodge of the B'nai B'rith, Szymon Seidenman (1878–1948), informed its members, who were mostly intellectuals, representatives and businessmen, about the recent events. The protocol of the meeting stated:

> Unfortunately, it looks like the news from there are true: The Jewish congregation in Berlin is closed, the Palestinian Office was destroyed, the certificates burned, the leaders of diverse social institutions are in prison, the majority of the Jewish shops have been destroyed, (. . .). This is the picture of German Jewry. And about those who were expelled: one part, around 6500 persons and more are situated in Zbąszyń under terrible conditions, without a roof over their head and without the right to leave. (. . .) A return to their homes is out of question.[62]

There is no clear information about where this detailed account came from, but the Warsaw lodge had stayed in close contact with members of lodges from Berlin and Breslau over the years and thereby remained well-informed.[63] Just one to two days before the members of the B'nai B'rith in Warsaw gathered together to discuss the events of October and November 1938, minor information on the expulsions and the pogroms had appeared in the Warsaw Jewish press.[64]

The November pogroms came as a shock to the people working in Warsaw's Jewish newspapers, but it was an expected one. Not the execution of the pogroms but rather the extent of the violence triggered feelings of fear and uncertainty.[65] For several days the newspapers' headlines were dedicated to the pogroms.[66] But compared to the press coverage during the first months after Hitler had come to power in 1933, the acquisition of detailed knowledge on the execution and intensity of the pogroms had become even more difficult in 1938. Thus, the coverage of the pogroms was less extensive both in terms of the quantity of articles published and the quality of the information featured therein. Apart from just a few correspondents who were still living in Berlin and working for the Yiddish press in Poland, most of the Jewish correspondents had left the city long before 1938.[67] In addition, communication with Jews living in Germany was often impossible, as most of them were even more unwilling to speak openly about their experiences than in 1933.[68] Not only did the Yiddish newspapers lack the reliable sources within Nazi Germany, they also lacked the financial resources to cover trips abroad of their own journalists as well as the necessary visas.[69] Before the German-Polish Non-Aggression declaration sprang into action in 1934, journalists had a chance to find support in their travels to Germany through the Polish Foreign Office.[70]

In 1938, however, support was replaced by widespread censorship. The censorship became most obvious in how the Polish government tried to ban all coverage of the *Polenaktion*, which explains why the first detailed reports from Zbąszyń were not published before late November 1938.[71] Even though censorship practices depended on the decisions of the voivodships and could therefore differ, the reasons behind the suppression of news were rooted in the same motivation. Following the argument of Jerzy Tomaszewski, the government wanted to avoid being seen as weak by showing any sympathy for the victims.[72] But the simple fact that the Polish government tried everything possible in order to avoid the influx of Jewish refugees beforehand, surely played a role, too. Furthermore, there is reason to believe that in oppressing critical comments on how bad the Polish state treated the incoming Jewish refugees, the Polish government hoped to avoid international criticism. This argument is supported by a confidential document from the JDC dated November 29, 1938. The anonymous author explained that the Polish government in fact forced former Jewish members of the Sejm to send a memorandum to various international Jewish organizations stating that the "government had displayed humanitarian treatment to the Jews from Germany exiled to Poland—this despite the fact that over 5,000 are still held prisoners in Zbonszyn [sic!] under the most pitiful conditions (. . .)."[73] However, only a few weeks later the Polish government changed their attitude and began to encourage newspapers to report extensively on the tragedy of the *Polenaktion*. With this strategy they hoped to draw international attention to the situation of Jews in Poland and away from Germany, in order to put pressure on the international community to include the Jews of Poland into their immigration quotas for refugees.[74]

But even after the press ban had been lifted, as it had proven to be ineffective anyway, information was still harder to get and less easy to verify. Thus, journalists relied more and more on information they received through official national and international newspapers or press agencies like the Jewish and the Polish Telegraphic Agencies. Equally important was the German illegal and émigré press. These publications were smuggled over the Polish border and sold openly at newspaper stands in Warsaw to the displeasure of the German Foreign Office.[75]

During October and November 1938, the journalists would visit the Journalists' Association more often than usual. Additionally, information from non-Jewish Polish colleagues became quite important. Zusman Segalovitsh remembered, that especially the staff of the Polish-language *Nasz Przegląd*, namely Nathan Szwalbe, Saul Wagman and Bernard Singer, often went to a cafeteria, where the non-Jewish Polish journalists used to gather. According to Segalovitsh, it was important to talk to these journalists because they had better networks.[76] In December 1938, *Der Moment* and *Nasz Przegląd* printed an exclusive multi-piece feature from Polish journalist Włodziemierz Lencki, who in early December 1938 traveled to Berlin to cover the aftermath of the pogroms.[77]

Not until the end of November, did they publish detailed political analyzes about anti-Semitic excesses. The topics discussed most intensely were the hidden intentions behind the pogrom and debates about the meaning of the events for the Polish-Jewish community and Jews in general.[78] Some journalists criticized also the notable absence of empathy in the Polish press.[79] The overall reactions of Jewish journalists in Warsaw were fear, disbelief, despair but also hope at the same time.[80] In a political column from January 1939 the political leader of the Bund and editor of the *Naye Folkstsaytung* Henryk Erlich argued, that "within the long list of years, which came to an end since the end of the [First; AK] World War, the year 1938—next to the year 1933—takes without any doubts the 'most prestigious' place: This relates to the general condition of the world and especially to Europe, to the conditions in Poland as well as to the conditions of the Jewish masses in Europe."[81] He goes on in listing all those political events that were for him the most crucial ones. Among them were the Annexation of Austria, the Sudeten crisis, the March crisis between Poland and Lithuania, the annexation of the Teschen province by Poland as well as the expulsion of Jews from Germany, the November pogroms and the implementation of anti-Jewish laws in Italy, Hungary, Romania and the Sudetenland. It was the overwhelming accumulation of events that had happened in just one year and changed radically the political and geographical situation of Europe, the reduction of civil rights for Jewish citizens as well as the increase of anti-Semitic violence in various European countries, which led the Jewish intellectuals from Warsaw into a state of desperation and disbelief.[82]

Deprived of their usual journalistic methods and rights, stories about the pogroms declined and the Jewish press focused its attention on more local concerns: the Jewish refugees in Poland, especially in Zbąszyń. On November 4 a new aid committee for Jewish refugees had been set up in Warsaw and the well-known journalists and public leaders Mark Turkow (*Der Moment*), Moshe Kleinbaum (*Der Moment*), Samuel Wolkowicz (*Nasz Przegląd*) and Natan Szwalbe (*Nasz Przegląd*) were among the members.[83] Yet again, Jewish journalists played a crucial role in helping the Warsaw central aid committee by launching a "propaganda campaign to make Polish Jewry conscious of the necessity of making contributions in favor of refugees" and a "publicity campaign in the press by means of articles, news items and features all especially written by competent journalists."[84] In the course of the press campaign for the refugees, Jewish newspapers from Warsaw began to collect money[85] and occasionally published protest notes from various Jewish organizations, lists of donors as well as lists with things, which were still needed, protocols and news from the various committees.[86] Journalists also donated a sum for the refugees by imposing a tax on their daily income to aid the persecuted.[87]

At the end of November, Jewish journalists from Warsaw began to travel to the make-shift camp in Zbąszyń.[88] To go to the places where help was needed was a common practice for the journalists. Mark Turkow explained, that the Jewish journalists not only felt obligated to go there because of their profession. In general, he remembered, the Jewish public expected journalists to visit places of terror and tragedy in order to encourage frightened Jews, who had become victims of anti-Semitic violence or persecution.[89] In the refugee camp, journalists talked to Jewish refugees and recorded their stories.[90] Because expelled Jews from Germany were still arriving in Poland over the course of the next year and because the refugees were in close contact with families and friends still living in Germany, journalists managed to secure more reliable information on the pogroms. The famous Jewish historian Emanuel Ringelblum from Warsaw, who organized the help in the refugee camp, encouraged refugees to write down their experiences and called on his colleagues to conduct interviews. As an historian and social worker, he was aware that the so-called *Polenaktion* and the November pogroms were important issues.[91] In his memoirs, Mendel Balberyszki, a journalist and colleague of Ringelblum, explained that it was "from them," the Jewish refugees, that they "learned of the anti-Jewish edicts, of persecution, of humiliation and of the executions."[92]

CONCLUSION

The question whether or not journalism needs to be objective and, if so, how this could be realized, has been discussed by journalists and researchers alike for many decades. To this day, there remains a strong belief that journalism needs to be objective, making the relation between the profession, the seeking of truth, and the journalist's own subjectivity a complex challenge.

As this article has shown, these standards did not apply to the Warsaw Jewish daily press of interwar Poland. On the contrary, objectivity was never their goal. Since the appearance of Warsaw's first Jewish daily newspaper in Yiddish, the *Haynt*, its purpose was to influence the lives of Jewish readers and to engage openly in discussions of all aspects of Jewish life, thereby making the journalist part of a Jewish intellectual elite.[93] Thus, the boundaries between journalism, activism, community leadership, and personal consternation were blurred for journalists, especially in times of crises. During the 1930s, the Jewish minority press was constantly observed, disciplined and censored by Polish and German authorities and faced constant threat of anti-Semitic violence and state-sanctioned discrimination. Consequently, journalists could not be passive observers of history, for they found themselves affected by it personally. Their Jewish readers eagerly hoped they would overcome their fears and help guide and support Jews, both morally and politically.[94]

This was also the case, when the National Socialists rose to power in Germany in early 1933 and when Jews from Germany were first persecuted and later expelled in October and November 1938. While in the first half of the year 1933 the Polish government supported the anti-Nazi boycott and protest of the Jewish community in Poland, Jewish journalists from Warsaw could openly and intensively report on the beginning persecution of Jews and political opponents in Nazi Germany. Through their various formal and informal networks, like Jewish correspondents in Berlin, who were working for the Jewish press, they were extremely well informed. But as time was moving on and Poland moved closer to its Western neighbor, the Jewish press was more and more criminalized by the German as well as the Polish authorities. At the same time, the newspapers faced a deep economic crisis and observation, repression and censorship made their work in 1938 even harder, as they also lost a lot of money due to the censorship. While most of the Jewish correspondents were forced to leave Berlin by the end of 1933, communication with Jews from Germany became more difficult as well as traveling to Nazi Germany had become nearly impossible by the end of 1938. Thus, the journalists relied more and more on information they got through international press agencies, the émigré press and their Polish colleagues.

These turbulent, unprecedented and closely linked developments in Poland and Germany made the Jewish community in Poland restless and made reporting on the situation in Germany a top priority for the Jewish press. Under the pressure of repression and challenging working conditions, Jewish journalists from Warsaw and Berlin tried their best to cover news from

Germany relying on the help of formal and informal networks. They were unable and unwilling to remain neutral in the face of oppression, as it was they and their people who were the oppressed. Together with other Jews from the Polish-Jewish intelligentsia, journalists promoted and organized a coordinated protest and aid movement. As a result, they left their observation posts on the sidelines and became active participants of history.

Notes

1. The author of this article is currently a Claims Conference Saul Kagan Fellow in Advanced Holocaust Studies and is finishing her doctoral thesis at Freie Universität Berlin, which deals with individual and collective reactions of Polish-Jewish journalists, who were mainly working for the Yiddish press in Warsaw, during the beginning persecution of Jews in Nazi Germany in 1933 and the outbreak of the Second World War in 1939. This article is part of her research findings.
2. Between October 27–29, 1938 about sixteen thousand to eighteen thousand Jews from all over Germany were under the pretense of the Polish March laws deported to Poland. At least nine thousand were sent to the Polish border town of Zbąszyń. These laws allowed Germans to revoke the citizenship of Polish citizens who had lived abroad permanently for longer than five years. The expulsions continued until summer 1939. For further detailed information, see Jerzy Tomaszewski, *Auftakt zur Vernichtung. Die Verteibung polnischer Juden aus Deutschland im Jahre 1938*, Klio in Polen, vol. 9 (Osnabrück: fibre verlag, 2002); (Polish version: *Preludium Zagłady. Wygnanie Żydów Polskich z Niemiec w 1938 r.* [Warsaw: Wydawnictwo Naukowe PWN, 1998]).
3. Yad Vashem Archives (hereafter YVA), Press Agency of the SIG, Die polnischen Juden im Niemandsland (not dated), 2. All translations from German, Polish and Yiddish are made by the author of this article. The Yiddish transliteration follows the YIVO system.
4. The Polish-Jewish press and their movers and shakers as an object of research has only recently become an area of interest to historians as Joanna Nalewajko-Kulikov noted in 2012, see "Prasa Żydowska na Ziemiach Polskich: Historia, Stan Badań, Perspektywy Badawcze," in *Studia z Dziejów Trójjęzycznej Prasy Żydowskiej na Ziemiach Polskich (XIX-XX w.)*, in cooperation with Grzegorz P. Bąbiak, Agnieszka J. Cieślikowa, and Joanna Nalewajko-Kulikov (Warsaw: Neriton, 2012), 25. Also Kenneth B. Moss ("Negotiating Jewish Nationalism in Interwar Warsaw," in *The Jewish Metropolis: Essays in Honor of the 75th Birthday of Professor Antony Polonsky*, ed. Glenn Dynner and François Guesnet [Leiden: Brill, 2015], 425) argued recently that both, comparative as well as systematic research on the Interwar Polish-Jewish press and the personal lives and networks of the journalists, are still missing, with the exception of Cohen's research (Nathan Cohen, *Sefer, Sofer ve-Iton. Merkaz ha-Tarbut ha-Yehudit be-Warse [1918–1942]* [Jerusalem: Magnes Press and Hebrew University, 2003]). For more information on individual profiles of the Warsaw Jewish newspapers see the various articles in the anthology of Nalewajko-Kulikov, *Studia z Dziejów*, and Marian Fuks, *Prasa żydowska w Warszawie* (Warsaw: Państwowe Wydawnictwo Naukowe, 1979).
5. While there is a vast literature on the November pogroms, the research on the *Polenaktion* is relatively clear and mostly directed to reconstructing the event itself.

See the works by Tomaszewski, *Preludium zagłady*; Sybil Milton, "The Expulsion of Polish Jews from Germany October 1938 to July 1939: A Documentation," *Leo Baeck Institute Year Book* 29, no. 1 (1984): 169–99; Trude Maurer, "Abschiebung und Attentat. Die Ausweisung der polnischen Juden und der Vorwand für die 'Kristallnacht,'" in *Der Judenpogrom 1938. Von der "Reichskristallnacht" zum Völkermord*, ed. Walter H. Pehle (Frankfurt am Main: Fischer Taschenbuch Verlag, 1988), 52–73; Bonnie Mae Harris, "From German Jews to Polish Refugees: Germany's Polenaktion and the Zbąszyń Deportations of October 1938," *Kwartalnik Historii Żydów* 230 (2009): 175–205; Izabela Skórzyńska and Wojciech Olejniczak, *Do zobaczenia za rok w Jerozolimie. Deportacje polskich Żydów w 1938 roku z Niemiec do Zbąszynia* (Zbąszyń: Fundacja TRES, 2012). However, in the last decade one can observe a growing scientific interest in the topic. In 2018 an exhibition on the *Polenaktion* was curated in the *Centrum Judaicum* in Berlin. See the catalog of the exhibition by Bothe and Pickhan (Alina Bothe and Gertrud Pickhan, *Ausgewiesen! Berlin, 28. 10. 1938. Die Geschichte der "Polenaktion"* [Berlin: Metropol, 2018]).

6. See the most recent works by L. Ruth Klein, *Nazi Germany, Canadian Responses: Confronting Anti-Semitism in the Shadow of War* (Montreal: McGill-Queen's University Press, 2012); Guy Miron, *The Waning of Emancipation. Jewish History, Memory, and the Rise of Fascism in Germany, France, and Hungary* (Detroit: Wayne State University Press, 2011); Colin McCullough and Nathan Wilson, *Violence, Memory, and History. Western Perceptions of Kristallnach* (New York: Routledge, 2015).

7. Ferenc Laczó, "Introduction," in *Catastrophe and Utopia: Jewish Intellectuals in Central and Eastern Europe in the 1930s and 1940s*, Europas Osten im 20. Jahrhundert, ed. Ferenc Laczó and Joachim von Puttkamer, vol. 7 (Berlin: de Gruyter, 2018), 1; Joanna Nalewajko-Kulikov, "When Goethe's Poetry Was Not Enough: Yehoshua Thon on Germany, Optimism and Anti-Semitism (1932–1933)," in *A Romantic Polish Jew. Rabbi Ozjasz Thon from Various Perspectives*, ed. Michał Galas and Shoshana Ronen (Kraków: Jagiellonian University Press, 2015), 95. The Polish-Jewish view on Nazi Germany is partly discussed in books by the historians Yfaat Weiss (*Deutsche und polnische Juden vor dem Holocaust. Jüdische Identität zwischen Staatsbürgerschaft und Ethnizität 1933–1940*, Schriftenreihe der Vierteljahreshefte für Zeitgeschichte, vol. 81 [Munich: Oldenburg Wissenschaftsverlag, 2000]), Nathan Cohen (*Sefer, Sofer ve-Iton*), and Katrin Steffen (Katrin Steffen, *Jüdische Polonität. Ethnizität und Nation im Spiegel der polnischsprachigen jüdischen Presse 1918–1939*, Schriften des Simon-Dubnow-Instituts, vol. 3 [Göttingen: Vandenhoeck & Ruprecht Verlage, 2004]); also see articles by Daniel Grinberg, "The Polish-Language Jewish Press and the Events in the Third Reich, 1933–1939," in *Why Didn't the Press Shout? American & International Journalism During the Holocaust*, ed. Robert Moses Shapiro (Jersey City: Yeshiva University Press with Ktav Publishing House, 2003), 429–46.; Ingo Loose, "Reaktionen auf den Novemberpogrom in Polen 1938–1939,"

in *Die Novemberpogrome. Versuch einer Bilanz*, ed. Stiftung Topographie des Terrors (Berlin: Stiftung Topographie des Terrors, 2009), 44–58; Daniel Blatman, "The National Ideology of the Bund in the Test of Antisemitism and the Holocaust, 1933–47," in *Jewish Politics in Eastern Europe: The Bund at 100*, ed. Jack Jackobs (London: Palgrave Macmillan, 2001), 197–212; Anna Landau-Czajka, "Adolf Hitler i III Rzesza w oczach czytelników Małego Przeglądu," in *Yesterday. Studia z Historii najnowszej. Księga dedykowana Prof. Jerzemu Eislerowi w 65. Rocznicę Urodzin*, ed. Jan Olaszek et al. (Warsaw: Instytut Pamięci Narodowej, Instytut Historii im. Tadeusza Manteuffla Polskiej Akademii Nauk, 2017), 307–24; Gertrud Pickhan, "Jakobs Berliner Kinder. Ein Warschauer Bundist im Jüdischen Berliner Theater 1935," in *"Der Fremde Im Dorf." Überlegungen zum Eigenen und zum Fremden in der Geschichte*, ed. Hans-Jürgen Bömelburg and Beate Eschment (Lüneburg: Institut Nordostdeutsches Kulturwerk, 1998), 196–210; Beate Kosmala, "Pressereaktionen in Polen auf den Novemberpogrom 1938 in Deutschland und die Lage der Polnischen Juden," *Zeitschrift für Geschichte* 46 (1998): 1034–45; Nalewajko-Kulikov, "When Goethe." However, the focus in the above-mentioned papers lies on the individual or collective reception by Polish Jews on selected events on Nazi Germany, while using superficially Polish or Yiddish language newspapers as source material.

8. Rebecca Margilos, "A Review of the Yiddish Media: Responses of the Jewish Immigrant Community in Canada," in *Nazi Germany, Canadian Responses*, 117–18.
9. For this article I worked mainly with articles from *Haynt, Naye Folkstsaytung, Der Moment* and *Nasz Przegląd*.
10. Susanne Marten-Finnis, "Die Jüdische Presse in der Osteuropäischen Diaspora: Eine Typologie," in *Die Jüdische Presse. Forschungsmethoden—Erfahrungen—Ergebnisse*, Jüdische Presse—Kommunikationsgeschichte im Europäischen Raum, ed. Susanne Marten-Finnis and Markus Bauer, vol. 2 (Bremen: Edition Lumiere, 2007), 77.
11. McCullough and Wilson, *Violence, Memory, and History*, 5.
12. On Jewish life, politics and anti-Semitism in the Second Polish Republic see, e.g., Emanuel Melzer, *No Way out: The Politics of Polish Jewry 1935–1939* (Cincinnati: Hebrew Union College Press, 1997); Antony Polonsky, *The Jews in Poland and Russia (1914–2008)* (Oxford: Littman Library of Jewish Civilization, 2012), 3:57–97.
13. See press coverage of the pogrom in the Berliner Scheunenviertel in November 1923; Abraham Goldberg, "Daytshe pogromen," *Haynt*, November 9, 1923, 3; Lidor Fishl, "Di ekstsesn gegn yidn in Berlin," *Der Moment*, November 11, 1923, 3. Anne-Christin Saß analyzed some of the articles written by Jewish correspondents who were working for the Warsaw Yiddish press in Berlin between 1920 and 1933 (*Berliner Luftmenschen. Osteuropäisch-jüdische Migranten in der Weimarer Republik*, Charlottengrad und Scheunenviertel, ed. Verena Dohrn and Gertrud Pickhan, vol. 2 [Göttingen: Wallstein Verlag, 2012], 411–32).

14. Gershon Swet, "With the Wurmbrands in Pre-Hitler Berlin," in *Michael Wurmbrand, The Man and His Work*, ed. Kurt R. Grossmann (New York: Philosophical Library, 1956), 18.
15. Yfaat Weiss, *Deutsche und polnische Juden vor dem Holocaust. Jüdische Identität zwischen Staatsbürgerschaft und Ethnizität 1933–1940*, Schriftenreihe der Vierteljahreshefte für Zeitgeschichte, vol. 81 (Munich: Oldenburg Wissenschaftsverlag, 2000), 16.
16. Szyja Bronsztein, "Polish-Jewish Relations as Reflected in Memoirs of the Interwar Period," *Polin* 8 (1994): 70–71.
17. E.g., Shlomo Mendelsohn, "Dos ponem fun hayntikn Daytshland," *Naye Folkstsaytung*, April 23, 1933, 5; Bernard Singer, *W krajach Hitlera i Stalina, Reportaże* (Warsaw: Biblioteka Midrasza, 2007), 19.
18. Joanna Nalewajko-Kulikov, "'Die Haynt-mishpokhe': Study of a Group Picture," in *The Jewish Metropolis: Essays in Honor of the 75th Birthday of Professor Antony Polonsky*, ed. Glenn Dynner and François Guesnet (Leiden: Brill, 2015), 266; idem, "When Goethe," 97–99.
19. Archive of the National Library of Israel (henceforth ANLI), Arkhion Melekh Ravitsh, ARC. 4* 1540 01 101, Kleyne togbikhler, not dated.
20. For various business-related travels of Polish-Jewish journalists to Germany, see the communication between editors of *Der Moment* and the *Polski Związek Wydawców, Dzienników i Czasopism w Warszawie* (Polish Association of Editors, Newspapers and Magazines in Warsaw), Archiwum Akt Nowych (henceforth AAN), PZWDz. i Cz., syg. 64/116.
21. Tobias Brinkmann, "Ort des Übergangs—Berlin als Schnittstelle der jüdischen Migration aus Osteuropa nach 1918," in *Transit und Transformation: Osteuropäisch-jüdische Migranten in Berlin 1918–1939*, ed. Verena Dohrn and Gertrud Pickhan (Göttingen: Wallstein Verlag, 2010), 41; Gennady Estraikh, "Weimar Berlin—An International Yiddish Press Center," in *Transit und Transformation. Osteuropäisch-jüdische Migranten in Berlin 1918–1939*, ed. Verena Dohrn and Gertrud Pickhan (Göttingen: Wallstein Verlag, 2010), 77–92.
22. Estraikh, "Weimar Berlin," 81.
23. Politisches Archiv des Auswärtigen Amts (henceforth PAAA), R 121606, Director of the German Parliament to the press department of the Foreign Office, February 5, 1929, enclosed list I and II regulating the press accreditation for the German parliament, not paginated.
24. Klinov joined the association in 1925 and Swet in 1926, see Archiv des Vereins der Ausländischen Presse zu Berlin e.V., DI: I, Medlemsmatriklar och föreningens gästbok 1912–43, Membership lists for the years 1925 and 1926. Other long-time members were e.g., Daniel Tsharny, Dovid Eynhorn, Jakob Lestschinsky and Raphael Rein Abramovitsh.
25. PAAA, R 121441, Swet, Hermann. Letter to Dr. von Saucken (Reichspressestelle),

May 30, 1931, not paginated; attached is an article written by Swet, "A par sheah mit'n daytshen kantsler un oysern-minister," *Der Moment*, May 17, 1931.

26. Samuel R Mozes, "Żydowska Agencja Telegraficzna w Polsce (1920-1939)," *Biuletyn Żydowskiego Historycznego w Polsce* 1, no. 97 (1976): 116; Mendelsohn, "Dos ponem fun," 5.
27. Hermann Swet, "Fun der berliner tog-teglikhkeyt," *Der Moment*, March 21, 1933, 3; Nathan Shnayder [Nathan Frenkel], "Der blutiker veg fun fashizm," *Naye Folkstsaytung*, March 21, 1933, 4.
28. Khaym Finkelshtayn, "Haynt (1918-1939)," in *Fun noentn ovar*, vol. 2, ed. Alveltlekhen yidishn kultur-kongres (New York, 1956), 210.
29. Dorothy Tompson, "Hitler hot dos blut fargosn," *Naye Folkstsaytung*, May 27, 1933, 4; Paul Arnsberg, "Di khurbes fun daytshishn tsionizm," *Der Nayer Veg*, September 1, 1932, 13-14; Lui Gothelf [Carlebach, Esriel], "Di hartsraysende stsenes in berliner palestina-amt," *Haynt*, May 3, 1933, 4. Beginning in 1926, journalist Esriel Carlebach (1908-56), who was one of the editors of the Hamburger *Israelisches Familienblatt*, wrote regularly for the *Haynt* and worked in 1933 in Germany as an investigative journalist under the pen-name Lui Gothelf for the paper. In spring 1933, he fled to Warsaw with the help of his colleges from *Haynt*. He stayed in Warsaw until 1935 and engaged himself there actively in the protest against Nazi Germany, see Joanna Nalewajko-Kulikov, "O Człowieku, który widział za dużo, czyli Historia Kryminalna z 'Hajntem' w Tle," in *Wiek Nienawiści. Księga dedykowana Prof. Jerzemu Borejszy*, ed. Jerzy Eisler, Edmund Dmitrów et al. (Warsaw: Instytut Pamięci Narodowej, 2014), 249-64; Esriel Carlebach, "Lomir zikh dermonen," *Fun noentn ovar*, vol. 2, ed. Alveltlekhen yidishn kultur-kongres (New York, 1956), 233-37.
30. In 1933 travelogues on Nazi Germany became quite a fashion among Jewish journalists and writers and the newspapers featured them prominently. See e. g. Mendelsohn, "Dos ponem fun," 5; Barukh Shefner, "Iber der daytsher grenets," *Naye Folkstsaytung*, June 5, 1936, 5; Shmuel-Leyb Shnayderman, "Farendig durkh Daytshland," *Der Moment*, April 10, 1933, 11.
31. Mark Turkow, "In'm land fun kemfender lagern," *Der Moment*, February 12, 1933, 4; Singer, *W krajach*.
32. E.g., Fishl Rotenshtraykh, "Der analiz fun barbaropa," *Haynt*, March 24, 1933, 4; Vladimir Kosovski, "Daytshland tsurikgevorfn in finstern mitlalter," *Naye Folkstsaytung*, April 4, 1933, 3; Yeshayahu Klinov, "Der shvartser montog," *Haynt*, February 1, 1933, 3; A. S. Lirik [Aaron-Levi Riklis], "Das land ohn yidn," *Haynt*, April 10, 1933, 5.
33. Yeshayahu Klinov, "Di 'zibete melukhe' firt milkhome mint dritn raykh: vi azoy arbeyten un leben ists yidish-oyslendishe zhurnalistn in Berlin," *Haynt*, June 23, 1933, 9-10. The arrest of Lestshinsky is discussed by Estraikh, "Weimar Berlin," 91 and Martin Herzer, *Auslandskorrespondenten und auswaertige Pressepolitik im*

Dritten Reich, Medien in Geschichte und Gegenwart, ed. Jürgen Wilke, vol. 27 (Köln: Böhlau Verlaug, 2012), 87–89.
34. Herzer, *Auslandskorrespondenten*, 34–39, 288.
35. See, for instance, the list on Berlin-based Eastern European Jewish and non-Jewish correspondents which circulated within the German Foreign Ministry in December 1932 and featured doubtful and anti-Semitic descriptions of the journalists; also see the protocol of the interrogation with Herman Swet, PAAA, R 121608 (Press Department, Meyer-Heydenhagen, alphabetical and national register of foreign correspondents, register of the 'Ostjournalisten,' December 28, 1932, 31–33) and R 121442 (Meyer-Heydenhagen, notes, talk with Herman Swet, April 5, 1933, not paginated). Yeshayahu Klinov himself fled to London and later went to Palestine, while Hermann Swet left Berlin for Paris.
36. "Farvaltung fun Varshever literatn-farayn protestirt kegn dem hitlerishn terror," *Literarishe Bleter*, no. 16 (1933): 265.
37. "6.000 osób w sali na dziedzińcu 'Nowości,'" *Nasz Przegląd*, March 28, 1933, 2; "Di grandieze montag'dige protest-mitingen," *Der Moment*, March 29, 1933, 6.
38. "Vos hert zikh in Varshe?" *Haynt*, April 19, 1933, 7. The Polish name of the committee was *Zjednoczony Narodowy Komitet Protestacyjny Żydostwa Polskiego przeciwko Prześladowaniu Żydów w Niemczech*. The committee later moved to ulica Orla nr. 6. In addition to that, some journalists from diverse newspapers were responsible for editing the central boycott magazine *Nasza Obrona/Unzer Obvehr* (Our defense), which appeared between 1933 and 1934 (*Nasza Obrona. Pismo Poświęcone antyhitlerowskiej Akcji gospodarczej*, ed. Leo Finkelshtayn, vol. 1 [November 1933] and vol. 2 [February 1934] [Yiddish and Polish]). The editor in chief was the journalist and Yiddish socialist activist Leo Finkelshtayn. The journalists Mark Turkow, Shaul Y. Stupnitski, Appolinary Hartglas and Samuel Wolkowicz supported the magazine with articles.
39. Mark Turkow, "Between Two World Wars," in *The Jewish Press That Was: Accounts, Evaluations and Memories of Jewish Papers in Pre-Holocaust Europe*, ed. David Flinker, Shalom Rosenfeld, and Mordechai Tsanin (Tel Aviv: World Federation of Jewish Journalists, 1980), 85.
40. Even though Assimilationists, Orthodox and Zionists became active in the movement, critics within the movement grew strong. Additionally, the Bund and with it the *Naye Folkstsaytung* called for a separated protest movement, even though they were aware of the fact, that their protest would be than regarded as part of the whole Jewish protest movement in Poland. For a more detailed description of the Bundist protest and its critics, see Henryk Erlich, "Der hayntike protest-tog," *Naye Folkstsaytung*, March 28, 1933, 3; Tsentrales bundishes anti-Hitler-komitet in Varshe: *Arbeter-klas in kampf kegn Hitler-Daytshland*, Warsaw, 1934.
41. E.g., Carlebach, "Lomir zikh dermonen," 233; "Sytuacja Żydów w Niemczech," *Nasz Przegląd*, April 24, 1933, 2–3; "Ayndrikn fun yidishn un arbeter-lebn in hitlerishn

Daytshland. Ayntsike varlezung fun bakantn yidishn zshurnalistn B. Zynger," *Naye Folkstsaytung*, May 12, 1933, 12; "Hitler (a literarisher portret). Forlezung fun dr. Yosef Kruk, montog, dem 6-tn februar, tsayger 9 in ovnt, farayn fun yidishe literatn un zhurnalistn, tlomatske 13," *Naye Folkstsaytung*, February 6, 1933, 6.

42. Y. Mlatek, "Drey yor in daytshe kontsentratsie-lagern," *Naye Folkstsaytung*, July 25, 1938, 3; "Oysgenart a 'beruhigende' deklaratsie, dan tseshlogen un deportirt," *Haynt*, April 2, 1933, 2.

43. The Association was an amalgamation of Jewish merchants and businessmen in Poland. For more information, see Ignacy Schiper, *Dzieje handlu żydowskiego na ziemiach polskich* (Kraków: Związek Kupców, 1937).

44. AŻIH, Prace magisterskie o tematyce żydowskiej obronione po II wojnie światowej, syg. 347/392, Michał Maksymilian Majewski, "Działalność Centralnego Komitetu dla Antyhitlerowskiej Akcji Gospodarczej w Polsce 1933–35, 2010," MA thesis, 60–61; Melzer, *No Way Out*, 9.

45. Jerzy Tomaszewski, "Bojkot towarów niemieckich w Polsce w latach 1933–1935," *Acta Oeconomica Pragnesia* 15, no. 7 (2007): 449–50. Although, the Polish government supported the protest movement at first, it observed and hindered the Jewish protest from the first moment on, as various notes in the Jewish press proved. In an article of *Haynt* it was mentioned, that the Warsaw commissariat forbade rallies outside on the street, which is why all manifestations on March 27, 1933 had to take place inside; see Feraynigter natsionaler protest-komitet, "Morgen protest-tog fun poylishen yidentum," *Haynt*, March 26, 1933, 1; "Fun tsuzamenfar fun poylishn yidntum," *Naye Folkstsaytung*, April 25, 1933, 4. Additionally, the German consulate observed the Jewish protest movement, especially after the Non-Aggression-Declaration came into being. The declaration, which was meant to improve the relationship as well as the mutual perception of the two countries, regulated also the press coverage. This meant that both states could intervene if they were not satisfied with the representation of their country in the press. The German consulate did this frequently. They used articles in the Jewish press for evidence, trying to prove that the Polish side did not stick to the agreement and in order to silence the Jewish press; see: AAN, AMSZ, syg. 7139, Note on a talk with Dr. Schliep from the German Consulate in Warsaw, signed St. Włodarkiewicz, not dated (probably around spring 1935), 21–22. However, the historian Karina Pryt argued that only after the death of the state man Józef Piłsudski in June 1935 did Polish-German relations actually improve for a short period of time; see Karina Pryt, *Befohlene Freundschaft. Die deutsch-polnischen Kulturbeziehungen 1934–1939*, Einzelveröffentlichungen des DHI Warschau, ed. Eduard Mühle, vol. 22 (Osnabrück: fibre verlag, 2010), 129–30.

46. Grzegorz Krzywiec, "The Balance of Polish Political Antisemitism: Between 'National Revolution,' Economic Crisis, and the Transformation of the Polish Public Sphere in the 1930s," in *Right-Wing Politics and the Rise of Antisemitism in Europe 1935–1941*, European Holocaust Studies, ed. Frank Bajohr and Dieter Pohl, vol. 1

(Göttingen: Wallstein Verlag, 2019), 72; Polonsky, *The Jews in Poland*, 56–98; Jehuda Reinharz and Yaacov Shavit, *The Road to September 1939: Polish Jews, Zionists, and the Yishuv on the Eve of World War II* (Waltham: MA: Brandeis University Press, 2018), 38–39.

47. I. M. Neumann, "Outstreched on the Altar," *The Menorah Journal* 24, no. 3 (October–December 1936): 294.
48. Finkelshtayn, "Haynt (1918-1939)," 158; Bernard Goldstein, *Twenty Years with the Jewish Labor Bund: A Memoir of Interwar Poland*, ed. and trans. Marvin S. Zuckerman (West Lafayette, IN: Purdue University Press, 2016), 371–72.
49. On the regulation of the press in general see Michał Pietrzak, *Reglamentacja wolności prasy w Polsce (1918–1939)* (Warsaw: Książka i Wiedza, 1963).
50. Melech Ravitsh, "'Tlomackie 13.' Home of Jewish writers and journalists," in *The Jewish Press That Was: Accounts, Evaluations and Memories of Jewish Papers in Pre-Holocaust Europe*, ed. David Flinker, Shalom Rosenfeld and Mordechai Tsanin (Tel Aviv: World Federation of Jewish Journalists, 1980), 215; Gertrud Pickhan, *"Gegen den Strom": Der Allgemeine Jüdische Arbeiterbund "Bund" in Polen 1918-1939*, Schriften des Simon-Dubnow-Instituts Leipzig, ed. Dan Diner, vol. 1 (Stuttgart: Deutsche Verlags-Anstalt, 2011), 255.
51. The state visit provoked a vivid and united press campaign from all Jewish daily newspapers in Warsaw with the exception of the *Naye Folkstsaytung*. When on June 13, 1934, Josef Goebbels visited Warsaw, all newspapers printed the same front page, featuring only three lines: "Down with the Nazi regime! Down with the racist propaganda! Shame on the anti-Semites!" Most of the papers were confiscated that day, but some editions circulated beforehand, see Moshe Prager, "Dos yudishe togblat (1929–1939)," in *Fun noentn ovar*, vol. 2, ed. Alveltlekhen yidishn kultur-kongres (New York, 1956), 522–23 and Cohen, *Sefer, Sofer ve-Iton*, 267. See also the list of confiscates between June 1934 and June 1935. Most of the confiscates were directly linked to the visits of Goebbels and Göring, AAN, Ambasada RP w Berlinie, syg. 2252, Foreign Ministry, political press department to the Polish embassy in Berlin, list of newspaper confiscates between June 1, 1934 and June 30, 1935, August 3, 1935, 33–42.
52. Pinkhas Shvarts, "Folkstsaytung (1921–1939)," in *Fun noentn ovar*, vol. 2, ed. Alveltlekhen yidishn kultur-kongres (New York: 1956), 418. Bereza Kartuska: Famous prison for mostly political prisoners during the Second Polish Republic.
53. AAN, Komisariat Rządu na m st Warszawę, syg. 297/VII-11, Socio-political department, monthly report 10, Ludwik Wędolowski, October 1–31, 1938, 5 (90).
54. Nalewajko-Kulikov, "Die Haynt-mishpokhe," 269.
55. YVA, M.72/792, Report on activities of JDC Office in Poland for Months of September–October 1937, Appendix: Economic aid and relief, not paginated.
56. Putchero is a type of stew and considered as a lower or middle-class Argentinian dish. In this case, it is probably a playful way to talk about work and money.

57. ANLI, Arkhion Melekh Ravitsh ARC 4*1540 12 2957.3, Shefner, Barukh. Letter to Melekh Ravtish, January 1, 1938, not paginated.
58. Turkow, "Between," 84.
59. Before the Polish government decided to lock down the refugees in Zbąszyń, an uncertain number of refugees passed the border, making their way into the country, see Tomaszewski, *Auftakt*, 203.
60. AAN, Komisariat Rządu na m st Warszawę syg. 297/VII-11, 33–34. The majority of Jews in Warsaw believed probably that the Jewish refugees would not enter the Polish metropolis as quickly and numerously as they did in October 1938. This attitude was perhaps nourished by their experiences from the years before. When in February 1933 the first Jewish refugees entered Poland it took a while before the first refugees arrived in Warsaw. According to a report given by Mark Turkow at a conference of delegates from fifteen local Jewish aid committees in Katowice in June 1933, around three thousand Jewish refugees had reached Poland since February 1933, among them 2,600 Jews with Polish citizenship. Until then, the committee in Warsaw had registered eighty persons. Although between 1933 and 1935 up to ten thousand Jews from Germany came to Poland, the situation was not comparable with the one which had arisen in October 1938. In the following years Jewish refugees also made their way to Poland, but the numbers were slightly lower. Furthermore, hundreds went illegally back to Germany, see AŻIH, Żydowskie Stowarzyszenia Krakowskie, syg. 108/36, Komitet Pomocy Uchodźcom z Niemiec przy Gminie Wyznaniowej Żydowskiej w Krakowie 1933–35, protocol, conference of the delegates of Jewish aid committees for refugees from Germany, Katowice, June 4, 1933, 2; YVS, M.72/788, JDC, Condensed Report of Poland, signature illegible, April 1935, 25; YVS, M.72/819, Central Refugee Committee, Warsaw 1939, Report the Activity of the Refugees Committee (A. Hafftka), 1; "Pleytim fun Daytshland okupirt dos dzhoynt-biro," *Naye Folkstsaytung*, December 14, 1936, 6; Weiss, *Deutsche und polnische Juden*, 140–49 and Anna Kargol, *Zakon Synów Przymierza. Krakowska Loża "Solidarność" 1892–1938* (Warsaw: Oficyna Wydawnicya RYTM, 2013), 242–45.
61. Zusman Segalovitsh, *Tlomatske 13. Fun farbrentn nekhtn* (Buenas Aires: Tsentral farband fun poylishe yidn in Argentinie, 1946) (Polish version. *Tłomackie 13 [Z unicestwionej przeszłości]. Wspomnienia o Żydowskim Związku Literatów i Dziennikarzy w Polsce [1919–1939]*. [Wrocław: Wydawnictwo Dolonśląskie, 2001]), 221.
62. AAN, Braterstwo—B'nei B'rith, Stowarzyszenie Humanitarne w Warszawie, syg. 674/4, protocol, closed meeting, members of the board, November 14, 1938, 248–49.
63. Sometimes Jewish intellectuals from Germany, Poland or other countries were invited to give lectures on the condition of German Jewry, anti-Semitism or other topics that were of interest to the members, see the protocols of the Warsaw B'nai B'rith lodge from the 1930s in the Archiwum Akt Nowych. The members of the B'nai B'rith were also among the first Polish Jews, who conducted interviews with

Jewish refugees in Zbąszyń in 1933, see Kargol, *Zakon Synów Przymierza*, 242–45; Anna Novikov-Almagor, "Zbąszyń, 1933," *Scripta Judaica Cracoviensia* 7 (2009: 103–09.

64. "Shoyderlikher yiden-pogrom in Daytshland," *Haynt*, November 11, 1938, 2; "Di pogromen in Daytshland," *Haynt*, November 13, 1938, 1–2; "Der yudisher khurbn in Berlin," *Der Moment*, November 13, 1938, 6; Loose, "Reaktionen," 49.

65. Polish Jews already got used to the horrible news coming in from Nazi Germany over the years, as several journalists like Esriel Carlebach (Lui Gothelf) or A. Zeytiker (probably a pen-name) mentioned in their articles, see Lui Gothelf [Carlebach, Esriel], "Naye 5600 krobnes fun Hitler'n," *Haynt*, May 16, 1933, 3; A. Zeytiker, "5 yidn in grenets-vald . . . der shmues beym redaktsie-tishl," *Naye Folkstsaytung*, August 12, 1939, 5.

66. Arn Aynhorn, "Fun tog tsu tog," *Haynt*, November 14, 1938, 3; Bernard Zynger, "Di pogromen oyf yidn un di ekonomishe lage fun Daytshland," *Haynt*, November 13, 1938, 3; Ytskhak Katsenelson, "Hersh Feyvel Grinshpan," *Haynt*, November 18, 1938, 5; Henryk Erlich, "In der finstere nakht," *Naye Folkstsaytung*, November 18, 1938, 3.

67. At least two journalists worked until 1939 for the Yiddish press in Warsaw: Ytsakh-Mayer Gliksman worked, among other newspapers, for *Haynt* and Josef Lanczener wrote, for instance, for *Di Tsayt* (Vilna). In September 1942 Gliksman and his wife were deported to Theresienstadt, where he perished. After a short time in prison, Josef Lanczener managed to fly to Warsaw in 1939. From there he made his way to Palestine. The JTA had at least two correspondents in Berlin until 1937, namely Arno Herzberg and Boris Smolar, see Arno Herzberg, "The Jewish Press under the Nazi Regime—Its Mission, Suppression and Defiance—A Memoir," *The Leo Baeck Institute Year Book* 36, no. 1 (1991): 387; Jewish Telegraphic Agency (JTA), "Germany Defers Smolar's Deportation until Thursday," March 15, 1937, 1; Ytsekh-Mayer Gliksman, "Vi azoy leben itst di poylishe yidn in Daytshland?" *Haynt*, June 27, 1939, 3.

68. Włodzimierz Lencki, "Sklepa Berlina," *Nasz Przegląd*, November 20, 1938, 7.

69. The only travelogue for the year 1938 I could find so far is from August 1938 and was written by the Bundist Jacob Pat for *Naye Folkstsaytung*. On his way back from the United States to Poland he had a short layover in Berlin, Germany, see Yakov Pat, "A par teg in Berlin," *Naye Folkstsaytung*, August 19, 1938, 5. After August 1938 I have not yet found further information on travels by Polish Jews through Germany. Emanuel Ringelblum remembered in his diaries, that the German embassy in Warsaw denied the Polish delegation transit visas through Germany, in order to attend the Zionist Congress in Geneva in August 1939. The delegation had then to travel via Hungary, Yugoslavia and Italy to Switzerland. Such refusals probably affected other Jewish travelers from Poland earlier than 1939, see Reinharz and Shavit, *The Road to September 1939*, 234. In addition, the Berlin JTA correspondent

Arno Herzberg remembered, how difficult it was to smuggle news out of Germany, see Herzberg, "The Jewish Press," 383–88.

70. This was the case with Mark Turkow (*Der Moment*) in February 1933, when he traveled to Germany to cover the political overthrow. The press department of the Polish Foreign Office supported him financially by giving him reduced tickets for the train and providing him with visas and contacts in Berlin, see AAN, Ambasada RP w Berlinie, syg. 2392, German embassy in Warsaw to Polish embassy in Berlin regarding Mark Turkow's journey to Berlin, February 14, 1933, 11.

71. The Polish authorities confiscated articles on the "Polenaktion" and the pogroms likewise. On November 8, 1938 they confiscated for example the *Naye Folkstsaytung* (nr. 334b) due to an article with the title "How the National Socialists brought Jews with Polish Citizenship to the Border." On November 22 they again confiscated the *Naye Folkstsaytung* and the *Nowy Dziennik*, due to "articles on the pogroms in Germany," see AAN, MSW, syg. 968, Wydział Narodowościowym, Komunikaty dzienne, 1938, Department of nationalities, Department for Jewish affairs, press reports from November 9, 15 and 22, 1938, Warsaw, 80, 140. Despite censorship, Jewish newspapers found ways to cover the news. Instead of writing reports on the *Polenaktion* itself, they reported on the activities of the newly founded aid committees, see "Algemeyner retungs-komitet tsu helfen di pleytim fun Daytshland," *Haynt*, November 6, 1938, 7. Only in mid-November, did the first detailed reports appear. The *Nasz Przegląd* even apologized to their readers for their late reaction due to "reasons beyond our control." This statement most obviously pointed to the censorship, see "Jak odbyło się wysiedlenie Żydów polskich z Niemiec," *Nasz Przegląd*, November 20, 1938, 9.

72. Tomaszewski, *Auftakt*, 157, 199.

73. YVA, M.72/793, JDC, Administration, General, 1938, November 29, 1938, Situation of the Jews in Poland, not paginated.

74. Tomaszewski, *Auftakt*, 156–57.

75. PAAA, R 122816, von Moltke, Hans-Adolf, German Embassy Warsaw to the German Foreign Office regarding the free distribution of the emigre press in Warsaw, February 18, 1938, not paginated.

76. Segalovitsh, *Tlomatske 13*, 221.

77. Vlodzimierzsh Lentski, "A bezukh in hayntigen Berlin," *Der Moment*, December 2, 1938, 4; Lencki, "Sklepa," 7. In *Der Moment*, Lentski was introduced as a "well-known Polish journalist, who is currently visiting Nazi Germany" and it was said that he would publish several articles exclusively for the newspaper. Unfortunately, I could not find any more information on him.

78. Zynger, "Di pogromen oyf yidn," 3; Yikhezkl Moyshe Nayman, "Di naye 'luzitanye,'" *Haynt*, November 16, 1938, 3; Shaul Y. Stupnitski, "Di velt hot a tsiter getun," *Der Moment*, November 13, 1938, 3; Yoshua Gotlib, "Der emes'er protest," *Der Moment*, November 18, 1938, 3; Erlich, "In der finstere," 3.

79. "Vi azoy 'reagirt' di poylishe prese oyf di shoyderlikhe yuden-pogromen in Daytshland? . . ." *Der Moment*, November 14, 1938, 2; Tomaszewski, *Auftakt*, 225; Kosmala, "Pressereaktionen in Polen," 1036–41.
80. Zusman Segalovitsh, "In unzere teg . . . refleksen," *Der Moment*, November 18, 1938, 5.
81. Henryk Erlich, "Oyf der shvel fun 1939," *Naye Folkstsaytung*, September 1, 1939, 3.
82. For a more detailed description on how Jewish newspapers in Poland, namely the *Nasz Przegląd, Hayntige Nayes, Unzer Ekspres* and *Republika*, reacted to the November pogroms see also Loose, "Reaktionen," and Kosmala, "Pressereaktionen in Polen," 1041–45.
83. "Ogólny komitet pomocy uchodźcom z Niemiec," *Nasz Przegląd*, November 5, 1938, 2.
84. YVA, M.72/819, 13.
85. According to information provided by the Polish Ministry of Interior, *Nasz Przegląd* collected 65.217 zlotys, *Unzer Ekspres* 325, *Naye Folkstsaytung* 5.350 and *Haynt* 3.837 zlotys until November 13, 1938, see AAN, MSW, syg. 968, 127.
86. "Hilf far di aroysgeshikte fun Daytshland," *Naye Folkstsaytung*, December 23, 1938, 5; Editors, "Der 'Haynt' far di pleytim!" *Haynt*, November 6, 1938, 1; "Tsu hilf di aroysgeshikte yidn fun Daytshland," *Naye Folkstsaytung*, January 7, 1939, 4; "Algemeyner," 7.
87. YVA, P.13/120, Press Agency of the SIG, Die polnischen Juden im Niemandsland, not dated, 2. The Bund organized again its own committee. However, the various committees worked side by side in the refugee camp in Zbąszyń.
88. There was at least one organized trip to Zbąszyń for several reporters of various Jewish and non-Jewish Polish socialist and democratic dailies. It was organized through the Bundist *Arbeter-komitet tsu helfn di aroysgeshikte*, see "Tsvishn di aroysgeshikte yidn fun Daytshland," *Naye Folkstsaytung*, November 20, 1938, 3.
89. Turkow "Between," 84.
90. Pinkhas Shvarts, "In Zbanshin," *Naye Folkstsaytung*, November 21, 1938, 4; Barukh Shefner, "Friling in Zbanshin," *Naye Folkstsaytung*, May 7, 1939, 4; Mikhoel Burshtin, "Bey di fertribene, . . ." *Der Moment*, January 1, 1939, 4.
91. Samuel D. Kassow, *Who Will Write Our History? Rediscovering a Hidden Archive from the Ghetto* (Bloomington: Indiana University Press, 2007), 100.
92. Mendel Balberyszski, *Stronger than Iron: The Destruction of Vilna Jewry 1941–1945: An Eyewitness Account* (Jerusalem: Gefen Publishing House, 2010), 4.
93. Nalewajko-Kulikov, "Di Haynt-mishpokhe," 254, 268.
94. Turkow "Between," 84.

Bibliography

Archives

Archiwum Akt Nowych w Warszawie.
Archive of the National Library of Israel.
Archiv des Vereins der Ausländischen Presse zu Berlin e.V.
Archiwum Żydowskiego Instytutu Historycznego im. E. Ringelbluma w Warszawie.
Politisches Archiv des Auswärtigen Amts.
Yad Vashem Archives.

Newspaper Articles

"6.000 osób w sali na dziedzińcu 'Nowości.'" *Nasz Przegląd*, March 28, 1933, 2.
"Algemeyner retungs-komitet tsu helfen di pleytim fun Daytshland." *Haynt*, November 6, 1938, 7.
"Ayndrikn fun yidishn un arbeter-lebn in hitlerishn Daytshland. Antsike varlezung fun bakantn yidishn zshurnalistn B. Zynger." *Naye Folkstsaytung*, May 12, 1933, 12.
"Der yudisher khurbn in Berlin." *Der Moment*, November 13, 1938, 6.
"Di grandieze montag'dige protest-mitingen." *Der Moment*, March 29, 1933, 6.
"Di pogromen in Daytshland." *Haynt*, November 13, 1938, 1–2.
Editors. "Der 'Haynt' far di pleytim!" *Haynt*, November 6, 1938, 1.
"Farvaltung fun Varshever literatn-farayn protestirt kegn dem hitlerishn terror." *Literarishe Bleter*, no. 16 (1933): 265.
"Fun tsuzamenfar fun 'poylishn yidntum.'" *Naye Folkstsaytung*, April 25, 1933, 4.
"Hilf far di aroysgeshikte fun Daytshland." *Naye Folkstsaytung*, December 23, 1938, 5.
"Hitler (a literarisher portret). Forlezung fun dr. Yosef Kruk, montog, dem 6-tn februar, tsayger 9 in ovnt, farayn fun yidishe literatn un zhurnalistn, tlomatske 13." *Naye Folkstsaytung*, February 6, 1933, 6.
"Jak odbyło się wysiedlenie Żydów polskich z Niemiec." *Nasz Przegląd*, November 20, 1938, 9.
"Ogólny komitet pomocy uchodźcom z Niemiec." *Nasz Przegląd*, November 5, 1938, 2.
"Oysgenart a 'beruhigende' deklaratsie, dan tseshlogen un deportirt." *Haynt*, April 2, 1933, 2.
"Shoyderlikher yiden-pogrom in Daytshland." *Haynt*, November 11, 1938, 2.
"Sytuacja Żydów w Niemczech." *Nasz Przegląd*, April 24, 1933, 2–3.
"Tsu hilf di aroysgeshikte yidn fun Daytshland." *Naye Folkstsaytung*, January 7, 1939, 4.
"Tsvishn di aroysgeshikte yidn fun Daytshland." *Naye Folkstsaytung*, November 20, 1938, 3.
"Vi azoy 'reagirt' di poylishe prese oyf di shoyderlikhe yuden-pogromen in Daytshland?..." *Der Moment*, November 14, 1938, 2.

"Vos hert zikh in Varshe?" *Haynt*, April 19, 1933, 7.
Arnsberg, Paul. "Di khurbes fun daytshishn tsionizm." *Der Nayer Veg*, September 1, 1932, 13–14.
Aynhorn, Arn. "Fun tog tsu tog." *Haynt*, November 14, 1938, 3.
Burshtin, Mikhoel. "Bey di fertribene. . . ." *Der Moment*, January 1, 1939, 4.
Erlich, Henryk. "Der hayntike protest-tog." *Naye Folkstsaytung*, March 28, 1933, 3.
———. "In der finstere nakht." *Naye Folkstsaytung*, November 18, 1938, 3.
———. "Oyf der shvel fun 1939." *Naye Folkstsaytung*, September 1, 1939, 3.
Feraynigter natsionaler protest-komitet. "Morgen protest-tog fun poylishen yidentum." *Haynt*, March 26, 1933, 1.
Fishl, Lidor. "Di ekstsesn gegn yidn in Berlin." *Der Moment*, November 11, 1923, 3.
Gliksman, Ytsekh-Meyer. "Vi azoy leben itst di poylishe yidn in Daytshland?" *Haynt*, June 27, 1939, 3.
Goldberg, Abraham. "Daytshe pogromen." *Haynt*, November 9, 1923, 3.
Gothelf, Lui [Carlebach, Esriel]. "Di hartsraysende stsenes in berliner palestina-amt." *Haynt*, May 3, 1933, 4.
———. "Naye 5600 krobnes fun Hitler'n." *Haynt*, May 16, 1933, 3.
Gotlib, Yoshua. "Der emes'er protest." *Der Moment*, November 18, 1938, 3.
Jewish Telegraphic Agency (JTA). "Germany Defers Smolar's Deportation until Thursday." March 15, 1937, 1.
Katsenelson, Ytskhak. "Hersh Feyvel Grinshpan." *Haynt*, November 18, 1938, 5.
Klinov, Yeshayahu. "Der shvartser montog." *Haynt*, February 1, 1933, 3.
———. "Di 'zibete melukhe' firt milkhome mint dritn raykh: vi azoyy arbeyten un leben ists yidish-oyslendishe zhurnalistn in Berlin." *Haynt*, June 23, 1933, 9–10.
Kosovski, Vladimir. "Daytshland tsurikgevorfn in finstern mitlalter." *Naye Folkstsaytung*, April 4, 1933, 3.
Lencki, Włodzimierz. "Sklepa Berlina." *Nasz Przegląd*, November 20, 1938, 7.
Lentski, Vlodzimierzsh. "A bezukh in hayntigen Berlin." *Der Moment*, December 2, 1938, 4.
Lirik, A. S. [Aaron-Levi Riklis]. "Das land ohn yidn." *Haynt*, April 10, 1933, 5.
Mendelsohn, Shlomo. "Dos ponem fun hayntikn Daytshland." *Naye Folkstsaytung*, April 23, 1933, 5.
Mlatek, Y. "Drey yor in daytshe kontsentratsie-lagern." *Naye Folkstsaytung*, July 25, 1938, 3.
Nayman, Yikhezkl Moyshe. "Di naye 'luzitanye.'" *Haynt*, November 16, 1938, 3.
Pat, Yakov. "A par teg in Berlin." *Naye Folkstsaytung*, August 19, 1938, 5.
Rotenshtraykh, Fishl. "Der analiz fun barbaropa." *Haynt*, March 24, 1933, 4.
S. "Pleytim fun Daytshland okupirt dos dzhoynt-biro." *Naye Folkstsaytung*, December 14, 1936, 6.
Segalovitsh, Zusman. "In unzere teg . . . refleksen." *Der Moment*, November 18, 1938, 5.
Shefner, Barukh. "Friling in Zbanshin." *Naye Folkstsaytung*, May 7, 1939, 4.

———. "Iber der daytsher grenets." *Naye Folkstsaytung*, June 5, 1936, 5.
Shnayder, Nathan [Nathan Frenkel]. "Der blutiker veg fun fashizm." *Naye Folkstsaytung*, March 21, 1933, 4.
Shnayderman, Shmuel-Leyb. "Farendig durkh Daytshland." *Der Moment*, April 10, 1933, 11.
Shvarts, Pinkhas. "In Zbanshin." *Naye Folkstsaytung*, November 21, 1938, 4.
Stupnitski, Shaul Y. "Di velt hot a tsiter getun." *Der Moment*, November 13, 1938, 3.
Swet, Hermann. "Fun der berliner tog-teglikhkeyt." *Der Moment*, March 21, 1933, 3.
Tompson, Dorothy. "Hitler hot dos blut fargosn." *Naye Folkstsaytung*, May 27, 1933, 4.
Turkow, Mark. "In'm land fun kemfender lagern." *Der Moment*, February 21, 1933, 4.
Zeytiker, A. "5 yidn in grenets-vald . . . der shmues beym redaktsie-tishl." *Naye Folkstsaytung*, August 12, 1939, 5.
Zynger, Bernard. "Di pogromen oyf yidn un di ekonomishe lage fun Daytshland." *Haynt*, November 13, 1938, 3.

Secondary Sources

Balberyszski, Mendel. *Stronger than Iron: The Destruction of Vilna Jewry 1941–1945: An Eyewitness Account*. Jerusalem: Gefen Publishing House, 2010.
Blatman, Daniel. "The National Ideology of the Bund in the Test of Antisemitism and the Holocaust, 1933–47." *Jewish Politics in Eastern Europe: The Bund at 100*, edited by Jack Jackobs, 197–212. London: Palgrave Macmillan, 2001.
Bothe, Alina and Gertrud Pickhan. *Ausgewiesen! Berlin, 28. 10. 1938. Die Geschichte der "Polenaktion."* Berlin: Metropol, 2018.
Brinkmann, Tobias. "Ort des Übergangs—Berlin als Schnittstelle der jüdischen Migration aus Osteuropa nach 1918." In *Transit und Transformation. Osteuropäisch-jüdische Migranten in Berlin 1918-1939*, edited by Verena Dohrn and Gertrud Pickhan, 25–44. Göttingen: Wallstein Verlag, 2010.
Bronsztein, Szyja. "Polish-Jewish Relations as Reflected in Memoirs of the Interwar Period." *Polin* 8 (1994): 66–88.
Carlebach, Esriel. "Lomir zikh dermonen." In *Fun noentn ovar*, vol. 2, edited by Alveltlekhen yidishn kultur-kongres, 233–37. New York, 1956.
Cohen, Nathan. *Sefer, Sofer ve-Iton. Merkaz ha-Tarbut ha-Yehudit be-Warse (1918–1942)*. Jerusalem: Magnes Press and Hebrew University, 2003.
Erlich, Henryk. *In kamf farn revolusionern sotsializm. Arbeter-klas in kamf kegn Hitler-Daytshland, Warsaw 1934*. Warsaw: Farlag Di Naye Folkstsaytung, 1934.
Estraikh, Gennady. "Weimar Berlin—An International Yiddish Press Center." In *Transit und Transformation. Osteuropäisch-jüdische Migranten in Berlin 1918-1939*, edited by Verena Dohrn and Gertrud Pickhan, 77–92. Göttingen: Wallstein Verlag, 2010.
Finkelshtayn, Khaym. *Haynt—a tsaytung bay yidn*. New York: Farlag Perets, 1978.

Finkelshtayn, Khaym. "Haynt (1918–1939)." In *Fun noentn ovar*, vol. 2, edited by Alveltlekhen yidishn kultur-kongres, 3–237. New York, 1956.

Fuks, Marian. *Prasa żydowska w Warszawie*. Warsaw: Państwowe Wydawnictwo Naukowe, 1979.

Goldstein, Bernard. *Twenty Years with the Jewish Labor Bund: A Memoir of Interwar Poland*. Translated and edited by Marvin S. Zuckerman. West Lafayette, IN: Purdue University Press, 2016.

Grinberg, Daniel. "The Polish-Language Jewish Press and the Events in the Third Reich, 1933–1939." In *Why Didn't the Press Shout? American and International Journalism during the Holocaust*, edited by Robert Moses Shapiro, 429–46. Jersey City: Yeshiva University Press with Ktav Publishing House, 2003.

Harris, Bonnie Mae. "From German Jews to Polish Refugees: Germany's Polenaktion and the Zbąszyń Deportations of October 1938." *Kwartalnik Historii Żydów* 230 (2009): 175–205.

Herzberg, Arno. "The Jewish Press under the Nazi Regime—Its Mission, Suppression and Defiance—A Memoir." *The Leo Baeck Institute Year Book* 36, no. 1 (1991): 367–88.

Herzer, Martin. *Auslandskorrespondenten und auswaertige Pressepolitik im Dritten Reich*. Medien in Geschichte und Gegenwart, edited by Jürgen Wilke, vol. 27. Köln: Böhlau Verlaug, 2012.

Kargol, Anna. *Zakon Synów Przymierza. Krakowska Loża "Solidarność" 1892–1938*. Warsaw: Oficyna Wydawnicya RYTM, 2013.

Kassow, Samuel D. *Who Will Write Our History? Rediscovering a Hidden Archive from the Ghetto*. Bloomington: Indiana University Press, 2007.

Klein, L. Ruth. *Nazi Germany, Canadian Responses: Confronting Anti-Semitism in the Shadow of War*. Montreal: McGill-Queen's University Press, 2012.

Kosmala, Beate. "Pressereaktionen in Polen auf den Novemberpogrom 1938 in Deutschland und die Lage der Polnischen Juden." *Zeitschrift für Geschichte* 46 (1998): 1034–45.

Krzywiec, Grzegorz. "The Balance of Polish Political Antisemitism: Between 'National Revolution,' Economic Crisis, and the Transformation of the Polish Public Sphere in the 1930s." In *Right-Wing Politics and the Rise of Antisemitism in Europe 1935–1941*. European Holocaust Studies, edited by Frank Bajohr and Dieter Pohl, vol. 1, 61–80. Göttingen: Wallstein Verlag, 2019.

Laczó, Ferenc. "Introduction." In *Catastrophe and Utopia. Jewish Intellectuals in Central and Eastern Europe in the 1930s and 1940s*. Europas Osten im 20. Jahrhundert, edited by Ferenc Laczó and Joachim von Puttkamer, vol. 7, 1–12. Berlin: de Gruyter, 2018.

Landau-Czajka, Anna. "Adolf Hitler i III Rzesza w oczach czytelników Małego Przeglądu." In *Yesterday. Studia z Historii najnowszej. Księga dedykowana Prof. Jerzemu Eislerowi w 65. Rocznicę Urodzin*, edited by January Olaszek et al., 307–24. Warsaw: Instytut Pamięci Narodowej, Instytut Historii im. Tadeusza Manteuffla Polskiej Akademii Nauk, 2017.

Loose, Ingo. "Reaktionen auf den Novemberpogrom in Polen 1938-1939." In *Die Novemberpogrome. Versuch einer Bilanz*, edited by Stiftung Topographie des Terrors, 44-58. Berlin: Stiftung Topographie des Terrors, 2009.

Margilos, Rebecca. "A Review of the Yiddish Media: Responses of the Jewish Immigrant Community in Canada." In *Nazi Germany, Canadian Responses. Confronting Anti-Semitism in the Shadow of War*, edited by L. Ruth Klein, 114-43. Toronto: McGill-Queen's University Press, 2012.

Marten-Finnis, Susanne. "Die Jüdische Presse in der Osteuropäischen Diaspora: Eine Typologie." In *Die Jüdische Presse. Forschungsmethoden—Erfahrungen—Ergebnisse*. Jüdische Presse—Kommunikationsgeschichte im Europäischen Raum, edited by Susanne Marten-Finnis and Markus Bauer, vol. 2, 75-86. Bremen: Edition Lumiere, 2007.

Maurer, Trude. "Abschiebung und Attentat. Die Ausweisung der polnischen Juden und der Vorwand für die 'Kristallnacht.'" In *Der Judenpogrom 1938. Von der "Reichskristallnacht" zum Völkermord*, edited by Walter H. Pehle, 52-73. Frankfurt am Main: Fischer Taschenbuch Verlag, 1988.

Melzer, Emanuel. *No Way out: The Politics of Polish Jewry 1935—1939*. Cincinnati: Hebrew Union College Press, 1997.

McCullough, Colin and Nathan Wilson. *Violence, Memory, and History: Western Perceptions of Kristallnach*. New York: Routledge, 2015.

Milton, Sybil. "The Expulsion of Polish Jews from Germany October 1938 to July 1939: A Documentation." *Leo Baeck Institute Year Book* 29, no. 1 (1984): 169-99.

Miron, Guy. *The Waning of Emancipation. Jewish History, Memory, and the Rise of Fascism in Germany, France, and Hungary*. Detroit: Wayne State University Press, 2011.

Moss, Kenneth B. "Negotiating Jewish Nationalism in Interwar Warsaw." In *The Jewish Metropolis: Essays in Honor of the 75th Birthday of Professor Antony Polonsky*, edited by Glenn Dynner and François Guesnet, 390-434. Leiden: Brill, 2015.

Mozes, Samuel R. "Żydowska Agencja Telegraficzna w Polsce (1920-1939)." *Biuletyn Żydowskiego Historycznego w Polsce* 1, no. 97 (1976): 109-21.

Nasza Obrona. Pismo Poświęcone antyhitlerowskiej Akcji gospodarczej, edited by Leo Finkelshtayn, vol. 1 (November 1933) and vol. 2 (February 1934) (Yiddish and Polish).

Nalewajko-Kulikov, Joanna. "'Die Haynt-mishpokhe': Study of a Group Picture." In *The Jewish Metropolis: Essays in Honor of the 75th Birthday of Professor Antony Polonsky*, edited by Glenn Dynner and François Guesnet, 252-70. Leiden: Brill, 2015.

———. "O Człowieku, który widział za dużo, czyli Historia Kryminalna z 'Hajntem' w Tle." In *Wiek Nienawiści. Księga dedykowana Prof. Jerzemu Borejszy*, edited by Jerzy Eisler, Edmund Dmitrów et al., 249-64. Warsaw: Instytut Pamięci Narodowej, 2014.

———. "Prasa Żydowska na Ziemiach Polskich: Historia, Stan Badań, Perspektywy Badawcze." In *Studia z Dziejów Trójjęzycznej Prasy Żydowskiej na Ziemiach Polskich (XIX-XX w.)*, in cooperation with Grzegorz Bąbiak and Agnieszka J. Cieślikowa, 7-30. Warsaw: Neriton, 2012.

———. *Studia z Dziejów Trójjęzycznej Prasy Żydowskiej na Ziemiach Polskich (XIX–XX w.)*, in cooperation with Grzegorz Bąbiak and Agnieszka J. Cieślikowa. Warsaw: Neriton, 2012.

———. "When Goethe's Poetry Was Not Enough: Yehoshua Thon on Germany, Optimism and Anti-Semitism (1932–1933)." In *A Romantic Polish Jew: Rabbi Ozjasz Thon from Various Perspectives*, edited by Michał Galas and Shoshana Ronen, 95–106. Kraków: Jagiellonian University Press, 2015.

Neumann, I. M. "Outstreched on the Altar." *The Menorah Journal* XXIV, no. 3 (October–December 1936): 294–301.

Novikov-Almagor, Anna. "Zbąszyń, 1933." *Scripta Judaica Cracoviensia* 7 (2009): 103–09.

Pickhan, Gertrud. *"Gegen den Strom": Der Allgemeine Jüdische Arbeiterbund "Bund" in Polen 1918–1939*." Schriften des Simon-Dubnow-Instituts Leipzig, edited by Dan Diner, vol. 1. Stuttgart: Deutsche Verlags-Anstalt, 2011.

———. "Jakobs Berliner Kinder. Ein Warschauer Bundist im Jüdischen Berliner Theater 1935." In *"Der Fremde Im Dorf." Überlegungen zum Eigenen und zum Fremden in der Geschichte*, edited by Hans-Jürgen Bömelburg and Beate Eschment, 196–210. Lüneburg: IInstitut Nordostdeutsches Kulturwerk, 1998.

Pietrzak, Michał. *Reglamentacja wolności prasy w Polsce (1918–1939)*. Warsaw: Książka i Wiedza, 1963.

Polonsky, Antony. *The Jews in Poland and Russia (1914-2008)*. Vol. 3. Oxford: Littman Library of Jewish Civilization, 2012.

Prager, Moshe. "Dos yudishe togblat (1929–1939)." In *Fun noentn ovar*. Vol. 2, edited by Alveltlekhen yidishn kultur-kongres, 443–529. New York: 1956.

Pryt, Karina. *Befohlene Freundschaft. Die deutsch-polnischen Kulturbeziehungen 1934–1939*. Einzelveröffentlichungen des DHI Warschau, edited by Eduard Mühle, vol. 22. Osnabrück: fibre, 2010.

Ravitsh, Melech. "'Tlomackie 13'. Home of Jewish Writers and Journalists." In *The Jewish Press That Was: Accounts, Evaluations and Memories of Jewish Papers in Pre-Holocaust Europe*, edited by David Flinker, Shalom Rosenfeld, and Mordechai Tsanin, 205–18. Tel Aviv: World Federation of Jewish Journalists, 1980.

Reinharz, Jehuda, and Yaacov Shavit. *The Road to September 1939: Polish Jews, Zionists, and the Yishuv on the Eve of World War II*. Waltham: MA: Brandeis University Press, 2018.

Saß, Anne-Christin. *Berliner Luftmenschen. Osteuropäisch-jüdische Migranten in der Weimarer Republik. Charlottengrad und Scheunenviertel*, edited by Verena Dohrn and Gertrud Pickhan, vol. 2. Göttingen: Wallstein Verlag, 2012.

Schiper, Ignacy. *Dzieje handlu żydowskiego na ziemiach polskich*. Kraków: Związek Kupców, 1937.

Segalovitsh, Zusman. *Tlomatske 13. Fun farbrentn nekhtn*. Buenas Ares: Tsentral farband fun poylishe yidn in Argentinie, 1946. (Polish version. *Tłomackie 13 [Z unicestwionej przeszłości]. Wspomnienia o Żydowskim Żwiązku Literatów i Dziennikarzy w Polsce [1919–1939]*. Wroclaw: Wydawnictwo Dolonśląskie, 2001).

Shvarts, Pinkhas. "Folkstsaytung (1921–1939)." In *Fun noentn ovar*. Vol. 2, edited by Alveltlekhen yidishn kultur-kongres, 303–425. New York, 1956.

Singer, Bernard. *W krajach Hitlera i Stalina, Reportaże*. Warsaw: Biblioteka Midrasza, 2007.

Skórzyńska, Izabela, and Wojciech Olejniczak. *Do zobaczenia za rok w Jerozolimie. Deportacje polskich Żydów w 1938 roku z Niemiec do Zbąszynia*. Zbąszyn: Fundacja TRES, 2012.

Steffen, Katrin. *Jüdische Polonität. Ethnizität und Nation im Spiegel der polnischsprachigen jüdischen Presse 1918–1939*. Schriften des Simon-Dubnow-Instituts, vol. 3. Göttingen: Vandenhoeck & Ruprecht Verlage, 2004.

Swet, Gershon. "With the Wurmbrands in Pre-Hitler Berlin." *Michael Wurmbrand, The Man and His Work*, edited by Kurt R. Grossmann, 17–21. New York: Philosophical Library, 1956.

Tomaszewski, Jerzy. *Auftakt zur Vernichtung. Die Verteibung polnischer Juden aus Deutschland im Jahre 1938*. Klio in Polen, vol. 9. Osnabrück: fibre, 2002. (Polish version: *Preludium Zagłady. Wygnanie Żydów Polskich z Niemiec w 1938 r.* Warsaw: Wydawnictwo Naukowe PWN, 1998.)

———. "Bojkot towarów niemieckich w Polsce w latach 1933–1935." *Acta Oeconomica Pragnesia* 15, no. 7 (2007): 448–59.

Tsentrales bundishes anti-Hitler-komitet in Varshe: *Arbeter-klas in kampf kegn Hitler-Daytshland*, Warsaw, 1934.

Turkow, Mark. "Between Two World Wars." In *The Jewish Press That Was: Accounts, Evaluations and Memories of Jewish Papers in Pre-Holocaust Europe*, edited by David Flinker, Shalom Rosenfeld, and Mordechai Tsanin, 79–85. Tel Aviv: World Federation of Jewish Journalists, 1980.

Weiss, Yfaat. *Deutsche und polnische Juden vor dem Holocaust. Jüdische Identität zwischen Staatsbürgerschaft und Ethnizität 1933–1940*. Schriftenreihe der Vierteljahreshefte für Zeitgeschichte, vol. 81. Munich: Oldenburg Wissenschaftsverlag, 2000.

CHAPTER 7

What Did Soviet Jews Make of Kristallnacht? The Nazi Threat in the Soviet Press

by Jeffrey Koerber

On November 11, 1938, the Soviet Yiddish newspaper *Oktyabr* (Minsk) published a front-page photo of Stalin and the Soviet leadership gathered on the platform atop Lenin's Tomb. They were there to review the parade on Red Square marking the anniversary of the October Revolution. Below the photo ran a startling news item: "Jewish Pogroms in Germany." Nazi Stormtroopers had beaten Jews in their homes and in the streets, it reported. Many were killed. Synagogues had been vandalized or destroyed by fire. The story noted the unprecedented scope of these actions.[1] More reports in the following days gave specific details of attacks in Berlin, Frankfurt, Vienna, and other cities, as well as the arrest of tens of thousands of Jewish men and their imprisonment in concentration camps.

News items like these of what later became known as Kristallnacht were readily available in the Soviet press under Stalinism. Indeed, Jewish readers had long been able to follow developments in Nazi Germany. Whether they interpreted this news as presenting any specific danger to their lives is another matter. This chapter explores the content of the Soviet news stories that examined the unfolding stages of antisemitic persecution in Nazi Germany, and it begins to assess what meaning these reports had for Jews living under Stalinism. Perspectives from the Belarusian Soviet Socialist Republic, one of the western border regions to completely fall under Nazi rule in 1941, are the focus. In addition to the Yiddish- and Russian-language press originating from Minsk, the Belarusian capital, it examines the recollections of witnesses from across Soviet Belarus and Ukraine.

BACKGROUND: SOVIET JEWS' SHIFTING FORTUNES

During the 1920s, the Bolsheviks sought to advance Jews from an oppressed minority to equal status alongside other Soviet nationalities. Antisemitism was denounced as "anti-Soviet." Jews and Gentiles increasingly lived side by side in communal apartments as crowded cities rapidly industrialized under the Five-Year Plans during the following decade. Leading the political and cultural campaign was the *Yevsektsiya*, the Jewish section of the Communist Party, which dismantled Jewish communal institutions, seized synagogues, and promoted anti-religious propaganda. Among the institutions that took their place were Yiddish-language theaters, publications, and school systems promoting a constructed Soviet Jewish identity.[2] Although distanced from their heritage, many young Jews plunged ahead into the opportunities on offer. Hirsh Reles (1913–2004), a young writer mentored during the 1930s, remembered the decade as "a glittering epoch" for Soviet Jewish intellectual life.[3]

By the mid-1930s, the Communist Party's support for Yiddish-language institutions waned considerably as minorities in the Soviet borderland regions came under suspicion of disloyalty. The *Yevsektsiya* had already been disbanded in 1929. During the Great Terror of 1937–38, wave of purges targeted perceived "enemies and wreckers" within the ranks of the Communist Party, Red Army officer corps, intelligentsia, and industrial sector management. Purges extended to ordinary citizens, bringing the numbers of arrested and executed to more than one million. The purges of the late 1930s also attacked ethnic minorities residing in the Soviet borderlands under the guise of the NKVD's "national operations." Tens of thousands of ethnic Poles, Germans, and Latvians were arrested and either executed or imprisoned.[4] Although Jews fell victim under the same program, they were not explicitly cited in NKVD decrees, probably to avoid outward appearances of antisemitism. Tens of thousands of Jews were arrested under charges of counterrevolutionary conspiracies, alleged ties to Polish or German intelligence services, or both.[5] Several of the leading Yiddish writers in Minsk were among those who "disappeared" during these years.[6]

The era's oppressions further shifted the identities of Soviet Jews. Many Jewish families already wanted their children to use Russian, not Yiddish, in their daily lives to access the best education and employment opportunities. In Soviet Belarus, decisions made concurrently with the Great Terror accelerated the abandonment of Yiddish. Party leaders in Minsk closed the Yiddish-language schools in the summer of 1938 and reopened them in the fall as Belarusian-language institutions.[7] Soviet Belarus retained its Yiddish newspaper, *Oktyabr*, which continued circulating from Minsk up to the German invasion in June 1941. Several members of its editorial staff fell victim to the Great Terror.[8] My research found that after the Great Terror the paper varied little from the Russian-language *Sovetskaya Belorussiya*, also published in Minsk, and even promoted Russian- and Belarusian-language culture.

In this context, news reports arrived describing events in Nazi Germany. Soviet Jews had experienced two decades of shifting fortunes, from marginalization to equality tempered by the embargo of their religious and cultural heritage. The purge period saw the status of Jews shift once again, as elements of the constructed Soviet Jewish identity came under attack. The Party's open expressions of antisemitism emerged later under wartime conditions, but Jews in the prewar years faced a dynamic situation with mounting bias. Still, most Jewish families had to remain focused on daily life in the Stalin era, aware of the concessions and compromises that the Soviet system demanded but deeply absorbed in the challenges of making a living. Little wonder that in this context news from Nazi Germany seldom penetrated into an awareness that Soviet Jews could use to perceive the potential dangers that lay ahead.

NAZI ANTISEMITISM IN THE SOVIET PRESS

Soviet Jews could read international news drawn from Reuters and other western wire services, albeit chosen with editorial selectivity to highlight the failures of the capitalist world. Many stories focused on the west's economic depression and resulting political turmoil. The crises of 1931 and 1932 had led the Communist Party in Moscow to believe that Germany in particular was headed for proletarian revolution. Even after Hitler's appointment as Chancellor and the Reichstag Fire in the first months of 1933, newspaper readers were assured that German Communists presented a formidable challenge.[9] As the Nazis consolidated power and successfully suppressed all opposition (not clearly depicted in the Soviet press), the narrative soon shifted to tales of Nazi brutality. A serial in *Oktyabr* later in 1933 told of a German Communist's experiences in the "protective custody camp," in reality an early concentration camp, at Leipzig Police Prison.[10]

Actions targeting Jews also appeared in the Soviet press. *Oktyabr* told of the Nazi Party's plans for a boycott of Jewish businesses across Germany on Saturday, April 1, 1933.[11] The same newspaper gave details the next day of the actions of the April Boycott. Groups of Stormtroopers stood outside Jewish stores to warn away prospective customers. Some shops closed that Saturday, typically the busiest shopping day of the week.[12]

Over the following years, sporadic news items kept Soviet Jews up to date. In July 1935, Nazi hooligans vandalized Jewish-owned stores in Berlin, Augsburg, and Breslau.[13] Readers learned not only about attacks on property but efforts to forcefully isolate German Jews from "Aryans." *Der emes,* the Communist Party's Yiddish newspaper in Moscow, reported on July 24, 1935, on the arrests of Jews accused of miscegenation with "arishe" (Aryan) women.[14]

Indeed, this wave of violence coupled with efforts to prohibit marriage between Jews and Aryans motivated the Nazi leadership to codify new legal measures. These were the Nuremberg Laws, issued on September 15, 1935. *Oktyabr* reported briefly how these were enacted by Hitler in the presence of Reichstag deputies during the Nazi Party's annual rally at Nuremberg. The Reich Citizenship Law declared that a citizen can only be "'a German with German or similar blood.'" The Law for the "protection of German blood and honor" forbade marriage between Germans and Jews.[15]

The brevity of this news story raises a significant issue. How well did the Soviet press educate its readers on the basis for these laws—Nazi racial theory? How were ordinary readers of *Oktyabr* supposed to interpret what "German blood" meant? Bolshevik ideology rejected biological determinism, making the new German laws all the more obscure to Soviet Jews. While a close reading of reports coming out of Germany might have revealed the irrationalism inherent in Nazism, detailed Soviet analyses of racial antisemitism appear to have been reserved for academic journals. Even here, Bolshevik polemic framed explanations. "The race propaganda of fascism has a goal to justify 'biologically' the warlike nationalism of dark capital," argued one researcher in a Yiddish-language journal put out by the Belarusian Academy of Sciences in 1934.[16] Little wonder, perhaps, that the Soviet press in Minsk failed to report on the "First Regulation" of the Nuremberg Laws (November 14, 1935), which advanced a legal definition of Jew based on the individual's grandparents with "Jewish blood."

REPORTS OF KRISTALLNACHT

While the editors of the Party newspapers avoided discussion of racial classifications, they could not ignore the widespread violence of November 9–10, 1938. We know, although Soviet readers could not, that the chain of events leading to Kristallnacht began with the Nazis' expulsion of thousands of Polish Jews at the end of October. The Russian-language *Sovetskaya Belorussiya* reported on the first days of November that Germany had deported thousands of Polish passport holders, almost exclusively Jews.[17] Marooned in fields near border posts, the deportees had no access to food, clean water, or medicine. Some had already died. Another report on the crisis appeared ten days later giving further details.[18]

Hershel Grynszpan's name remained unknown to readers in Minsk, but not his actions. *Oktyabr* for November 11 explained the pogrom as a disproportionate act of retribution for the shooting of Ernst vom Rath. "The German fascists have exploited the dispatches about the attack on the Third Secretary of the German Embassy in Paris into a drastic intensification of the terror against Jews," opened the account originating from Geneva on November 10.[19] The scope of violence was unprecedented, reported the newspaper. Jews had been beaten in their homes and in the streets. Horrible scenes unfolded in the streets of Berlin, as "fascists" vandalized Jewish stores. A nearly identical account ran the same day in *Sovetskaya Belorussiya*.[20] Both Minsk newspapers closed their reportage with the descriptions of merchandise scattered over Friedrichstrasse, as Berliners stood by in silence.

More details emerged in the November 12 issues of *Oktyabr* and *Sovetskaya Belorussiya*. In a Reuters story relayed from London, police in Berlin were observed standing by as attackers ransacked Jewish stores. Similar scenes occurred in Munich, Nuremberg, Frankfurt, and Cologne. Damage to synagogues was widespread. In Vienna, regular police aided Stormtroopers in arresting adult Jewish men. Not fewer than ten thousand were rounded up across Greater Germany.[21] Within days, *Oktyabr* elevated the figure to not fewer than 35,000, as reported in the English press.[22]

Oktyabr and *Sovetskaya Belorussiya* also carried reports (November 14) about new laws banning German Jews from engaging in private enterprise, part of the effort to "Aryanize" the economy. In addition, Jews were forbidden from collecting on insurance policies for property damage. The German government confiscated all payouts, leaving Jews to pay for repairs themselves.[23]

Readers of *Oktyabr* also learned about the pogrom's impact in Western Europe. *Oktyabr* reported on November 14, "The English press is full of communiques from their correspondents in different German cities describing the details of the bloody slayings of the defenseless Jewish population."[24] As before, *Sovetskaya Belorussiya* printed a nearly identical story on the same day.[25] The French paper *Ce Soir* told of sixty suicides among Jews in Munich and Vienna.[26] A Swiss news report reprinted in *Oktyabr* ascribed the organizing role of the pogrom to the German government, contradicting the Ministry of Propaganda's assertions of a popular uprising.[27] *Sovetskaya Belorussiya* printed a similar news item relayed from Paris.[28]

The flurry of reports highlighted other difficulties that German Jews faced. The London *Daily Telegraph and Morning Post* reported that six thousand Munich Jews were ordered to leave the country in twenty-four hours, the rest to be gone in forty-eight hours.[29] Although the order was not carried out, it revealed to Soviet Jewish readers that would-be expellees lacked visas to enter another county. *Ce Soir* also reported that the German government intended to create a ghetto to confine remaining Jews.[30] This was not implemented by the Nazi security services, but it revealed to Soviet audiences the possibilities for the future.

DID SOVIET JEWS PERCEIVE ANY DANGER?

What impact did these reports have on Soviet Jews? This is difficult to assess. In the USC Shoah Foundation Institute's collection of testimonies, few mention Kristallnacht by name compared to Holocaust survivors raised across the border in the Second Polish Republic. Then again, Soviet Jews were not exposed to postwar remembrance of the Holocaust and so lack the vocabulary possessed by Polish Jewish survivors, many of whom migrated to the west.

Some interviewers asked Holocaust survivors and other witnesses about their recollections of Soviet media, while others volunteered this information. Aleksandr Lyubich, born in Minsk in 1928, recalled that he learned about events outside of the Soviet Union by following reports in the newspaper. "I don't know why," he reflected, given his youth in the late 1930s, "but I happened to be interested in that." He also remembered learning about the 1938 pogrom in Germany, but not fully understanding its meaning. "We cannot—uh—know what has happened, how it happened," Lyubich admitted, his hesitation a further indication of his past incomprehension.[31] Alexander Feldman, born in 1929 in Vinnitsa oblast, Ukraine, shared this perception. Single copies of newspapers circulated hand to hand in his *shtetl* and their contents spread by word of mouth. By such means his family learned about Kristallnacht and other events across Europe. Still, he and his family did not quite understand the broader ideological motivations for Nazi antisemitism.[32]

Many Soviet Jews did not appear to have the luxury to devote much attention to events in Germany. Bronia Gofman (born in 1918), deeply engaged in her studies at the Jewish Pedagogical Tekhnikum in Minsk, read reports from across the western Soviet border but did not have the time to fathom their meaning. "We read newspapers, we listened to the radio, but we didn't take it seriously," she remembered. The German invasion of Poland changed her perspectives.[33] Pesia Aizenshtadt, born in 1921, remembered hearing from a Minsk newspaper about *Mein Kampf* and Hitler's plans for Eastern Europe. Still, she felt secure. "We were all sure that Stalin would protect us."[34]

When asked about fears of a German invasion, many former Soviet citizens, Jews and Gentiles, remembered their sense of security. "I didn't think that the Germans will come to us!" Elizabeth Bershad, a Jew born 1923 in Vinnytsia, Ukraine, admitted decades later. "We were thinking that we were very strong, and we have a lot of munitions and everything. Nobody can come to our country."[35] Some were aware of Germany's rearmament and realized the threat Hitler posed for the rest of Europe, especially the Soviet Union. A young ethnic Belarusian émigré interviewed after the war by the Harvard Refugee Interview Project knew something about this (his statements were recorded anonymously, hence we do not know his name). He had learned about German militarization from his father's Jewish acquaintances who tracked such reports. This young man told an interviewer, "Before the war, for example, there were conversations about Hitler's rearmament, about the crusade against the Soviet Union, and so forth. Since my father was in contact with Jews, he got most of his information from them."[36]

Instances such as this anonymous account, where information was transformed into knowledge, appear to have been few. Nazi aggression was a European affair, the Soviet press seemed to imply. Despite the rhetoric building up to war with the capitalist world, including daily coverage of the Spanish Civil War, nothing pointed toward the possibility of German conquest of Soviet territory. The Third Reich was a remote land and the Soviet frontier was well guarded—or so newspapers asserted repeatedly. Frequent newspaper reports during the 1930s touted the strength of the Red Army and its border defenses. This posturing filtered into many media. Soviet Yiddish poet Zelik Akselrod penned a verse in 1939 titled "Lager" (camp), recounting the thoughts of an alert border guard. He closes with the lines:

> For bold Red Army fighters,
> For bravery,
> For clearheaded judgment,
> For secure borders of our land,
> To the last battle,
> For life and for death!
> We are ready!
> We are vigilant![37]

Soviet cinema also conveyed reassuring messages. Sergei Eisenstein's *Alexander Nevsky,* which premiered soon after Kristallnacht, told the medieval tale of Germanic defeat in the face of Slavic resistance. Director Eisenstein drew inspiration from the growing need to protect the Soviet Union from external aggression. In an English-language piece titled "My Subject Is Patriotism," published in 1939 in the Soviet journal *International Literature,* Eisenstein warned of the dangers present outside the Soviet Union: "The suppression of the independence of the so-called small countries, blood-drenched Spain, dismembered Czechoslovakia, China gasping in desperate struggle, these realities appear like a gory nightmare." He also connected the film's message to the events of Kristallnacht. "But every new day brings us news of greater outrages, greater savagery," Eisenstein noted. "It is hard to believe your eyes when you read of the unbridled ferocity of the Jewish pogroms in Germany, where before the eyes of the world hundreds of thousands of downtrodden people, shorn of human aid, are being wiped from the face of the earth."[38] Yet this article was not meant for Soviet readers. Furthermore, what warnings for the present could theater audiences find in this medieval tale, especially with its triumphalist ending?

At least one other film released in 1938, the less cinematically accomplished *If War Comes Tomorrow* (*Yesli zavtra voina . . .*), set its story in the present day. Here too, the inevitable victory did little to alert viewers of the true dangers posed by Nazi Germany. The film's format mixed a dramatized invasion by an unnamed aggressor (wearing stylized swastikas) with existing footage of the Red Army on maneuvers. Not only were the invaders easily repelled, they were beaten back to their own territory. The counter-invasion provoked a workers' uprising in the invaders' capital city (more existing footage, this time of German Communist rallies in pre-Hitler Berlin).[39] The film's drift into the fantastic undercuts the realities of the moment. The escapism offered by such films, especially for young people, is reflected in the recollections of Boris Falevich, a Jew from Slutsk. "Everyone dreamed to become a tank driver or a pilot," he remembered about how he and his friends were swept up by this propaganda.[40]

CENSORSHIP UNDER THE MOLOTOV-RIBBENTROP PACT

The Molotov-Ribbentrop Pact, announced to the world on August 24, 1939, was sold to the Soviet people as securing the Soviet Union's western border by eliminating the threat from "fascist Poland" and neutralizing any potential one posed by Hitler. Stalin had wanted better relations with Germany since the mid-1930s, and this desire increased in the aftermath of the Munich Agreement between Germany, Great Britain, France and Italy in September 1938. In practical terms, the Molotov-Ribbentrop Pact gave the Soviet Union the eastern half of Poland and beneficial trade opportunities with Nazi Germany. Yet the "liberation" of "western Belarus" and "western Ukraine" meant that the western border and associated defenses had to be shifted some three hundred kilometers. The Molotov-Ribbentrop Pact also brought the Third Reich up to the Soviet Union's doorstep.[41]

The pact also meant that criticism of Nazi Germany disappeared from Soviet public discourse to avoid angering Hitler. *Alexander Nevsky* and *If War Comes Tomorrow,* for example, were withdrawn from circulation. News of the persecution of Jews under German rule rapidly declined in Soviet media as early as May 1939 with the developing rapprochement with Hitler; it then disappeared with the signing of the pact.[42] Rumors took their place, delivered by the hundreds of thousands of refugees from western Poland, most of them Jews, who fled German rule into Soviet-occupied eastern Poland to escape Nazi brutality. Unfortunately, their audience among the native Jewish population frequently dismissed these stories, despite the reports on Kristallnacht and other events they had read before the war in Poland's Yiddish press. Older Jews in the territories newly annexed from Poland remembered the Germans to be good masters during the First World War. Why should it be different now, they rationalized. Most younger Jews were too engrossed in the new daily activities offered by the Soviets to pay attention to the refugees.[43]

Some of these Jewish refugees passed east of the pre-September 1939 Soviet border in fulfillment of education or labor commitments. They encountered Soviet populations that had read the newspaper accounts outlined above. Yet again their experiences during the first months of German rule in Poland were met with disbelief. Leon Shulkin (born 1923) encountered a few of these refugees in his home city of Minsk. They conveyed the terrible things the Germans were doing to Jews. "We couldn't imagine that it's going to happen in Russia because they had a—the Ribbentrop with Molotov—to sign an agreement," Shulkin recalled, halting phrases that seem to reflect his rationalized dismissal.[44]

Others gave more thought to the presence of these refugees. Raisa Gringauz (born 1932) was sent from Leningrad to her grandparents in Vitebsk in the summer of 1940. "Vitebsk started to be crowded with some strange people," she remembered decades later, "and when I started to ask my grandparents, they told me [these were] Polish people who are running from Germany." Their presence alerted the girl to Jews who lived outside the Soviet Union. But why were they running? Was Germany a threat to all Jews? Raisa's grandfather spoke misinformed words of reassurance. "'The *daytchen* [Germans] are educated people, are high-cultured people—they will not do anything wrong to us,'" she recalled her grandfather saying. Others retorted, what about these refugees? Has something changed?[45]

To Irina Zhivliuk, a Gentile born in 1925 in Minsk, the arrival of refugees after the annexation of eastern Poland prompted her to think something indeed had changed.[46] Yet where could she go to find believable information to confirm or dismiss her fears? Just as a news blackout barred any official reports about the treatment of Polish Jews, warnings of German aggression disappeared as well. This changed after the fall of France in June 1940. Thereafter oblique allusions reemerged in the press. By autumn 1940, Soviet newspapers printed short news items on the Germans' sustained campaign of aerial bombing of London and other cities.[47] The tone of these reports hinted at sympathy for the British. A story on the passage in March 1941 of the Lend-Lease Act in the United States was described as an example of international cooperation, not collaboration between capitalist exploiters as might be expected.[48]

But what inferences could readers draw from such stories? Could war come tomorrow? Unlike the bellicose rhetoric shouted in the 1930s, the subtle references in the Soviet press do not seem to have caught most people's attention. Instead, rumor overshadowed official narratives. The Germans' treatment of Jews in occupied countries remained solely the domain of gossip, although most tales were too strange or horrible to believe. This left the threat posed by German aggression. "Most of the people, they felt this way, yeah, most of them," Eli Schupak (born 1924) remembered about the belief that war between the Soviet Union and German was inevitable. But he was also old enough to know that this commonly held notion needed to remain secret. "It was against the policy to talk about it."[49] Bella Vaysman, although only a nine-year-old child, also was aware that talk of war between Germany and the Soviet Union not only carried risk, nobody truly believed it. "Some noises we got," she recalled, referring to a story published in a wall newspaper that she overheard some adults talking about. An alleged spy was caught spreading the rumor that Germany will attack the Soviet Union. "They called those people *provokatorii* [provocators]," she recalled. "That's why we were calmly living, and we didn't expect nothing!"[50] Still others simply could not believe that the Germans posed a threat. Elena Zibert, born in 1930 in Vitebsk, recalled in a 1998 interview that her family "didn't feel that there would be a war."[51] To put it another way, the war would not reach them, reflecting the false sense of security that many Soviet citizens continued to feel into 1941.

And the Soviets promoted such notions. "We didn't feel that we were in jeopardy," remembered Zelda Gordon, a native of Grodno in eastern Poland, who by June 1941 had lived under Soviet rule for only twenty months. "We never thought that Germany will attack the Russian army and we felt . . . more secure."[52] Indeed, as the Soviet media seemed to suggest, "We will protect you." Images of happy, safe children figured prominently in the pages of *Oktyabr* during the first months of 1941. One photo shows Białystok school students sharing a snowball fight with their teacher.[53] In another, toddlers eyed the camera as they were photographed in a Gomel crèche.[54] The same issue of the newspaper carried a picture of children in Britain, hiding in a trench and looking skyward in fear of German bombs.[55] To drive the point home, *Oktyabr* printed a series of articles on Soviet military forces in February 1941 under the bold headline "For Our Children."[56]

CONCLUSION

All dismissals and delusions shattered once the bombs started falling in the early morning of June 22, 1941. As Red Army forces retreated in chaos, Jews in the western borderland regions came to the stark realization that the Soviet system was not prepared to protect them. Soviet leaders in the previous two decades labored to convince their citizens that they acted to secure their homeland from internal and foreign attack. Newspapers kept readers informed of the growing dangers beyond the Soviet borders. Yet a certain hubris underlies these reports. Stories of the April Boycott and Nuremberg Laws told of what happened to Jews under capitalism and fascism in the west. Whether in the Yiddish- or Russian-language press, the news one column over on the page offered reassuring views of the Soviet Union as a land of opportunity. The Red Army was invincible. The high price was life under a harsh regime, compounded for Jews by emerging persecution.

Even with the extensive reportage on Kristallnacht, Soviet Jews seldom understood what specific threat the Nazis posed for their lives. Within six months, news of the persecution of German Jews declined and then ceased in the Soviet press due to Stalin's wish to draw up a non-aggression agreement with Nazi Germany. This news embargo continued after the Molotov-Ribbentrop Pact and Soviet occupation of eastern Poland in August–September 1939. Only rumors of German atrocities against Jews in western Poland reached Soviet Jews, and these were seldom believed. Hints of the military threat presented by Nazi Germany reemerged in newspapers after the fall of France in June 1940, but this was coupled with propaganda reinforcing trust in the strength of the Red Army. Soviet citizens, and Soviet Jews in particular, were left tragically vulnerable.

Notes

1. "Yidishe pogromen in Daytshland" [Jewish pogroms in Germany], *Oktyabr,* November 11, 1938, 1.
2. Elissa Bemporad, *Becoming Soviet: The Bolshevik Experiment in Minsk* (Bloomington: Indiana University Press, 2013); Gennady Estraikh, *In Harness: Yiddish Writers' Romance with Communism* (Syracuse: Syracuse University Press, 2005); David Shneer, *Yiddish and the Creation of Soviet Jewish Culture, 1918–1930* (Cambridge: Cambridge University Press, 2004); Anna Shternshis, *Soviet and Kosher: Jewish Popular Culture in the Soviet Union, 1923–1939* (Bloomington: Indiana University Press, 2006); Jeffrey Veidlinger, *The Moscow State Yiddish Theater: Jewish Culture on the Soviet Stage* (Bloomington: Indiana University Press, 2000).
3. Hirsh Reles, *Di yidish-sovetishe shrayber fun Vaysrusland* [The Soviet Yiddish writers of Belarus] (Minsk: I. P. Logvinov, 2004), 8.
4. Nicolas Werth, "The NKVD Mass Secret National Operations (August 1937–November 1938)," May 20, 2010, *SciencesPo, Mass Violence and Resistance—Research Network,* accessed November 14, 2017, http://www.sciencespo.fr/mass-violence-war-massacre-resistance/en/document/nkvd-mass-secret-national-operations-august-1937-november-1938; Nikita Petrov and Arsenii Roginskii, "The 'Polish Operation' of the NKVD, 1937–8," in *Stalin's Terror: High Politics and Mass Repression in the Soviet Union,* ed. Barry McLoughlin and Kevin McDermott (New York: Palgrave Macmillan, 2003), 153–72.
5. Hiroaki Kuromiya, *The Voices of the Dead: Stalin's Great Purges in the 1930s* (New Haven: Yale University Press, 2007), 204–16.
6. Bemporad, *Becoming Soviet,* 194; Estraikh, *In Harness,* 169.
7. Viacheslav Selimenev and Arkadii Zeltser, "The Liquidation of Yiddish Schools in Belorussia and Jewish Reaction," *Jews in Eastern Europe* 41, no. 1 (2000): 77.
8. Viacheslav Selimenev and Arkadii Zeltser, "The Jewish Intelligentsia and the Liquidation of Yiddish Schools in Belorussia, 1938," *Jews in Eastern Europe* 43, no. 3 (2001): 80 n. 7.
9. "Di KomPartay rufn tsu an algemaynem shtreyk kegn der fashistisher Hitler-regirung" [The Communist Party call for a general strike against the fascist Hitler government], *Oktyabr,* February 2, 1933, 1; "Kryvavaya sutychka pamizh pabochymi i natsyyanal-satsyyalistami ŭ Breslaŭli" [Crooked clashes between workers and National Socialists in Breslau], *Vitsebski praletarii,* April 12, 1933, 4; "Ablavy, aryshty i katarzhnyya prysudy" [Round-ups, arrests, and floods of verdicts], *Vitsebski praletarii,* April 27, 1933, 4.
10. "Tsvishn toyznter andere" [Among thousands of others], *Oktyabr,* December 17 and 19, 1933, January 18 and 19, 1934; Joseph Robert White, "Leipzig," in *The United States Holocaust Memorial Museum Encyclopedia of Camps and Ghettos, 1933–1945,* vol. 1, *Early Camps, Youth Camps, and Concentration Camps and Subcamps*

under the SS-Business Administration Main Office (WVHA), Part A, ed. Geoffrey P. Megargee (Bloomington: Indiana University Press, 2009), 117.
11. "Organizirter fashistisher anti-Yidisher boikot" [Organized fascist anti-Jewish boycott], *Oktyabr*, April 1, 1933, 1.
12. "Der anti-Yidisher boikot viklt zikh fanander" [The anti-Jewish boycott winds up], *Oktyabr*, April 2, 1933, 1.
13. "Pratim vegn der neyer pogrom-khvalie in Daytshland" [Details about the new pogrom-wave in Germany], *Oktyabr*, July 17, 1935, 1; "Di pogrom-khvalie in Daytshland doyert" [The pogrom-wave in Germany continues], *Oktyabr*, July 24, 1935, 1.
14. "Vayterdike farsharfung fun der inerlekher politisher lage in Daytshland" [Successive intensifications of the domestic political situation in Germany], *Der emes*, July 24, 1935, 1.
15. "Mitlalterlekhe gezetsn in Hitler-reykhstag" [Medieval laws in Hitler's Reichstag], *Oktyabr*, September 17, 1935, 1.
16. S. Volfson, "Di rasn-teories fun fashizm un der klasnkamf" [The racial theories of fascism and the class struggle], *Afn visnshaftlekhn front* [On the scientific front], *Biuleten fun institut far yidisher proletarisher kultur ba der Vaysrusisher visnshaftakademie* [Bulletin of the institute for Jewish proletarian culture with the Belarus science academy] no. 5–6 (Minsk, 1934): 30.
17. "Vyseleniye Polyakov iz Germanii" [Eviction of Poles from Germany], *Sovetskaya Belorussiya*, November 1, 1938, 4; "Izgnaniye yevreyev iz Germanii" [Expelled Jews from Germany], *Sovetskaya Belorussiya*, November 2, 1938, 1.
18. "Izdevatel'stva germanskikh vlastei and polyakami" [Harassment of Poles by German authorities], *Sovetskaya Belorussiya*, November 11, 1938, 1.
19. "Yidishe pogromen in Daytshland," *Oktyabr*, November 11, 1938.
20. "Yevreiskiye pogrom v Germanii" [Jewish pogroms in Germany], *Sovetskaya Belorussiya*, November 1, 1938, 1.
21. "A khvalie fun Yidishe pogromen in Daytshland" [A wave of Jewish pogroms in Germany], *Oktyabr*, November 12, 1938, 1; "Volna yevreiskikh pogromov v Germanii" [Wave of Jewish pogroms in Germany], *Sovetskaya Belorussiya*, November 12, 1938, 1.
22. "Yidishe pogromen in Daytchland" [Jewish pogroms in Germany], *Oktyabr*, November 15, 1938, 1.
23. "Naye gezetsn vegn yidn in fashistishn Daytshland" [New laws against Jews in fascist Germany], *Oktyabr*, November 14, 1938, 1; "Razul band fashistskikh pogromshchikov" [Riotous bands of fascist pogromists], *Sovetskaya Belorussiya*, November 14, 1938, 1.
24. "Di oyslendishe prese vegn di yidishe pogromen in Daytshland" [The foreign press on the Jewish pogroms in Germany], *Oktyabr*, November 14, 1938, 1.
25. "Angliiskaya pechat' o yevreiskikh pogromakh v Germanii" [English reports about Jewish pogroms in Germany], *Sovetskaya Belorussiya*, November 14, 1938, 1.

26. "Yidishe pogromen in fashistishn Daytshland" [Jewish pogroms in fascist Germany], *Oktyabr,* November 14, 1938, 1.
27. "Ayntslheytn fun di Yidishe pogromen in Daytshland" [Particulars of the Jewish pogroms in Germany], *Oktyabr,* November 15, 1938, 1.
28. "Vozmushcheniye vo frantsik" [Outrage among the French], *Sovetskaya Belorussiya,* November 14, 1938, 1.
29. "Di oyslendishe prese," *Oktyabr,* November 14, 1938.
30. "Yidishe pogromen in fashistishn Daytshland," *Oktyabr,* November 14, 1938.
31. Aleksandr Lyubich, San Mateo, California, November 7, 2005, interview 52926, segments 23–24, JFCS Holocaust Center collection, USC Shoah Foundation Institute, Visual History Archive, 22:25–23:05.
32. Alexander Feldman, Dedham, Massachusetts, December 15, 1996, interview 23356, segment 7, USC Shoah Foundation collection, USC Shoah Foundation Institute, Visual History Archive (hereafter USC SF/VHA), tape 2, 11:20–12:40.
33. Bronia Gofman, Minsk, Belarus, April 12, 1997, interview 30315, USC SF/VHA, tape 1, segments 8–9, 6:10–7:45.
34. Pesia Aizenshtadt, Minsk, Belarus, February 14, 1997, interview 29732, USC SF/VHA, tape 2, segments 37–38, 5:55–6:15.
35. Elizabeth Bershad, Brooklyn, New York, November 16, 1998, interview 48164, USC SF/VHA, tape 2, segments 31–32, 0:53–1:21.
36. Harvard Project on the Soviet Social System, Schedule A, Vol. 11, Case 142, Male, 27, Byelorussian, Elementary school teacher, Widener Library, Harvard University, 30.
37. Zelik Akselrod, "Lager" [Camp], in *Ordentregerishe Vaysrusland* [Valorous worker Belarus], ed. Zelik Akselrod and Hirsh Kamenetski (Minsk: Melukhe-farlag fun Vaysrusland, 1939), 240.
38. Sergei Eisenstein, "My Subject is Patriotism," *International Literature* (1939): no. 2, 90–93, repr. in *The Film Factory: Russian and Soviet Cinema in Documents, 1896–1939,* ed. Richard Taylor and Ian Christie (New York: Routledge, 1994), 398.
39 *Alexander Nevsky,* dir. Sergei Eisenstein and Dmitri Vasilyev, Mosfilm, 1938, DVD; Catherine Merridale, *Ivan's War: Life and Death in the Red Army, 1939–1945* (New York: Picador, 2006), 24–26.
40. Boris Falevich, Slutsk, Belarus, September 5, 1997, interview 39468, USC SF/VHA, tape 2, segments 36–37, 4:50–5:20.
41. Jan Gross, *Revolution from Abroad: The Soviet Conquest of Poland's Western Ukraine and Western Belorussia* (Princeton: Princeton University Press, 2002); Dov Levin, *The Lesser of Two Evils: Eastern European Jewry under Soviet Rule, 1939–1941,* trans. Naftali Greenwood (Philadelphia: Jewish Publication Society, 1995); Roger Moorhouse, *The Devils' Alliance: Hitler's Pact with Stalin, 1939–1941* (New York: Basic Books, 2014); Timothy Snyder, *Bloodlands: Europe Between Hitler and Stalin* (New York: Basic Books, 2010); Keith Sword, ed., *The Soviet Takeover of the Polish Eastern Provinces, 1939–41* (New York: St. Martin's Press, 1991).

42. Mordechai Altshuler, "The Distress of Jews in the Soviet Union in the Wake of the Molotov-Ribbentrop Pact," *Yad Vashem* 36, no. 2 (2008): 76; Matityahu Mintz, "The Soviet State and the Plight of the Jews during the 'Classified Period'—September 1939–June 1941—Rescue or Abandon?" *Moreshet: Journal of the Study of the Holocaust and Antisemitism* 11 (2014): 85; Ben-Cion Pinchuk, "Soviet Media on the Fate of Jews in Nazi-Occupied Territory (1939–1941)," *Yad Vashem Studies* 11 (1976): 222–23; Feldman, interview, segment 7, tape 2; 12:45–13:37.
43. Jeffrey Koerber, *Borderland Generation: Soviet and Polish Jews under Hitler* (Syracuse: Syracuse University Press, forthcoming).
44. Leon Shulkin, Vaucluse, Sydney, New South Wales, Australia, May 9, 1996, interview 14779, USC SF/VHA, tape 1, segment 25, 24:25–24:55.
45. Raisa Gringauz, Casper, Wyoming, March 10, 2000, interview 50727, USC SF/VHA, tape 1, segments 17–19, 16:08–18:55.
46. Irina Zhivliuk, Kyiv, Ukraine, October 22, 1998, interview 50057, USC SF/VHA, tape 1, segments 19–20, 18:55–19:25.
47. "Angla-Germanskaya vaina—Germanskiya pavedamlenni" [Anglo-German war—German reports], *Vitsebski rabochy*, September 7, 1940, 1.
48. "Tsvishnfelkerlekher iberzikht" [Cooperation between peoples], *Oktyabr*, March 29, 1941.
49. Eli Schupak, New York, New York, June 20, 1995, interview 3399, USC SF/VHA, tape 1, segment 29, 28:12–28:23.
50. Bella Vaysman, Morton Grove, Illinois, November 13, 1995, interview 8603, USC SF/VHA, tape 1, segment 10, 9:32–10:11.
51. Elena Zibert, Vitebsk, Belarus, May 3, 1998, interview 49456, USC SF/VHA, segment 16, tape 1, 15:10–15:15.
52. Zelda Gordon, Beverly Hills, California, July 15, 1994, interview 15, USC SF/VHA, tape 1, segment 5, 15:15–15:26.
53. *Oktyabr*, January 1, 1941.
54. *Oktyabr*, January 12, 1941, 3–4.
55. Ibid.
56. "Far undzere kinder" [For our children], *Oktyabr*, February 18, 1941, 3.

Bibliography

Newspapers

Nearly complete print runs of *Oktyabr* (Minsk) on microfilm are found at the Dorot Jewish Division of the New York Public Library (late 1920s through 1935) and the YIVO Institute for Jewish Research at the Center for Jewish Research (1935 through spring 1941). The Library of Congress (European Reading Room, Thomas Jefferson Building) has microfilms of *Sovetskaya Belorussiya* (Minsk), also in a nearly complete print run. Very limited surviving paper copies of local Vitebsk newspapers are found at the *Gosudarstvennyi Arkhiv Vitebskoi Oblasti* (State Archive Vitebsk Oblast), Vitebsk, Belarus: *Vitsebski praletarii* (Fond 2285, opus 2, delo 125), in a partial print run for 1933; *Vitsebski rabochy* (Fond 2289, opus 2, delo 132), in single issues for 1940.

"A khvalie fun Yidishe pogromen in Daytshland" [A wave of Jewish pogroms in Germany]. *Oktyabr,* November 12, 1938, 1.

"Ablavy, aryshty i katarzhnyya prysudy" [Round-ups, arrests, and floods of verdicts]. *Vitsebski praletarii,* April 27, 1933, 4.

"Angla-Germanskaya vaina—Germanskiya pavedamlenni" [Anglo-German war—German reports]. *Vitsebski rabochy,* September 7, 1940, 1.

"Angliiskaya pechat' o yevreiskikh pogromakh v Germanii" [English reports about Jewish pogroms in Germany]. *Sovetskaya Belorussiya,* November 14, 1938, 1.

"Ayntslheytn fun di Yidishe pogromen in Daytshland" [Particulars of the Jewish pogroms in Germany]. *Oktyabr,* November 15, 1938, 1.

"Der anti-Yidisher boikot viklt zikh fanander" [The anti-Jewish boycott winds up]. *Oktyabr,* April 2, 1933, 1.

"Di KomPartay rufn tsu an algemaynem shtreyk kegn der fashistisher Hitler-regirung" [The Communist Party call for a general strike against the fascist Hitler government]. *Oktyabr,* February 2, 1933, 1.

"Di oyslendishe prese vegn di yidishe pogromen in Daytshland" [The foreign press on the Jewish pogroms in Germany]. *Oktyabr,* November 14, 1938, 1.

"Di pogrom-khvalie in Daytshland doyert" [The pogrom-wave in Germany continues]. *Oktyabr,* July 24, 1935, 1.

"Far undzere kinder" [For our children]. *Oktyabr,* February 18, 1941, 3.

"Izdevatel'stva germanskikh vlastei and polyakami" [Harassment of Poles by German authorities]. *Sovetskaya Belorussiya,* November 11, 1938, 1.

"Izgnaniye yevreyev iz Germanii" [Expelled Jews from Germany]. *Sovetskaya Belorussiya,* November 2, 1938, 1.

"Kryvavaya sutychka pamizh pabochymi i natsyyanal-satsyyalistami ŭ Breslaŭli" [Crooked clashes between workers and National Socialists in Breslau]. *Vitsebski praletarii,* April 12, 1933, 4.

"Mitlalterlekhe gezetsn in Hitler-reykhstag" [Medieval laws in Hitler's Reichstag]. *Oktyabr,* September 17, 1935, 1.

"Naye gezetsn vegn yidn in fashistishn Daytshland" [New laws against Jews in fascist Germany]. *Oktyabr,* November 14, 1938, 1.

Oktyabr, January 1, 1941.

Oktyabr, January 12, 1941, 3–4.

"Organizirter fashistisher anti-Yidisher boikot" [Organized fascist anti-Jewish boycott]. *Oktyabr,* April 1, 1933, 1.

"Pratim vegn der neyer pogrom-khvalie in Daytshland" [Details about the new pogrom-wave in Germany]. *Oktyabr,* July 17, 1935, 1.

"Razul band fashistskikh pogromshchikov" [Riotous bands of fascist pogromists]. *Sovetskaya Belorussiya,* November 14, 1938, 1.

"Revoliutsionere protest-demonstratsies in gants Daytshland" [Revolutionary protest demonstrations in all of Germany]. *Oktyabr,* February 2, 1933, 1.

"Tsvishn toyznter andere" [Among thousands of others]. *Oktyabr,* December 17 and 19, 1933, January 18 and 19, 1934.

"Tsvishnfelkerlekher iberzikht" [Cooperation between peoples]. *Oktyabr,* March 29, 1941.

"Vayterdike farsharfung fun der inerlekher politisher lage in Daytshland" [Successive intensifications of the domestic political situation in Germany]. *Der emes,* July 24, 1935, 1.

"Volna yevreiskikh pogromov v Germanii" [Wave of Jewish pogroms in Germany]. *Sovetskaya Belorussiya,* November 12, 1938, 1.

"Vozmushcheniye vo frantsik" [Outrage among the French]. *Sovetskaya Belorussiya,* November 14, 1938, 1.

"Vyseleniye Polyakov iz Germanii" [Eviction of Poles from Germany]. *Sovetskaya Belorussiya,* November 1, 1938, 4.

"Yevreiskiye pogrom v Germanii" [Jewish pogroms in Germany]. *Sovetskaya Belorussiya,* November 1, 1938, 1.

"Yidishe pogromen in Daytchland" [Jewish pogroms in Germany]. *Oktyabr,* November 15, 1938, 1.

"Yidishe pogromen in Daytshland" [Jewish pogroms in Germany]. *Oktyabr,* November 11, 1938, 1.

"Yidishe pogromen in fashistishn Daytshland" [Jewish pogroms in fascist Germany]. *Oktyabr,* November 14, 1938, 1.

Interviews

Aizenshtadt, Pesia. Minsk, Belarus, February 14, 1997. Interview 29732. Segments 37–39. USC Shoah Foundation collection, USC Shoah Foundation Institute, Visual History Archive.

Bershad, Elizabeth. Brooklyn, New York, November 16, 1998. Interview 48164. Segments 31–32. USC Shoah Foundation collection, USC Shoah Foundation Institute, Visual History Archive.

Falevich, Boris. Slutsk, Belarus, September 5, 1997. Interview 39468. Segment 37. USC Shoah Foundation collection, USC Shoah Foundation Institute, Visual History Archive.

Feldman, Alexander. Dedham, Massachusetts, December 15, 1996. Interview 23356. Segment 7. USC Shoah Foundation collection, USC Shoah Foundation Institute, Visual History Archive.

Gofman, Bronia. Minsk, Belarus, April 12, 1997. Interview 30315. Segments 8–10. USC Shoah Foundation collection, USC Shoah Foundation Institute, Visual History Archive.

Gordon, Zelda. Beverly Hills, California, July 15, 1994. Interview 15. Segment 4. USC Shoah Foundation collection, USC Shoah Foundation Institute, Visual History Archive.

Gringauz, Raisa. Casper, Wyoming, March 10, 2000. Interview 50727. Segment 17. USC Shoah Foundation collection, USC Shoah Foundation Institute, Visual History Archive.

Harvard Project on the Soviet Social System, Schedule A, Vol. 11, Case 142. Male, 27, Byelorussian, Elementary school teacher. Widener Library, Harvard University.

Lyubich, Aleksandr. San Mateo, California, November 7, 2005. Interview 52926. Segments 23–24. JFCS Holocaust Center collection, USC Shoah Foundation Institute, Visual History Archive.

Schupak, Eli. New York, New York, June 20, 1995. Interview 3399. Segments 29–31. USC Shoah Foundation collection, USC Shoah Foundation Institute, Visual History Archive.

Shulkin, Leon. Vaucluse, Sydney, New South Wales, Australia, May 9, 1996. Interview 14779. Segment 25. USC Shoah Foundation collection, USC Shoah Foundation Institute, Visual History Archive.

Vaysman, Bella. Morton Grove, Illinois, November 13, 1995. Interview 8603. Segments 10–11. USC Shoah Foundation collection, USC Shoah Foundation Institute, Visual History Archive.

Zhivliuk, Irina. Kyiv, Ukraine, October 22, 1998. Interview 50057. Segments 19–20. USC Shoah Foundation collection, USC Shoah Foundation Institute, Visual History Archive.

Zibert, Elena. Vitebsk, Belarus, May 3, 1998. Interview 49456. Segments 15–16. USC

Shoah Foundation collection, USC Shoah Foundation Institute, Visual History Archive.

Secondary Sources

Akselrod, Zelik. "Lager" [Camp]. In *Ordentregerishe Vaysrusland* [Valorous worker Belarus], edited by Zelik Akselrod and Hirsh Kamenetski, 240. Minsk: Melukhefarlag fun Vaysrusland, 1939.

Altshuler, Mordechai. "The Distress of Jews in the Soviet Union in the Wake of the Molotov-Ribbentrop Pact." *Yad Vashem* 36, no. 2 (2008): 73–113.

Bemporad, Elissa. *Becoming Soviet: The Bolshevik Experiment in Minsk*. Bloomington: Indiana University Press, 2013.

Davies, Sarah. *Popular Opinion in Stalin's Russia: Terror, Propaganda, and Dissent, 1934–1941*. Cambridge: Cambridge University Press, 1997.

Eisenstein, Sergei. "My Subject is Patriotism." *International Literature* (1939): no. 2, 90–93. Reprinted in *The Film Factory: Russian and Soviet Cinema in Documents, 1896–1939*, edited by Richard Taylor and Ian Christie, 398–401. New York: Routledge, 1994.

Estraikh, Gennady. *In Harness: Yiddish Writers' Romance with Communism*. Syracuse: Syracuse University Press, 2005.

Figes, Orlando. *The Whisperers: Private Life in Stalin's Russia*. New York: Metropolitan Books, 2007.

Fitzpatrick, Sheila. *Everyday Stalinism. Ordinary Life in Extraordinary Times: Soviet Russia in the 1930s*. Oxford: Oxford University Press, 1999.

Gross, Jan. *Revolution from Abroad: The Soviet Conquest of Poland's Western Ukraine and Western Belorussia*. Princeton: Princeton University Press, 2002.

Kenez, Peter. *Cinema and Soviet Society: From the Revolution to the Death of Stalin*. London: I. B. Tauris, 2008.

Koerber, Jeffrey. *Borderland Generation: Soviet and Polish Jews under Hitler*. Syracuse: Syracuse University Press, forthcoming.

Kuromiya, Hiroaki. *The Voices of the Dead: Stalin's Great Purges in the 1930s*. New Haven: Yale University Press, 2007.

Levin, Dov. *The Lesser of Two Evils: Eastern European Jewry under Soviet Rule, 1939–1941*. Translated by Naftali Greenwood. Philadelphia: Jewish Publication Society, 1995.

Merridale, Catherine. *Ivan's War: Life and Death in the Red Army, 1939–1945*. New York: Picador, 2006.

Mintz, Matityahu. "The Soviet State and the Plight of the Jews during the 'Classified Period'—September 1939–June 1941—Rescue or Abandon?" *Moreshet: Journal of the Study of the Holocaust and Antisemitism* 11 (2014): 63–97.

Moorhouse, Roger. *The Devils' Alliance: Hitler's Pact with Stalin, 1939–1941*. New York: Basic Books, 2014.

Moss, Kenneth B. *Jewish Renaissance in the Russian Revolution*. Cambridge: Harvard University Press, 2009.

Petrov, Nikita, and Arsenii Roginskii. "The 'Polish Operation' of the NKVD, 1937–8." In *Stalin's Terror: High Politics and Mass Repression in the Soviet Union*, edited by Barry McLoughlin and Kevin McDermott, 153–72. New York: Palgrave Macmillan, 2003.

Pinchuk, Ben-Cion. "Soviet Media on the Fate of Jews in Nazi-Occupied Territory (1939–1941)." *Yad Vashem Studies* 11 (1976): 221–33.

Reles, Hirsh. *Di yidish-sovetishe shrayber fun Vaysrusland* [The Soviet Yiddish writers of Belarus]. Minsk: I. P. Logvinov, 2004.

Selimenev, Viacheslav, and Arkadii Zeltser. "The Jewish Intelligentsia and the Liquidation of Yiddish Schools in Belorussia, 1938." *Jews in Eastern Europe* 43, no. 3 (2000): 78–97.

———. "The Liquidation of Yiddish Schools in Belorussia and Jewish Reaction." *Jews in Eastern Europe* 41, no. 1 (2000): 74–111.

Shneer, David. *Yiddish and the Creation of Soviet Jewish Culture, 1918–1930*. Cambridge: Cambridge University Press, 2004.

Shternshis, Anna. *Soviet and Kosher: Jewish Popular Culture in the Soviet Union, 1923–1939*. Bloomington: Indiana University Press, 2006.

Snyder, Timothy. *Bloodlands: Europe Between Hitler and Stalin*. New York: Basic Books, 2010.

Sword, Keith, ed. *The Soviet Takeover of the Polish Eastern Provinces, 1939–41*. New York: St. Martin's Press, 1991.

Veidlinger, Jeffrey. *The Moscow State Yiddish Theater: Jewish Culture on the Soviet Stage*. Bloomington: Indiana University Press, 2000.

Volfson, S. "Di rasn-teories fun fashizm un der klasnkamf" [The racial theories of fascism and the class struggle], *Afn visnshaftlekhn front* [On the scientific front]. *Biuleten fun institut far yidisher proletarisher kultur ba der Vaysrusisher visnshaft-akademie* [Bulletin of the institute for Jewish proletarian culture with the Belarus science academy] no. 5–6. Minsk, 1934.

Werth, Nicolas. "The NKVD Mass Secret National Operations (August 1937–November 1938)." May 20, 2010. *SciencesPo, Mass Violence and Resistance—Research Network*. Accessed November 14, 2017. http://www.sciencespo.fr/mass-violence-war-massacre-resistance/en/document/nkvd-mass-secret-national-operations-august-1937-november-1938.

White, Joseph Robert. "Leipzig." In *The United States Holocaust Memorial Museum Encyclopedia of Camps and Ghettos, 1933–1945*. Vol. 1, *Early Camps, Youth Camps, and Concentration Camps and Subcamps under the SS-Business Administration Main Office (WVHA), Part A*, edited by Geoffrey P. Megargee, 117–18. Bloomington: Indiana University Press, 2009.

Films

Alexander Nevsky. Dir. Sergei Eisenstein and Dmitri Vasilyev. Mosfilm, 1938. DVD.
Yesli zavtra voina . . . (*If War Came Tomorrow*). Dir. Lazar Antsi-Polovskiy, Georgiy Beryozko, Efim Dzigan, and Nikolay Karmazinskiy. Mosfilm, 1938. Accessed 24 July 2018. https://www.youtube.com/watch?v=NidxI8xyaPk.

CHAPTER 8

The Absence of "Kristallnacht" and Its Aftermath in BBC German-language Broadcasts during 1938–1939

by Stephanie Seul

The anti-Jewish pogrom staged by the Nazis during the night of November 9–10, 1938 was carried out in the full glare of world publicity.[1] The Nazis made no attempt to conceal evidence of the atrocities, which subsequently became known as Kristallnacht, or Night of Broken Glass.[2] The Nazi terror deeply shocked the British government and public, particularly as it came only a few weeks after the Munich Agreement, which Prime Minister Neville Chamberlain considered a first step towards a peaceful settlement with Hitler. The pogrom helped, more than anything else, to harden British opinion towards Germany.[3]

Given the development of Nazi anti-Jewish policy, the role of anti-Semitism in Nazi domestic propaganda,[4] and the revulsion felt in Great Britain about the pogrom, one might presume that Kristallnacht would have played a crucial role in the British radio broadcasts addressed to the German people. However, while the British press reported extensively and critically, the pogrom never took on prominence in German-language broadcasts. In order to understand the factors that influenced the British Broadcasting Corporation's (BBC) reporting on Kristallnacht, and indeed on all Jewish topics, one needs to take a closer look at British diplomacy towards Germany during 1938–39 and the role the BBC played therein.

At the request of the government, the BBC started broadcasting in German at the height of the Sudeten crisis on September 27, 1938, when war and peace hung in the balance.[5] Chamberlain's principal reason for continuing the broadcasts after the Munich Agreement on September 29, 1938 was the realization that Britain and France were militarily unprepared for war against Germany. "Propaganda"—a term widely used at that time for British government publicity—offered a small chance to avert war by winning over the German public. Still, the Munich Agreement did not dispel Chamberlain's mistrust regarding Hitler's intentions. The BBC broadcasts therefore aimed to inform the German public of British efforts to appease Hitler and to avoid war. They sought to strengthen the desire of the Germans for peace and to arouse doubts and criticism in regard to Hitler's aggressive foreign policy. Moreover, the propaganda campaign was to warn Hitler that he would risk opposition from his own people if he provoked a war involving the British Empire and France, and thus induce the dictator to seek a peaceful solution to his territorial claims.

The newly created German Service was closely supervised by the Foreign Office. Whitehall never made it a secret that it considered the BBC broadcasts a propaganda instrument of the state. The close collaboration between the BBC and Whitehall meant that a consensus evolved in both institutions regarding the BBC's treatment of the Nazi Jewish persecution. Although with hindsight one might assume that the terror against the Jews would seem to offer a strong moral argument against Nazism, reporting the Jewish persecution ran counter to the British propaganda strategy. Importantly, all information broadcast had to serve the aim of supporting Chamberlain's appeasement policy by stimulating the resistance of the German public against the Nazi regime. As we shall see, continually informing the Germans about Nazi anti-Jewish policy was thought to have the opposite effect. In considering the representation of Kristallnacht and its aftermath in the BBC's German-language broadcasts, we therefore have to bear in mind that the coverage of the pogrom was determined by Chamberlain's foreign policy. Moreover, in order to better understand the limitations of the reporting, we also need to take a look at responses of the British domestic media to Kristallnacht.

BRITISH RESPONSES TO KRISTALLNACHT

The reaction of the British government to Kristallnacht was muted.[6] While the United States recalled its ambassador—without, however, breaking off diplomatic relations altogether—London did not issue any official protest to Berlin. Certainly, the British government was well-informed. The British embassy and consulates in Germany reported extensively about Kristallnacht, the reaction of the German public to it, and Goebbels' anti-British propaganda campaign in the aftermath of the pogrom accusing British politicians of warmongering and attacking British policy in Palestine. On November 13, Oliver Harvey, the Private Secretary of Foreign Secretary Lord Halifax, noted in his diary: "The Jewish pogroms have shaken up world opinion—even the City—as to the character of the criminal regime we are up against in Germany. Every scrap of information, secret and public, we get from Germany now shows that the German Government are laughing at us, despising us and intending to dispossess us morally and materially from our world positions."[7]

There are three possible explanations as to why the British government refrained from officially protesting against Kristallnacht.[8] First, Whitehall feared that any public condemnation would only worsen the situation of the Jews. Sir George Ogilvie-Forbes, the head of the British embassy in Berlin, warned on November 13 "that inevitable public condemnation and censure should be tempered by consideration that it will be visited on the unfortunate Jews whose sufferings will be increased."[9] Second, London viewed Nazi anti-Jewish policy as an internal German affair, which should not stand in the way of an Anglo-German understanding. Antisemitism was regarded as one of the central dogmas of the Nazi faith, and as long as the majority of the German people supported Nazism, Great Britain had no right to interfere.[10] Ogilvie-Forbes informed Foreign Secretary Halifax on November 10 that "the treatment of German Jews is fiercely and jealously regarded as a purely internal matter. As you are aware from his recent speeches, the Chancellor is at present in an aggressive and anti-British mood [...]. In short, it is a wasp's nest in which we would be ill-advised in our own interests and that of the Jews themselves gratuitously to poke our fingers."[11] And third, Chamberlain was concerned not to aggravate the already tense relations between Great Britain and Germany. Provoking the Nazi regime had to be avoided at all costs; it was therefore out of the question to criticise the pogrom in official statements. At a meeting of the Cabinet's Foreign Policy Committee on November 14, 1938 Chamberlain ruled out any official protest against Nazi anti-Jewish policy because Great Britain was militarily not in a position to frighten Germany.[12]

Parliament debated the pogrom on November 14 and 21, condemning in strong terms the Nazi atrocities and calling on the British government to secure a common refugee policy amongst the nations. When the Prime Minister was asked by a Labour MP whether he would consider issuing a statement condemning the pogrom and making known to the German government the deep feeling of horror aroused in Britain, Chamberlain replied evasively and stressed instead that the British embassy had been instructed to protest to the German Foreign Office against the allegations in the German press that former British ministers such as Winston Churchill, Duff Cooper and Anthony Eden had been involved in the murder of Ernst vom Rath. Goebbels apologized reluctantly in a statement made to the British news agency Reuters, but no German newspaper was allowed to reprint it.[13]

Still, as a result of Kristallnacht, Great Britain relaxed its immigration policy. About forty thousand Jewish refugees were admitted before the outbreak of war, among them some ten thousand unaccompanied children, who arrived under the *Kindertransport* scheme.[14] Yet, entry of Jewish refugees into Palestine—a League of Nations mandated territory under British rule since 1920—remained strictly limited. Palestine was the scene of the Arab rebellion during 1936–39, which developed into a major revolt against the British (and the Jews) in 1937. Hence, London did all it could to limit Jewish immigration for fear of alienating the Arabs and endangering its strategic interests in the Middle East.[15]

While the British government sought to maintain friendly relations with Berlin and therefore refrained from openly criticizing the Nazis, Kristallnacht caused an outcry of indignation in the press. British newspapers brought detailed reports on their front and inside pages, and they printed photographs of the damage inflicted on Jewish property. As several studies have shown, the bulk of British press opinion reflected the public outrage felt in regard to the pogrom and unanimously condemned the events.[16] In their extensive reportage, quality papers as well as tabloids made no secret that they disbelieved the official German story of a spontaneous public reaction against the Jews. Rather, they held the view that the murder of Ernst vom Rath in Paris was used as a pretext by the German government for encouraging the attack on the Jews. In the days and weeks after Kristallnacht, British papers continued to report extensively; the coverage included editorials, letters to the editors as well as reports about world reactions. Headlines in the *Manchester Guardian* read, among others: "Reprisals against Jews" (November 12), "Germany's Brutal Treatment of the Jews: Reaction of World Opinion" (November 18), "Reign of

Terror for German Jews: Organised Destruction of Property and Thousands of Arrests" (November 18).[17] As Andrew Sharf put it, "the dominant note struck by the British Press [...] was one of genuine moral outrage."[18]

Unlike the press, British newsreels were cautious in their treatment of the pogrom. As two studies have shown, this attitude was in part caused by the anti-Semitism prevalent in Great Britain at that time and reflected by the newsreels, and in part by Chamberlain's appeasement policy, which complicated the reporting on the Nazi persecution of the Jews and on Jewish refugees. Newsreel publicity given to refugees could be seen as criticizing the German government for its treatment of the Jews, while some sections of the British public disliked the arrival of more Jews in Great Britain.[19] Thus, with the exception of *British Paramount*, British newsreels did not report on Kristallnacht. The *Paramount* newsreel of November 21, 1938 focused on the international criticism of the pogrom and presented, among others, an American protest march followed by a statement from Rabbi Stephen Wise, the president of the American Jewish Congress and ardent critic of Nazi anti-Jewish policy, and Roosevelt's recalling of the American ambassador in Berlin to Washington.[20]

The Jewish refugee crisis in the aftermath of Kristallnacht received more attention. During December 1938 and January 1939, several sympathetic stories were brought about the arrival of Jewish refugee children in Britain. In this case, newsreels could be sure of public and government support: images of refugee children were more acceptable and raised less controversial concerns than those of adult refugees. Using emotive language, on December 5, a *Gaumont-British* newsreel focused on the need for the children to come to Great Britain and encouraged a sympathetic response of the British public to these unaccompanied minors.[21]

The response of the BBC Home Service to Kristallnacht was equally cautious. The BBC had been founded as an independent institution committed to impartial political reporting. With the rise of the totalitarian dictatorships in Europe during the 1930s, the BBC and the Foreign Office developed an informal agreement concerning foreign affairs, whereby the BBC had to obtain clearance of all news content concerning controversial issues. In order to comply with the needs of Chamberlain's appeasement policy, and because the BBC was widely perceived abroad as the official voice of the government, the Corporation developed an editorial policy which avoided negative publicity about Germany, and hence criticism of the persecution of the Jews. Moreover, as Guy Raz has argued in his study of the BBC's responses, "News of anti-Jewish persecution was never considered a broadcast priority by the BBC and the issue of its dissemination was never a source of contention between the BBC and the Foreign Office."[22] Both Raz and Jean Seaton have emphasized that latent anti-Semitism within the BBC was instrumental in preventing a more detailed and critical reporting on the Nazi persecution of the Jews.[23]

Hence, the BBC Home Service did not condemn Kristallnacht. On November 10, the pogrom was mentioned in one news bulletin without comment, but with considerable detail:

> After the death of Herr vom Rath [. . .], a national campaign of anti-Jewish rioting and arson began throughout Germany on November 10. Nine out of eleven synagogues in Berlin were set on fire, and synagogues were destroyed in many other parts of the country. Shop windows throughout Germany were smashed and goods destroyed or looted, and many shops and restaurants were also set on fire (. . .) all damage done during the attacks on Jewish property would be made good by the Jews themselves, and that from the beginning of next year no Jews would be allowed to engage in retail trades, export, business, commercial affairs or independent handicraft businesses or to act as managers.[24]

Moreover, on November 19 the Home Service reported in three news bulletins the press criticism in Germany of British reactions to the pogrom, and on November 21 three news bulletins recounted the statements made during the House of Commons debate on Jewish refugees.[25] However, the Home Service did not condemn the pogrom. In a letter to the Corporation, British Jews criticized the BBC for its failure to adequately convey the extent of the Nazi atrocities and the foreign reactions to them.[26] This criticism could also be applied to the BBC's German transmissions: nothing was broadcast that might have aroused the resentment of the Nazis.

KRISTALLNACHT IN THE BBC'S GERMAN-LANGUAGE BROADCASTS

During the first weeks of British German-language broadcasting little was reported about the plight of the German Jews.[27] The period not only witnessed a surge in Nazi anti-Jewish terror, but also the climax of Chamberlain's appeasement policy. As we have seen, Kristallnacht caused an outrage in the British press. This in turn provoked a massive press campaign by the Nazis against Great Britain in general, and against British policy in Palestine in particular. British diplomats gave a detailed account of Goebbels' anti-Jewish and anti-British propaganda campaign, which apparently was aimed at stirring up anti-Jewish and anti-British feelings among the German public.[28] An internal Foreign Office memorandum of November 23 stated: "The reaction of the democratic states to the recent anti-Jewish excesses in Germany has led to an outburst of anti-British sentiment in the German press. [. . .] The German press has concentrated on lurid accounts of terrorism throughout British imperial history, calling special attention to British military action in Palestine."[29] A British consul in Germany warned that this kind of propaganda would soon effectively poison the minds even of those Germans who had thus far been friendly to Great Britain.[30] Not surprisingly, in the aftermath of Kristallnacht, the BBC seemed more concerned about countering Goebbels' anti-British propaganda campaign than about reporting on the pogrom.

Little archival evidence is available to reconstruct what the BBC German Service did broadcast. There was certainly no lack of information. The British embassy and consulates in Germany reported extensively about Kristallnacht, the reaction of the German public to it, and Goebbels' anti-British press campaign.[31] On November 16, 1938, Ogilvie-Forbes informed Halifax that the aim of the anti-Jewish pogrom, which in his view was instigated and organized by the Nazi regime, was the complete elimination of the Jews. He also reported that the mass of the German people apparently did not support the anti-Jewish policy of the regime.[32] However, the BBC German Service refrained from criticizing the Nazi regime. The most it did was to report the reaction to, and condemnation of, the pogrom in foreign countries. Goebbels had forbidden German newspapers to publish foreign press criticism of the pogrom; all they were allowed was to reprint a news agency statement on the foreign press reports by *Deutsches Nachrichtenbüro*.[33] For the German public, the BBC German-language broadcasts were thus the only source of "uncensored news in their own language," as the Berlin correspondent of *The Scotsman* explained: "This afternoon a taxi-driver told me that he had heard the BBC account of the reaction in the United States and in European countries to the German pogrom, and it had been an 'eye-opener' for him."[34]

While the German Service refrained from critically reporting on the pogrom, the British government and the BBC seemed to be more concerned about German press attacks on Great Britain and British policy in Palestine than about the fate of German Jewry. Sources documenting the BBC's coverage of Kristallnacht are scarce, but there is ample evidence of the response given to the Nazi anti-British press campaign. Nazi propaganda sought to undermine British prestige and authority in Palestine and in the Arab world as a whole; it was therefore considered a serious threat to British political and strategic interests in the Middle East. It is thus not surprising that in the aftermath of Kristallnacht, Whitehall opposed any talk of a "Jewish problem" in the BBC German Service. Appeals for sympathy towards the Jews, the London government feared, would only have alarmed the Arabs further and were likely to undermine British policy towards Palestine.[35]

From the second half of November 1938 onwards, Whitehall launched a vigorous campaign to counter Nazi allegations of British terrorism in Palestine and to improve the negative image of Britain among the German public. As part of its concerted propaganda campaign against the Third Reich, the Foreign Office sent five hundred reprints of a speech in the House of Commons by Malcolm MacDonald, the Secretary of State for the Colonies, to Berlin for distribution to the German public by the British embassy and consulates.[36] It is possible that extracts of MacDonald's speech were also broadcast on the German Service. In his speech—explicitly designed to answer Goebbels' propaganda—MacDonald praised the conduct of British forces in Palestine despite difficult circumstances. He made also clear that the persecution of Jews in Germany could not be solved by allowing more Jews into Palestine.[37] Moreover, the BBC German Service broadcast four *Sonderberichte* (special reports) on the subject of Palestine in February 1939. Unfortunately, their content is lost.[38]

THE BBC GERMAN SERVICE AND THE "JEWISH PROBLEM" IN THE AFTERMATH OF KRISTALLNACHT

Although Ogilvie-Forbes, the head of the Berlin embassy, had condemned Kristallnacht in the strongest possible terms—"I can find no words strong enough in condemnation of the disgusting treatment of so many innocent people,"[39] he wrote—there is no evidence to show that British propaganda also condemned the pogrom. There were, however, voices urging Whitehall to report more critically about the Jewish persecution. On November 19, 1938, the Manchester branch of the League of Nations Union urged the British government "to broadcast by radio to the German nation the world's revulsion from the increased persecution and suffering of the Jews" and to call "on the humanitarian section of the German people to bring pressure on their Government with a view to calling a halt to the present forms of barbarism and cruelty on a helpless minority."[40] Moreover, on January 23, 1939, the Cabinet's Foreign Policy Committee had before them a memorandum by the Foreign Secretary containing information derived from secret German informants.[41] They urged the British government to intensify their German-language broadcasting. Kristallnacht, they said, had caused a great revulsion among the German people and accordingly the Nazi regime had suffered a loss of prestige. This opened the possibility for British propaganda to drive a wedge between the Nazi regime and the German people.[42] However, both suggestions to exploit Kristallnacht for the purpose of discrediting the Nazi regime in the eyes of the German public were not followed up. Whitehall felt that propaganda concerning Jews and a public condemnation of the pogrom would not only upset the Nazi regime and hence aggravate Anglo-German relations and the situation of the Jews in the Reich even further, but that it would also be resented by the German people and thus render British propaganda as a whole ineffective.

How the Nazis reacted to BBC reports about Jews was demonstrated on February 3, 1939, when the German Service told its listeners that since last September six thousand German refugees and 2,400 German refugee children had arrived in Great Britain. This is a rare and well-documented case of a BBC German broadcast concerning the Nazi persecution of the Jews and will therefore be discussed in more detail. The BBC Home Service, the German broadcast announced, would offer the same evening an electrical recording of the landing of a party of German refugee children and of their first impressions of England.[43] The broadcast titled "Children in Flight" and transmitted at 9:25 pm was widely publicized in the BBC magazine *Radio Times* (including a photograph of Jewish refugee children) and in the national and regional press.[44] The broadcast of the German Service was worded in the most inoffensive language and avoided to mention that the children were Jewish and fleeing from Nazi persecution. However, it also indirectly invited German listeners to tune in to the broadcast, as information was provided on the relevant transmitters and wavelengths. An extract of the broadcast, preserved in the Foreign Office archive, reads as follows:

> Last December the BBC recording van went to Dovercourt near Harwich where refugee children from Germany are looked after as they land in England, and where they are housed in the wooden chalets of a camp built for British holiday makers. A number of recordings were made of what these children had to say about their impressions of England, and their plans for the future. A programme of

these recordings, without any commentary, is being broadcast by the BBC tonight at 9.25 p.m. G.M.T. (10.25 p.m. central European time) on the Droitwich wave length (1500 metres) and also on the medium wave length (262.1 metres).[45]

As could be expected, Berlin protested sharply and Goebbels launched yet again a retaliatory press campaign attacking British imperial history and British policy in Palestine.[46] Several British newspapers reported on the broadcast and the Nazi reactions to it (frequently quoting a Reuter news agency message) and praised the Nazi protest as proof of the effectiveness of the BBC's German transmissions.[47] *The Courier and Advertiser* from Dundee in Scotland cited the *Völkischer Beobachter* saying: "Every method of wireless production was used to make political capital out of sympathy for the refugees. The broadcast was maliciously done and an indirect incitement against Germany."[48] The broadcast led to a diplomatic incident between Great Britain and the Third Reich; Berlin accused London of interfering illegally in internal German affairs.[49] Whitehall took this charge seriously, as in 1936 the League of Nations had passed a "Convention on the Use of Broadcasting in the Cause of Peace" which explicitly banned broadcasts intended "to incite the population of any territory to acts incompatible with the internal order or the security of a territory of a High Contracting Power."[50] Ogilvie-Forbes reported that the German ambassador in London had been instructed to make representations to Halifax."[51] The British embassy considered it unwise that the BBC had, on its own initiative, given "a propagandist value to the news."[52] Ogilvie-Forbes told the Foreign Office: "it was a mistake for the BBC to include in their broadcast a Jewish item of this kind which was bound to give the German Government an opportunity which was otherwise difficult to find to protest against our news bulletins. Such inclusion might weaken effect and popularity of these bulletins. I consider that we should concentrate on straight and objective news."[53]

It is remarkable that a British diplomat argued without a moment's hesitation that reports about the persecution of the Jews were not "straight and objective news," but anti-Nazi propaganda. In a further report, Ogilvie-Forbes came back to his charge that it had been a mistake of the BBC to broadcast a Jewish item, as this was "liable to [. . .] alienate the sympathies of German listeners."[54] His views were widely shared inside the Foreign Office. Rex Leeper of the News Department commented: "I think the BBC were not wise in doing this & we are warning them to keep off Jews."[55]

Apart from the necessities of foreign policy there was yet another factor limiting the coverage of the Jewish persecution. This was the widespread belief in Whitehall and in the BBC that the majority of Germans held anti-Semitic views and that propaganda sympathizing with Jews or appearing to be under Jewish influence was doomed to be ineffective. In August 1939 H. H. Stewart, the Director of the BBC Overseas Intelligence Department, reported after a visit to Berlin "that it was extremely damaging to mention or use talks by or about Jews [. . .]. People were still inclined to prefer anti-Jewish propaganda."[56] This view even led the BBC to decide that German-Jewish refugees should not be employed as speakers on the German Service, as it was thought that Germans were able to recognize Jews by the way they wrote or spoke.[57] The fact that the Foreign Office and the BBC uncritically accepted such reports—often amounting to no more than unverified gossip—testifies to the anti-Semitic views prevailing among the British governing elite and the BBC. The allusion to "Jewish accents" belongs to the standard repertoire of anti-Semites eager to show that Jews are different from the society they live in.[58] As Jean Seaton argued, "The BBC displayed, both before and during the war, views and decisions that were quite simply anti-Semitic."[59]

Consequently, British propaganda never attempted to combat anti-Semitism in German society or called for sympathy for the persecuted Jews. Its main target was the mass of politically indifferent Germans, not the small minority of those critical of the Nazi regime. For this reason, the Foreign Office and the BBC also opposed direct appeals to the German people on behalf of the Jews. Christopher Warner of the News Department explained in the summer of 1939 that "any direct appeal savours of subversive propaganda [. . . W]e shall indispose more listeners than we shall appeal to by playing up to the disaffected in Germany; if they are already disaffected they are not the people whom we most want to get at."[60] Hence, while the persecution of the Jews rapidly intensified during the last months of peace, driving tens of thousands of Jews into emigration, and many into suicide, the plight of German Jewry was rarely given publicity in the BBC's German-language broadcasts.[61]

EPILOGUE

Political events during 1939—the German invasion of Prague, the Allied military guarantee to Poland, and the German-Soviet non-aggression pact—soon eclipsed Kristallnacht. After the outbreak of war, the Nazis not only intensified the persecution of Jews inside the Reich, but extended it to the occupied territories, and especially to Poland. As before, however, the ongoing Nazi persecution of the Jews enjoyed only a low priority on the British political and propaganda agenda. Although Whitehall was well informed about each new step in Nazi anti-Jewish policy, very little was reported about the systematic persecution and murder of the Jews inside the Third Reich and throughout Europe.[62] Still, after the outbreak of war the constraints of the appeasement policy no longer applied. The BBC German Service was therefore more open in its criticism of the Nazi regime. This new liberty also found, among others, expression in the treatment of Kristallnacht.

While during 1938–39 the BBC had avoided references to the pogrom, in the first two years of the war it broadcast a number of talks and features in remembrance of Kristallnacht, which it denounced as "the biggest pogrom against Jews of all times."[63] On October 26, 1939 the Planning Committee of Department EH (as the British propaganda organization was called during 1939–41) discussed at length the vom Rath murder case "with a view to broadcasting the events which led to pogrom" on the occasion of the first anniversary of Kristallnacht.[64]

On the pogrom's first anniversary, the German Service broadcast a *Sonderbericht* in which a British officer, who had been in Vienna when the violence broke out, gave an account of his impressions. Offering a detailed description of the synagogue burning he witnessed, he declared that the fires had not been the acts of an angry populace but had been deliberately arranged by the Nazis.[65] "Die Ungehängten," a feature broadcast of mid-July 1941, described how under Himmler and Heydrich political murder and the murder of the insane and mortally ill had become daily practice in Germany. Importantly, it also described Himmler's directive regarding the pogrom—his instructions that the wealthy and influential male Jews were to be arrested—about three thousand in every larger city—and Jewish property destroyed; that the police and fire brigades were not to aid the Jews but rather see to it that deliberately-set fires did not damage non-Jewish houses.[66] A few months later a directive of the British propaganda organization Political Warfare Executive (PWE) for the German Service stated: "The anniversary of vom Rath"—the reference was to the November 1938 assassination in Prague of Nazi diplomat Ernst vom Rath by the Jewish youth Herschel Grynszpan, an event that served as an excuse for the November pogrom—"will enable us to stress the barbarism of reprisals on a whole people for an individual action and the conclusion that those who act on this policy unite everyone against them in hatred."[67]

An explanation for the curious focus on November 1938, rather than on the horrendous crimes the Nazis were committing during the war, might be that Kristallnacht had involved large numbers of German civilians witnessing what was happening to the German Jews. They could thus personally relate to what was described in the broadcasts, and hence the BBC sought to appeal to their moral conscience. In contrast, during 1939–41 Jews were not being assaulted and murdered on German streets and so the British propagandists did not consider it a useful propaganda strategy to confront the German public directly with all the details of the Nazi persecution of *Polish* Jews in the General Government.

CONCLUSION

Kristallnacht represented a turning point in the Nazi persecution of the Jews and an important step towards genocide. As Alan E. Steinweis argued, "It was the single instance of large-scale, public, and organized physical violence against Jews inside Germany before the Second World War. It unfolded in the open, in hundreds of German communities, even those with very few Jewish residents, and took place partly in broad daylight [. . .]."[68] The pogrom marked the passage from economic, political and social discrimination and disenfranchisement to systematic persecution, robbery, beatings, incarceration, murder and expulsion. It was a massive, state-sponsored attack on a minority on a national scale.[69] Since the pogrom was carried out in the full glare of world publicity—newspapers around the world reported on their front pages about the destruction of Jewish synagogues, businesses and homes, and the killing and arrest of countless Jews—ordinary people in foreign countries were confronted "for the first time with the immensity of the Jewish plight."[70]

Although the persecution of the Jews reached a new peak with Kristallnacht, the pogrom and its implications were not adequately reflected in the BBC's German-language broadcasts. If Jews were mentioned at all, this was done using inoffensive language and avoiding any appearance that Great Britain was criticizing Berlin for its anti-Jewish policy. The BBC not only failed to explain to German listeners why Jews were persecuted by the Nazis, namely, for irrational racist and anti-Semitic reasons. It also failed to call on the Germans to show their sympathy for the Jews and to help stop their persecution. At no time did British broadcasts indicate that Jewish refugees were welcome in Britain or encourage their emigration. The nearest thing to a sympathetic presentation of the refugee crisis was the Jewish children's broadcast of February 3, 1939, which promptly roused the criticism of the Foreign Office.

The failure to report Kristallnacht and the almost complete exclusion of all Jewish topics in its aftermath cannot be explained by a lack of information, as British diplomats in Germany and the British press reported fully about the persecution. Sure, the historical evidence is fragmentary and it is possible that the BBC did broadcast more information than is known to date. It can be no coincidence, however, that an internal BBC document listing all the *Sonderbericht* titles of the first half of 1939 does not contain a single item on the Nazi persecution of the Jews, but as many as six items on Palestine.[71]

The reluctance to talk about the Jewish persecution in British propaganda must therefore be attributed to a deliberate choice on the part of the British government and the BBC. Four factors stand out: The first and most influential factor was considerations of foreign and defense policy. Chamberlain feared that public criticism of the Nazis might provoke Hitler and increase the probability of war for which Great Britain was militarily unprepared. An additional factor was British fears of alienating the Arab population in Palestine and the need to appease the governments in the Middle East and in the British Empire, on whose support Great Britain would depend in case of war with Germany. To acknowledge publicly that a "Jewish problem" existed and thus create sympathy for the Jews would only have led to public demands for the opening of Palestine to Jewish refugees. Therefore, the less said about Kristallnacht the better. A second factor was British fears of playing into the hands of Nazi propaganda, which was feverishly attacking British policy in Palestine. This campaign not only threatened London's political influence in a region of vital strategic importance, but also sought to convince the German people of British decadence and weakness. The BBC therefore went to great lengths to explain to the German public the conflict between Jews and Arabs in Palestine and British policy in the Mandate. A third factor was British assumptions about the spread of anti-Semitic attitudes among the German public and the belief that Germans were likely to reject propaganda concerning Jews. Most of the internal discussions did not center on the question of how Jews could be helped by giving more publicity to their plight, but whether or not the German public would react negatively to British reports about Jews. A fourth factor was latent anti-Semitism in the British government and the BBC. The very fact that "Jewish accents" were frequently reported to exist and to be easily discernible by German listeners, and that these reports were taken at their face value, can be taken as a sign of anti-Jewish attitudes. There was little sympathy for the Jews in British government circles; many held the view that the Jews themselves were responsible for their persecution because they refused to assimilate. Whitehall feared that appeals for sympathy for, and rescue of, German Jews would lead to a resurgence of anti-Semitism among the British public.

Thus, during 1938–39 the BBC's primary concern was not to awaken the German public to the Nazi persecution of the Jews and to appeal for their moral and material support, but to support Great Britain's foreign policy aim of averting war with Germany. In other words, the coverage of Kristallnacht fell victim to Chamberlain's appeasement policy.

Notes

1. Tony Kushner, *The Holocaust and the Liberal Imagination: A Social and Cultural History* (Oxford: Blackwell, 1994), 49–50, 59, 272; Raphael Gross, *November 1938: Die Katastrophe vor der Katastrophe* (Munich: C. H. Beck, 2013), 80–81.
2. A critical reflection on the usage of the term Kristallnacht is offered in Christoph Kreutzmüller and Bjoern Weigel, *Kristallnacht? Bilder der Novemberpogrome 1938 in Berlin* (Berlin: Kulturprojekte Berlin GmbH, 2013), 4–6, 9; Gross, *November 1938*, 10–11; and Alan E. Steinweis, *Kristallnacht 1938* (Cambridge, MA: The Belknap Press of Harvard University Press, 2009), 1–6. The anti-Jewish violence was not limited to one night, but in some regions started as early as November 7 and lasted until November 13.
3. Donald Cameron Watt, *How War Came: The Immediate Origins of the Second World War, 1938–1939* (London: Heinemann, 1989), 88–92; Tony Kushner, "Beyond the Pale? British Reactions to Nazi Antisemitism, 1933–1939," in *The Politics of Marginality: Race, the Radical Right and Minorities in Twentieth Century Britain*, ed. Tony Kushner and Kenneth Lunn (London: Frank Cass, 1990), 143, 148; Kushner, *Liberal Imagination*, 49–50; David Dutton, *Neville Chamberlain* (London: Arnold, 2001), 58.
4. Jeffrey Herf, *The Jewish Enemy: Nazi Propaganda during World War II and the Holocaust* (Cambridge, MA: The Belknap Press of Harvard University Press, 2006).
5. The following draws on Stephanie Seul, "Appeasement und Propaganda 1938–1940: Chamberlains Außenpolitik zwischen NS-Regierung und deutschem Volk" (PhD diss., European University Institute, Florence, 2005), accessed June 15, 2019, http://cadmus.eui.eu/handle/1814/5977; idem, "Journalists in the Service of British Foreign Policy: The BBC German Service and Chamberlain's Appeasement Policy, 1938–1939," in *Journalists as Political Actors: Transfers and Interactions between Britain and Germany since the Late 19th Century*, ed. Frank Bösch and Dominik Geppert (Augsburg: Wißner, 2008); and idem, "'Plain, Unvarnished News'? The BBC German Service and British Propaganda Directed at Nazi Germany, 1938–1940," *Media History* 21, no. 4 (2015): 378–96.
6. Jodi Burkett, "Antisemitism and Racism in Britain: Assessing the Reaction to and the Legacy of *Kristallnacht*," in *Violence, Memory, and History: Western Perceptions of Kristallnacht*, ed. Colin McCullough and Nathan Wilson (New York: Routledge, 2015), 18–21; David Cesarani, "Great Britain," in *The World Reacts to the Holocaust*, ed. David S. Wyman and Charles H. Rosenzveig (Baltimore: The Johns Hopkins University Press, 1996), 602–03; Stephanie Seul, "'Any Reference to Jews on the Wireless Might Prove a Double-edged Weapon': Jewish Images in the British Propaganda Campaign towards the German Public, 1938–1939," in *Jewish Images in the Media*, ed. Martin Liepach, Gabriele Melischek, and Josef Seethaler (Vienna: Austrian Academy of Sciences, 2007), 204–08.

7. John Harvey, ed., *The Diplomatic Diaries of Oliver Harvey, 1937-40* (London: Collins, 1970), 218.
8. Seul, "Any Reference," 207-08.
9. No. 681 telegraphic, Ogilvie-Forbes to Halifax, November 13, 1938, in Ernest Llewellyn Woodward and Rohan Butler, eds., *Documents on British Foreign Policy 1919-1939. Third Series: 1938-1939*, vol. 3 (London: H.M.S.O., 1967), 271.
10. Franklin Reid Gannon, *The British Press and Germany, 1936-1939* (Oxford: Clarendon Press, 1971), 227; Kushner, "Beyond the Pale?" 155; Kushner, *Liberal Imagination*, 50.
11. No. 662 telegraphic, in Woodward and Butler, *Documents*, 266-67.
12. Louise London, *Whitehall and the Jews, 1933-1948: British Immigration Policy, Jewish Refugees and the Holocaust* (Cambridge: Cambridge University Press, 2000), 99.
13. *Parliamentary Debates (Hansard), House of Commons, Official Report, Fifth Series*, vol. 341 (London: H.M.S.O., 1938), November 14, 1938, 504; "German Attacks on British Press," *The Times of India*, November 16, 1938, 10; Seul, "Any Reference," 206-07; idem, "Appeasement," 236; Burkett, "Antisemitism," 20-21.
14. David Cesarani, "British Jewry," in *The Holocaust Encyclopedia*, ed. Walter Laqueur and Judith Tydor Baumel (New Haven: Yale University Press 2001), 83-90; London, *Whitehall*.
15. Shlomo Aronson, *Hitler, the Allies, and the Jews* (Cambridge: Cambridge University Press, 2004) 6, 14, 17-21.
16. Andrew Sharf, *The British Press and Jews under Nazi Rule* (Oxford: Oxford University Press, 1964); Gannon, *British Press*; Kushner, *Liberal Imagination*; Marianne Hicks, "R. Selkirk Panton, an Australian in Berlin: A Foreign Correspondent for the Daily Express in Europe, 1929-1950" (PhD diss., The University of Western Australia, Perth, 2005), accessed 15 June 2019, https://research-repository.uwa.edu.au/files/3388354/Hicks_Marianne_2005.pdf; Burkett, "Antisemitism."
17. Burkett, "Antisemitism," 22, 32.
18. Sharf, *British Press*, 58.
19. Susan H. Szczetnikowicz, "British Newsreels and the Plight of European Jews, 1933-1945" (PhD diss., University of Hertfordshire), 121, 132, accessed June 15, 2019, https://uhra.herts.ac.uk/handle/2299/14274; John A. S. Grenville, "British Propaganda, the Newsreels and Germany 1933 to 1939," in *Studien zur Geschichte Englands und der deutsch-britischen Beziehungen: Festschrift für Paul Kluke*, ed. Lothar Kettenacker, Manfred Schlenke, and Helmut Seier (Munich: Wilhelm Fink, 1981), 290.
20. Szczetnikowicz, "British Newsreels," 136-39.
21. Ibid., 140-43; Grenville, "British Propaganda," 290-91.
22. Guy Raz, "The BBC and Appeasement: Broadcast Coverage of Nazi Persecution of the Jews, 1933-1938" (MPhil diss., University of Cambridge, 1997), 4, 30-31,

84, quotation 2, accessed June 15, 2019, https://www.repository.cam.ac.uk/handle/1810/269790.
23. Ibid., 2–4; Jean Seaton, "The BBC and the Holocaust," *European Journal of Communication* 2, no. 1 (1987): 66–67.
24. "Anti-Jewish Rioting in Germany," BBC Script in *The Listener*, quoted in Raz, "The BBC and Appeasement," 3.
25. Szczetnikowicz, "British Newsreels," 139–40.
26. Raz, "The BBC and Appeasement," 75.
27. This analysis is based on Seul, "Any Reference"; idem, "The Representation of the Holocaust in the British Propaganda Campaign Directed at the German Public, 1938-1945," *Leo Baeck Institute Year Book* 52 (2007): 267–306.
28. Seul, "Appeasement," 236, 317–21.
29. "Summary of recent speeches by German leaders and of German Press articles hostile to the United Kingdom," The National Archives, Kew, London (TNA), FO 371/21659, C 14558/42/18.
30. No. 97, Robinson to Ogilvie-Forbes, 2 Dec. 1938, forwarded to Halifax December 7, 1938, TNA, FO 371/21659, C 15163/42/18.
31. Martin Gilbert, "British Government Policy towards Jewish Refugees (November 1938-September 1939)," *Yad Vashem Studies* 13 (1979): 127–31; London, *Whitehall*, 98.
32. No. 1224, Ogilvie-Forbes to Halifax, November 16, 1938, Woodward and Butler, *Documents*, 275–77.
33. Seul, "Appeasement," 317.
34. "Continued Persecution of German Jews." *The Scotsman*, November 15, 1938, 11.
35. Bernard Wasserstein, *Britain and the Jews of Europe 1939-1945* (Oxford: Oxford University Press, 1979), 1–17, 163; Cesarani, "Great Britain," 605.
36. No. 1956, Strang to Ogilvie-Forbes, December 1, 1938, TNA, FO 371/21791, C 14793/13064/18; minute Cadogan, November 28, 1938, ibid; Seul, "Appeasement," 215–18, 243–46, 303–09.
37. *Parliamentary Debates*, November 24, 1938, 1989.
38. "The BBC's German News Talks," July 21, 1939, TNA, FO 395/631, P 3336/6/150. The memorandum by A. E. Barker lists the titles, but not the content of the *Sonderberichte* broadcast on February 3, 9, 14, and 16, 1939. *Sonderberichte* consisted of talks, political commentaries or press reviews on current political events or on subjects of general interest to the German public. Seul, "Appeasement," 297–98, 341.
39. No. 681 telegraphic, Ogilvie-Forbes to Halifax, November 13, 1938, Woodward and Butler, *Documents*, 270–71.
40. "World Horror of the German Terror: A Broadcast Suggestion," *Manchester Guardian*, November 19, 1938, 15.
41. "Possible German Intentions," January 19, 1939, TNA, CAB 27/627, FP (36)74; Seul, "Appeasement," 294–95, 326–27, 332–34.

42. "Notes of a Conversation with a German Who Occupies a Responsible Official Position, December 20, 1938." TNA, CAB 27/627, FP (36)74, p. 23.
43. "From BBC German Broadcast of February 3rd," TNA, FO 395/625, P 377/6/150.
44. See *Radio Times*, issue 800, January 29–February 4, 1939, programme of February 3, 1939; "To-night's Broadcasting," *Northern Daily Mail* (Hartlepool, England), February 3, 1939, 10; "Today's Home Programmes," *The Nottingham Evening Post*, February 3, 1939, 8. The text of the broadcast is in part reproduced in London, *Whitehall*, 118–20. The "Children in Flight" broadcast was transmitted a second time on April 7, 1939 at 2.45 p.m., see *Radio Times* issue 809, p. 2 April 2, 1939–April 8, 1939.
45. "From BBC German Broadcast of February 3rd," TNA, FO 395/625, P 377/6/150. See also Seul, "Any Reference," 213.
46. Ogilvie-Forbes to Foreign Office, No. 56 telegraphic, February 6, 1939, TNA, FO 395/625, P 377/6/150; No. 185, February 9, 1939, TNA, FO 395/626, P 440/6/150.
47. "B.B.C. Broadcasts in German. Nazi Criticism," *The Times*, February 8, 1939, 13; "Children in Flight. B.B.C. Broadcast Angers German Press," *Liverpool Daily Post*, February 4, 1939, 11; "B.B.C. Angers Germans. Jewish Children's Arrival," *Sheffield Telegraph and Daily Independent*, February 6, 1939, 7.
48. "Nazis Dig Up Scots History. Angry Retort to B.B.C.," *The Courier and Advertiser*, February 6, 1939, 7.
49. "An 'Interference.'" *The Scotsman*, February 8, 1939, 14.
50. Quoted in Seul, "Appeasement," 123 n. 36.
51. No. 56 telegraphic, Ogilvie-Forbes to Foreign Office, February 6, 1939, TNA, FO 395/625, P 377/6/150.
52. No. 170, Ogilvie-Forbes to Halifax, February 8, 1939, TNA, FO 395/625, P 439/6/150, p. 2.
53. No. 56, Ogilvie-Forbes to Foreign Office, February 6, 1939, TNA, FO 395/625, P 377/6/150.
54. No. 170, Ogilvie-Forbes to Halifax, February 8, 1939, TNA, FO 395/625, P 439/6/150, p. 2.
55. Minute Leeper, February 7, 1939, TNA, FO 395/625, P 377/6/150.
56. "German News," August 25, 1939, BBC Written Archives Centre, Caversham, Reading (BBC WAC), E 9/12/5.
57. "Bulletins in Foreign Languages," BBC memorandum, undated, BBC WAC, R 34/325, 2; Murray to J. B. Clark, September 29, 1938, BBC WAC, R 28/270/1.
58. Tony Kushner, *The Persistence of Prejudice: Antisemitism in British Society during the Second World War* (Manchester: Manchester University Press, 1989); idem, "The Impact of British Antisemitism, 1918–1945," in *The Making of Modern Anglo-Jewry*, ed. David Cesarani (Oxford: Basil Blackwell, 1990), 191–208; idem, "Beyond the Pale"; idem, *Liberal Imagination*.
59. Seaton, "The BBC and the Holocaust," 66.

60. Minute Warner to Lord Perth, June 29, 1939, TNA, FO 395/630, P 2966/6/150.
61. For a list of the BBC's German news talks and press reviews for the period late January to mid-July 1939 see A. E. Barker, "The BBC's German News Talks," July 21, 1939, TNA, FO 395/631, P 3336/6/150. Likewise, a list containing suggestions for future *Sonderberichte* does not contain a single proposal for a talk about Jews, apart from one suggestion mentioning Jewish scientists and exiles such as Freud and Einstein: "Provision of Material for BBC German News Bulletins through Speeches and Publications," July 24, 1939, BBC WAC, E 9/12/5. Since only few sources survived it is impossible to state with certainty how often a Jewish topic was taken up in British propaganda.
62. On the reporting of the BBC German Service on the Holocaust see Seul, "Representation."
63. "'Die Ungehängten': Himmler." Manuscript of feature broadcast on the BBC German Service, July 15, 1941, BBC WAC, ES 22, 8. The following analysis is based on Seul, "Representation," 286–87.
64. Planning and Broadcasting Committee, 37th meeting, TNA, FO 898/7, minute 14.
65. "Daventry deutsch, 22.30 Uhr." Evening monitoring report of 'Sonderdienst "Landhaus,"' November 10, 1939, Bundesarchiv Berlin, R 74/347, pp. 105–10.
66. "'Die Ungehängten': Himmler." Manuscript of feature broadcast on the BBC German Service, July 15, 1941, BBC WAC, ES 22, 8. A recording of this broadcast (dated July 18, 1941) is kept at Deutsches Rundfunkarchiv, Frankfurt/M., Band Nr. 79 U 3702/2. This recording is also included in the published edition of wartime broadcasts by Hans Sarkowicz and Michael Crone, eds., *Der Kampf um die Ätherwellen: Feindpropaganda in Zweiten Weltkrieg* (Frankfurt am Main: Eichborn, 1990).
67. PWE weekly directive for the BBC German Service, November 9–15, 1941, TNA, FO 371/26533, C 11508/154/18, 2.
68. Steinweis, *Kristallnacht 1938*, 3–4.
69. Gross, *November 1938*, 9–11; Beth A. Griech-Polelle, *Anti-Semitism and the Holocaust: Language, Rhetoric and the Traditions of Hatred* (London: Bloomsbury Academic, 2017), 124–25.
70. Kushner, *Liberal Imagination*, 49.
71. A. E. Barker, "The BBC's German News Talks," July 21, 1939, TNA, FO 395/631, P 3336/6/150. The talks on Palestine were broadcast on February 3, 9, 14 and 16, and on May 16 and 19, 1939.

Bibliography

Archives

BBC Written Archives Centre, Caversham, Reading.
Bundesarchiv Berlin.
Deutsches Rundfunkarchiv. Frankfurt am Main.
The National Archives. Kew, London.

Newspapers and Radio Broadcasts

"An 'Interference.'" *The Scotsman*, February 8, 1939, 14.
"B.B.C. Angers Germans. Jewish Children's Arrival." *Sheffield Telegraph and Daily Independent*, February 6, 1939, 7.
"B.B.C. Broadcasts in German: Nazi Criticism." *The Times*, February 8, 1939, 13.
"Children in Flight. B.B.C. Broadcast Angers German Press." *Liverpool Daily Post*, February 4, 1939, 11.
"Continued Persecution of German Jews." *The Scotsman*, November 15, 1938, 11.
"German Attacks on British Press." *The Times of India*, November 16, 1938, 10.
"Nazis Dig Up Scots History. Angry Retort to B.B.C." *The Courier and Advertiser*, February 6, 1939, 7.
Radio Times 800 (January 29–February 4, 1939).
Radio Times 809 (April 2–April 8, 1939).
"Today's Home Programmes." *The Nottingham Evening Post*, February 3, 1939, 8.
"To-night's Broadcasting." *Northern Daily Mail* (Hartlepool, England), February 3, 1939, 10.
"World Horror of the German Terror: A Broadcast Suggestion." *Manchester Guardian*, November 19, 1938, 15.

Secondary Sources

Aronson, Shlomo. *Hitler, the Allies, and the Jews*. Cambridge: Cambridge University Press, 2004.
Burkett, Jodi. "Antisemitism and Racism in Britain: Assessing the Reaction to and the Legacy of *Kristallnacht*." In *Violence, Memory, and History: Western Perceptions of Kristallnacht*, edited by Colin McCullough and Nathan Wilson, 16–33. New York: Routledge, 2015.
Cesarani, David. "British Jewry." In *The Holocaust Encyclopedia*, edited by Walter Laqueur and Judith Tydor Baumel, 83–90. New Haven: Yale University Press, 2001.
———. "Great Britain." In *The World Reacts to the Holocaust*, edited by David S.

Wyman and Charles H. Rosenzveig, 599–641. Baltimore: The Johns Hopkins University Press, 1996.
Dutton, David. *Neville Chamberlain*. London: Arnold, 2001.
Gannon, Franklin Reid. *The British Press and Germany, 1936–1939*. Oxford: Clarendon Press, 1971.
Gilbert, Martin. "British Government Policy towards Jewish Refugees (November 1938–September 1939)." *Yad Vashem Studies* 13 (1979): 127–67.
Grenville, John A. S. "British Propaganda, the Newsreels and Germany 1933 to 1939." In *Studien zur Geschichte Englands und der deutsch-britischen Beziehungen: Festschrift für Paul Kluke*, edited by Lothar Kettenacker, Manfred Schlenke, and Helmut Seier, 281–93. Munich: Wilhelm Fink, 1981.
Griech-Polelle, Beth A. *Anti-Semitism and the Holocaust: Language, Rhetoric and the Traditions of Hatred*. London: Bloomsbury Academic, 2017.
Gross, Raphael. *November 1938: Die Katastrophe vor der Katastrophe*. Munich: C. H. Beck, 2013.
Harvey, John, ed. *The Diplomatic Diaries of Oliver Harvey, 1937–40*. London: Collins, 1970.
Herf, Jeffrey. *The Jewish Enemy: Nazi Propaganda during World War II and the Holocaust*. Cambridge, MA: The Belknap Press of Harvard University Press, 2006.
Hicks, Marianne. "R. Selkirk Panton, an Australian in Berlin: A Foreign Correspondent for the Daily Express in Europe, 1929–1950." PhD diss., The University of Western Australia, Perth, 2005. Accessed June 15, 2019. https://research-repository.uwa.edu.au/files/3388354/Hicks_Marianne_2005.pdf.
Kreutzmüller, Christoph, and Bjoern Weigel. *Kristallnacht? Bilder der Novemberpogrome 1938 in Berlin*. Berlin: Kulturprojekte Berlin GmbH, 2013.
Kushner, Tony. "Beyond the Pale? British Reactions to Nazi Antisemitism, 1933–1939." In *The Politics of Marginality: Race, the Radical Right and Minorities in Twentieth Century Britain*, edited by Tony Kushner and Kenneth Lunn, 143–60. London: Frank Cass, 1990.

———. *The Holocaust and the Liberal Imagination: A Social and Cultural History*. Oxford: Blackwell, 1994.

———. "The Impact of British Antisemitism, 1918–1945." In *The Making of Modern Anglo-Jewry*, edited by David Cesarani, 191–208. Oxford: Basil Blackwell, 1990.

———. *The Persistence of Prejudice: Antisemitism in British Society during the Second World War*. Manchester: Manchester University Press, 1989.
London, Louise. *Whitehall and the Jews, 1933–1948: British Immigration Policy, Jewish Refugees and the Holocaust*. Cambridge: Cambridge University Press, 2000.
Parliamentary Debates (Hansard), House of Commons, Official Report, Fifth Series. Vol. 341. H.M.S.O., 1938.
Raz, Guy. "The BBC and Appeasement: Broadcast Coverage of Nazi Persecution of the Jews, 1933–1938." MPhil diss., University of Cambridge, 1997. Accessed June 15, 2019. https://www.repository.cam.ac.uk/handle/1810/269790.

Sarkowicz, Hans, and Michael Crone, eds. *Der Kampf um die Ätherwellen: Feindpropaganda in Zweiten Weltkrieg*. Frankfurt am Main: Eichborn, 1990.

Seaton, Jean. "The BBC and the Holocaust." *European Journal of Communication* 2, no. 1 (1987): 53–80.

Seul, Stephanie. "'Any Reference to Jews on the Wireless Might Prove a Double-edged Weapon': Jewish Images in the British Propaganda Campaign towards the German Public, 1938-1939." In *Jewish Images in the Media*, edited by Martin Liepach, Gabriele Melischek, and Josef Seethaler, 203–32. Vienna: Austrian Academy of Sciences, 2007.

———. "Appeasement und Propaganda 1938–1940: Chamberlains Außenpolitik zwischen NS-Regierung und deutschem Volk." PhD diss., European University Institute, Florence, 2005. Accessed June 15, 2019. http://cadmus.eui.eu/handle/1814/5977.

———. "Journalists in the Service of British Foreign Policy: The BBC German Service and Chamberlain's Appeasement Policy, 1938–1939." In *Journalists as Political Actors: Transfers and Interactions between Britain and Germany since the Late 19th Century*, edited by Frank Bösch and Dominik Geppert, 89–109. Augsburg: Wißner, 2008.

———. "'Plain, Unvarnished News'? The BBC German Service and British Propaganda Directed at Nazi Germany, 1938–1940." *Media History* 21, no. 4 (2015): 378–96.

———. "The Representation of the Holocaust in the British Propaganda Campaign Directed at the German Public, 1938–1945." *Leo Baeck Institute Year Book* 52 (2007): 267–306.

Sharf, Andrew. *The British Press and Jews under Nazi Rule*. Oxford: Oxford University Press, 1964.

Steinweis, Alan E. *Kristallnacht 1938*. Cambridge, MA: The Belknap Press of Harvard University Press, 2009.

Szczetnikowicz, Susan H. "British Newsreels and the Plight of European Jews, 1933–1945." PhD diss., University of Hertfordshire. Accessed June 15, 2019. https://uhra.herts.ac.uk/handle/2299/14274.

Wasserstein, Bernard. *Britain and the Jews of Europe 1939–1945*. Oxford: Oxford University Press, 1979.

Watt, Donald Cameron. *How War Came: The Immediate Origins of the Second World War, 1938–1939*. London: Heinemann, 1989.

Woodward, Ernest Llewellyn, and Rohan Butler, eds. *Documents on British Foreign Policy 1919–1939. Third Series: 1938–1939*. Vol. 3. H.M.S.O., 1967.

CHAPTER 9

Orthodox Jewish Reflective Responses to Kristallnacht

by Gershon Greenberg

he study of real-time Orthodox Jewish responses can help to apprehend and comprehend the point of encounter between Nazism and Judaism known as the Kristallnacht. The responses belonged to a sanctified universe whose sacraments were largely obliterated. Textual research cannot retrieve the in-themselves meaning of the responses. But it can position one at the threshold to the sacred realm, from which the responses emerged. It enables one to look in the direction of sanctity's disappearance, and even apprehend a dimension of its reality. There, one might gaze in the direction of the disappearance, to perhaps catch a glimpse of that lost universe.[1]

Orthodox reactions began epistemologically, in the sense that thinkers sought to comprehend the event rationally. Orthodox thinkers realized they could not and drew a perimeter around humanly-based understanding. Ultimately, they addressed the disaster in transcendental terms of apocalyptic dualism. In between there was a metahistorical narrative, rooted in biblical scripture and the dialectical relation between God and the history of the people of Israel.[2] It raised temporal and spatial events to a spiritual realm, and expressed them in terms of a revelatory, mythic drama advancing toward the metaphysical reality of redemption.

The various streams of Orthodox Jewish responsive thinking coalesced around four themes: The Kristallnacht was without precedent and contrary to human natural behavior and reason. Given divine providence, understanding was nevertheless possible—but in metahistorical or mythic terms. These explanations centered on the premise that the Jewish people had sinned, and that suffering came from above to address the transgressions. But the uniqueness of the horrors was such, that such a traditional path of explanation did not resolve the religious turmoil brought about by the destruction. Our thinkers turned to radically dualistic apocalyptic considerations—and a quest to identify means to survive and to share in the redemption to follow.

Over the course of the history of the people of Israel, when historical events could not be understood in terms of natural human behavior or reason, the metahistory provided a refuge for traditional religious thought. In turn, this opened a space for Judaism to endure on a spiritual level—and perhaps, given that pious Jews blended physical with spiritual existence, on the physical as well. In modern times, the metahistorical dimension was largely abandoned by Reform and Conservative Judaism—which confined themselves to the data of empirical history and universalistic, humanistic values.

Thus, when Reform Rabbi Ferdinand Isserman of St. Louis preached on the second Sabbath eve (1st November, *Torah* portion *Hayei sarah*) following the Kristallnacht assaults "at the special service of prayer for the persecuted people of all groups," he stated:

> If need be, perhaps by the wounds and stripes of Jews in Germany and Austria, the suffering and woes of all men will be healed.... The Jews of the past knew how to suffer with dignity. The Jews of the present will know how to suffer with equal dignity.[3]

By contrast, on the same Sabbath, Rabbi Tobias Geffen of Atlanta, Georgia, thinking metahistorically, sublated the 400 million dollar (one billion *Reichsmark*) fine imposed on Jews for the destruction, into the scriptural narrative of the 400 shekels which Abraham had to pay for Sarah's plot when Ephron reneged on his offer to gift it. Hitler, Geffen predicted, would end up like Ephron—a leper, isolated from mankind.[4]

The Orthodox writers (predominantly rabbis) who responded from across Eastern Europe, the Land of Israel, and the United States included Hasidic, religious nationalist, *Da'at torah*-based (committed to the revealed scriptural tradition, identified with the Agudat Yisrael world rabbinical organization) streams. But they shared a common frame of reference, crossing sectarian lines. Cohesive patterns may be discerned. 1) The authors did not expect the calamity, especially because it emerged from what they regarded as an enlightened culture. It was unprecedented and inexplicable in terms of human nature and rationality. However, it did take place in the universe which God created. Accordingly, there had to be an explanation in divinely-rooted, mythic terms, i.e., through metahistorical narrative. 2) Insofar as God's special people, the Jews, were positioned at the sacred *axis mundi* of humankind, they were the primary movers of world events. In the minds of these writers, Jews were not the "objects" of actions taken by other nations. They were the "subjects"—and in this sense not the "victims" but the generators of whatever happened to them. Specifically, the thinkers believed that Jews who assimilated and abandoned *Torah*, were responsible for the Kristallnacht. God intervened in history, and punished Jews (indiscriminately) with Amalek-like human instruments (Amalek was the paradigmatic enemy of the people of Israel), so that His people would return to *Torah*. Once they did, the divinely imposed suffering would end. 3) The developing troubles were breaking all boundaries of earlier agonies, they were so uncontrolled that these thinkers were left to resort to a transcendental, apocalyptic dualistic drama between metaphysical good and evil. By doing so, they could set aside any ambiguities about God's role in history. They ceded rational or sequential explanation to a drama beyond the grasp of either historical or metahistorical explanation. The apocalyptic battle would end with the onset of redemptive reality. Redemption would balance out the destruction and assure that the universe was indeed ordered under God. Along with this, and in tandem with the transcendental drama, Jews were called upon to act: to conduct themselves benevolently, live and think according to the *Torah*, repent (*Teshuvah*, i.e, the turn back to God through a process of penitence).

THE THRESHOLD TO HIGHER TRUTHS
The cruelty of the Kristallnacht, in the face of the enlightenment of modernity, directed the *Admo"r* of Bobov, Poland, Bentsion Halberstam, to reach to the outer border of natural behavior and reason for understanding. He issued a massively distributed statement on January 3, 1939 (100,000 copies were reportedly distributed) that such a torrent of fury, where Jews were expelled from their homes and left with nothing; where righteous fathers and sons, and innocent weanlings were slaughtered, defied comprehension in an era of enlightenment and belief in natural compassion:

> We believe in full faith, that the creator Himself, may His name be blessed, has made, does make, and will make all events happen. Further, anything which befalls a nation or individual is a matter of providence. The present generation is proud and boastful of the enlightenment, which has spread its wings across all lands. The enlightenment has refined human nature to be sympathetic and righteous—to have compassion even for animals. Who would believe that humans could become so cruel, and so suddenly? Like ostriches in the wilderness [Lamentations 4:3], they slaughter the righteous, fathers and sons, innocent weanlings. Does this not make us realize that this is not a matter of natural law or judgment?[5]

Halberstam did not offer his thoughts about what lay beyond natural law or judgment and how to access it.

Others did. Elhanan Wasserman (*Da'at torah*), head of the Baranowicz, Poland yeshivah who was then in Baltimore, wrote that any attempt to understand the events surrounding Kristallnacht could drive one insane. But by looking to *Torah*, one would understand—and one should not remove one's "finger" from its text for a moment.[6]

In Palestine, the Chief Rabbi of Petah Tikvah, Reuven Katz (*Da'at torah Agudat Yisrael*) wrote that no rational explanation was possible as to why and how, in such a cultured era, the greatest tyrant in all the history of Israel could arise. How, in an age of socialism and democracy, could decrees of annihilation be issued? In a world where nations and races were mixed, how could racial madness erupt? Asking "Was all this meaningless? Do not such hard facts make us think? Is the hand from above not hidden in all this?" Katz responded that God had brought a Haman to induce Israel to return to its better self. (*Sanhedrin* 97b). Redemption would follow.[7] Chief Rabbi of Tel Aviv Mosheh Avigdor Amiel (religious nationalist) posited that ongoing hatred towards Jews and the intent to annihilate them went beyond human understanding. Still, it had to be asked. "Why did God do this?" The answer was unavoidably tied to sinning: "If a man sees that powerful sufferings visit him, let him examine his conduct" (*Berakhot* 5a).[8]

In Jerusalem, Y. A. Dvorkes (Tseirei Agudat Yisrael—Youth Agudat Yisrael), referring to the current decline of civilization and the awakening of bestial-like inclinations, suggested that factors of punishment and repentance were involved, and that one had to look to higher providence:

> Our era is one of decline after generations of civilization. Base human inclinations, those of the beast, have been awakened. Who would

ever have thought . . . ? A great and small era together. . . . Great technology and small ethics. Airplanes, created to join the hearts of neighbors, turning into birds of prey. There are great minds in the generation. But the mind does not overcome the small heart. In this era, we, the small and humble people, "The sheep among the seventy wolves" must set a path for itself between billowing waves of evil. We should know that "Punishment comes into the world only on Israel's account" (*Yebamot* 63a) . . . The era is not yet behind us. Higher providence has yet to have the "open for me an opening of repentance no bigger than the eye of a needle and I will widen it into an opening to a hall" (*Song of Songs R. Parashah* 5 *Siman* 3). We await the "If the people of Israel would observe two Sabbaths they would be redeemed immediately (*Shabbat* 118a) from above. Each and every moment of weakness and inattention is grievous.[9]

In America, Rabbi Mordekhai Schwartz of Cleveland iterated the Kristallnacht destruction of synagogues, the burning of *Torah* scrolls and rabbinic texts; how tens of thousands of Jews were forced into homelessness and imprisoned in concentration camps. How, he asked, was it possible for some Austrian painter and low-ranked soldier, who was jailed in Germany for perverse activities to dissolve the *Reichstag*, annul state laws, dismiss judges and ministers, kill hundreds of army officers overnight and take over the treasury, all in enlightened Germany? It could all be traceable, only to God: "Knowest thou not, that it is Heaven that has ordained this Roman nation to reign?" (*Avodah Zara* 18a).[10]

Thus, Orthodox rabbis across the globe arrived independently at the same conclusion: comprehension in human terms was not possible. These thinkers set a boundary around the natural and rational mind, and once they did, they were open to higher, trans-natural understanding. It came from *Torah*, truths about God's relationship with His people, and about divine oversight and governance.

METAHISTORICAL DISCLOSURES

Orthodox thinkers held that the people of Israel were a sacred nation; rooted in an a-temporal and a-spatial point at the center of the creative energy of the world, *axis mundi*. Accordingly, whatever unfolded in world history centered around them—and their relationship with God. According to the spirit of the covenant, the welfare of the Jews would be assured as long as they adhered to divine commands. Alternatively, sin spelled disaster—and all was under divine control. Across the globe, with rare exceptions (Bentsion Halberstam, and Ya'akov Mosheh Harlap, see below) Jewish thinkers held that the Kristallnacht was brought by God in response to Israel's transgressions. As such, it did not upset Israel's metahistorical relationship with God. To the contrary, the Kristallnacht confirmed it.

In some instances, the blame was general. The Chief Rabbinate of London composed a prayer for Sunday, November 20, 1938, which included the phrases:

> You, the pious God have ordered tyrants to rule over the nation Israel, and have the nation suffer by the rod for its transgression. The people annulled the covenant of Your peace. For each of its sins, the nation is receiving doubly from Your hand. And the heart of the nation is humbled.[11]

In New York, President Joseph Konvitz and Secretary Yehudah Layb Seltser of the Union of Orthodox Rabbis (*Agudat harabbanim*) described the Kristallnacht as an attack upon the sanctity of the people of the covenant—killing children and the elderly, leaving them to wander in hunger and cold, destroying synagogues, *Batei midrash* and *Torah* scrolls, dragging rabbinic scholars and pious Jews through the streets.[12] On behalf of the *Agudat harabbanim*, they called for a public fast to help the unfortunate brethren and to repent for sin.

> At the same time, we must not show helplessness, or despair. We must be strong and decisive in the critical moment. We have the promise, "And yet for all that, when they are in the land of their enemies, I will not reject them, neither will I abhor them, to destroy them utterly, to break my covenant with them." [*Leviticus* 26:44]. We draw from the ways utilized by our forefathers, "Out of the depths have I called Thee, O Lord." [*Psalms* 130:1] "Repentance, prayer and charity remove the evil decree" ["*Unetaneh tokef*" prayer, Day of Atonement] ... The *Agudat harabbanim* has called for a public fast for all America and Canada, for Monday, 28 November 1938. Fellow Jews! Gather in the synagogues, recite *Selihot*. Pray. The primary purpose of prayer is *Teshuvah*. Return Israel. To help our unfortunate brethren, we call for doing *Teshuvah* for sins for which we are responsible. The sanctity of our Sabbath has been weakened. Protect the Sabbath. Our feet

have trampled the sanctity of our synagogues. Keep the sanctity of the synagogues. Marriage and divorce by the ignorant have increased illegitimate children in Israel. Family purity, the basis of our existence, has been ridiculed. *Teshuvah* for all sins![13]

In most instances, assimilants were held culpable. Dvorkes correlated the growth of anti-Semitism with assimilation. When the granting of equal rights evoked anti-Semitism, spiritual leaders sounded the alarm to return to Jewish sources. They were ignored, in the mistaken belief that assimilation was the cure-all. When the eruption of evil did in fact take place, the assimilants were left unprepared.[14] In Vilnius, Hayim Ozer Grodzensky (*Da'at torah*) found a causal connection between assimilation and disaster: the plight of thousands of Jews now stranded on the German-Polish border and threatened by death, was the long-term result of assimilationist Reform in Western Europe. Grodzensky called for *Teshuvah*—which also implied redemption.[15]

Schwartz in Cleveland and Amiel in Tel Aviv spoke of a "backfire" effect. Jews who abandoned the *Mitsvot* of *Torah* (including Sabbath, *Kashrut*, family purity, *Talmud torah*) hoped to integrate into non-Jewish culture and join its professions. Integration did not follow; to the contrary, Jews were beaten and forced into concentration camps. It was true that pathological hatred for Jews remained latent among the nations. But absent the misguided attempt to co-opt this animosity through intimacy, the hatred would have remained dormant. Intimacy became a catalyst for its outbreak—and the deeper the intrusion into non-Jewish culture, the harsher the repulsion. In turn, the repulsion was a punishment by God intended to have Jews return to *Torah*. Schwartz held that if *Teshuvah* were performed, the suffering would ebb and be followed by redemption.[16] Amiel observed that German-born Reform Judaism, with its assimilationist character and side-effect of conversion to Christianity, failed to bring equal rights as the Reformers assumed. Instead, assimilation brought Hitler's racial doctrine and the determination to eliminate Jews and Judaism altogether.[17] Eliezer Gershon Fridenzon of Lodz added the element of self-deception. The Kristallnacht was divine punishment for assimilation by Reform Jews, whose immersion into Gentile German culture amounted to a "wild devil's dance of Jewish denial," and delusion, that immersion would bring security.[18]

Wasserman constructed the assimilation-disaster relation dialectically. In traditional Orthodox Jewish thought Amalek—the paradigmatic enemy of ancient Israel, who had been destroyed physically with his people in ancient times (Deut. 25:17–19; 1 Sam. 15:3)—had been transformed into a timeless category of absolute evil. The mythic evil assumed the form of historical personalities, ranging from Haman to Chmielnitzky to Petliura and now to Hitler. In modern times, the essence of Amalek manifest itself in the Berlin *Haskalah* and loss of *Torah* within the Jewish people. Currently, the internal Amalek was projecting itself outward, in the external form of Hitler, who punished Israel back to its *Torah* self. (A cyclical dynamic echoed by Schwartz.) Punishment was measure-for-measure specific: Nazi national-socialism reacted to Jewish nationalism and socialism. The closing of Jewish theaters was a response to Jews' having attended theaters to the neglect of *Torah* study. As the universe was ultimately enveloped by *Torah*, the external served to annul the internal Amalek.[19]

The motives behind blaming fellow Jews and focusing on the theme of assimilation were not made explicit. While echoing the ancient prophetic tradition of transmitting God's messages, denouncing sin and calling for repentance, the rationale behind the rebukes is left to speculation. Was there an ongoing animosity towards assimilants? Was there a fear that, unless an intra-covenantal explanation were to be found, the covenant itself would be under threat? Was blaming part of an attempt to find and diagnose a cause so that a remedy could be sought? The undercurrent of expected redemption following *Teshuvah* (Dvorkes, Katz, Grodzensky, Wasserman, Schwartz) suggests that a remedial intention was behind the accusations.

APOCALYPTIC DUALISM

The metahistorically-framed reflections by Orthodox thinkers who gazed beyond empirical history and reason were not a final stage. The increasing horrors tested the underlying logic of metahistory of a one-to-one relationship between transgression and punishment. Metahistory was implicitly fragile: If suffering was God's response to sin, why did the pious suffer? How could the evil perpetrator be employed by a good God? What was the relationship (causal? coincidental?) between *Teshuvah*, the ebbing of persecution and redemption? Movement to trans-metahistorical, apocalyptic dualism indicated that the metahistorical narrative was not enough for the faithful.

In Chicago, in the December 1938 edition of *Hapardes*, Shemuel Aharon Pardes (identified with *Da'at torah*) described the Kristallnacht as a war of Hitler against Holy Scripture and God:

> We lament and sigh over the great, shameful and terrible *Shoah* which has come upon our brethren in the lands of slaughter, Germany and Austria. . . . The people of Israel have been murdered and slaughtered by Hitler and his fellow killers. The heart rages, with a great and bitter cry over the vengeance and terrible oppression erupting from *Sheol*. But the cry is choked in our throats, and we have become mute. We can only be deadly silent. How can our lips express our disaster? The acts of their slaughter have traversed all boundaries and shocked all lands. State organs have been on the attack. They conduct pogroms; beat and torture people unto death. They burn synagogues and *Torah* scrolls, they destroy houses and demolish stores, starve their victims and drive them to insanity and suicide. Then they imposed decrees of annihilation of their wretched victims. 12,000 Jews, Polish subjects, have been expelled from Germany in the darkness of night. And many of them are still on the German-Polish border, naked and with nothing. The evil Hitler taunts and blasphemes *Hashem*, the God of Israel, and has issued a decree to erase the name of God from the *Tanakh*. We believe that the war of Hitler against *Hashem* will bring his fall near.[20]

In Lodz, Eliezer Gershon Fridenzon described the Kristallnacht as a volcanic like eruption of a barbaric, primitive evil—one which had devoured Germany's culture, science and art. But redemption was imminent, with the extinction of the evil realm. Amalek's "death's head" was rising out of its grave to see the light of the world one last time. Amalek mocked and spit at the majestic image of God. Knowing that he was about to lose his battle with God's light, he convulsed with death throes filled with insanity, theft and sadism.[21] Ya'akov Moshe Harlap, Head of the Merkaz Harav Kook in Jerusalem, who echoed Friedenzon's dualism and the insanity of evil forces at the brink of death, identified the perpetrators as manifestations of the Kabbalist's realm of negative, other being (*Sitra ahra*). Sensing the onset of the redemption—to be preceded by the annihilation of evil—the perpetrators sought to destroy the people of Israel through whom redemption would come.[22]

The apocalyptic battle unfolded at the edge of metahistory, where metahistorical narrative yielded to a cosmic struggle between metaphysical entities. The struggle involved the transition from temporality and sequence to eternity. It was also the era of messianic suffering—prior to the birth of the messiah. While the battle was abstract and trans-empirical, Jews did have a role such that the cosmic and metahistorical touched. A life of *Torah*, benevolence, *Teshuvah* and prayer were all imperative.

Wasserman spoke of adhering to *Torah* as a way to survive. He identified events surrounding the Kristallnacht as those of the onset of the messiah (*Ikveta dimeshiha*; the footsteps of the messiah), filled with the agonies of the messiah's birth. Citing "and I will sift the House of Israel among all the nations, like as corn is sifted in a sieve" (Amos 9:9) he wrote:

> Jews will be scattered like wheat kernels being sifted. The Hofets Hayim of Blessed memory used to say: In the sieve one kernel falls closer and one further, but none remains in its original place. So it will be with Jews in the era of "footsteps of the messiah." He reported in the name of R. Abraham ben David of Posquieres *ad Mishnah Eduyot* 8:7 that before the messiah comes, Jewish families will be separated. The parents will be in one land and each of the children in another land, and they will not be able to come together until Elijah will come [Malachi 3:24].

In the past, Wasserman continued, when Jews were being persecuted in one country, there was always a second place to which they could escape. During the Spanish expulsion for example, Turkey and Poland were open for Jews, as was Catholic Holland. During the era of the birth pangs of the messiah, however, they will be pursued everywhere and admitted nowhere. Currently Jews can do nothing to avert the tragedy. But they could survive by adhering to *Torah*, which enabled passage out of time and into eternity: "Thousands of years of Jewish history have demonstrated that with the power of *Torah*, Jews would be able to remain intact through fire and water."[23] Fridenzon also spoke of *Torah* study. When the second Temple was destroyed, a yeshiva was built in Yavneh. Now, Amalek was setting synagogues and houses of learning aflame—and the response should be similar—that of cultivating *Torah* education.[24]

The *Admor* of Bobov, Bentsion Halberstam, wrote that with events of *Ikveta dimeshiha* underway it was incumbent upon Jews to act benevolently (*Gemilut hasadim*). Israel's metahistory was one of the proportional descents and ascents. Now, during the era of *Ikveta dimeshiha*, they were deepest and highest. The ascent would finally be so dramatic as to transcend the descent-ascent pattern altogether. The people of Israel would endure the agony, if they understood the radical change. They also had to act benevolently.

> Take pity on the unfortunate. Support them as much as possible, until the time will come for release from prison (and for redemption). God will recompense the generous of the nation well.... The rich should increase their giving, the poor should not lessen acts of

grace (*Hesed*)—each according to ability. As this was the era of *Ikveta dimeshiha*, we must make the greatest effort to increase acts of benevolence (*Gemilut hasadim*), the third of the three pillars of the world.[25]

Others spoke of *Teshuvah*. In Lodz, citing "Let the sufferings come, but let me not see them" (*Sanhedrin* 98a), B[inyami]n held that the current sufferings were those of *Ikveta dimeshiha*. Suffering and relief were dialectically interrelated. As the era of *Asarah harugei malkhut* (the ten rabbis said to have been martyred during Hadrian's reign) was followed by a period of mending, the Kristallnacht would be followed by messianic redemption. *Teshuvah* below by the people of Israel must correspond to the salvational mending above.[26] Katz identified the bestial behavior aimed at the Jewish people and the descent of the world into a flood of fire as sufferings preceding redemption (*Hevlei geulah*). Citing *Sanhedrin* 97b–98a he explained that because redemption was imminent and the people were unworthy, God had set "a king as cruel as Haman" to force Israel to do *Teshuvah* and thereby become worthy.[27]

Lastly, in Brooklyn, NY, the religious nationalist Menahem Risikoff called upon the Levites to convene for a day of prayer and *Teshuvah*. According to the rabbinic sages, world history would yield to redemption in the year 6000, according to the Hebrew calendar (*Sanhedrin* 98a). The temporal path to redemption would begin three hundred years before. The current flood of fire, blood, and ruination of Jewish life (during the Hebrew months of *Kislev-Tammuz*, 1937–38) belonged to the final nine months of intense suffering.

> There are eighty-nine days in the months of *Ellul*, *Tishrei* and *Heshvan* leading up to *Kislev*. Then come nine months from *Kislev* through *Tammuz*, ending with the onset of the month of *Av*. The Ba'al Shem Tov wrote that redemption would come at that onset. . . . He also wrote that the troubles of the two hundred seventy-six days, *Kislev* through *Tammuz*, would be so difficult as to be unbearable. The period of *Be'ita* would end, and with *Av*, *Be'ita* would be transformed into *Ahishena*. [R. Joshua b. Levi: 'It is written that the messiah will come in his time (*Be'ita*). It is also written "I the Lord will hasten it. If the people are worthy, I will hasten it (*Ahishena*). If not, the messiah will come at the end of time (*Be'ita*). *Sanhedrin* 98a].[28]

With *Ahishena*, Nazism would collapse, and redemption would begin. When the second Temple was set aflame, Risikoff recalled, young priests ascended to the roof and handed its keys to heaven (*Ta'anit* 29a). By convening now during the month of *Av* for a day of prayer filled with mourning and atonement, attired in white robes and wrapped in *Tefillin*, and imploring God for redemption, the priests of Israel could bridge between disaster and salvation. The keys would be returned to history—for history to blend with redemption.[29]

REVERBERATIONS

Having found a path of thought to respond to the Kristallnacht, Orthodox Jews now had the wherewithal to respond to the unprecedented events to come. Namely: 1) The epistemological process where a boundary is drawn around naturalistic and rational explanation and opening reflection to metahistorical explanation. 2) The focus on accusing Jewish assimilants for setting off the persecution, under divine *aegis*. 3) Setting limits to metahistorical explanation and yielding to a transcendental battle between good and evil. 4) The need for Jews to participate from below, in tandem with the battle above between evil and good and its conclusion with redemption.

In Simleul-Silvaniei, Transylvania, Shelomoh Zalman Ehrenreich drew a perimeter around attempted explanations of God's relationship to history in February 1939. He fell silent, and then turned to await future redemption for understanding.[30] In Bratislava, Shelomoh Zalman Unsdorfer suspended all questions related to God's intentions with regard to historical events. A leap of faith was required—which could access the apocalyptic drama underway between suffering and redemption.[31] In Jerusalem, the Gur *Hasid* Yitshak Meir Levin wrote (on October 29, 1942) that

> All events, good and bad, can be understood through *Torah* alone. Is there any clearer way (human or natural) to really comprehend all that has happened to us since the day we became a nation and until today? [To grasp our survival] for thousands of years of exilic wandering, despite what the enemy and persecutor who rose up to destroy us sought? Certainly, we suffered as no other. But we have remained standing erect. Meanwhile, how many nations have been lost from the world, with nothing but fragile "historical" vestiges left? We have survived millennia without our own territory, exiled and exiled. Even the most severe tyrant cannot deny the eternity within us; the power of our existence. Is it possible to explain this through any natural calculations or humanistic research?[32]

Also in Jerusalem, in December 1944, Yehezkel Sarna, unable to find an explanation for the calamity based upon Israel's past, turned to God above. God's tears over Israel's plight opened a path of explanation.[33] In the wake of the catastrophe, Simhah Elberg, who escaped to Shanghai from Warsaw, declared that no language existed to articulate the catastrophe. He turned to the *Akedah*, the virtual sacrifice of Isaac, which he identified as Israel's timeless, metaphysical essence.[34]

METAHISTORICAL DISCLOSURES

The correlation between assimilation and catastrophe was present, for example, in Unsdorfer's sermons in Bratislava at the end of 1941 and the beginning of 1942. He observed that when Jews did away with traditional garb for modern dress, the enemy forced them to dress with patches of the yellow star; that after Jews joined Christmas celebrations, they were forced to remain inside during the Christmas holiday.[35] In Brooklyn, NY, the Lubavitch Rebbe Yosef Yitshak Schneersohn claimed that assimilationist denials of Jewish election and of divinely chosen prophets set off Nazi measure-for-measure assaults at the end of 1939.[36] Also in New York, Joseph Henkin of the *Ezrat torah* relief society wrote that Gentiles were, by nature, animals of prey with enmity for Jews. Sooner or later they would have attacked. Assimilation by Jews provoked them—for they interpreted it as an underhanded maneuver to both undermine Christianity and to become rich and politically important.[37]

APOCALYPTIC DUALISM

Examples of apocalyptic visions include those offered by Schneersohn. He described the exile of the people of Israel from their land in 70 AD as divine punishment for sin. Its purpose was to evoke *Teshuvah*. When *Teshuvah* did not take place, God radicalized the past choice between suffering and *Teshuvah* to one between death and life. Those who did *Teshuvah* would find refuge in the spiritual "camp of Israel" ("Mahaneh Yisrael") for a rapture-like return to the land for redemption. Those who did not return would be destroyed—along with all humans who had not adhered to the seven Noahide Laws.[38]

In Mexico City and then Brooklyn, NY, beginning in 1948, the Jerusalemite Mordekhai Atiyah identified the Holocaust as a cataclysmic turning point from exile to redemption. With the exile, sacred sparks descended into darkness, where the tension between sacred night and profane, material darkness (*Kelippot*, or shells) intensified more and more. The sparks were indestructible. When they descended to a point where further descent would have destroyed them, because they were indestructible, redemption became imminent. The explosive violence with which the sparks were liberated from the depths constituted the Holocaust.[39]

The earlier imperative of pious conduct in conjunction with the apocalyptic struggle, which was articulated in response to the Kristallnacht found its way through the war. Schneersohn called out for *Teshuvah*, as did Atiyah—for whom *Teshuvah* (penitent return) became subsumed into return to the Land of Israel. While not as apocalyptically dramatic, others expected redemption and called for *Teshuvah*—to participate in and contribute to the higher process. Yehezkel Sarna wrote that the realms of redemption (*Geulah*), *Teshuvah* and disaster (*Hurban*) were displayed across Israel's metahistorical path of development, and that *Geulah* was now imminent. It was, however, contingent upon Israel's *Teshuvah* below.[40] In 1943 Ehrenreich admonished his congregants not to reflect upon whether or how the tragedies were divine judgment, and instead to do *Teshuvah* as their forefathers had done in Egypt.[41]

CONCLUDING REMARKS

The existence of religious responses to the Kristallnacht demonstrated the creative vitality of Orthodox Judaism's spiritual dimension of a metahistorical narrative that endured incomprehensible historical events, as well as of apocalyptic drama (which had its parallels, in reverse, in Nazism)[42] which opened to redemption. The pattern of response to the Kristallnacht: recognition of the unprecedented character of the destruction, the search for higher truth and conviction that it existed; the metahistorical narrative, and the apocalyptic dualism opening to redemption, would reverberate into and through the Holocaust itself. The fact that there was a spiritual, reflective response to the Kristallnacht could well have enabled Orthodox thinkers to continue to respond as the tragedy became increasingly catastrophic. The contemporaneous responses from across the globe also belonged to a cohesive whole—evidencing the strength and breadth of the unified tradition of Orthodox thought. Ingredients of the responses could be traced to earlier cataclysmic events, but insofar as the Kristallnacht was unique, so were the responses.[43]

Notes

1. For further details on the American Ultra-Orthodox response see Gershon Greenberg, "*Kristallnacht*: The American Ultra-Orthodox Jewish Theological Response," in *American Religious Responses to Kristallnacht*, ed. Maria Mazzenga (New York: Palgrave Macmillan, 2009), 145–81.
2. The term "metahistory" was initiated by Jacob Rosenheim and Isaac Breuer in the interwar years. See Gershon Greenberg, "Sovereignty as Catastrophe: Jacob Rosenheim's *Hurban Weltanschauung*," *Holocaust and Genocide Studies* 8, no. 2 (1994): 202–24 and Gershon Greenberg, "The *Yishuv* of History vs. the *Yishuv* of Revelation: Jacob Rosenheim's 1934 Response to Isaac Breuer," *Judaica* 75, no. 3 (2018): 12–21.
3. Ferdinand M. Isserman, "Assassination—Not the way of Judaism," sermon delivered at Temple Israel, St. Louis, at the special service of prayer for the persecuted people of all groups. November 18, 1938, 1.
4. Tobias Geffen, "Derush leparashat hayei sarah 5699," in *Nahalat Yosef* (New York: Moyneshter Publishing, 1946), 60–64.
5. Bentsion Halberstam, "Igeret kodesh 3 leseder lishuateha kiviti hashem, 5699 Bobov," in *Sha'ar hatefillah*, ed. Shelomoh Czernowitz (Jerusalem: H. Grinfeld, 1955), 157–59.
6. Elhanan Wasserman, *Ma'amar ikveta dimeshiha. Ah belaykhtung fun der yetstike tekufah* (New York: Publisher unknown, 1938).
7. Reuven Katz, "Hevlei geulah," *Hayesod* 8, no. 259 (1939): 2.
8. Mosheh Avigdor Amiel, "Nehapesah darkenu: Hirhurei teshuvah," *Hatsofeh* 2, no. 318 (1939): 6.
9. Y. A. Dvorkes, "Tekufatenu: Hirhurim lamatsav," *Diglenu* (April 3, 1939): 15.
10. Mordekhai Schwartz (Martin Herman), "Yafeh liyemei hateshuvah ulekhal et," in *Derushei hokhmah veda'at* (Quality Printing and Publishing, 1940): 163–69.
11. Office of the Chief Rabbi, London. A Service of Prayer and Intercession for the Jews in Germany. Sunday, November 20, 1939.
12. Joseph Konvitz and Yehudah Layb Seltser, "Letsom, liteshuvah utefillah utsedakah," *Hapardes* 12, no. 9 (1938): 3.
13. Joseph Konvitz and Yehudah Layb Seltser, "Ruf fun agudas harabanim for dem ta'anis tsibur komenden Montag," *Morgen Zshurnal—Togblat* 38, no. 11, 278 (1938): 5.
14. Dvorkes, "Tekufatenu," 15.
15. Hayim Ozer Grodzensky, "Be'ezrat hashem. 31 May 1959," *Sefer ahiezer*, vol. 3 (Vilna: S. P. Grober, 1939), preface. After Germany invaded Poland (September 1, 1939) and Jews sought refuge in Vilnius (Vilnius was returned to independent Lithuania on October 10, 1939), Grodzensky sent an urgent appeal to the United States. It led to an emergency Agudat harabbonim conference and the creation of the *Va'ad Hatsalah* rescue organization. Editor, "Hakhrazat agudat harabanim in amerika," *Hapardes* 14, no. 7 (October 1940): 2.

16. Schwartz, "Yafeh," 163–69.
17. Amiel, "Nehapesah," 6.
18. Eliezer Gershon Fridenzon, "For der antshaydung," *Beit ya'akov* 16, no. 152 (1938): 1.
19. Wasserman, *Ma'amar*.
20. Shelomoh Pardes, "Al hurban hamikdash, hurban hatorah, ve'al am hashem ki naflu baherev . . . Ve'anu shoalim ben adam ayyekah?" *Hapardes* 12, no. 9 (1938): 2–3.
21. Fridenzon, "For der antshaytung," 1.
22. Ya'akov Mosheh Harlap, "Beni yakiri mahmadi [15 November 1938]," *Or hamizrah* 10, nos. 1–2 (1962): 14–15.
23. Wasserman, *Ma'amar*.
24. Fridenzon, "For der antshaydung," 1.
25. Halberstam, "Igeret," 157–59.
26. B[inyami]n, "An aktuel vort," *Beit Ya'akov* 16, no. 155 (1939): 1–2.
27. Katz, "Hevlei hageulah," 2.
28. Menahem Risikoff, *Palgei shemen* (New York: Publisher unknown, 1939): 171a–73b.
29. Risikoff, *Palgei shemen*, 103b–08b, 170b–73b.
30. Shelomoh Zalman Ehrenreich, "Mah shedarashti beyom alef parashat tetsaveh 7 Adar 5699 (29 February 1939)," in *Derashot lehem shelomoh*, ed. Y. Kats (Brooklyn: Y. Kats, 1976), 283–85.
31. Shelomoh Zalman Unsdorfer, "Parashat va'era: Or leyom le'erev shabbat kodesh vayera shenat 5702," in *Siftei shelomoh* (Brooklyn: Publisher unknown, 1972), 308–10.
32. Isaac Meir Levin, "Heshbono shel olamenu," *Haderekh* 7 (October 29, 1942): 2.
33. Yehezkel Sarna, *Liteshuvah velitekumah. Devarim sheme'emru bakinus lemasped uteshuvah shehitkayem ba'ir biyeshivat hevron-keneset yisrael beyom 8 Kislev 5705* (Jerusalem: Tevunah, 1944).
34. Simhah Elberg, *Akedas treblinka* (Shanghai, 1946).
35. Shelomoh Zalman Unsdorfer, "Vayehi . . . Erev shabbat kodesh lesidra vayehi shenat 5702," in *Seftei shelomoh* (Brooklyn: Publisher unknown, 1972), 81–89 and idem, "Parashat vayera," 308–10.
36. Yosef Yitshak Schneersohn, "Ferter kol kore fun dem lubavitsher rabin shlita [11 September 1942]," *Hakeriyah vehakedushah* 3, no. 25 (1942): 12–13.
37. Joseph Henkin, "Sinat ha'umot," *Hamesilah* 4, nos. 11–12 (1939): 4–6.
38. Gershon Greenberg, "Mahaneh yisrael—Lubavitch, 1940–1945," *Modern Judaism* 12, no. 1 (1992): 61–84.
39. Gershon Greenberg, "Mordekhai Yehoshua Atiyah's Kabbalistic Response to the Holocaust," *Iggud: Mivhar ma'amarim bemada'ei hayahadut. Kerekh beit. Toledot am yisrael vehevrah hayehudit bat zemanenu. Ha'igud ha'olami lemada'ei hayahadut* 2 (2009): 137–56.
40. Sarna, *Liteshuvah*.
41. Shelomoh Zalman Ehrenreich, "Mah shedarashti beshabbat hagadol shenat 5703," in *Derashot lehem shelomoh*, ed. Y. Kats (Brooklyn: Y. Kats, 1976), 212–16.

42. The apocalyptic mindset, transcending empirical and meta-empirical explanations, aligned with Nazi apocalyptisicm. In *Mein Kampf*, Hitler pronounced "By defending myself against the Jew, I am fighting for the work of the Lord" (Adolf Hitler, *Mein Kampf* [Boston: Houghton Mifflin, 1943], 65). The German historian Helmut Krausnick wrote that while for Christians the Jew was a symbol of evil, and Judaism a rotting remnant which was superseded by true faith and had been destroyed, Nazism performed the hypostatic charge which substituted content for symbol, Jew for Judaism, evil for the symbol of evil. The Jew was evil itself (Helmut Krausnick, "The Persecution of the Jews," in *Anatomy of the SS State*, ed. Helmut Krausnick, Hans Buchheim, Martin Broszat and Hans-Adolf Jacobsen [London: Collins, 1968], 1–124). The Jew, for Nazism, was the devil incarnate, a satanic force out to rule and destroy the world (Yehudah Bauer, "The *Kristallnacht* as Turning Point: Jewish Reactions to Nazi Policies," in *The Origins of the Holocaust*, ed. Michael Marrus [Westport: Meckler, 1989], 553–69).

43. In turn, the vitality of response reflected the strength of faith. Eliezer Schweid of Jerusalem explores this from the perspective of his position as the leading historian of Jewish thought of our era. His observations include the following:

> Grappling with the reality of the Holocaust was a factor that turned the faith in divine providence into an absolute need, as if it were the only hope or saving way out for humanity . . . In the face of the Holocaust [believers] were able to enlist the reserves of moral energy that were necessary in order to resist, to survive, and to look forward in hope, solely on the basis of their tottering faith. If they were to give up on it, they would be giving up on the hope of life and on life itself. They refused. The need for faith became for them the source of its validity" (Eliezer Schweid, "Faith Confronting the Experiences of Our Age," in *Eliezer Schweid: The Responsibility of Jewish Philosophy*, ed. Hava Tirosh-Samuelson and Aaron W. Hughes, trans. Leonard Levin [Leiden: Brill, 2013], 81–87).

Bibliography

Amiel, Mosheh Avigdor. "Nehapesah darkenu: Hirhurei teshuvah." *Hatsofeh* 2, no. 318 (1939): 6.

Bauer, Yehudah. "The *Kristallnacht* as Turning Point. Jewish Reactions to Nazi Policies." In *The Origins of the Holocaust*, edited by Michael Marrus, 553-69. Westport: Meckler, 1989.

B-n. "An aktuel vort." *Beit Ya'akov* 16, no. 155 (1939): 1-2.

Dvorkes, Y. A. "Tekufatenu: Hirhurim lamatsav." *Diglenu* (April 3, 1939): 15.

Editor. "Hakhrazat agudat harabanim in amerika." *Hapardes* 14, no. 7 (October 1940): 2.

Ehrenreich, Shelomoh Zalman. "Mah shedarashti beshabbat hagadol shenat 5703." In *Derashot lehem shelomoh*, edited by Y. Kats, 212-16. Brooklyn: Y. Kats, 1976.

———. "Mah shedarashti beyom alef parashat tetsaveh 7 Adar 5699 (29 February 1939)." In *Derashot lehem shelomoh*, edited by Y. Kats, 283-85. Brooklyn: Y. Kats, 1976.

Elberg, Simhah. *Akedas treblinka*. Shanghai, 1946.

Fridenzon, Eliezer Gershon. "For der antshaydung." *Beit ya'akov* 16, no. 152 (1938): 1.

Geffen, Tobias. "Derush leparashat hayei sarah 5699." In *Nahalat Yosef*, 60-64. New York: Moyneshter Publishing, 1946.

Greenberg, Gershon. "*Kristallnacht*: The American Ultra-Orthodox Jewish Theological Response." In *American Religious Responses to Kristallnacht*, edited by Maria Mazzenga, 145-81. New York: Palgrave Macmillan, 2009.

———. "Mahaneh yisrael—Lubavitch, 1940-1945." *Modern Judaism* 12, no. 1 (1992): 61-84.

———. "Mordekhai Yehoshua Atiyah's Kabbalistic Response to the Holocaust." *Iggud: Mivhar ma'amarim bemada'ei hayahadut. Kerekh beit. Toledot am yisrael vehevrah hayehudit bat zemanenu*. Ha'igud ha'olami lemada'ei hayahadut 2 (2009): 137-56.

———. "Sovereignty as Catastrophe. Jacob Rosenheim's *Hurban Weltanschauung*." *Holocaust and Genocide Studies* 8, no. 2 (1994): 202-24.

———. "The *Yishuv* of History vs. the *Yishuv* of Revelation: Jacob Rosenheim's 1934 Response to Isaac Breuer." *Judaica* 75, no. 3 (2018): 12-21.

Grodzensky, Hayim Ozer. "Be'ezrat hashem. 31 May 1959." In *Sefer ahiezer*, vol. 3, preface. Vilna: S. P. Grober, 1939.

Halberstam, Bentsion. "Igeret kodesh 3 leseder lishuateha kiviti hashem, 5699 Bobov." In *Sha'ar hatefillah*, edited by Shelomoh Czernowitz, 157-59. Jerusalem: H. Grinfeld, 1955.

Harlap, Ya'akov Mosheh. Beit Zevul—Harlap Archives. "Beni hayakar [27 October 1938]. Letter 158.

———. "Beni yakiri mahmadi [15 November 1938]." *Or hamizrah* 10 nos. 1-2 (1962): 14-15.

Henkin, Joseph. "Sinat ha'umot." *Hamesilah* 4, nos. 11-12 (1939): 4-6.

Hitler, Adolf. *Mein Kampf.* Boston: Houghton Mifflin, 1943.

Isserman, Ferdinand M. "Assassination—Not the way of Judaism." Sermon delivered at Temple Israel, St. Louis, at the special service of prayer for the persecuted people of all groups. November 18, 1938.

Katz, Reuven. "Hevlei geulah." *Hayesod* 8, no. 259 (1939): 2.

Konvitz, Joseph, and Yehudah Layb Seltser. "Letsom, liteshuvah utefillah utsedakah." *Hapardes* 12, no. 9 (1938): 3.

———. "Ruf fun agudas harabanim for dem ta'anis tsibur komenden Montag." *Morgen Zshurnal—Togblat* 38, no. 11, 278 (1938): 5.

Krausnick, Helmut. "The Persecution of the Jews." In *Anatomy of the SS State*, edited by Helmut Krausnick, Hans Buchheim, Martin Broszat, and Hans-Adolf Jacobsen, 1–124. London: Collins, 1968.

Levin, Isaac Meir. "Heshbono shel olamenu." *Haderekh* 7 (October 29, 1942): 2.

Office of the Chief Rabbi, London. A Service of Prayer and Intercession for the Jews in Germany. Sunday, November 20, 1939.

Pardes, Shelomoh. "Al hurban hamikdash, hurban hatorah, ve'al am hashem ki naflu baherev . . . Ve'anu shoalim ben adam ayyekah?" *Hapardes* 12, no. 9 (1938): 2–3.

Risikoff, Menahem. *Palgei shemen.* New York: Publisher unknown, 1939.

Sarna, Yehezkel. *Liteshuvah velitekumah. Devarim sheme'emru bakinus lemasped uteshuvah shehitkayem ba'ir biyeshivat hevron-keneset yisrael beyom 8 Kislev 5705.* Jerusalem: Tevunah, 1944.

Schneersohn, Yosef Yitshak. "Ferter kol kore fun dem lubavitsher rabin shlita [11 September 1942]." *Hakeriyah vehakedushah* 3, no. 25 (1942): 12–13.

Schwartz, Mordekhai (Martin Herman). "Yafeh liyemei hateshuvah ulekhal et." In *Derushei hokhmah veda'at*, 163–69. St. Louis: Quality Printing and Publishing, 1940.

Tirosh-Samuelson, Hava, and Aaron W. Hughes, eds. *Eliezer Schweid: The Responsibility of Jewish Philosophy*, translated by Leonard Levin. Leiden: Brill, 2013.

Unsdorfer, Shelomoh Zalman. "Parashat va'era: Or leyom le'erev shabbat kodesh vayera shenat 5702." In *Siftei shelomoh*, 308–10. Brooklyn: Publisher unknown. 1972.

———. "Vayehi . . . Erev shabbat kodesh lesidra vayehi shenat 5702." In *Seftei shelomoh*, 81–89. Brooklyn: Publisher unknown. 1972.

Wasserman, Elhanan. *Ma'amar ikveta dimeshiha. Ah belaykhtung fun der yetstike tekufah.* New York: Publisher unknown. 1938.

CHAPTER 10

1938: American Jews Respond to a Very Bad Year

by Hasia Diner

The historian and prolific author, Dorothy Zeligs, published *A History of Jewish Life in Modern Times for Young People* in 1938. Released by Bloch Publishing Company, one of the signature houses for American Jewish books, this volume told its story in a decidedly somber tone despite the generally upbeat voice common to this genre of writing, one which shared with Jewish youngsters the positive aspects of Jewish life and Judaism, stressing Jewish achievements. Zeligs had, however, no choice but to conclude her chapter, "The Story of the Jews in Germany," in an ominous tone. "At the present," she declared, "under the Hitler rule ... anti-Semitism has reached such a high point that the future of the Jews in Germany seems very gloomy." She advised teachers to stage a classroom drama for students to enact, "Elsa's house before she leaves Nazi Germany for the United States," hoping it would convey to these American Jewish youngsters that Elsa and her family could not remain at home. Yet despite these somber pronouncements, Zeligs, like so many writers of American Jewish texts published that year, strove to end on an optimistic note. "Jews have gone through difficult periods before. They will not lose hope now."[1]

1938, the year Zelig's little book came out, from the point of view of the Jews' recent history, could not have been worse. The horrors visited upon the Jews in Germany in November, 1938 with mass arrests, street attacks, invasions of their homes, destruction of their businesses and communal institutions, and the burning of so many synagogues, followed a year-by-year unfolding crisis, starting in 1933 with Hitler's accession to power.

The disturbing events of 1938, month-by-month, in particular captured the attention of American Jews, horrifying them and making them increasingly frantic about the fate of their co-religionists in Europe. Their horror at Kristallnacht's fury served as a capstone to a half-decade of worry and almost a year of escalating anxiety. It in itself did not wake up these already worried American Jews, but rather served as an unmistakable, very real marker of the spreading threats which loomed against the Jews living under German domination.

The ways in which Kristallnacht, which took place near the very end of 1938—November—registered to American Jews reflected the growing realities which they had been living with for five years. They saw that each year after 1933 had chipped away at the lives of Germany's Jews. But 1938 gave American Jews, the rank-and-file and the community leaders, much to terrify them. These included the German absorption of Austria, the *Anschluss*, in March, which immediately launched a coordinated set of actions against the Jews; the German incorporation of parts of Czechoslovakia in October; the November promulgation of the *leggi razialli*, the racial laws, which stripped the Jews of Italy of their citizenship, and that same month, the most dramatic moment of all in that terrible year, the "night of the broken glass," Kristallnacht.

The last of these loomed largest but altogether the horrors of 1938, as well as the whole cascade of assaults upon the Jews which had begun earlier in the 1930s, left their marks on the Jewish people in the United States despite the ocean, which separated them from those living directly with these attacks. The changes which took place during 1938 can be less attributed to this one blazing event but rather to the steady accretion of recognition that the Jewish people faced a much altered, and for the worse, future.

Their newspapers, whether English or Yiddish, carried details of the evolving degradation of the status of Jews in Germany and they organized meetings, symposia, and public gatherings to ask how they could address the ever-growing specter. Some of them who came out of the labor movement, for example, formed as early as 1933 the Jewish Labor Committee to both rescue Jewish labor leaders and socialists from Germany and to inform the American unions about the threat emanating from Germany.

American Jews responded to the assaults engulfing the Jewish people in Europe. They issued direct political appeals to those who held the reins of power, including but not limited to members of congress, officials of the

Department of State, and President Franklin D. Roosevelt, whom the vast majority had voted for in 1932 and in the recent election in 1936, when he sought his second term.

How did these Jews, living so far away from the scenes of physical violence, lost rights, mass incarcerations in concentration camps, and stolen property, change their own institutional practices to respond to what they read about in the Jewish and general press and heard in their synagogues and other communal Jewish organizations? How did they rearrange their institutional practices and ideologies in the face of 1938?

BETWEEN RIGHTS AND FEARS

American Jewish actions in response to the events of 1938 in Europe, Germany most importantly, reflected both their increasing integration and the unmistakable proliferation of anti-Jewish rhetoric which resounded in their America. On the one hand they had experienced no diminishing of rights, legal or civic. They constituted one of the largest Jewish population centers in the world, generally enjoying the full privileges of white citizenship. While Jews experienced discrimination in a range of settings, whether private colleges and universities, social clubs, hotels, resorts, and residential neighborhoods, in the eyes of the law they possessed the full bundle of rights of all white people. In terms of their economic condition in 1938, while they had, like all Americans, suffered from the still raging economic depression, they could not be described as having been particularly stung by it. In some ways, Jews suffered less, given that farmers, African Americans, and laborers in the heavy industries like mining, steel, and automobile manufacturing felt its impact most severely. By 1930 a majority of Jews had been born in the United States and experienced, despite the economic downturn, a slow but measurable movement out of the working class into the middle class.

By the 1930s the Jews of the United States constituted the largest, freest, richest, and institutionally robust Jewish population in the world, with more organizations, institutions, and communal bodies than any other Jewry at the time. Their economic resources, channeled through global bodies such as the American Jewish Joint Distribution Committee provided most of the funds to aid the Jews of Europe and the Middle East during and after World War I. In the 1920s American Jewish money rebuilt Jewish communal life in eastern

Europe. Hadassah, among other American Jewish philanthropic bodies, raised millions of dollars for the Jews of Palestine in the interwar years. Jewish women in America under Hadassah's auspices enabled the work of Youth Aliyah, which as of 1935 sent youngsters from Germany, Austria, and Czechoslovakia to Palestine. HIAS (the Hebrew Immigrant Aid Society) and subsidiary offshoots of the Joint facilitated Jewish resettlement out of Nazi-dominated Europe to far flung global havens, even before 1938 when the refugee crisis mushroomed to previously unimaginable proportions. Their communal coffers facilitated the movement of Jews to Shanghai, the Dominican Republic, Portugal, parts of Africa, indeed wherever refuge could be located.[2]

No other Jewish community in the world could accomplish this. As the situation of Jews in one European nation after another deteriorated with the economic depression, fascism and antisemitism, Jews in America raised money. Their ability to function like this depended on the efforts of both the very wealthy elite at the top and the masses below who contributed small but not irrelevant amounts of money. It also required that they marshal the support of powerful non-Jews to speak for and with them. Yet in 1938 much gave them pause. An opinion poll taken in 1938 found that sixty percent of Americans considered Jews "pushy" and "greedy" while other surveys revealed sizable percentages who declared that Jews had too much power and benefitted from the suffering of others.[3] The mid-1930s catapulted the radio priest, Father Charles Coughlin, into celebrity status with audiences numbering by some estimates to eleven million. His publication, *Social Justice,* like his airwave broadcasts, spewed hatred of Jews as parasites and exploiters of the poor. He expressed great admiration for Hitler, claimed that Jews pulled Roosevelt's strings, and might himself be one. Coughlin, like other, lesser demagogues, labelled the New Deal the "Jew Deal," charging that Roosevelt acted for the Jews, at their behest.[4]

Commenting on Kristallnacht, Coughlin insisted that the Jews of Germany had brought it upon themselves. "Jewish persecution," he declared a few weeks later, "only followed after Christians first were persecuted." The following month the radio priest fired up over two thousand followers to join a protest march in New York, demanding that the United States government not open its doors to Jewish refugees. Their banners warned, "Wait until Hitler comes over here!"[5]

Coughlin alone did not create the anti-Jewish barrage of the mid-1930s. William Dudley Pelley with his Silver Shirt Legion of America and Gerald Winrod, founder of the Defenders of the Christian Faith, along with other local hate-mongers, sent a collective shiver down the backs of American Jews. So, too, members of the German-American Bund, founded in 1936, took to the streets in Nazi uniforms and filled auditorium halls in New York, Newark, Milwaukee, Cincinnati, St. Louis and elsewhere, bringing Berlin's message to America's main streets.[6]

Anti-Jewish activities of the 1930s followed the spectacular rise of the 1920s Ku Klux Klan, which enrolled millions nationally. The Klan whipped up Americans in every region with arguments about the Jews' pernicious ability to control the media, entertainment, Wall Street, and the government. It ran and elected local and state candidates, registering successes well beyond its initial base in the South.[7]

The *American Jewish Yearbook*, a widely distributed compendium of Jewish news and statistics published since 1898, noted in its 1938–39 volume that, "the past year saw attempts on the part of the various native Jew-baiting organizations to unite," and warned that they managed to "join forces with the foreign provocateurs, chiefly the German American Bund." It commented that, "the Nazi infiltration among the native anti-Jewish groups," had become so dense, "that it is . . . increasingly difficult to separate one from the other."[8]

American Jews, as articulated in their publications, the reports of organizations, statements and deeds of communal bodies, and pronouncements of religious institutions, found this frighteningly real. While they lacked an official, central agency that could issue authoritative statements and despite sharp organizational competition and heated differences of opinion as to how to address the problems they faced, a near unanimity pervaded community life. Across deep divisions a consensus prevailed that American Jews had to do something and that understanding spanned women and men, Reform, Conservative, Orthodox, Reconstructionist, socialist, Communist, Zionist, anti-Zionist, English-speaking, Yiddish-speaking, American born, immigrant, of Central European background, of east European background, rich, middle class, and working class Jews, who converged on a few facts.

Across fundamental divides, American Jews recognized that many Jews outside the United States lived under the sword of Nazism. Jewish life in Europe, especially Poland and Rumania, teetered on the brink of disaster, and American Jews believed their own security threatened. How, with the increasingly audible ugly rhetoric swirling around them, could they as Jews accomplish two ends: preserve their own security, and, fulfill their responsibilities towards Jews elsewhere, their literal and metaphoric kin? As they saw it, the two could not be disaggregated. To accomplish the latter they had to ensure the former. Their political and communal actions in 1938 involved the mutuality of those concerns and while they did not agree how to accomplish these ends, they did all recognize their responsibilities.

Certainly millions of American Jews, regardless of class, ideology, gender, or region, lived undisturbed by European traumas. They went to work, ran businesses, invested in new enterprises, attended school, married, gave birth to children, raised them, enjoyed leisure, and participated in Jewish and general communal activities. Some contributed to American culture through literature, theater, the movies and music.

1938 proved a banner year for the latter of these endeavors. One American Jew, Irving Berlin, provided the nation with a stirring patriotic anthem, "God Bless America," which revealed the difference between it and Europe, where, "the storm clouds gather far across the sea." Berlin had originally written the song in 1918 as American entered World War I, but revised it in the year of Kristallnacht. The immigrant Jewish songwriter asked the popular performer Kate Smith to premier the song on the radio on Armistice Day, November 11, 1938. The hymn urged Americans: "Let us swear allegiance to a land that's free,/ Let us all be grateful for a land so fair./ As we raise our voices in a solemn prayer." "God Bless America" contrasted by implication the United States with Europe, a horror chamber defined by the Vienna pogroms and Kristallnacht.

The work of American Jews in the public sphere reflected their disturbed consciousness as they faced 1938 and that work operated on two levels. As they went about figuring out what they could do, American Jews sought ways to reach out to Americans of good-will to speak with and for them while at the same time they recognized a need to reshape Jewish communal life itself in order to act on their own behalf.

REACHING OUT

Jewish outreach to non-Jews, allies and potential allies whom they hoped to advocate for endangered Jews in Germany and elsewhere, reflected a reasonable assessment of reality. Knowing that they constituted less than five percent of the American people, Jews recognized that their own fate, and that of European Jewry, lay in the hands of others.

Engagement with non-Jewish comrades did not arise out of nowhere in 1938 or in the half decade after Hitler's accession to power. American Jews, rabbis and self-appointed leaders of local and national defense bodies had been doing so since the nineteenth century. When Jewish crises erupted in the United States or abroad, they consistently turned to non-Jews to speak with and for them. A monster rally organized, for example, by the American Jewish Congress on March 27, 1933, held at a packed Madison Square Garden in New York City, featured Catholic, Protestant and Jewish clergy, public officials, leaders of the labor movement and civic personalities. This rally in its own way resembled rallies they held in the first decade of the twentieth century after the Kishinev pogrom, when they had also sought out notable non-Jews to stand at their sides.[9]

The German crisis of 1938, however, accelerated such activity, rendering the task ever more critical. American Jewish publications and institutions widely publicized the deeds of their non-Jewish fellow Americans, Christian clergy or others, who supported the Jews of Europe and publicly opposed the spread of Fascist anti-Semitism, abroad and at home. Awareness of the larger American public's widespread good will and its aversion to the persecution of the Jews, they wagered, would inspire other non-Jews, unaware of the exigencies of the moment, to join. As more Americans awoke to the plight of the Jews in Germany, opinion makers among American Jews hoped the government would respond in kind. Those with power would realize that Jews did not stand alone in calling for vigorous action against Hitlerism.

The *American Jewish Yearbook* offers one source from which to survey this kind of wishful thinking. Its reliability as an historical record reflects its careful research, accuracy of reporting, meticulous statistics, geographic breadth, and wide circulation to government officials, academicians, libraries, and others. Its editors, as they prepared each volume, scanned the Jewish and general press, redacted articles and editorials, gleaning news nationally and globally.[10]

In the two volumes bridging 1938 and Kristallnacht, 1937–38 and 1938–39, its editors balanced news of the harsh realities of anti-Jewish violence abroad and anti-Jewish agitation in America with reportage on the many hopeful signs signaling that American non-Jews stood up to combat anti-Semitism. Upsurges in good-will, evidence of Americans' revulsion against Nazi hatred of the Jews, allowed American Jews to claim that their nation occupied a very different and special place in the world. As the 1937–38 *Yearbook's* section, "Movements for Better Understanding" noted, even after "appraising the influence of the forces of ill-will . . . and the anti-Jewish agitation promoted by them," readers should recognize that, "the forces of good will are much more numerous and active, and the wholesome inter-group attitudes generated by them are much more in harmony with the American spirit than the heresy of inter-group hostility."[11]

Pages upon pages listed meetings, publications, petitions, articles, sermons, radio broadcasts, and statements made in city councils, state legislatures, and the halls of Congress by non-Jewish allies in support of the Jews. The editors positively glowed describing anti-Nazi rallies held in New York and Los Angeles in January 1938, events that marked the fifth anniversary of Hitler's accession to power. The Los Angeles meeting, it reported, brought ten thousand to the Shrine Auditorium to listen to the Jewish actor Eddie Cantor, but also author Dorothy Parker and Congressman Jerry O'Connell.[12] It provided book titles of the year authored by non-Jews, which documented the hideous actions visited upon Jews in Germany and elsewhere under Nazi rule, hailing authors like John Haynes Holmes, Dorothy Thompson, William Harman Black, among many others, whose works like, *Through Gentile Eyes, Refugees: Anarchy or Organization,* and *If I Were a Jew,* empathized with the Jews.[13]

Unitarian minister, Holmes, after all, declared himself in the title, a "Gentile," who considered it his responsibility to issue a *Plea for Tolerance and Good Will.*[14] Notably Holmes, a close collaborator with Stephen Wise, issued his book through the Jewish Opinion Publishing Company, an offshoot of Wise's magazine, *Jewish Opinion.* Throughout 1938, Jews repeatedly sought out non-Jews to speak for them. William Harman Black, a justice of the Supreme Court of New York and Honorary Chairman of the Interfaith Movement, declared in his *If I Were a Jew,* that this organization had been founded with the aid of the Wall Street Synagogue. The movement and its official publication, "The Beacon Light," existed to warn the American public that the "prairie fire of intolerance has been lighted in Germany," where the Jews "find themselves again the almost helpless victims of the conflagration."[15]

The *Yearbook* lauded the ways Jewish notables, organization leaders, and communal figures turned to their Catholic and Protestant colleagues to write on behalf of the Jews, to speak at rallies, and to form organizations and committees to advocate for Jews abroad in distress. These same political acts, undertaken by Jews alone, Jews calculated, would have smacked of Jewish pleading, playing into the hand of the critics of the Jews who long argued that Jews had too much power and cared only for themselves. But outrage against anti-Semitism in Germany, articulated by a Catholic priest or a Protestant lay person, appeared humanitarian and selfless.

Larger and smaller pieces of writing by Christians in support of Jews merited attention. The 1938–1939 *Yearbook* highlighted magazine articles and other pieces, which it claimed had "resulted in arousing public interest." Among many, it ticked off:

> "Good Will to Men," by Alvin Johnson, in *Atlantic Monthly*, December, 1938; "Jewish Pawns in Power Politics," by Demaree Bess, in *Saturday Evening Post*, March 18, 1939; "Star-Spangled Fascists," by Stanley High, in *Saturday Evening Post*, May 27; "Why Hate the Jews," by Struthers Burt, in *Forum*, May and June; and "Why the Jews are Persecuted," by Stanley High, in *Look*, July 18. The *Survey Graphic*, for February, 1939, in an issue entitled "Calling America," and the *Atlantic Monthly*, in a special issue entitled, "We Americans," part of a series bearing the general title *Atlantic Presents*, were devoted to studies of the subject of group relations in a democracy.[16]

The descant of hope embedded in these articles, essays, books, lectures and sermons represented wishful thinking about Americans' good-will towards Jews and their sympathy for the Jews facing Nazism abroad. It constituted evidence, real or imaginary, that Americans would never behave like Germans, Austrians, Italians, and Czechs and turn on their Jewish fellow citizens. After all, as of December 1938, a few weeks following the devastation that took place in Germany, "an official joint Protestant-Catholic statement" went forth in America "denouncing religious and racial persecution." Furthermore, "virtually every prominent Protestant communion condemned anti-Semitism during the year in official resolutions, through denominational publications or in other forms of action."[17]

The Jewish leadership fantasized that an awoken American public would spur the United States government to intervene on behalf of the imperiled Jews. With no idea as to how this might happen, Cyrus Adler, President of the American Jewish Committee, the body responsible for the *Yearbook*, sounded an optimistic tone in his address to the AJC's 1938 annual meeting. "America," he declared, "will struggle for and I believe maintain, its system of civilization and that it may sometime again be willing to take the opportunity to spread democratic ideals throughout the world." To Adler, that spread of consciousness among the American people would push the government to act and to "interfere in the domestic affairs of another State." Naming Germany and Italy, Adler called upon the American people and government to act when foreign nations "force large numbers of people to migrate, create a great mass of refugees, émigrés, stateless people who with the best will find it difficult sometimes to adjust themselves in other States, or whom other States sometimes find it difficult to digest."[18]

The *Yearbook* editors additionally noted that most German Americans, as well as Czech and Italian Americans, abhorred the actions of their old homelands, reporting that "many Americans of German origin openly disapprove and strongly resent the importation of Nazi doctrines in this country." In the aftermath of the promulgation of the racial laws in Italy, the *Yearbook* highlighted the negative reaction of Italian Americans *vis-à-vis* the actions of their country of origin. That surely gave American Jews something to savor. The heretofore pro-Fascist "Generoso Pope, the most prominent and influential of the Italian-American publishers," expressed disbelief that his country would act so brutally towards the Jews. Pope, it noted, broke ranks with the Mussolini government that had been funding his New York newspaper, *Il Progresso*. As "a concrete manifestation" of the Italian Americans' revulsion against anti-Semitism back home, it pointed to the establishment of The Sons of Italy Grand Lodge in June 1939. Among its first acts, the Italian fraternal order with two hundred branches throughout New York State, created a bureau to foster good will between the two groups.[19]

The message here emphasized America's essential difference and exceptionalism. They marshalled what evidence they had to prove American disgust at the anti-Jewish violence undertaken by Nazi Germany in 1938. All the New York daily newspapers, and in fact most papers across the country, editorialized against Nazi brutality. As Saul Friedman wrote, prominent American people and institutions, including, "the Catholic monthly *Wisdom*, the *Messenger* (national organs of the Evangelical and Reform Churches in the United States), the National Methodist Student Conference, the YMCA, the World Conference of the Society of Friends, Bishop William Manning of the Cathedral of St. John the Divine in New York, Harry Emerson Fosdick, Al Smith . . . . Vito Marcantonio, a New York Republican," lent their public voices to the chorus.[20] The National Catholic Welfare Conference News Service broadcast a message on NBC and CBS on November 16, 1938, expressing solidarity with the Jews of Germany and revulsion against the actions of Hitler's Reich.[21]

We cannot know to what extent the Jewish leaders actually believed in the beneficence of the American people and their government or if they manufactured their hopeful words to calm a jumpy Jewish population. Likely they veered between these two poles, clutching at straws as they cast their eyes across the Atlantic and as they heard the hoof beats of an anti-Jewish stampede at home. Either way the American Jewish world itself produced an avalanche of texts to educate itself on the crisis it faced.

1938, for example, saw the release of books such as Morris S. Lazaron's, *Common Ground: A Plea for Intelligent Americanism*; Oscar I. Janowsky and Melvin Fagen's, *International Aspects of German Racial Policies* (published the year before); Oscar Janowsky's, *People at Bay: The Jewish Problem in Central Europe*—all written by Jewish communal insiders, and published by major American presses.[22] All were intended to reveal the horrors of Jewish life in Europe and to try, through logic, rational arguments, and appeals to the nation's core values, to enlist Americans' sympathies and convince them to stand aloof from anti-Semitism. These represent just a small sampling of those books, let alone the virtual tsunami of articles printed in general and Jewish publications.[23]

No issue of Chicago's *Jewish Sentinel*, Wisconsin's *Jewish Chronicle*, Boston's *Jewish Advocate* or the hundreds of other papers around the country contained less than one or two articles on the deterioration of Jewish life in Europe under the Nazi menace. The daily Yiddish press covered the events in and graphic harrowing detail.

The year's events impelled American Jews to organize protest meetings in communities large and small, to which they invited local Jews along a broad spectrum as well as non-Jewish notables. Those meetings, like the ones that took place in such communities as New Haven and Waterbury, Connecticut, not only brought Jews and non-Jews together in outrage, but received press coverage, widening the net of those who knew of the plight of Germany's Jews and of Jewish mobilization at home.[24] Jewish spokespeople took to the airwaves, utilizing local stations and national broadcasting networks to answer the question, as posed by Rabbi Samuel Goldenson in an April, 1938 sermon on NBC, "What Shall We Jews Do These Days?"[25]

1938: A YEAR OF AMERICAN JEWISH ACTION

Rabbi Goldenson's sermon asked his co-religionists, "What Shall We Jews Do," and in asking this he reflected the reality that Jews in 1938, should not sit back and wait for American non-Jews to act for them. Indeed it did not take Kristallnacht to motivate them to act. Rather American Jewish organizations geared up for heightened outreach work, preparing texts to foster positive American support. In 1938 the American Jewish Committee hired Richard Rothschild, of the Walter Thompson and the Lord and Thomas advertising agencies to organize and supervise a broad coalition of Jewish and non-Jewish opponents of Nazism and anti-Semitism. Rothschild generated a steady stream of propaganda materials, using every genre at his command, to deliver the message to the American people that anti-Semitism was wrong, that Jews did not differ from other people, and that hatred of the Jews violated American norms and harmed America in the process.[26]

Other Jewish organizations added their voices. The Jewish Theological Seminary, under the leadership of Cyrus Adler, organized in 1938 the Institute for Religious and Social Studies, creating the first ongoing forum for Jewish, Protestant and Catholic clergy to engage in dialogue to lessen tensions based on faith traditions. The previous year Professor Abraham Katsch at New York University created the Jewish Culture Foundation, specifically to disseminate positive and truthful information about Jews and Judaism to the non-Jews on his campus and beyond. The Jewish Culture Foundation brought together a distinguished group of Jewish and non-Jewish public figures to contemplate how the Nazi government tried to influence "Americans of German origin." The Foundation published the papers in a book "intended to expose the purposes of National Socialist propaganda outside the Reich," in order "to inform the American public of the attitude of the German government toward American institutions and particularly toward American principles of citizenship." The following year, 1939, the newly created National Federation of Temple Brotherhoods, an arm of the Reform movement, prepared materials, including booklets, radio shows, articles, and films for distribution to libraries, churches, Christian summer camps and universities about Judaism, to spread good-will for the Jews. It also took over the somewhat moribund Jewish Chautauqua Society, and through it sent out rabbis to lecture to Christian groups in hopes of shattering the lies being spewed forth by Coughlin and Hitler.[27]

Joining this Jewish-inspired chorus, Jewish Opinion Publishing Company convened a symposium of Jews and non-Jews in its magazine, *Jewish Opinion*. The symposium was based on an essay contest, launched in 1937, "How to Combat Anti-Semitism in America." *Jewish Opinion* published the six winning submissions. All the contest participants referred to the looming threat of Germany and the danger it posed to Jews everywhere.[28] The Anti-Defamation League of the B'nai B'rith did its work, producing pamphlets in 1938 for use in its chapters around the country and for its "Fireside Discussion Group" activities. Women and men sitting around a table or in a living room, with sympathetic non-Jews invited to participate, contemplated such topics as, "The Aryan and Nordic Myths," "The Myth of Jewish Economic Dominance,"

"Hitler's Communism Unmasked," and in light of the recently enacted racial laws under Mussolini, "The Jews of Italy." These discussions never strayed far from the tragic events unfolding almost daily in the lives of Europe's Jews, set against a fear that maybe they could happen in America too.[29]

Such work infused American Jewish organizations and institutions, each working to spread the message. Maurice Karpf, a faculty member of the Graduate School for Jewish Social Work New York, made a direct connection in his 1938 compendium, *Jewish Community Organization in the United States*, between all the outreach activity and the "present German government's activities against the Jews." The American Jewish campaign of "propaganda against the Nazis," according to Karpf, focused on "the identification of the type of discrimination against Jews, with discrimination either immediate or ultimate against other minority groups; the stimulation of labor and other liberal groups to the realization that Nazi Germany and its program represent a threat to them." This work had been undertaken to combat, "the German influence in this country," set against, "anti-Semitism and intolerance in whatever guise."[30]

Karpf, writing in the year of Kristallnacht could only speculate on the efficacy of such actions. "It is," he almost sighed in conclusion, "impossible to estimate these activities" and their impact, adding a cautionary note, perhaps directed at those Jews who felt frustrated at the limited weapons in their arsenal. Some Jews "believe that were Jews to present a united front to the world in these and other efforts, however much they might differ internally," they could make a real difference as they faced the hostile situation of the 1938 moment.[31]

That quest for unity and the widely shared assumption that a less fractious and fractured American Jewish polity could more effectively combat Nazism at home and abroad than a complex, multi-vocal, chaotic, disorganized, and anarchic American Jewry, provides a second way by which they responded to the Nazi persecution of the Jews. American Jews, through communal bodies, began to redefine how they did their work and initiated a series of changes which informed their subsequent work. They did so by taking on new functions, creating more united fronts, and working to lessen previously held divisive beliefs.

In some cases, Jewish agencies reorganized or refined their organizational structure so as to respond more quickly to the rapid-fire events in Europe. The Joint Distribution Committee, conscious that in the face of 1938 and of "an emergency of huge proportions," demanded that familiar structures for fundraising and disbursement of monies be refined. Since it would "have to render assistance without delay," the Joint needed a more efficient structure. It became much less driven by a handful of wealthy and well-placed individuals.[32] Instead it took "several notable steps toward increasing the opportunities for community leaders throughout the country to participate in its work," setting up regional offices, and expanding its board in response to the "anti-Jewish outrages throughout Germany and Austria on November 10, 1938."[33] Similarly the Jewish War Veterans took on tasks it had never assumed before. In 1938 it picked up responsibility for aiding in the resettlement of the veterans who came to America among the Germany Jewish refugees, ironically providing aid to their former battlefield foes.[34] The B'nai B'rith established a Washington, DC office in 1938, making it the first American Jewish organization to set up a permanent presence in the nation's capital.

From the perspective of the ideological changes inspired by the German horror, the decision of the Reform movement's Central Conference of American Rabbis (CCAR) in 1937 to alter, however gingerly, its position on Zionism generated much attention. At its meeting in Columbus, Ohio, the CCAR announced that it now looked positively on the project of, the "upbuilding of a Jewish homeland and the rehabilitation of Palestine," thereby reversing its stance adopted at the end of the nineteenth century. Similarly the American Jewish Committee moved itself closer to the Zionist position. So, too, the Joint Distribution in 1939 began cooperating for the first time, although not without discord, with Zionists, easing the gap that had divided them since the end of World War I. The Jewish Labor Committee (JLC), founded by anti-Zionist Bundists in 1933 as an anti-Nazi organization, also shifted focus in 1938. While it had always co-operated with the Zionist left, in 1938 it broadened its vision by drawing attention to and actively supporting Jewish workers of Palestine; it also started participating in other kinds of Zionist projects. In 1939, the JLC joined with a broad coalition of American Zionists in protesting the British issuance of the White Paper, which severely curtailed Jewish migration from Germany. The emergence of a consensus on Palestine among American Jews, including those previously lukewarm or hostile to Zionism, made 1938 a turning point as American Jews focused on rescue and resettlement for the beleaguered Jews of Central Europe.[35]

As late as 1937, Jewish women's groups like National Council of Jewish Women, the National Federation of Temple Sisterhoods, the Women's League of the United Synagogue of America, and the Women's Branch of the Union of Orthodox Jewish Congregations, along with some of the male-dominated bodies, still publicly identified with the agenda of the American peace movement. Within a year, that support withered as pacifism seemed a less compelling ideology, peace a less persuasive agenda, and a belief that only military force would topple Nazism in Germany.[36]

That ability, or willingness, first manifest in 1938 among American Jews to co-operate along previously profound ideological and organizational divides also inspired some notable local and national innovations. Some proved short-lived and failed. The National Council of Jewish Federations and Welfare Funds, whose origins lay in the early twentieth century along with the American Jewish Committee, helped launch the General Council for Jewish Rights. While the AJC, the B'nai B'rith and the Jewish Labor Committee initially balked at the idea of a single defense agency to represent American Jewry, the forces in favor of such a coordinated body prevailed. They considered that it might help "mobilize the strength of American Jews in the struggle against Hitlerism."[37] The former naysayers overcame their opposition and in June, 1938, signed on to the Pittsburgh Agreement which led to the founding of the General Jewish Council. Organizers of the Council envisioned a broad-based forum for all American Jews to share in the fight against Nazism. They decided that after paying a ten-cent fee, any adult Jew could cast a ballot for delegates to the Council, which in turn would hammer out a general consensus on the momentous events of the day.

It never worked. The Council disbanded two years later, but even in its failure it demonstrated how 1938 compelled American Jews to consider the impact of their scattered communal structure and to search for antidotes to it.[38]

Of greater longevity and more measurable achievement, the United Jewish Appeal (UJA) also owed its birth to the global Jewish crisis of 1938. In January 1939, the United Palestine Appeal, the fundraising body of the Zionists, along with the Joint Distribution Committee and the National Coordinating Committee Fund, which had been formed to address the needs of the German Jewish refugees who made it to America, banded together to create the United Jewish Appeal for Refugee and Overseas Needs. To show that the fissures of the past paled in the face of the Hitler menace, the newly born body functioned under the tripartite joint leadership of Rabbi Abba Hillel Silver, a Zionist, William Rosenwald, son of the philanthropist and decidedly non-Zionist Julius Rosenwald, who represented the National Coordinating Committee, and Rabbi Jonah B. Wise, head of the Joint. Wise in 1938 served at President Roosevelt's request as a delegate to the international refugee conference in Evian, France. The initial goal of the UJA, to triple or quadruple the money which the three partners had raised individually in 1937, succeeded and the UJA went on to become a powerhouse of fund-raising for the Jews of Europe over the following decades. It is no exaggeration to say that nearly every penny used to fund the flight of Jews from Nazi-dominated countries, to resettle them in places on nearly every continent, and to provide food and other supplies to Jews still in Europe and who during the war languished in the ghettoes, came from the UJA. Despite internal dissension, organizational competition, and territorial squabbling, it served as the rallying point for large, medium, and small Jewish donors who considered giving money to the UJA a way to help their sisters and brothers under the threat of Hitler and Germany.[39]

So, too, against the specter of 1938, the Jewish communal service activists, donors, administrators, and social workers who provided direct assistance to Jews in need formed themselves into the National Refugee Service (NRS). Although it also assisted non-Jewish refugees and adopted a religiously neutral name, its purpose could not have been more decidedly Jewish. Within months of its founding in early 1939, it created liaison relationships with Jewish social service agencies in five hundred communities around the country, standing ready to provide housing, jobs, legal advice, and other services to the German, Czech, Austrian, and Polish Jewish refugees coming to the United States. NRS facilitated their settlement in New York and their dispersal to cities beyond which could accommodate the newcomers. Wherever they went, the local Jewish social service agencies, assisted by the New York office of NRS, worked with potential employers to provide jobs, while local bodies like the Associated Jewish Charities of Chicago or the Jewish Child and Family Services of Milwaukee secured and helped subsidize housing, clothing, medical care, and other essentials.[40]

On the local level, a number of Jewish communities formed themselves into community councils in 1938. Seeking a way to be able to speak authoritatively for all, or at least most Jews, community councils, some of which had started before 1938, got a boost in the face of the events of that year. These councils, in which all Jewish organizations sent representatives and collectively forged a communal consensus, heralded the fading of a significant divide between the American-born Jews of central European origins and the more recently arrived eastern Europeans, particularly their children. These two segments of American Jewry recognized a common enemy—Hitler abroad and Hitlerian anti-Jewish activity at home—and in cities like Washington, DC, they came together precisely in 1938, to do what they could.

Indeed, its first organizational meeting in Washington took place after Minnie Goldsmith, long a patron of the city's Jewish Social Service Agency, assembled a group because of the arrival of German Jewish refugees to

Washington. She understood that JSSA could meet some of their material needs, but the Jews of the city needed a constituent body "to speak for the Jewish community in matters of community concern."[41]

The proliferation of councils in 1938 and 1939 caught the attention of the editors of the *American Jewish Yearbook,* who deemed the increase "one of the most significant trends in the field of social welfare." The forty new such bodies represented a way "to cope on a unified basis with the greater needs at home and abroad."[42]

Kristallnacht sparked those "greater needs," although the events of 1938 that preceded it, also caused them to act. But it loomed most dramatically in their minds. As the editors of the *Yearbook* declared, "the single event which shocked American public opinion more profoundly than any other . . . since the rise of Hitlerism, was the campaign of pillage and destruction let loose against the Jews of Germany, on "Thursday, November 10, 1938." The editors, careful observers of the American Jewish scene, may very likely have deliberately chosen to declare that "the American public," and not just America's Jews had recoiled in horror. By putting it this way, they could confirm at least to themselves the support they understood they needed from the non-Jews with whom they had to work with. Kristallnacht burnt into their awareness the truth that they had to restructure community life so as to be able to respond to the grave challenges they faced and to shoulder the desperate chores thrust on them. But it alone did not put them on that course. The events of the half decade before got them started.[43]

Notes

1. Dorothy Zeligs, *A History of Jewish Life in Modern Times for Young People* (New York: Bloch, 1938), 183.
2. Marion Kaplan, *Dominican Haven: The Jewish Refugee Settlement in Sosua, 1940–1945* (New York: Museum of the Jewish Heritage and a Living Memorial to the Holocaust, 2008); Tom Schachtman, *"I Seek My Brethren": Ralph Goldman and the Join: Rescue, Relief and Reconstruction: The Work of the American Jewish Joint Distribution Committee* (New York: Newmarket Press, 2001).
3. Cited in, Leonard Dinnerstein, *Anti-Semitism in America* (New York: Oxford University Press, 1994), 113, 127.
4. Ibid., 109.
5. Ibid., 115.
6. On Coughlin, see, Donald I. Warren, *Radio Priest, Charles Coughlin, the Father of Hate Radio* (New York: Free Press, 1990); on American Nazism, see, Sander I. Diamond, *The Nazi Movement in the United States, 1934–1941* (Ithaca, NY: Cornell University Press, 1974); Warren Grover, *Nazis in Newark* (New Brunswick, NJ: Transaction Publishers, 2003).
7. Linda Gordon, *The Second Coming of the KKK: The Ku Klux Klan of the 1920s and the American Political Tradition* (New York: Liveright, 2017).
8. *American Jewish Yearbook* (henceforth, *AJY*) *5699: September 26, 1938 to September 13, 1939*, vol. 40 (Philadelphia: Jewish Publication Society of America, 1938), 120. A thorough review of the *AJY*, in particular volumes 39 and 40 in and of themselves, reveals a constant concern, monitoring, and analysis of the situation of the Jews under Nazi rule in Europe and the impact of that situation on the Jews of the United States.
9. *AJY 5694: September 21, 1933–September 9, 1934*, vol. 35 (Philadelphia: Jewish Publication Society of America, 1938), 2, 43; on American Jewish outreach to notable non-Jews since the middle of the nineteenth century, see, Gary Dean Best, *To Free a People: American Jewish Leaders and the Jewish Problem in Eastern Europe, 1890–1914* (Westport, CT: Greenwood Press, 1982).
10. The *AJY* followed the Hebrew calendar rather than the general one and therefore a year on the Gregorian calendar, 1938, split into two volumes, September 1937 to September 1938 (Volume 39) and then September 1938 to September 1939 (Volume 40).
11. *AJY*, vol. 40, 129.
12. *AJY*, vol. 40, 93–94.
13. *AJY*, vol. 40, 148–49, 509, 593, 617.
14. Dorothy Thompson, *Refugees: Anarchy or Organization* (New York: Random House, 1938); William Harman Black, *If I Were a Jew* (New York: Real Books, 1938); John Haynes Holmes, *Through Gentile Eyes: A Plea for Tolerance and Good Will* (New York: Jewish Opinion Publishing Corporation, 1938).

15. Black, *If I Were a Jew*, 277.
16. *AJY*, vol. 41, 217.
17. Ibid., vol. 40, 222–23.
18. Ibid., 651–52.
19. Ibid., 126; *AJY*, vol. 41, 199.
20. Saul S. Friedman, *No Haven for the Oppressed: United States Policy toward Jewish Refugees, 1938–1945* (Detroit: Wayne State University Press, 1973), 42; see also, Maria Mazzenga, ed., *American Religious Responses to Kristallnacht* (New York: Palgrave Macmillan, 2009).
21. Mark Pattison, "Archival Find at Catholic U. Leads to Kriistallnacht Remembrance," *Catholic News Service*, November 9, 2018.
22. Morris S. Lazaron, *Common Ground: Plea for Intelligent Americanism* (New York: Liveright, 1938); Oscar I. Janowsky and Melvin M. Fagen, *International Aspects of German Racial Policy* (New York: Oxford University Press, 1937); Oscar I. Janowsky, *People at Bay: The Jewish Problem in Central Europe* (New York: Oxford University Press, 1938).
23. *AJY*, vol. 40, 91–92, 95–99, 589, 601–05.
24. Kenneth Wolk, "New Haven and Waterbury, Connecticut Jewish Communities' Public Response to the Holocaust, 1938–1944: An Examination Based on Accounts in the Public Printed Press and Local Jewish Organizational Documents," PhD diss., New York University, 1995.
25. Rabbi Samuel Goldenson, "What Shall We Jews Do These Days? A Sermon Delivered on the Message of Esrael Hour, National Broadcasting Company, Saturday, April 9, 1938" (Center for Jewish History).
26. Frederick A. Lazin, "The Response of the American Jewish Committee to the Crisis of German Jewry, 1933–1939," *American Jewish Historical Quarterly* 68 (March, 1979): 283–305.
27. Jewish Culture Foundation, New York University, *The German Reich and Americans of German Origin* (New York: Oxford University Press, 1938), v–vi; "Jewish Chautauqua Society," in *Jewish American Voluntary Associations*, ed. Michael Dobkowsk (New York: Greenwood Press, 1986), 210.
28. *How to Combat Anti-Semitism in America: The Six Prize Winning Essays in the Contest Conducted by OPINION—a Journal of Life and Letters* (New York: Jewish Opinion Publishing Corporation, 1937).
29. Fireside Discussion Group of the Anti-Defamation League, B'nai B'rith, *Introduction* (Chicago: Anti-Defamation League, 1938).
30. Maurice J. Karpf, *Jewish Community Organizations in the United States: An Outline of Types of Organizations, Activities, and Problems* (New York: Bloch, 1938), 26.
31. Ibid.
32. Joseph C. Hyman, *Twenty-Five Years of American Aid to Jews Overseas: A Record of the Joint Distribution Committee* (New York: 1939), 51–52.

33. *AJY*, vol. 41, 205–08.
34. Ibid., 229.
35. *AJY*, vol. 40, 229.
36. Melissa Klapper, "'Peace Is Truly Our Mission': NFTS and the Peace Movement," in *Sisterhood: A Centennial History of Women of Reform Judaism*, ed. Carole B. Balin, Dana Herman, Jonathan D. Sarna, and Gary P. Zola (Cincinnati: Hebrew Union College Press, 2013), 281.
37. *AJY*, vol. 40, 138, 229.
38. "General Jewish Council," in *Jewish American Voluntary Organizations*, ed. Michael Dobkowski (New York: Greenwood Press, 1986), 147–49.
39. Abraham J. Karp, *To Give Life: The UJA in the Shaping of the American Jewish Community* (New York: Schocken Books, 1981).
40. Maurice R. Davie, *Refugees in America* (New York: Harper and Brothers, 1947).
41. Hasia R. Diner, *Fifty Years of Jewish Self-Governance: The Jewish Community Council of Greater Washington, 1938–1988* (Washington, DC: Jewish Community Council of Greater Washington, 1989), 29–30.
42. *AJY*, vol. 41, 226–27.
43. *AJY*, vol. 40, 190.

Bibliography

American Jewish Yearbook, 5694: September 21, 1933 to September 9, 1934, vol. 35. Philadelphia: Jewish Publication Society of America, 1933.

American Jewish Yearbook, 5699: September 26, 1938 to September 13, 1939, vol. 40. Philadelphia: Jewish Publication Society of America, 1938.

American Jewish Yearbook, 5700: September 14, 1939 to October 2, 1940, vol. 41. Philadelphia: Jewish Publication Society of America, 1939.

Best, Gary Dean. *To Free a People: American Jewish Leaders and the Jewish Problem in Eastern Europe, 1890–1914*. Westport, CT: Greenwood Press, 1982.

Black, William Harman. *If I Were a Jew*. New York: Real Books, 1938.

Davie, Maurice R. *Refugees in America*. New York: Harper and Brothers, 1947.

Diamond, Sander I. *The Nazi Movement in the United States, 1934–1941*. Ithaca, New York: Cornell University Press, 1974.

Diner, Hasia R. *Fifty Years of Jewish Self-Governance: The Jewish Community Council of Greater Washington, 1938–1988*. Washington, DC: Jewish Community Council of Greater Washington, 1989.

Dinnerstein, Leonard. *Anti-Semitism in America*. New York: Oxford University Press, 1994.

Fireside Discussion Group of the Anti-Defamation League, B'nai B'rith. *Introduction*. Chicago: Anti-Defamation League, 1938.

Friedman, Saul S. *No Haven for the Oppressed: United States Policy toward Jewish Refugees, 1938–1945*. Detroit: Wayne State University Press, 1973.

"General Jewish Council." In *Jewish American Voluntary Organizations*, edited by Michael Dobkowski, 147–49. New York: Greenwood Press, 1986.

Goldenson, Rabbi Samuel. "What Shall We Jews Do These Days? A Sermon Delivered on the Message of Esrael Hour, National Broadcasting Company, Saturday, April 9, 1938." Center for Jewish History.

Gordon, Linda. *The Second Coming of the KKK: The Ku Klux Klan of the 1920s and the American Political Tradition*. New York: Liveright, 2017.

Holmes, John Haynes. *Through Gentile Eyes: A Plea for Tolerance and Good Will*. New York: Jewish Opinion Publishing Corporation, 1938.

How to Combat Anti-Semitism in America: The Six Prize Winning Essays in the Contest Conducted by OPINION—a Journal of Life and Letters. New York: Jewish Opinion Publishing Corporation, 1937.

Hyman, Joseph C. *Twenty-Five Years of American Aid to Jews Overseas: A Record of the Joint Distribution Committee*. New York: 1939.

Janowsky, Oscar I. *People at Bay: The Jewish Problem in Central Europe*. New York: Oxford University Press, 1938.

Janowsky, Oscar I., and Melvin M. Fagen. *International Aspects of German Racial Policy*. New York: Oxford University Press, 1937.

"Jewish Chautauqua Society." In *Jewish American Voluntary Organizations*, edited by Michael Dobkowski, 210. New York: Greenwood Press, 1986.

Jewish Culture Foundation, New York University. *The German Reich and Americans of German Origin*. New York: Oxford University Press, 1938.

Kaplan, Marion. *Dominican Haven: The Jewish Refugee Settlement in Sosua, 1940–1945*. New York: Museum of the Jewish Heritage and a Living Memorial to the Holocaust, 2008.

Karp, Abraham J. *To Give Life: The UJA in the Shaping of the American Jewish Community*. New York: Schocken Books, 1981.

Karpf, Maurice J. *Jewish Community Organizations in the United States: An Outline of Types of Organizations, Activities, and Problems*. New York: Bloch, 1938.

Klapper, Melissa. "'Peace Is Truly Our Mission': NFTS and the Peace Movement." In *Sisterhood: A Centennial History of Women of Reform Judaism*, edited by Carole B. Balin et al., 270–88. Cincinnati: Hebrew Union College Press, 2013.

Lazaron, Morris S. *Common Ground: Plea for Intelligent Americanism*. New York: Liveright, 1938.

Lazin, Frederick A. "The Response of the American Jewish Committee to the Crisis of German Jewry, 1933–1939." *American Jewish Historical Quarterly* 68 (March, 1979): 283–305.

Maria Mazzenga, ed. *American Religious Responses to Kristallnacht*. New York: Palgrave Macmillan, 2009.

Pattison, Mark. "Archival Find at Catholic U. Leads to Kriistallnacht Remembrance." *Catholic News Service*, November 9, 2018.

Schachtman, Tom. *"I Seek My Brethren": Ralph Goldman and the Joint: Rescue, Relief and Reconstruction: The Work of the American Jewish Joint Distribution Committee*. New York: Newmarket Press, 2001.

Thompson, Dorothy. *Refugees: Anarchy or Organization*. New York: Random House, 1938.

Warren, Donald I. *Radio Priest, Charles Coughlin, the Father of Hate Radio*. New York: Free Press, 1990.

Wolk, Kenneth. "New Haven and Waterbury, Connecticut Jewish Communities' Public Response to the Holocaust, 1938–1944: An Examination Based on Accounts in the Public Printed Press and Local Jewish Organizational Documents." PhD diss., New York University, 1995.

Zeligs, Dorothy. *A History of Jewish Life in Modern Times for Young People*. New York: Bloch, 1938.

CHAPTER 11

The Ambiguous Legacy of Kristallnacht: Nazis, Jewish Resistors, and Anti-Semitism in Los Angeles

by Steven J. Ross

Kristallnacht had an impact in the United States, but not in the way we think. Scholars have documented reactions in the public realm, but in Los Angeles, the most consequential responses to Kristallnacht occurred in the often hidden world of private actions taken both by Nazis and by resistors.[1]

The initial American response to Kristallnacht came from President Franklin D. Roosevelt who denounced the pogroms and recalled his ambassador to Germany, Hugh Wilson, and US commercial attaché Douglas Miller. Roosevelt also demanded that the German government pay compensation for damages to the property of American Jews and that they reverse their decision to forbid foreign Jews from doing business in Germany. Yet, rhetoric aside, the American government took no real action to stop German territorial aggression or the persecution of European Jews. Congress rejected a bill that would have allowed twenty thousand Jewish children to emigrate to the United States, and while Roosevelt recalled his ambassador to Germany, he did not break off diplomatic relations. Jews would have to fend for themselves. "Extermination" was the goal of the November pogroms, warned the Los Angeles *B'nai B'rith Messenger*. "Unless the democracies evacuate the German Jews at once and at their own expense, they will be starved into crime and then exterminated with 'fire and sword.'"[2]

The tepid response of the American government was matched by the ambivalent response of the American public. Kristallnacht, numerous scholars have insisted, marked a turning point in American public opinion toward the Hitler regime.[3] That is true, but only to a limited extent and one that had little significant impact on American Nazi and fascist leaders. Politicians, clergy, and civic leaders throughout the nation denounced the pogroms, and a Gallup poll taken that November revealed ninety-four percent of respondents disapproved of the Nazi treatment of Jews. Americans condemned anti-Semitism abroad, but they remained more equivocal in their attitude about Jews at home. A Roper poll taken after Kristallnacht revealed only thirty-nine percent believed Jews should be treated like everyone else; fifty-three percent believed Jews were different and should be restricted; and ten percent believed Jews should be deported.[4]

Kristallnacht was not an isolated incident and responses to it need to be seen in the context of a series of European events that began with the Anschluss in March 1938. The lack of any serious reaction to Hitler's take over of Austria during the Anschluss, the subsequent capitulation of western leaders at Munich later that September, and Germany's seizure of the Sudetenland in October emboldened Nazis and fascists throughout the United States and reinforced their belief that Hitler could not be stopped by faint-hearted western leaders.

Nazi aggression abroad was accompanied by Nazi aggression in the United States. In Los Angeles, members of the German-American Bund reacted to news of the pogroms with unfettered joy. On Wednesday evening, November 16, 1938, an ebullient Hermann Schwinn, leader of the local Bund and the number two Nazi in America, addressed an excited crowd of several hundred who had come to attend a special meeting celebrating Kristallnacht. Surrounded by storm troopers dressed in full uniform, the slender thirty-three-year-old führer with a thin Hitler mustache blamed Jews for causing the massacre. Hitler and the German people, he told the sympathetic audience, had simply given "the Jews what is coming to them." Schwinn denounced the "Jew controlled press" for its "malicious campaign against Germany" and insisted that American Christians were finally waking up to the Jewish menace. "I predict that within less than five years we will see Jews dangling from telephone posts and trees."[5]

Los Angeles was one of many Nazi strongholds in the United States. Hitler's American minions, operating as the Teutonia Association, established

The Ambiguous Legacy of Kristallnacht 239

German-American Bund Celebrating Hitler's Birthday at Deutsches Haus, April 1935 (Jewish Federation Council of Greater Los Angeles, Community Relations Committee Collection, Part 2, Special Collections and Archives, Oviatt Library, California State University, Northridge).

their initial beachhead in Chicago in 1924. In the spring of 1933, Heinz Spanknöbel, head of the Friends of New German (renamed the German-American Bund in 1936), sent German veteran Captain Robert Pape to Los Angeles to organize Nazi branches along the Pacific Coast. Several months later, Pape was succeeded by Hamburg-born Hermann Schwinn, who moved to Canton, Ohio, in 1924 with his parents and worked as a bank clerk until settling in Los Angeles in 1928. Schwinn soon rose to become head of the entire western region of the German-American Bund and the number two Nazi in the United States.[6]

Inspired by Kristallnacht, Schwinn and his Nazi cohort began working toward *Der Tag*, "the day" when Nazis and their supporters would seize control of the American government—either through force or the ballot box. Once in power, they would eliminate the dual threats of communism and Judaism. Unafraid of blustering national politicians, Schwinn and his lieutenants were far more concerned that local Jews and their allies would respond to the Kristallnacht massacre with violence. Following the November 16 Deutsches Haus celebration, *Ordnungsdienst* leader (OD, or uniformed service, a militia equivalent to the storm troopers) Mike Drey gathered his men and warned,

"Things are rapidly coming to a point where physical violence will be the order of the day." Fearing that "bombs or rocks may be thrown by 'enemies,'" Schwinn ordered all Deutsches Haus windows to be covered with sturdy wooden shutters.[7]

The overt physical attacks and violence Schwinn feared never occurred, but Angelinos did voice their anger at Kristallnacht with a series of highly publicized anti-Nazi meetings. On November 18, 3,500 local residents flocked to Philharmonic Auditorium for a "Quarantine Hitler" rally to hear actor John Garfield and director Frank Capra give speeches condemning Germany. Speakers called upon the crowd to send President Roosevelt telegrams denouncing western "capitulation to Hitler" and demanding that he take action to express "the horror and the indignation of the American people."[8] Ten days later, over one thousand men and women turned out for a similar mass protest at Grace Methodist Church organized by Jewish and Protestant clergy and leaders of the United Anti-Nazi Conference.[9]

Hermann Schwinn and his Nazi cohort remained unmoved by such actions. Anti-Nazi protestors believed words and rhetoric could serve as effective weapons. Schwinn believed that guns and well-drilled troops would prove far more useful in attaining his vision of a Jew-free America—a vision shared by Fritz Kuhn, the German-American Bund's national leader. The Munich-born Kuhn moved to the United States in 1928 and worked as a chemist for Henry Ford before assuming control of the Bund in 1936.[10]

On November 30, 1938, nearly three weeks after Kristallnacht, Mike Drey read a twenty-one-page set of secret orders sent from Bund headquarters in New York instructing local *Ordnungsdienst* members to begin rigorous training in firearms and hand-to-hand combat. All training activities, the orders warned, must be camouflaged and appear to be private practice and not Bund sponsored. Schwinn called upon all Bund members who were American citizens to join the National Rifle Association, from whom they could then purchase new guns for $14 and second-hand weapons for $7.50 each. Over the next several months, the Bund's storm trooper unit began secretly training in hand-to-hand combat in the Hollywood Hills far away from prying eyes. "It seems we are in the Army now," quipped Schwinn lieutenant Reinhold Kusche.[11]

Raising and training a well-drilled military force was only a part of Schwinn's strategy for bringing National Socialism to the United States. Following Kristallnacht, Bundists created a network of local secret cells among sympathetic Americans, each no larger than ten men that would be spread across the country. Modeled on the cell system used by the Nazi party in the

Hans Diebel Prepares for Der Tag *Leading Secret Pistol Practice (Jewish Federation Council of Greater Los Angeles, Community Relations Committee Collection, Part 2, Special Collections and Archives, Oviatt Library, California State University, Northridge).*

1920s, all meetings were held in secret and no cell knew of the existence of the other. By the end of December 1938, the Los Angeles Bund had organized eighteen cells and anticipated more. Each member of the cell, according to Hans Diebel, Schwinn's closest lieutenant, "can be relied upon in an uprising. It is to be done exactly as it was done in [1920s] Germany."[12]

Knowing the importance of swaying public opinion to their cause, Schwinn and Diebel also organized "private discussion groups" in the homes of sympathetic Americans who supported the Nazis but did not want that fact known to neighbors and acquaintances. Bund meetings were regularly attracting 250–300 people, but Schwinn wanted to build a support network that ran into the thousands. By early 1939, Diebel succeeded in organizing one hundred discussion groups throughout Los Angeles and nearby Pasadena and Glendale. Much to the Bund's delight, the leaders of these groups included prominent members of the city's social register, such as wealthy Beverly Hills socialite Mrs. Preston Harris Fisher, who recruited like-minded people from the city's Women's Club.[13] Schwinn also worked to gain additional supporters by hosting a weekly program of news and music featuring National Socialist songs that could be heard on the German Radio Hour every Friday night and Sunday morning on KRKD.[14]

German-American Bundists in Los Angeles were not the only ones working toward *Der Tag*. Hitler's forces threatened the city on multiple fronts. The vapid response of the American government to Kristallnacht led Germany to step up its spying activities along the Pacific coast. The Los Angeles port proved a godsend for the German government. Unlike the docks of New York City ("Jew York" as Nazis called it) that were closely monitored by the city's outspoken half-Jewish mayor Fiorello LaGuardia, Nazis discovered they could funnel money, propaganda, and secret agents through the western city's ports without detection. Following the Anschluss, and especially after Kristallnacht, Berlin sent unprecedented numbers of highly trained spies to assess the nation's readiness for war and to scope out military installations and defense plants along the Pacific Coast. "We have no difficulties at all," Hans Diebel boasted to friends in December 1938, "in getting certain people into this country with or without papers."[15]

Hermann Schwinn knew he had to forge a broad coalition of similarly minded men and women if he was to succeed in convincing Americans to join his cause. Several years earlier, he created the United Front, an alliance of the city's many fascist groups. That alliance grew far stronger after Kristallnacht. With Hitler's forces seemingly invincible, Schwinn found it easy to assemble a consortium of anti-Semites prepared to take militant action: Silver Shirts, Ku Klux Klan, Japanese and Italian fascists, Mexican Gold Shirts, and White Russians who had participated in pogroms in Russia and were anxious to do the same in the United States.[16]

With over 750 Nazi and fascist groups operating in the United States in 1939, Schwinn's vision of establishing a Jew-free nation did not seem so far-fetched. "So thorough has been the Nazi infiltration among the native anti-Jewish groups," the *American Jewish Yearbook* reported in 1939, "that it is becoming increasingly difficult to separate one from the other."[17] Public denunciations of Kristallnacht and subsequent anti-Nazi rallies did little to stem rising Nazi and fascist aggression in Los Angeles. Concerned about Nazi activities on American soil, Congress gave the FBI $300,000 in October 1938 to increase their counter-espionage activities. However, the FBI's Red-obsessed director J. Edgar Hoover did not think Nazis posed a serious threat to the nation. Despite pleas from local agents, Hoover did not order the Los Angeles bureau to put Hermann Schwinn—the number two Nazi in the nation—under surveillance until November 28, 1941, nine days before the attack on Pearl Harbor.[18]

In the aftermath of Kristallnacht, Hermann Schwinn and his fascist allies felt confident that the New Year would bring more good news and more converts to the cause. His confidence was misplaced. The Nazi defeat in Los Angeles would not come from public protests or the actions of government agencies. Rather, Schwinn and his cohort would be brought down by a small group of men and women led by Leon Lewis, the man Nazis referred to as "the most dangerous Jew in Los Angeles."[19]

JEWISH RESISTANCE
Local resistance to Nazism began on July 26, 1933, when Los Angeles Nazis, operating as the Friends of New Germany, held their first open meeting and announced their intention to save America from its two greatest threats, communists and Jews. Several days later, as national organizations such as the American Jewish Congress and American Jewish Committee continued debating what to do about Adolf Hitler, Jewish attorney and World War I veteran Leon L. Lewis took direct action. Approaching four fellow members of the Disabled American Veterans, he asked them and their wives to risk their lives by going undercover and spying on every Nazi and fascist group in the city and then sending him daily reports describing their activities. Lewis and his Community Committee (a small advisory board of local Jewish leaders) maintained their undercover spy operation from summer 1933 until the end of World War II. Often rising to leadership positions, his spies foiled a series of Nazi plots to kill the city's Jews and to sabotage the nation's military installations: plans existed for murdering twenty-four Hollywood actors and power figures such as Al Jolson, Eddie Cantor, Charlie Chaplin, Louis B. Mayer and Samuel Goldwyn; for driving through Boyle Heights and machine-gunning as many Jewish residents as possible; for fumigating Jewish homes with cyanide; and, for blowing up defense installations and seizing munitions from National Guard armories on the day Nazis planned to launch their American putsch.[20]

There was nothing in Lewis's past to indicate he would one day become a highly successful spymaster. Born in Hurley, Wisconsin on September 5, 1888 to German-Jewish immigrants Edward and Rachel Lewis, Leon attended public school in Milwaukee, went to college at the University of Wisconsin and George Washington University, and earned a law degree from the University of Chicago Law School in 1913.[21] Upon graduating, he accepted a position as the founding executive secretary of the recently organized Anti-Defamation League—a position he maintained until 1925. Suffering from a variety of war-induced health issues, Lewis moved his family from Chicago to Los Angeles in the early 1930s.[22]

Lewis's spy activities, which are thoroughly described in *Hitler in Los Angeles: How Jews Foiled Nazi Plots Against Hollywood and America*, took on a new urgency in the months between the Anschluss and Kristallnacht. Until then, he ran a one-man operation assisted only by his part-time volunteer, Hollywood story editor Joseph Roos. Unlike Lewis, the Vienna-born, Berlin-raised Roos was familiar with the worlds of espionage and counter-espionage. In 1933, after learning that he and his uncle Julius Klein had been spying on Nazis in Chicago and fearing the untrained Roos was likely to be discovered, Army Colonel George C. Marshall ordered his men to train him in espionage and counterespionage techniques. Over the course of several weeks, Marshall's army intelligence operatives taught their Jewish pupil to "keep your eyes wide open, never get into any arguments with anybody, talk as though you are in agreement with them, don't egg them on in order to have a better story to tell." His instructors also took him out on night maneuvers and taught him how to evade detection.[23]

Arriving in Los Angeles in the spring of 1934, Roos went to work as a story editor for Carl Laemmle and then for Jesse Lasky and Mary Pickford. The former newspaper reporter earned a good living in the movie business, but the work left him unsatisfied. The diminutive twenty-five-year-old writer with a heavy accent and bottle-like eyeglasses began spending evenings and weekends assisting Lewis, whom he met through mutual friends. "Before I knew it, I was his one and only volunteer who trained his under-cover people, taught them how to watch even for the smallest details, how to write reports, etc."[24]

For the next several years, Lewis urged Roos to work for him full time. Roos resisted until the evening of April 10, 1938, when he went to Deutsches Haus to observe 450 Bundists, Silver Shirts, White Russians, and Italian and Spanish fascists celebrate Hitler's triumphant entry into Vienna following the Anschluss. "The reaction of the populace," Roos reflected, "was as if Jesus Christ had arrived."[25] That evening changed the course of his life. "I felt it wasn't fair for me to continue thinking up nice boy-meets-girl stories for the movies, because I understood what Nazism stood for." Encouraged by his wife Alvina, Roos gave up his cushy job at United Artists and became Lewis's full-time associate spymaster.[26]

Following Kristallnacht, Lewis and Roos found themselves involved in a deadly race between two opposing forces: Nazis who called for eliminating communists and Jews, and, a small group of Jews and their spies who worked to stop them. With the FBI dragging its feet, and with Los Angeles police chief James Davis and county sheriff Eugene Biscailuz showing little interest in monitoring anyone other than communists, it was up to Lewis and Roos to stop the Nazi assault on Los Angeles.[27]

As news of Nazi militancy at home and abroad increased, Roos expanded the scope of Lewis's undercover operation by bringing in several new full-time spies as well as a number of trusted informants. By January 1939, he succeeded in placing three undercover operatives inside Deutsches Haus. In addition to recruiting former Burns Detective Agent William Bockhacker, who rose to become Schwinn's right-hand American advisor, Roos also enlisted Charles Young, a German-born naturalized citizen and financial investigator who deplored the bad name Germans were getting because of Hitler, and life insurance salesman Roy Arnold, who loathed the city's Nazi cohort and was happy to feign being one of Schwinn's desired American followers.[28]

Roos recruited four other informants who worked for him on a sporadic basis: Mrs. Anna Friedman, a German American who provided important information gleaned from mingling with Bund women; Harwood E. Park, an American-born aircraft mechanic who alerted the spymasters to potential sabotage at local aircraft factories; Walter Hadel, who investigated incidents of anti-Semitism and tracked Nazis and fascists working in the movie studios; and Jimmy Frost, an investigator who acted as a go-between with a number of local and federal officials.[29]

With his spies in place, Roos began reorganizing Lewis's chaotic system for filing spy reports. "Everybody was identified by [code] number, and you had to figure out who is this and who is that. It was terrible." Roos created individual index cards with the names, addresses, and vital information about hundreds of local Nazis and fascists, as well as separate cards for the many right-wing organizations to which they belonged. Roos soon turned himself into a "walking encyclopedia" who knew the name of every Nazi and what he or she looked like.[30] More importantly, he sent his extensive list of Nazis, fascists, and suspected spies to the FBI, Army Intelligence, and Naval Intelligence—and updated them on a regular basis.[31]

Until Kristallnacht, most of Lewis's work had been confined to the secret world of espionage. But Roos changed that. Taking a page from Joseph Goebbels, a man he considered the "most clever, ablest propaganda operator in the world," the Austrian-born Jew began his own propaganda campaign by launching the News Research Service in January 1939. Drawing upon his considerable skills as a newspaperman and Hollywood story editor, Roos's weekly *News Letter* turned his spy reports into a read as gripping as any detective thriller. Over the next three years he sent copies to myriad government agencies, newspapers, popular magazines, and influential political columnists.[32]

Roos slowly transformed Leon Lewis's local spy ring into a successful national operation whose *News Letter* "reached millions practically every week because of the 'pickup'" by syndicated columnists such as Walter Winchell and the team of Robert Allen and Drew Pearson.[33] The popular political columnists regularly used material from the *News Letter* to provide newspaper readers with an often-frightening look at Nazi activity inside and outside the nation's borders. The normally modest Roos insisted that as a result of these exposés, several "slow-moving government forces were compelled to take action against a number of Nazi propaganda agents who had failed to register as foreign agents with the State Department."[34]

In the months between the Anschluss, and especially after Kristallnacht, Lewis and Roos began fighting their enemies on two fronts: a secret undercover operation, and a public relations campaign aimed at alerting Americans to the threat Nazism posed to democracy. The strategy in both cases was to weaken, if not destroy the Nazi movement in Los Angeles, by discrediting Hermann Schwinn, sowing dissension within the Bund, and creating so much national publicity through the use of Winchell, Allen, and Pearson that government officials would be forced to take action against the Bund. Their strategy worked, though it would take several years before Lewis and Roos would enjoy their ultimate victory.

Following Hitler's many European triumphs, William Bockhacker reported that the local Bundists were growing increasingly divided between militants such as storm trooper leader Michael Drey, who wanted to pursue a more aggressive National Socialist course of action, and those who favored Hermann Schwinn's more accommodationist plan aimed at enticing Americans to join the Bund. As a result of the open feud, many local Bundists grew disillusioned with both sides. Members accused the warring leaders of being too arrogant and insufficiently *kameradschaftlich* (comradely). Worse yet, they suspected Schwinn was pocketing money belonging to the Bund. Resentment against Schwinn grew so great that the Bund leader kept his home address secret from all but his trusted confidantes Diebel and Bockhacker. Only obedience to the *Führer-Prinzip* (unquestioning loyalty to the leader) prevented opponents from ousting him.[35]

Lewis and Roos's plan of action was simple: have Bockhacker pit rivals against one another so as to weaken the Bund and stifle its ability to carry out plots against the city's Jews. Bockhacker ingratiated himself with leaders on both sides of the divide and slowly turned them against one another. When Drey bitterly complained about Schwinn's inability to stop Jewish spies from penetrating Deutsches Haus, Bockhacker agreed to track them down. But he was playing a very dangerous game, for Drey warned that when they caught the spy, "he would have nothing to laugh at."[36] He was deadly serious. Three of Lewis's spies would die under highly suspicious circumstances.

Knowing that the *Führer-Prinzip* would make it nearly impossible to dislodge Schwinn from office, Lewis and Roos pursued a second strategy: convince government authorities to revoke his citizenship and, in so doing, throw the Bund into chaos. In September 1938, acting on information provided by Lewis and Roos's spy Neil Ness, the Department of Naturalization and Immigration began taking steps to revoke Schwinn's citizenship. Apparently, when Schwinn signed his naturalization papers in July 1932, he perjured himself by swearing he had been in Los Angeles since October 1926; in fact, he moved to Los Angeles in October 1927, which left him three months shy of the required five years residency in the same city. The Bund leader also failed to disclose his Nazi activities in Germany and the United States when he filed his papers, an oversight that provided a possible second reason for denial of citizenship.[37]

On December 14, 1938, acting on the recommendation of the chief of the US Immigration Service, the US Attorney General began proceedings to revoke Schwinn's citizenship. A week later, Assistant US District Attorney Ira Brett filed formal charges in Los Angeles Federal Court claiming that Schwinn's citizenship had been "illegally procured."[38] The flustered Nazi downplayed the charges, explaining, "It was merely a mistake which I made while filling out my application of citizenship papers."[39]

Simple mistake or not, Schwinn had to shift his attention away from laying the groundwork for *Der Tag* and focus instead on remaining in the United States. Lewis was playing the long game—and it worked. In June 1939, federal prosecutors, armed with evidence provided by Lewis and Roos, persuaded judge Ralph Jenney to revoke the Bund leader's citizenship on the grounds that the witnesses signing his papers had made false statements about the length of his residency in Los Angeles and that Schwinn was not of "good moral character."[40] Two hours after the verdict, Leon Lewis received more good news from his informant Jimmy Frost: the Immigration and Naturalization Service was now preparing deportation proceedings against Schwinn.[41] Schwinn's reign as *Gauleiter* (district leader) of all Bund branches in the western United States and the nation's number two Nazi had effectively come to an end.

After removing Schwinn from the scene, Lewis and Roos worked hard to convince the three major government intelligence agencies—the FBI, Army Intelligence (G2), and Naval Intelligence (ONI)—that Nazis in Germany and the United States posed a serious threat to national security. Knowing the FBI had little interest in using their scarce resources to monitor domestic Nazis and their fascist allies, Lewis and Roos provided all three intelligence agencies with a steady stream of information about potential sabotage in the city's aircraft factories. Los Angeles produced more than half the nation's airplanes and storm trooper leader Mike Drey repeatedly urged members who had citizenship papers to apply for jobs at the Lockheed plant in Burbank or "any other airplane factory." Drey assured them they would be okay if they kept "their mouths shut about politics" and did not let anyone know they were connected to the Bund.[42]

Anna Friedman provided a chilling account of what Nazis and Fifth Columnists intended to do once inside the aircraft factories. Establishing herself as a regular patron at Charlie's T-Bone Steak House on 54th and Broadway, a popular haunt of Bundists, Friedman became friendly with a waitress who told her how a number of Germans got rip-roaring drunk one evening and "boasted about their sabotage activities at the Douglas Aircraft plant. It appears that they have taken bolts out of planes which will endanger the safety of the planes." Chuck Slocombe, Lewis's ace spy, filed an equally disturbing report in April 1939, warning that fascist Silver Shirts were securing positions at the Douglas factory and were planning to subvert production if Germany went to war. Lewis sent the information to grateful security officers at the airplane factories, who placed potential subversives under surveillance.[43]

The two spymasters also assigned their agents to monitor the city's ports, looking for evidence of Japanese and German plots to sabotage local docks. In February 1939, after completing the enormous task of systematizing the office files, Roos began sending Commander Ellis Zacharias, head of Naval Intelligence for the Pacific Coast and a Jew, the first of many updated reports on "Nazi Spies and Agents in the United States." His initial eighteen-page memorandum contained the names, addresses, and activities of 157 suspected Nazi and Japanese spies and their fascist allies scattered across the United States. Zacharias forwarded the report to Naval Intelligence headquarters in Washington, DC with a note explaining that the data he received from a "private source" in Los Angeles contained valuable information "that has never reached this office." Obeying President Roosevelt's executive order to share information, Naval Intelligence sent the reports to Army Intelligence and to the FBI.[44]

Following the outbreak of war on September 1, 1939, Lewis and Roos compiled a several-hundred-page "Summary Report on Activities of Nazi Groups and their Allies in Southern California." The report described in great detail the activities of every Nazi and fascist organization in Los Angeles and contained equally extensive profiles of their leaders. Lewis and Roos revised their report every September and sent it to the FBI, Army Intelligence, and Naval Intelligence hoping someone would pay attention.[45]

On December 7, 1941, Japanese forces attacked the American Naval base at Pearl Harbor, killing more than 2,400 Americans and damaging or destroying eight Navy battleships and 188 airplanes. Three hours later, the Japanese government declared war on the United States and Great Britain. At 4:35 p.m., December 8, FBI Los Angeles Special Agent in Charge Richard Hood received a teletype from J. Edgar Hoover with the names of people "recommended for custody." Four hours later, Hoover sent a second teletype ordering the arrest of all German and Italian aliens who posed a threat to the "Internal Security of this country."[46] Heading the "A" list of dangerous suspects were Hermann Schwinn and Hans Diebel.

In the days and weeks after Pearl Harbor, Hoover's men received nationwide acclaim for the speed and efficiency with which they rounded up suspected German, Italian and Japanese spies and fifth columnists. Yet, as Roos would later reflect, the Los Angeles FBI "had scant security information of their own."[47] Hoover had not ordered a thorough investigation of Hermann Schwinn until less than a month before Pearl Harbor. What material the local FBI had compiled on the west coast Nazi leader was filled mainly with newspaper clippings; Los Angeles agents gathered virtually no important information on their own. The bureau had even less material on Schwinn's lieutenants. What useful information they did have came almost exclusively from Lewis and Roos's operatives William Bockhacker and Charles Young.

So how did authorities know whom to arrest? Justice Department arrests lists in Los Angeles were compiled from the massive amounts of information that Lewis and Roos sent them after Kristallnacht. The FBI simply retyped the data provided by Lewis and Roos and claimed it as their own. Hoover's agency received all the glory, while the two Jews quietly basked in the knowledge of what they had achieved. The Jews' spy reports were put in the service of national security as Bureau agents began rounding up Los Angeles' most dangerous Nazis and fifth columnists.[48]

With the FBI, Naval Intelligence, and other authorities on the alert for espionage and subversive activities, Lewis and Roos no longer needed to run the extensive spy network they employed from 1933 until 1941. But the two men did not trust local authorities to protect the city's Jews from harm, so they relied on a series of undercover agents—most notably Charles Slocombe and the mother and daughter spy team Grace and Sylvia Comfort—to monitor hate groups that openly called for violence against Jews, blacks, and Catholics.[49]

Without ever firing a weapon, the two Jewish leaders managed to keep Los Angeles and its citizens safe. They and the men and women who risked their lives to spy on Nazis and fascists understood that when a government failed to stem the rise of extremists bent on violence, it was up to every citizen to protect the lives of every American no matter their race, ethnicity or religion.

CONCLUSION

The full history of American Jewish response to Kristallnacht and resistance to Nazism remains to be told. As the story of Leon Lewis and Joseph Roos suggests, we need to reconsider the nature of American Jewish resistance before World War II. American Jews were far more active in opposing Nazism and fascism during the 1930s, and especially after the Anschluss and Kristallnacht, than we previously thought. Much of the scholarship about American reaction to Hitler has focused on the responses of national groups and leaders—responses that have led many to condemn Jews for not opposing Hitler's minions more aggressively. The Los Angeles story reveals that American Jews were often highly successful in resisting Nazism, more so than most government agencies and public protest groups.

Eighty years have passed since the events of November 9–10, 1938. And eighty years later, we still need to know more about the ground-level actions of Nazis and resistors in places where Bund leaders were given a warm reception, especially in cities with German strongholds such as New York, Chicago, and Milwaukee. If scholars are to raise questions about passivity and cowardice, the proper focus should not be on the nation's Jews but on an American government that did little to stop the spread of Nazism and fascism at home. Let us flip traditional questions about Jewish passivity on their head and ask instead what did Jewish resistors accomplish and why did "patriotic" government authorities in so many cities turn a blind eye to Nazi activities in their own backyards? The answers are as important today as they were eighty years ago.

Notes

1. For American reactions to Kristallnacht, see Arthur D. Morse, *While Six Million Died: A Chronicle of American Apathy* (New York: Random House, 1968); Haskel Lookstein, *Were We Our Brothers' Keepers? The Public Response of American Jews to the Holocaust* (New York: Hartmore House, 1985); Deborah Lipstadt, *Beyond Belief: The American Press and the Coming of the Holocaust, 1933-1945* (New York: Free Press, 1986); Maria Mazzenga, ed., *American Religious Responses to Kristallnacht* (New York: Palgrave Macmillan, 2009); Barry Trachtenberg, *The United States and the Nazi Holocaust* (New York: Bloomsbury Academic, 2018).
2. Los Angeles, *B'nai B'rith Messenger*, December 2, 1938.
3. See sources in note 1.
4. Gallup and Roper polls are quoted in Glen Yeadon with John Hawkins, *The Nazi Hydra in America* (Joshua Tree, CA: Progressive, 2008), 187.
5. For reports of meeting, see Agent W2 (William Bockhacker) Reports, November 17, 21, 1938, in CRC2 box 66, folder 25: David Hall Jr., 1938–40, Jewish Federation Council of Greater Los Angeles, Community Relations Committee (CRC) Collection, Special Collections and Archives, Oviatt Library, California State University Northridge; *Los Angeles Times*, November 17, 1938. For general local coverage of Kristallnacht and responses, see ibid., November 12-17, 1938; *B'nai B'rith Messenger*, November 18, December 2, 1938; Thomas Doherty, *Hollywood and Hitler 1933-1939* (New York: Columbia University Press, 2013), 290.
6. For a general history of Nazi activity in the United States, see Sander A. Diamond, *The Nazi Movement in the United States 1924-1941* (Ithaca: Cornell University Press, 1974); for Schwinn's background and rise to power, see Steven J. Ross, *Hitler in Los Angeles: How Jews Foiled Nazi Plots Against Hollywood and America* (New York: Bloomsbury Press, 2017).
7. Bockhacker Report, November 17, 1938, CRC2 box 66, folder 25. Schwinn's activities are documented in the spy reports collected by Leon Lewis and housed in the special collections department at California State University Northridge mentioned in n. 5.
8. A description of the rally and telegrams can be found in Doherty, *Hollywood and Hitler 1933-1939*, 290.
9. *B'nai B'rith Messenger*, December 2, 1938.
10. For Kuhn's background, see Arnie Bernstein, *Swastika Nation: Fritz Kuhn and the Rise and Fall of the German-American Bund* (New York: St. Martin's Press, 2013); Diamond, *Nazi Movement in the United States 1924-1941*.
11. "Summary Report on Activities of Nazi Groups and Their Allies in Southern California, September 1939" (henceforth "Summary Report"), 484, box 10, Joseph Roos Papers, Special Collections, USC Libraries, University of Southern California. The NRA sold weapons to citizens who joined their organization and paid $3 in

annual dues. For a description of the increased militarization of the Bund after Kristallnacht, see "Summary Report September 1939," 479–84.
12. Ibid., 509.
13. Ibid., 727.
14. The German Radio Hour ran for only thirty minutes from 7:45–8:15pm. The show repeated on Sundays. For Leon Lewis's efforts to halt the radio show, see "Confidential Memo: *Herald Examiner*," March 5, 1938, in Leon Lewis File, *Los Angeles Examiner* Clippings, Special Collections, University of Southern California.
15. "Summary Report," 549. The Gestapo was training spies at espionage-sabotage schools in Berlin, Dresden, and Hamburg and funneling money for their American operations through consular offices. For the training and funding of German and fascist spies, see Michael Sayers and Albert E. Kahn, *The Plot Against Peace: A Warning to the Nation* (New York: Dial Press, 1947), 172; Richard Wilmer Rowan, *Secret Agents against America* (New York: Doubleday, Doran & Co., Inc., 1939), 8.
16. For the United Front and Schwinn's forging a fascist cohort bent on violence, see Ross, *Hitler in Los Angeles*.
17. Harry Schnedierman, ed., *American Jewish Yearbook, 1938-1939*, vol. 40 (Philadelphia: The Jewish Publication Society of America, 1938–39), 120.
18. J. Edgar Hoover to Special Agent in Charge, LA, June 17, 1941: "Re: H. Schwinn, Internal Security," P. E. Foxworth, Washington D.C., "Memorandum for Mr. E. A. Tamm," September 8, 1941, Hermann Schwinn folder, box 75, Charles Higham Papers, Cinema-Television Collection, University of Southern California. For orders to investigate Schwinn, see R. B. Hood, SAC, to Director, J. Edgar Hoover, November 28, 1941, "FBI Report: Subject: Herman Schwinn; File No. 65-9483; section 2; Serials 39–67, Herman Schwinn Folder, box 72, Higham Papers. When I requested Hermann Schwinn's FBI file under the Freedom of Information Act, the only files I was sent began in 1942. For general works on Hoover and the FBI, see Don Whitehead, *The FBI Story: A Report to the People* (New York: Random House, 1956); Richard Gid Powers, *Secrecy and Power: The Life of J. Edgar Hoover* (New York: Free Press, 1988).
19. Ross, *Hitler in Los Angeles*, 16.
20. The full story of Leon Lewis and his undercover operation is told in ibid.
21. Biographical material on Lewis drawn from Julius Schwartz, Solomon Aaron Kaye, and John Simons, *Who's Who in American Jewry, 1926* (New York: The Jewish Biographical Bureau, Inc., 1927), 382–83; *American Jewish Year Book* 56 (1955), accessed July 20, 2013, http://www.ajcarchives.org/AJC_DATA/Files/1955_16_DirectoriesLists.pdf.
22. For Lewis's background and the beginning of his spy operation, see Ross, *Hitler in Los Angeles*, 7–20.
23. Joseph Roos, interview #2996, June 7, 1995, USC Shoah Foundation Visual History

Archive (USC SF/VHA). For Roos's background and subsequent training by Marshall's men, see Ross, *Hitler in Los Angeles*, 135–39.
24. Joseph Roos, "Chapter Headings—For Identification Only," box 7, folder: "Outline for the Book, 'Under the Crooked Cross,'" Roos Papers, USC.
25. Folder "Background of Joseph Roos," box 6, Roos Papers, USC.
26. Ibid.
27. Not only did Police Chief James Davis and Sheriff Eugene Biscailuz ignore Lewis's calls for help, but several members of their departments were implicated in various Nazis plots; a number of their men also belonged to the Silver Shirts and/or Ku Klux Klan. Ross, *Hitler in Los Angeles*.
28. The backgrounds of Bockhacker, Young, and Arnold are described in Ross, *Hitler in Los Angeles*, 235, 248–49.
29. The backgrounds of these informants are described in ibid., 249.
30. Joseph Roos, Oral History Interview, 10, 15, conducted December 18, 1979, January 7 and 28, 1980, February 14, 1980, Interview conducted by Dr. Leonard Pitt, Professor Department of History, CSUN, and Murray Wood, Executive Director, Community Relations Committee, box 6, Roos Papers, USC.
31. The Los Angeles FBI bureau was so dependent on Lewis and Roos for information that they eventually asked if they could have Bockhacker spy directly for them.
32. Selected copies of Roos's *News Letter* can be found online at http://jfk.hood.edu/Collection/White%20Materials/Weisberg%20Harold%20Dies%20Committee%20Files/News%20Research%20Service%20Inc%20News%20letters/.
33. Roos, interview, USC SF VHA; Roos, oral history interview, 14, Roos Papers, USC.
34. Folder "Background of Joseph Roos," box 6, Roos Papers, USC.
35. "Summary Report, September 1938," 33. For the Bund's financial status, suspicion of Schwinn's larcenous activities, and hiding his home address, see Bockhacker Report, May 5, 23, 1938, CRC2 box 32, folder 13.
36. Bockhacker Report, April 28, 1938, CRC2 box 32, folder 13; also see Verbal Report W2: April 4, 1938, CRC2 box 32, folder 12.
37. Bockhacker Report, Sept 28, 1938, CRC2 box 32, folder 17.
38. *Los Angeles Examiner*, December 20, 1938.
39. *Los Angeles Times*, December 15, 1938; also see *Los Angeles Examiner*, December 15, 16, 20, 1938.
40. Bockhacker Memo, "Schwinn Loses Citizenship Papers," June 22, 1939, CRC2 box 64, folder 16.
41. Ibid. For further coverage of the trial and deportation preparations, see *Los Angeles Examiner*, June 23, 1939; *Jewish Telegraphic Agency*, June 25, 1939; "Summary Report, Sept.1939," 437–38, box 10, Roos Papers, USC.
42. Memo from Lewis to Ellis Zacharias, April 20, 1939, CRC2 42-2.

43. Friedman Report, April 3, 1939, CRC2 box 39, folder 22. For Slocombe, see Slocombe Report, April 28, 1939, CRC2 box 40, folder 20: Slocombe, Charles: Reports, April–May 1939.
44. Ellis Zacharias Memorandum, February 9, 1939, CRC2 box 42, folder 1. For more reports from Lewis and Roos to Zacharias, see correspondence in CRC2 box 42, folder 2. Copies of these and other reports sent by the spymasters to American intelligence agencies can be found in Navy Department Office of Naval Intelligence, Washington, DC, September 10, 1940: "Memorandum, for Mr. Clegg, FBI, Colonel Lester, MID," from E. B. Nixon, Capt. US Navy, file 2801-943, folder 2801-943/1 [Arno Risse], Box 166, RG165: Military Intelligence Division General Correspondence, 1917–41, National Archives, College Park, MD. Lewis and Roos kept sending updated reports that were in turn forwarded to other intelligence agencies.
45. For the original and updated copies of their reports, see "Summary Report," box 10, Roos Papers, USC.
46. Memo to: Mr. Ladd from J. F. Buckley, May 26, 1944, 65-94-107, Hermann Schwinn FBI file, obtained through Freedom of Information Act; also see, Telemeter: to Director from LA Office, May 13, 1944, 65-9483-110, Schwinn FBI file. The 1944 memo reported on local FBI activities following Pearl Harbor.
47. Joseph Roos, Outline for Book, "Shadows of the Crooked Cross: An Untold Story about Nazis and Anti-Nazis in America, 1933 to 1945," Leonard Pitt and Joseph Roos, penciled dated January 20, 1990, box 7, Roos Papers, USC.
48. Most of their reports were sent to Lewis' favored contacts at Naval Intelligence, who then forwarded them to Army Intelligence and the FBI. Those lists can be found in Army and Naval Intelligence files at the National Archives in College Park, Maryland. For examples of various reports, see "German Known Suspects," "Navy Dept. Office of Naval Intelligence, Washington, D.C., 10 September 1940: Memorandum for Mr. Clegg, FBI, Colonel Lester, Military Intelligence Division, from E. B. Nixon, Capt. U. S. Navy, Subject: Suspect Lists," RG 165: War Dept.: Military Intelligence Division, Correspondence, 1917–41, Entry 65: MID General Correspondence, 1917–41; File #2801-943; Box 1866; Folder 2801-943/1 "Supplementary List— Known German Suspects," RG 165: War Dept.: Military Intelligence Division, Correspondence, 1917–41, Entry 65: MID General Correspondence, 1917–41; File #2801-943; Box 1866; Folder 2801-943/1; "German Agents," Entry 65: MID. General Correspondence, 1917–41, File #10110-2723-62, Box 2857, RG 165: War Dept.: Military Intelligence Division, Correspondence, 1917–41, NA, College Park, MD.
49. The activities of Lewis, Roos, and their operatives after Pearl Harbor are described in Ross, *Hitler in Los Angeles*, 316–40.

Bibliography

Archives

Federal Bureau of Investigation. Hermann Schwinn file.
Jewish Federation Council of Greater Los Angeles. Community Relations Committee (CRC) Collection. Special Collections and Archives. Oviatt Library. California State University Northridge.
Higham, Charles. Papers. Cinema-Television Collection. University of Southern California.
Los Angeles Examiner Clippings. Special Collections. University of Southern California.
Navy Department Office of Naval Intelligence, Washington, DC. National Archives.
Roos, Joseph. Papers. Special Collections. USC Libraries. University of Southern California.
University of Southern California Shoah Foundation Visual History Archive.

Newspapers

B'nai B'rith Messenger. November 18, 1938.
———. December 2, 1938.
Jewish Telegraphic Agency. June 25, 1939.
Los Angeles Examiner. December 15, 1938.
———. December 16, 1938.
———. December 20, 1938.
———. June 23, 1939.
Los Angeles Times. November 12–17, 1938.
———. December 15, 1938

Secondary Sources

American Jewish Year Book 56 (1955). Accessed July 20, 2013. http://www.ajcarchives.org/AJC_DATA/Files/1955_16_DirectoriesLists.pdf.
Bernstein, Arnie. *Swastika Nation: Fritz Kuhn and the Rise and Fall of the German-American Bund.* New York: St. Martin's Press, 2013.
Diamond, Sander A. *The Nazi Movement in the United States 1924–1941.* Ithaca: Cornell University Press, 1974.
Doherty, Thomas. *Hollywood and Hitler 1933–1939.* New York: Columbia University Press, 2013.
Lipstadt, Deborah. *Beyond Belief: The American Press and the Coming of the Holocaust, 1933–1945.* New York: Free Press, 1986.

Lookstein, Haskel. *Were We Our Brothers' Keepers? The Public Response of American Jews to the Holocaust.* New York: Hartmore House, 1985.

Mazzenga, Maria, ed. *American Religious Responses to Kristallnacht.* New York: Palgrave Macmillan, 2009.

Morse, Arthur D. *While Six Million Died: A Chronicle of American Apathy.* New York: Random House, 1968.

Powers, Richard Gid. *Secrecy and Power: The Life of J. Edgar Hoover.* New York: Free Press, 1988.

Ross, Steven J. *Hitler in Los Angeles: How Jews Foiled Nazi Plots Against Hollywood and America.* New York: Bloomsbury Press, 2017.

Rowan, Richard Wilmer. *Secret Agents against America.* New York: Doubleday, Doran & Co., Inc., 1939.

Sayers, Michael, and Albert E. Kahn. *The Plot Against Peace: A Warning to the Nation.* New York: Dial Press, 1947.

Schnedierman, Harry, ed. *American Jewish Yearbook, 1938–1939*, vol. 40. Philadelphia: The Jewish Publication Society of America, 1938–39.

Schwartz, Julius, Solomon Aaron Kaye, and John Simons. *Who's Who in American Jewry, 1926.* New York: The Jewish Biographical Bureau, Inc., 1927.

Trachtenberg, Barry. *The United States and the Nazi Holocaust.* New York: Bloomsbury Academic, 2018.

Whitehead, Don. *The FBI Story: A Report to the People.* New York: Random House, 1956.

Yeadon, Glen, with John Hawkins. *The Nazi Hydra in America.* Joshua Tree, CA: Progressive, 2008.

CHAPTER 12

Jewish Anti-Fascism? "Kristallnacht" Remembrance in the GDR between Propaganda and Jewish Self-Assertion

by Alexander Walther

The memory of the terror events on November 9, 1938 can serve as a litmus test of the East German regime's view on the Holocaust. When the German Democratic Republic (GDR) was founded in 1949, its ruling elite was facing a fundamental dilemma: establishing a Socialist country was seen as the result of the previous anti-fascist struggle against Nazi Germany, and, based on a Marxist view of history, as the only possible consequence in a history of class struggles. While the GDR had that fact in common with other Socialist regimes taking over all over Eastern Europe, there was one crucial difference: the GDR was one of two successor states of the German Reich, and, thus, the land of the perpetrators. Both German governments tried to solve this problem in a similar way, although with a different tone to it. Both were very eager to grant amnesties to all those willing to help build a new state. Questions of guilt and responsibility were soon discarded, and a small set of villains and perpetrators was presented to the people: in the West, these included mostly Hitler and his henchmen, in the East it was Hitler, and, more importantly, capitalists and West German industrialists.[1]

After the collapse of the GDR, some historians have argued that the Holocaust was mostly a taboo topic in East German memory culture.[2] If it was addressed, it supposedly only served as a means of propaganda. Previous research on the memory of November 9, 1938, in the GDR mostly reflected this, arguing that the date was appropriated by the regime for its purposes while other actors, such as the Jewish communities, if they are mentioned at all, are portrayed as amenable accomplices to state propaganda.[3] New research on Holocaust memory in the GDR, however, paints a more differentiated picture.[4] Thus, the memory of November 9 may provide an opportunity to shed new light on this topic. This article will show how the commemoration in the GDR of the 1938 events tells us something about the regime's stance on the memory of Jewish victims of Nazi crimes, and, more importantly, how other groups, especially East Germany's Jewish minority, used the date to implement their very own agenda.

CONFRONTING THE PUBLIC

November 9 has been a day for commemoration in Germany ever since 1918. However, in 1945 it was unclear what exactly was to be remembered that day. Two events had been addressed during the Third Reich: the failed putsch by Hitler in 1923 which was glorified by the Nazis as the first attempt to overthrow the state, and the official announcement of the Kaiser's abdication and the proclaiming of the republic in 1918 following the German revolution, which was, in contrast, demonised. After 1945, in East Germany, the Socialist Unity Party of Germany (Sozialistische Einheitspartei Deutschlands, SED), was eager to point out the revolution of 1918, highlighting the Communist's role in the toppling of monarchy and criticising the missed opportunity of erecting a Socialist state. The events of 1938 had to be integrated into that sample.[5]

During the early postwar years, it was almost exclusively survivors who took action and initiated commemorative events. Already in November 1945, a Berlin based radio station hosted a public event featuring a speech by the mayor, and an interview on the pogrom and its causes by Fritz Katten, a Jewish survivor and later the Chief of Police in Berlin up until his arrest in 1948. Similar events were held on every anniversary in subsequent years.[6] These events all over Germany were usually hosted by a small group of Jewish survivors, and mostly attended by Jews only.

Non-Jewish Germans reacted to these events in diverse ways, ranging from approval and praise to strong rejection and hatred. When a newspaper in Halle printed an article on the fate of the city's Jewish population in 1938, it received various letters from readers scornfully asking whether it would be right to only report about Jewish victims, especially since National Socialism had shown that they were "parasites to the people" as one reader put it.[7] Staging commemorative events for Jewish victims in postwar Germany always meant confronting the still virulent anti-Semitism within the population.

Furthermore, these events automatically confronted the public with its own role during National Socialism. The term "collective guilt" became a buzzword all over Germany, and soon people began discussing its implications. The defensive reactions of so many ordinary Germans were an expression of a common feeling of guilt, or at least shame and acknowledgment of some responsibility for the crimes and the stability of the regime.[8] The persecution of the Jewish population especially was a trigger of such reactions as the overall acceptance or appraisal of National Socialism by the majority could most impressively be addressed via this issue, especially in commemorative events on November 9 both by Jewish and non-Jewish speakers. The reactions of the population to the terror events of November 1938 had ranged from appraisal to—probably more common—rejection, not necessarily due to compassion for the attacked, however, but out of moral outrage over such "dishonourable" behaviour of a "civilised people."[9] Yet, from a victim's perspective this was irrelevant. Accordingly, the indifference of most Germans to the entire persecution of the Jewish population became a key element of the commemoration of November 9. In an internal report to the party about an event in the small city of Plauen in Saxony in 1950, the reactions of the audience is especially revealing: "Some concertgoers staged a concert of coughing so loud that comrade Friedrich remarked: 'You should have coughed in 1938, but you remained silent then. Today, you will have to listen to what I have to say to you.'"[10] Similar remarks could be found in newspaper articles concerning November 9 as well.[11] This occasion especially revealed how deeply rooted anti-Semitic mindsets still were within the people, and how unwilling most non-Jewish Germans were to confront the past.

While the annual *Day of the Victims of Fascism*, established already in 1945, was conceived as a tribute to all Nazi victims and perceived accordingly, albeit with a distinct focus on Communists, November 9 soon became a metaphor for the entire Holocaust. Still, there were limitations. The global dimension of the Nazi genocide was rarely realised by the public or addressed by the officials, and the persecution mostly remained closely linked to German, and not necessarily European Jewry.

ALLIES

Jewish survivors all over Germany were not entirely alone in their attempts to raise awareness of Jewish persecution under Nazi rule, yet their allies were scarce. The nature of the postwar discourse on the Nazi past was paradoxical: it was entirely dominated by former Nazi victims and survivors, yet it had to incorporate the vastly different experience of the majority as well. Already in 1948, the formerly persecuted came into conflict with the SED. Since the regime did not justify its own existence via elections, but derived their claim to power from history, their governmental position was fairly weak. In order to ensure the population's consent, the party's elite soon opted for conciliatory gestures, just as the West German government did. Reminding the population of its own role in National Socialism was not among these strategies. Rather, the SED granted permission to the founding of the National Democratic Party as a gathering place for former Nazis, and welcomed former Nazi party members—who amounted to up to ten percent of all SED members in the early 1950s—into their own ranks.[12] Those insisting that Germans should be confronted with Nazi crimes and their own role in it became less visible.

Accordingly, the Association of Nazi Persecutees (*Vereinigung der Verfolgten des Naziregimes*, VVN), which existed in all parts of Germany, soon became a thorn in the SED inner circle's flesh. It was the VVN that assisted Jewish survivors in their struggle for recognition. Between its founding in 1947 and its forced dissolution in 1953, one-third to half of the association's members were Jewish or had been defined as such and persecuted accordingly by the Nazis. The leadership was distinctly Communist, but Jews, some of them Communists themselves, always played a role.[13]

Two years after the war, the severity of German anti-Semitism became evident as dozens of Jewish cemeteries in all occupation zones were desecrated and destroyed. The VVN initiated various events all over Germany on November 9, 1947 where Jewish and non-Jewish survivors could address their concerns.[14] Julius Meyer, chairmen of the East German Association of Jewish Communities and high ranking member of the VVN, announced that "Jewish cemeteries have been desecrated not just during the Nazi time, but again today. We now know that the fight must continue."[15] Meyer's plea was shared by politicians in all zones who promised a fierce fight against anti-Semitism.[16] Yet, most of the public—and high-ranking politicians as well—seemed fairly unimpressed with the new violent outbursts. Apart from ceremonies on November 9, the mantra that anti-Semitism had been overcome could be heard in all parts of Germany. Already in February 1947, Kurt Schumacher, head of the Social

Democratic party in the Western zones, declared that a "Jewish question does not exist anymore" for most Germans as a result of the "evocative education ["Anschauungsunterricht"] sparked by the persecution of the Jews, especially since November 1938. In fact, today Germany is probably the country with the weakest anti-Semitic stirring of all."[17] He could not have been more wrong. Schumacher's assessment was shared and uttered even more vigorously by East German Communists; yet, this was more an expression of an envisaged future than a realistic representation of the present situation. Anti-Semitism was still an integral feature of the German population, and politicians knew that.

During an event in Dresden on November 9, 1947, Leon Löwenkopf, head of the local Jewish community and member of the VVN's inner circle, painted a grim picture: "Nine years have passed and we, the few surviving Jews, stand here forlorn and alone, surrounded by millions of corpses of our murdered children, fathers, and mothers." Disregarding the claim of collective guilt, he still stressed that "Germans, numbering millions, were actively or passively involved in the murder of millions of Jews." Despite that bleak outlook, Löwenkopf still saw a possibility for Jewish life in postwar Germany, but was unsure whether the Germans were willing to let that happen.[18] Löwenkopf pointed to a pressing issue for most Jewish survivors and returnees for whom the question of remaining in Germany had not been answered in the mid-1940s. Reminding the German population of its responsibility and hoping for a change in their attitude was certainly a way for many survivors to ensure themselves that returning to Germany was right. Yet, the overall lack of outrage over postwar anti-Semitic attacks and defaced cemeteries seemed proof enough that Germans had not changed at all.

Moreover, these commemorative events never attracted as many people as the annual *Day of the Victims of Fascism*. Although the VVN and the churches assisted the Jewish communities in their events around November 9, attendance was scarce, and the outreach negligible. Commemorating Jewish victims together with non-Jews was a welcomed token for the VVN as it publicly indicated the alleged cohesion of all Nazi victims. However, since its leadership consisted mainly of non-Jewish SED members who mostly agreed with the newly established East German government's course of integrating former Nazis into the society and refraining from addressing German guilt, Jewish survivors felt increasingly estranged from the association. Some VVN members even opposed highlighting the Jewish victim's perspective. In 1949, the VVN regional board in Dresden deemed it "inadvisable" to stage a rally on November 9 in memory of Kristallnacht since the effect would eventually "peter out. [...] We would probably address the same group of people, and with this the effort and effect would be amiss."[19] For some Nazi victims, addressing the public and commemorating Nazi crimes did not necessarily include a distinct Jewish perspective. However, they correctly ascertained a reluctance within the public to attend events commemorating Jewish victims, so urging the population to do so anyway might affect the VVN's reputation.

There are, however, also examples of non-Jewish members eager to call public attention to Jewish suffering under Nazi rule. In 1951, Kurt Schatter, a non-Jewish politician and resistance fighter from Berlin, tried to initiate a research project on the November 1938 events, and suggested browsing municipal archives for relevant documents. He wanted the historians' findings published in a "black book" that would be made available at every "public or school library," and featured in history education. Schatter was deeply concerned that these "horrible deeds" would be forgotten, and he regarded such a book "as a cultural document and warning" and an effort to redeem "our guilt" from "the Jews"—something the world would surely recognise.[20] Although the project was never realized, Schatter's impulse hints at the need some non-Jewish Germans felt to redeem themselves from feelings of guilt. An annual reminder of the population's consent to violence was, after all, a constant reminder of one's own bad conscience, and accordingly fairly unpopular within both German societies.

November 9 soon emerged as a fixed date in the calendar of commemoration, but it never reached an importance befitting its cause. For the most part, members of the Jewish communities observed and organized the event amongst themselves. Occasionally, local, mostly Protestant churches invited Jews to stage a common event in memory of Kristallnacht. Church groups, Jewish communities, and the VVN, thus, formed an alliance of Nazi victims or opponents eager to acknowledge the suffering of Jews under Nazi rule.[21] These events featured a mixture of music, recitals of poetry, and (mostly Christian) prayers. In Bautzen in Saxony, for example, Lewandowski's *Kol Nidre* was played next to Beethoven's *Fidelio*, a poem by a "Jewish mother who perished in Auschwitz" was recited after the "Ring Parable" from the play *Nathan the Wise* by German-Jewish Enlightenment era dramatist Gotthold Ephraim Lessing.[22] Lessing's play, a plea for religious tolerance between Christianity, Islam, and Judaism, was one of the first to be staged at German theatres after the war, and a common choice at commemorative events.[23] Choosing this play hints at the importance of mediating religious, and thus ethnical, tolerance ascribed by cultural officials in postwar Germany. The audience's reactions to the play seemed to prove them right as the writer Willi Bredel described it: "Previously the narrative of the ring was the core and free-spirited high point of the play. How that had changed! Today it was the story of the massacre of Jews at Gath that shook audiences most."[24] Still, despite the overall solidarity by non-Jewish Nazi victims and logistical help by the local administration, Jewish communities had to rely on themselves to mount most commemorations.

1953—A TURNING POINT?

Following anti-Semitic campaigns and show trials in Eastern Europe in 1953, mostly in Czechoslovakia and the GDR, a vast number of Jews left East Germany. Almost every leading figure of the Jewish communities fled, leaving the remaining members in dire need to reorganise themselves quickly.[25] Yet, even in this hostile situation, commemoration continued. Only half a year after the hasty flight of its board members, East Berlin's Jewish community unveiled a new memorial stone at its biggest cemetery in Weißensee. Others in the GDR as well as in the Federal Republic acted similarly, and availed themselves of November 9 as an opportunity to unveil new memorial stones, mostly at the sites of destroyed synagogues. In 1960, this happened at Große Hamburger Straße in East Berlin, in Leipzig in 1951 and again in 1966, or in Halle on the occasion of the thirtieth anniversary in 1968.[26]

Contrary to what some historians have claimed, Jewish communities organized events around November 9 every year during the GDR's existence.[27] Yet, after the dissolution of the VVN in 1953, public awareness of these events plummeted.[28] Still, Jewish communities were eager to stage dignified events, and often asked acclaimed artists for their assistance. The writer Peter Edel, for instance, a Jewish-Communist survivor of Auschwitz and Sachsenhausen, frequently assisted the Jewish community in East Berlin by giving speeches on November 9 or on the *Day of the Victims of Fascism* in September at which the Jewish community usually held their events at the cemetery in Weißensee separate from the main, SED dominated event.[29]

The most frequently requested artist was the Dutch-Jewish singer and actress Lin Jaldati. A performer of mostly Yiddish songs, Jaldati had joined the Dutch-Communist resistance together with her husband, Eberhard Rebling, a German Communist. Eventually, they were betrayed, and while Rebling escaped, Jaldati was deported with her family and others (among them Anne

Frank and her family) from Westerbork to Auschwitz, and later to Bergen-Belsen. There, Jaldati and her sister were among the few who took care of Anne and Margot Frank, and eventually buried both of them in a mass grave.[30] After the liberation, Jaldati returned to Amsterdam and started working as a singer again, but the family struggled, and when Jaldati's husband was offered a job as chief editor of a music journal in East Berlin in 1952 he gladly accepted. Only seven years after the war, Jaldati moved to the country of the perpetrators. Unlike her husband, Jaldati's career was uncertain. The demand for Yiddish songs in postwar Germany was very low, but Jaldati, accompanied by her husband on the piano, nevertheless found an audience. Although she never became a member of the local Jewish community, Jaldati often performed at their cultural events. In 1952, they participated in a theatrical show commemorating Kristallnacht, the first of many to come.[31]

In 1953, Jaldati took part in the inauguration of a memorial plaque at a train station in West Berlin's Grunewald from where Jews had been deported in the 1940s. The police tried to prevent this, mostly due to the involvement of the Communist dominated VVN, which, already dissolved in the GDR, was a prohibited organisation at the time in West Berlin. GDR newspapers praised Jaldati's actions as part of an anti-fascist resistance fight against a supposedly neo-fascist West German government. Yet, Jaldati was not merely a passive pawn in the party's game, but an individual genuinely interested in the commemoration of Jewish victims. When the police tried to dissolve the rally at which all speeches were restricted, she started singing Hirsch Glik's hymn to the Jewish partisans, *Zog nit keyn mol*.[32] Although Jaldati soon incorporated German folk songs into her programme to attract a larger audience and to contribute to the anti-fascist narrative, she always stuck to the core of her repertoire of Yiddish songs, many of them with reference to the Holocaust such as Mordechai Gebirtig's *S'brent* which soon became her theme song. Her growing reputation helped raise awareness of commemorative events in which she participated, but it never really altered the small, intimate character of them except for major anniversaries.[33]

ALL PROPAGANDA?

It took years for the East German regime to realise that these events could be exploited in a propagandistic fashion. In 1958, on the twentieth anniversary of Kristallnacht, an employee of the State Secretary for Church Affairs complained that unlike their counterparts in West Germany, no high-ranking politicians participated in the commemorative event.[34] This would change in 1963. That year, the State Secretary organised a grand ceremony staged shortly before the opening of the Auschwitz trial in West German Frankfurt—the largest trial against Nazi perpetrators being held in the Federal Republic against former personnel from the Auschwitz concentration camp—and following a campaign against Hans Globke who had authored the legal commentary on the Nuremberg Race Laws in 1935, and in the 1960s served as the most influential state secretary of the West German Chancellery under Adenauer. In this setting, the SED took the opportunity of presenting the GDR as a place where Nazis were vigorously persecuted and Jews could live happily and safely. The Federal Republic, on the other hand, was demonised by speakers.[35]

The official event was held on November 11, 1963 at the German Hygiene Museum in Dresden. A few days prior, the Association of Jewish Communities in the GDR had published an "Appeal to the Jews of the World and all Men of Good Will," condemning neo-Fascist activities in West Germany and praising the GDR where "fascism, anti-Semitism, and racism have been uprooted."[36] The speeches delivered at the event were similar. As the GDR's chief rabbi, Martin Riesenburger, put it: "We Jews always have a home where we find a home in the people's hearts. Our home is here in the GDR where the brown past has flat out been dealt with."[37] These remarks seem to prove the often uttered accusation that the Jewish communities, and Riesenburger in particular, succumbed to the regime's pressure, and assisted a dictatorship by lending themselves to propaganda.[38] This puts a misleading moral perspective on the Jewish minorities' behaviour, and suggests that they should have acted differently. Yet, Jewish GDR citizens often behaved just as the non-Jewish majority: at times they adopted the regime's views and policies, sometimes they compromised and went along, and sometimes they ignored them or resisted.

Furthermore, Riesenburger's statement cannot only be seen as propaganda. After 1945, socialism and anti-Fascism constituted the only condition under which Jewish life in Germany seemed possible at all to many survivors. The anti-Jewish actions of 1953 did not necessarily change that, for only a few months later, during the violent riots against the East German regime in June 1953, most Jews remaining in the GDR supported the regime suppressing the uprising. Too many remembered how an intractable mass of people could also pose a threat to the Jewish minority. Some were reminded of the events of 1938, and the few, but frightening instances of rioters chanting anti-Semitic slogans in 1953 seemed to prove their point.³⁹ While some certainly had their issues with the regime, there were few alternatives, if any. In 1950, Victor Klemperer noticed a "great divergence from the SED on all intellectual matters. But I cannot just move over to the West—it is even more repugnant to me."⁴⁰ While some were cross with the state, living in West Germany did not seem to be a viable alternative. Although reality often interfered, the desire for an anti-fascist Germany was strongly felt by many Jews, and one of the reasons they stayed.

Although the Jewish communities often assisted the SED by providing them with public statements of solidarity and support, they also retained some independence from the regime. They never publicly condemned Israel, for instance, something that the party often asked them to do, especially during various wars in the Middle East.⁴¹ Jewish groups also used whatever opportunity they had to highlight Jewish suffering under National Socialism. Since the Eichmann trial in 1961, the GDR government had appropriated the memory of the Holocaust for political campaigns against West Germany. Leading figures of the Jewish communities assisted them, but utilized these campaigns to implement their own agenda of fostering Holocaust memory. In 1963, the Association of Jewish Communities proposed a special stamp in memory of Kristallnacht which the GDR's post then issued. Although the effect of this was benign, it was still a success for the association in their strife for recognition.⁴² Accusing the Jewish communities' chairmen of complicity in retrospect ignores the complex historical reality which often required compromise.⁴³ Chairmen behaved the way they were supposed to at times, but received greater government focus on Jewish victims under National Socialism in return.

On some occasions, though, GDR Jewish communities were publicly forced to endorse state positions, such as in the period following the Six Day War in 1967. The State Secretary of Church Affairs, often manoeuvring between the party leadership's intentions and the Jewish communities' needs, suggested a public commemoration at the Ravensbrück memorial site. The commemoration, however, was not for Kristallnacht, but for the fiftieth anniversary of the October Revolution. At this ceremony, the Jewish communities were expected to proclaim their solidarity with the GDR. Helmut Aris, chairman of the Association of Jewish Communities, cunningly prevented this public humiliation. The date in October proposed by the State Secretary would collide with the Jewish holidays, he argued, so that only November 9, 1967, would be possible. Instead of Ravensbrück, Aris also suggested staging the event at the memorial site in Tröbitz in south Brandenburg.⁴⁴ In 1945, one of the "Lost Transports"—three trains carrying Jewish inmates from the cleared out Exchange Camp at Bergen-Belsen—ended in Tröbitz. Of the almost 2,500 people in the train, at least 133 died on the way, and some 320 more after the liberation in Tröbitz who were then buried in mass graves. A proper memorial site was inaugurated only in 1966, which soon became one of the most important sites in the GDR; the Association began holding events there, often around November 9.[45]

The Kristallnacht commemoration in Tröbitz in 1967 encapsulates the ambiguity of Holocaust remembrance in the GDR, and the intricate relationship between the state and its Jewish communities. In his statement, Helmut Aris pledged "a clear allegiance to the GDR," the "homeland where fascism and racism have been banned for ever."[46] In previous negotiations, however, both the Association and the State Secretary had agreed to leave out any remarks concerning the "Middle East problem" due to "different opinions." When Herbert Ringer, vice chairmen of the Association, asked whether a statement on the Jewish communities' "stance on West Germany" was really necessary, the State Secretary insisted on it.[47] Both groups benefitted from that compromise: while the government received a public appraisal by the communities—not so much as an act of heartfelt allegiance, but as a necessary measure to ensure the regime's toleration—the communities managed to stage a dignified event commemorating Kristallnacht in return.

NOVEMBER 9 AND THE GDR SOCIETY

For decades November 9 remained a date most relevant to the Jewish communities. Starting in the 1960s, though, other East German groups society began to realise its potential. The thirtieth anniversary of Kristallnacht in 1968 was celebrated not just by the Association, but also with a grand event hosted at East Berlin's Academy of Arts where the publisher Verlag der Nation presented an anthology of poetry on the Holocaust, some of which were recited by famous writers such as Stephan Hermlin or Christa Wolf.[48] Non-Jewish artists, writers, and intellectuals increasingly took an interest in the memory of the anti-Semitic persecution, contributing to a multi-faceted culture of remembrance about the Holocaust within the GDR.[49]

GDR churches were another protagonist that would later prove of vital importance in toppling the SED. From the 1960s onwards, church groups staged their own events around November 9, mostly in towns where no Jewish community could survive; church-owned papers often published sermons on or recollections of the event.[50] The Action Reconciliation Service for Peace, founded in 1958 in both Germanys, provided field trips to Holocaust memorials in Poland and Czechoslovakia to several thousand adolescents.[51] The cooperation of Jewish communities and church groups intensified from the 1970s onwards, especially in promoting the "Christian-Jewish Dialogue." In Leipzig, the fortieth anniversary of Kristallnacht was celebrated as a joint event by the local Jewish and the *Versöhnungskirche* community with its minister, Siegfried Theodor Arndt, one of the leading figures of Christian-Jewish relations in the GDR.[52]

November 9 evolved into an occasion for protests. The authorities were sceptical of this new-found interest in Jewish matters by the churches who sometimes led demonstrations of dissent. On November 9, 1983, a small group of adolescents gathered in Leipzig at the memorial stone for a destroyed synagogue. Following a prayer in the nearby Nikolai church, they placed candles next to the stone. Shortly afterwards, the police arrived, removed the candles, and arrested everyone. The next evening, the adolescents returned to the same spot, provoking another response from authorities. Criticism of the regime's policies and of an anti-fascist folklore that often tended to neglect Jewish and non-Communist victims was mixed with expressions of discontent with life in the GDR.[53] This episode highlights how people with no particular connection to Jewish remembrance appropriated the event and used it for their own purpose, thereby expanding its meaning. Commemorating a historical event is, after all, never only about the past, but also about the present.

NEW DIMENSIONS: 1978–1988

High ranking party officials were rarely involved in commemorative events on November 9. Yet, in both German states, the fortieth anniversary of Kristallnacht in 1978 proved a critical turning point. For the first time the memory of November 1938 was acknowledged as something truly meaningful by both governments. In the Federal Republic, Chancellor Helmut Schmidt and President Walter Scheel joined a festive ceremony in the main synagogue in Cologne while manifold other events were held.[54] Similar events, albeit with less prominent personnel, were staged throughout the GDR, and the completion of the refurbishment of the synagogue at East Berlin's Rykestrasse was used to open a special exhibition on the event, designed by the Museum for

German History. There are several reasons for this change: First, both governments reacted to a newly found interest in Jewish history and culture, an international trend at the time. Second, West Germany had been experiencing a new wave of interest for Hitler often with undisguised fascination, and a surge in right-wing extremism which was also felt, but not publicly acknowledged, in the GDR. Third, and probably most importantly, a new generation started to raise questions about the German past. The pressure of non-Jewish groups "from below" urged the political elite to react while often the groups took initiative themselves. Almost half of the forty-five plus events staged in memory of Kristallnacht in the GDR that year were organised by Protestant churches. Also, the party's preference of highlighting 1938 instead of 1918 coincided with a general growing disinterest in the 1918 revolution.[55] The Jewish communities gladly accepted this new form of attention, but kept a distance due to their experience with the state. Five years later, the forty-fifth anniversary was not celebrated, as it coincided with the five hundredth anniversary of the birth of Martin Luther. Helmut Aris refused to stage an event, referring to an "anti-Semitic atmosphere" in the GDR due to an "undifferentiated depiction of the situation in the Middle East"—the media coverage of the 1982 Lebanon War—which coincided with a noncritical appraisal of Luther and his anti-Semitic writings.[56]

The greatest efforts by the SED were put into the organisation of the fiftieth anniversary of Kristallnacht in 1988. The regime recognised its chance to start what Harald Schmid called a "charm offensive."[57] However, the many events, publications, and speeches honouring the day did not have the intended effect. On the contrary, this "epidemic of remembrance," as the Jewish journalist Salomea Genin noted, was the last grand effort of the regime to regain some international recognition and trust of the population, but failed eventually.[58] Nevertheless, the memory of Kristallnacht and of the Jewish victims of Nazi atrocities were prominently addressed in 1988. The founding of the Centrum Judaicum, a Jewish cultural institution, at Berlin's former synagogue at Oranienburger Straße was the clearest sign of a new appreciation of Jewish history. The connivance of *ordinary* Germans in the persecution of the Jews could now be expressed more clearly than before. A memorial plaque unveiled at a church in Dresden read: "We kept silent when their synagogues were burned, when Jews were deprived of their rights, expelled, and murdered. We did not recognise them as our brothers and sisters. We ask for forgiveness and shalom."[59] Such a clear acknowledgement of guilt had been mostly absent in the public since the 1940s, but speeches by Jewish dignitaries prior to 1988 included remarks to that effect.[60] Furthermore, GDR historiography had finally begun to address Kristallnacht in more detail. Kurt Pätzold, the GDR's leading historian on the Holocaust, published several articles on the subject in which he depicted the German population as beneficiaries of forcefully sold or confiscated Jewish property.[61] He also published an edition of unknown documents on Kristallnacht together with Jewish sociologist Irene Runge, whose introductory essay candidly reviewed the overall missing protest by non-Jewish observers in 1938.[62]

CONCLUSION

November 9 was an occasion for the commemoration of Kristallnacht and the Shoah throughout the GDR's existence, yet it rarely reached an importance similar to other anniversaries such as the founding of the GDR or even the *Day of the Victims of Fascism*. While the government soon opted for a highlighting of Communist resistance during the war and the blaming of a few high-ranking capitalists for the crimes, in order to deviate attention away from pressuring questions about German guilt and individual involvement in Nazi crimes, Jewish survivors chose a different approach. Torn between their own experiences of persecution, leading to a highly critical assessment of the postwar German society eager to forget its recent past, and their desire to believe in the possibility of a truly better, anti-fascist Germany, survivors and returned émigrés had to negotiate with the non-Jewish elite about their agenda. Contrary to what 1990s research on the Jewish communities suggested, the chairmen did not merely succumb to the regime's pressure, but managed to form compromises leaving all parties involved mostly satisfied with the outcome. Thus, the communities were able to shape the events in their will, eking out "a peripheral yet largely unmolested existence" in the GDR, as Jay Geller put it.[63] The memory of Kristallnacht in the GDR is a prime example of how negotiations between the state, Jewish communities, and other groups such as Protestant churches, unfolded, and how different parties strove to find the best possible solution for themselves and their members.

Furthermore, it shows that clear cut paradigms like *the state* and *the Jews* are insufficient in explaining the intricate historical situation. Using November 9 as an occasion to criticize West Germany's policies and neo-fascist activities, for instance, served the interests of both the Jewish communities and the government as it highlighted Jewish suffering during National Socialism, mostly unimpaired careers of perpetrators after 1945, and emphasized the GDR's anti-fascist aura. The commemorative events were the most explicit way of highlighting the experience of Jewish victims, though the public perception of this tragedy only became pronounced after the late 1970s, very similar to developments in the Federal Republic. Beforehand, Jewish survivors had to rely on themselves in organising commemorative events while public perception remained negligible.

On November 9, 1989, a large crowd of tens of thousands of people gathered in Leipzig to hold a silent protest at the memorial stone for the former synagogue. Speakers demanded a change in politics, and an improved relationship with Israel. A press conference held that same day in Berlin led to a very different kind of commemoration—and celebration: the fall of the Berlin wall, which initiated the end of the GDR. November 9 had once again become a relevant date in German history.

Notes

1. See Norbert Frei, *Adenauer's Germany and the Nazi Past. The Politics of Amnesty and Integration* (New York: Columbia University Press, 2002); Jeffrey Herf. *Divided Memory: The Nazi Past in the Two Germanys* (Cambridge: Cambridge University Press, 1997).
2. For an overview, see Helmut Peitsch, "Antifaschistisches Verständnis der eigenen jüdischen Herkunft in Texten von DDR-SchriftstellerInnen," in *Das Kulturerbe deutschsprachiger Juden. Eine Spurensuche in den Ursprungs-, Transit- und Emigrationsländern*, ed. Elke-Vera Kotowski (Berlin: de Gruyter Oldenbourg, 2015), 117–20.
3. See, among others, Tobias Grill, "Die Reichskristallnacht als DDR-Geschichtspolitik," in *Die Novemberpogrome 1938. Versuch einer Bilanz*, edited by Andreas Nachama (Berlin: Stiftung Topographie des Terrors, 2009), 105–16; Olaf Groehler. "Erinnerungen an die 'Reichskristallnacht' in der SBZ und DDR," in *Pogromnacht und Holocaust. Frankfurt, Weimar, Buchenwald. Die schwierige Erinnerung an die Stationen der Vernichtung*, ed. Thomas Hofmann, Hanno Loewy, and Harry Stein (Vienna / Cologne / Weimar: Böhlau, 1994), 172–97.
4. See, among others, Norbert Frei, Christina Morina, Franka Maubach, and Maik Tändler, *Zur rechten Zeit. Wider die Rückkehr des Nationalismus* (Berlin: Ullstein, 2019), 43–65; Bill Niven, "Remembering Nazi Anti-Semitism in the GDR," in *Memorialization in Germany since 1945*, ed. Bill Niven and Chloe Paver (Basingstoke / New York: Palgrave Macmillan, 2010), 205–213.
5. On November 9, 1947, for instance, the SED paper *Neues Deutschland* featured two articles on the proclamation of the republic in 1918, and only two days later a short note about the event on 1938. Heinz Schumann, "Die 'Kristallnacht' von 1938." *Neues Deutschland*, November 11, 1947, 2. Cf. Harald Schmid, *Erinnern an den 'Tag der Schuld.' Das Novemberpogrom von 1938 in der deutschen Geschichtspolitik* (Hamburg: Ergebnisse, 2001), 85–94.
6. Cf. Christoph Classen, *Faschismus und Antifaschismus. Die nationalsozialistische Vergangenheit im ostdeutschen Hörfunk (1945–1953)* (Cologne / Vienna / Weimar: Böhlau, 2004), 130–31; Gerd Kühling, *Erinnerung an nationalsozialistische Verbrechen in Berlin. Verfolgte des Dritten Reiches und geschichtspolitisches Engagement im Kalten Krieg 1945–1979* (Berlin: Metropol, 2016), 59.
7. Cited in Gudrun Goeseke, "Geschichte der Jüdischen Gemeinde zu Halle nach 1945," in *300 Jahre Juden in Halle. Leben, Leistung, Leiden, Lohn*, ed. Jüdische Gemeinde Halle (Halle: Mitteldt. Verlag, 1992), 277.
8. Norbert Frei, *1945 und wir. Das Dritte Reich im Bewusstsein der Deutschen* (Munich: Deutscher Taschenbuch Verlag, 2009), 161–63; Barbara Wolbring, "Nationales Stigma und persönliche Schuld. Die Debatte über Kollektivschuld in der Nachkriegszeit," *Historische Zeitschrift* 289, no. 2 (2009): 325–64.

9. See Otto Dov Kulka and Eberhard Jäckel, *The Jews in the Secret Nazi Reports on Popular Opinion in Germany, 1933-1945* (New Haven: Yale University Press, 2010), 340-433.
10. Sächsisches Staatsarchiv Chemnitz (SächsStA-C), 32672 VVN, Nr. 47.
11. See Alice Stettiner, "Zehn Jahre nach der 'Kristallnacht,'" *Deutscher Pressedienst*, November 11, 1948. Bundesarchiv Berlin (BArch), DY 55/V 278/2/139.
12. Cf. Henry Leide, *NS-Verbrecher und Staatssicherheit. Die geheime Vergangenheitspolitik der DDR* (Göttingen: Vandenhoeck & Ruprecht, 2005), 48; Jürgen Danyel, "Die SED und die 'kleinen PG's.' Zur politischen Integration der ehemaligen NSDAP-Mitglieder in der SBZ/DDR," in *Helden, Täter und Verräter. Studien zum DDR-Antifaschismus*, ed. Annette Leo and Peter Reif-Spirek (Berlin: Metropol, 1999), 177-96.
13. See Olaf Groehler, "Antifaschismus und jüdische Problematik in der SBZ und der frühen DDR," in *Die SED-Politik, der Antifaschismus und die Juden in der SBZ und der frühen DDR*, ed. Olaf Groehler and Mario Keßler (Berlin: Gesellschaftswissenschaftliches Forum, 1995), 5-31.
14. Cf. Harald Schmid, *Antifaschismus und Judenverfolgung. Die 'Reichskristallnacht' als politischer Gedenktag in der DDR* (Göttingen: V&R Unipress, 2004), 20-31.
15. *Unser Appell*, no. 5 (1947): 6. Cf. Olaf Groehler. "Die Diskussion um die Judenverfolgung in SBZ und DDR (1947-1953)," in *Arbeiterbewegung und Antisemitismus. Entwicklungslinien im 20. Jahrhundert*, ed. Mario Keßler (Bonn: Pahl-Rugenstein-Verlag Nachf., 1993), 80-81.
16. Cf. Schmid, *Erinnern*, 94-111.
17. Interview with Kurt Schumacher, cited in Verein Aktives Museum, ed., *1945. Jetzt wohin? Exil und Rückkehr* (Berlin: Verein Aktives Museum Faschismus und Widerstand in Berlin, 1995), 184.
18. Leon Löwenkopf, "Kristallnachtkundgebung," November 9, 1947. BArch, DY 55/V 278/2/139.
19. SED Kreisvorstand to SED Landesvorstand, October 26, 1949, Sächsisches Staatsarchiv Dresden (SächsSta-D), 11856 SED-Landesleitung Sachsen, IV/A/1800.
20. Letter from Kurt Schatter, the addressee is unclear, November 23, 1951, Centrum Judaicum Archive (CJA), Berlin, 5 B 1, Nr. 6.
21. See the invitations and reports for the early 1950s in CJA, 5 B 1, Nr. 68. Cf. Irena Ostmeyer, *Zwischen Schuld und Sühne. Evangelische Kirche und Juden in SBZ und DDR 1945-1990* (Berlin: Inst. Kirche und Judentum, 2002), 163-82.
22. It is unclear which poem was meant here. Yet, one year later, a poem under that title was published in the VVN paper *Die Tat* on November 5, 1949, 6. See the correspondence, announcements, and programme in SächsStA-C, 32672 VVN, Nr. 47; SächsStA-D, 11410, Kreisrat Bautzen, Nr. 868.
23. See the programmes in Landesarchiv Berlin (LAB), C Rep. 118-01, Nr. 38958; BArch, DY 54/V 277/1/45. Cf. Peter Monteath, "A Day to Remember: East Germany's Day

of Remembrance for the Victims of Fascism," *German History* 26, no. 2 (2008): 205-07.
24. Willi Bredel, *Die Enkel* (Berlin [East]: Aufbau-Verlag, 1953), 658. Translation quoted from Stephen Brockmann, *The Writers' State: Constructing East German Literature, 1945-1959* (Rochester: Camden House, 2015), 39-40.
25. Cf. Jay Howard Geller, *Jews in Post-Holocaust Germany, 1945-1953* (Cambridge: Cambridge University Press, 2005).
26. CJA, 2 A 2, Nr. 406; CJA, 2 A 2, Nr. 1931; LAB, C Rep. 104, Nr. 102. Cf. Schmid, *Antifaschismus*, 32-65. For West Germany see idem, *Erinnern*, 97, n. 53.
27. See Y. Michal Bodemann, *Gedächtnistheater. Die jüdische Gemeinschaft und ihre deutsche Erfindung* (Hamburg: Rotbuch-Verlag, 1996), 108. Newspaper articles prove that such events took place every year, at least in Berlin, but surely also in other communities.
28. Cf. Schmid, *Antifaschismus*, 32-40.
29. See the letters and invitations in Archiv der Akademie der Künste, Berlin (AdK), Peter-Edel-Archiv, Nr. 744; CJA, 2 A 2, Nr. 431; CJA, 5 A 1, Nr. 491; LAB, C Rep. 104, Nr. 2093.
30. See Willy Lindwer, *The Last Seven Months of Anne Frank* (New York: Anchor Books, 1992).
31. See David Shneer, "Eberhard Rebling, Lin Jaldati, and Yiddish Music in East Germany 1949-1962," in *Dislocated Memories: Jews, Music, and Postwar German Culture*, ed. Tina Frühauf and Lily E. Hirsch (New York: Oxford University Press, 2014) 161-86; idem, "Yiddish Music and East German Antifascism: Lin Jaldati, Post-Holocaust Jewish Culture and the Cold War," *Leo Baeck Institute Year Book* 60 (2015): 207-34.
32. "Jüdische Bürger erzwangen in Westberlin eine Gedenkfeier für die Opfer der Kristallnacht," *Neues Deutschland*, November 11, 1953, 8. Cf. Gerd Kühling,"Frühes Gedenken am ehemaligen Deportationsbahnhof Berlin-Grunewald. Ein Fund aus dem Bildarchiv," *Mitgliederrundbrief Aktives Museum* 74 (2016): 18-22.
33. Cf. Shneer, *Eberhard Rebling*, 172.
34. Cf. Angelika Timm, "Der 9. November 1938 in der politischen Kultur der DDR," in *Der Umgang mit dem Holocaust. Europa—USA—Israel*, ed. Rolf Steininger (Vienna / Cologne / Weimar: Böhlau, 1994), 253.
35. BArch, DY 30/J IV 2/3/920; BArch, DY 6/289; BArch, DY 6/2356. Cf. Michael Lemke, "Kampagnen gegen Bonn. Die Systemkrise der DDR und die Westpropaganda der SED 1960-1963," *Vierteljahrshefte für Zeitgeschichte* 41, no. 2 (1993): 153-74.
36. CJA, 5 B 1, Nr. 218. See also "Mahnung und Warnung. Zum 25. Jahrestag der Kristallnacht—Aufruf an die Juden der Welt und alle Menschen guten Willens," *Neue Zeit*, November 5, 1963, 4.
37. "'Unsere Heimat ist hier in der DDR.' Gedenkkundgebung zum 25. Jahrestag der

Kristallnacht in Dresden," *Neue Zeit*, November 13, 1963, 2. See also Schmid, *Antifaschismus*, 55–61.
38. See Michael Wolffsohn, *Die Deutschland-Akte. Juden und Deutsche in Ost und West. Tatsachen und Legenden*, 3rd ed. (München: Ed. Ferenczy bei Bruckmann, 1997); Jutta Illichmann, *Die DDR und die Juden. Die deutschlandpolitische Instrumentalisierung von Juden und Judentum durch die Partei- und Staatsführung der SBZ/DDR von 1945 bis 1990* (Frankfurt am Main: Lang, 1997); Stefan Meining, *Kommunistische Judenpolitik. Die DDR, die Juden und Israel* (Hamburg: Lit, 2002).
39. Cf. Kühling, *Erinnerung*, 253–58.
40. Victor Klemperer, "24 May 1950," in *The Diaries of Victor Klemperer 1945–59*, ed. Martin Chalmers (London: Phoenix, 2003), 317.
41. See Karin Hartewig, *Zurückgekehrt. Die Geschichte der jüdischen Kommunisten in der DDR* (Vienna / Cologne / Weimar: Böhlau, 2000), 562–74; Angelika Timm, *Hammer, Zirkel, Davidstern: Das gestörte Verhältnis der DDR zu Zionismus und Staat Israel* (Bonn: Bouvier, 1997), 171–332.
42. BArch, DM 3/5522. See also Schmid, *Antifaschismus*, 58; Thomas Fache,"DDR-Antifaschismus und das Gedenken an die Novemberpogrome 1938. Eine Lokalstudie," *Medaon* 2 (2008): 7, 20 n. 61.
43. Michael Wolffsohn deemed the Jews in the GDR "useful idiots": Wolffsohn, *Deutschland-Akte*, 12.
44. CJA, 5 B 1, Nr. 235, p. 22.
45. See Stefanie Endlich, "'Der verlorene Transport.' Gedenken an die Toten in Tröbitz zum 70. Jahrestag der Befreiung," *Gedenkstättenrundbrief*, no. 178 (2015): 18–25. On the events see CJA, 2 A 2, Nr. 749; CJA, 5 B 1, Nr. 219-220; CJA, 5 B 1, Nr. 236.
46. *Neues Deutschland*, November 10, 1967, 2.
47. CJA, 5 B 1, Nr. 235, Bl. 22.
48. See the invitation in BArch, DY 17/3998. "Klage und Ausweg. Matinee zum 30. Jahrestag der 'Kristallnacht,'" *Neues Deutschland*, November 11, 1968, 3.
49. See Alexander Walther, "Keine Erinnerung, nirgends? Die Shoah und die DDR," *Deutschland-Archiv* (July 15, 2019), http://www.bpb.de/293937; idem, "Distrusting the Parks: Heinz Knobloch's Journalism and the Shoah Memory in the GDR," in *Growing out of Antifascism's Shadow: Holocaust Memory in Socialist Eastern Europe since the 1950s*, ed. Kata Bohus, Peter Hallama, and Stephan Stach (forthcoming); idem, "Anti-Fascism without Jews? Aspects of Commemorating the Shoah in the GDR's Post-Perpetrator Society," in *The Afterlife of the Shoah in Central Eastern European Cultures: Concepts, Problems, and the Aesthetic of Postcatastrophic Narration*, ed. Anja Tippner, Anna Artwińska, and Katarzyna Adamczak (forthcoming).
50. See Günter Arndt and Christfried Berger, *"Als die Synagogen brannten . . .": Kristallnacht und Kirche. 40 Jahre Kristallnacht, 9 November 1938* (Magdeburg: Evangelisches Konsistorium, 1978); Karl Kleinschmidt, "Kristallnacht und Kirche,"

Glaube und Gewissen 9, no. 11 (1963): 205–06. Cf. Ostmeyer, *Schuld und Sühne*; Schmid, *Antifaschismus*, 61.

51. Cf. Anton Legerer, *Tatort: Versöhnung. Über die Aktion Sühnezeichen, Friedensdienste in der BRD sowie in der DDR und Gedenkdienste in Österreich* (Leipzig: Evangelische Verlagsanstalt, 2011), 255–320.
52. Nora Goldenbogen, "Jüdisches Leben in Sachsen 1945 bis 1989," in *Juden in Sachsen*, ed. Gunda Ulbricht and Olaf Glöckner (Leipzig: Edition Leipzig, 2013), 204–05; Ostmeyer, *Schuld und Sühne*, 242–47.
53. Stephan Stach, "Dissidentes Gedenken. Der Umgang Oppositioneller mit Holocaustgedenktagen in der Volksrepublik Polen und der DDR," in *Gegengeschichte. Zweiter Weltkrieg und Holocaust im ostmitteleuropäischen Dissens*, ed. Peter Hallama, and Stephan Stach (Leipzig: Leipziger Universitäts Verlag, 2015), 210–11.
54. Schmid, *Erinnern*, 325–93.
55. BArch, DY 30/J IV 2/3/2781; BArch, DY 30/J IV 2/3/2815. Cf. Schmid, *Antifaschismus*, 78–103; Hartewig, *Zurückgekehrt*, 542–49.
56. BArch, DO 4/448. See also Timm, "9. November 1938," 259.
57. Schmid, *Antifaschismus*, 108.
58. Salomea Genin, "Erinnerungen einer Jüdin in der DDR," *Horch und Guck* 12 (1994): 50.
59. *Gedenkstätten für die Opfer des Nationalsozialismus*, ed. Bundeszentrale für Politische Bildung, vol. 2 (Bonn: Bundeszentrale für Politische Bildung, 2000), 649.
60. Cf. Timm, "9. November 1938," 255.
61. Kurt Pätzold, "Der Novemberpogrom 1938. Die Täter—Die Opfer—Die Mehrheit der Deutschen," *Archivmitteilungen* 38, no. 5 (1988): 145–48. Some of the sources that Pätzold used were pointed out to him by his student Wolf Gruner. Ibid., 148 n. 13.
62. Kurt Pätzold and Irene Runge, *Pogromnacht 1938* (Berlin [East]: Dietz, 1988).
63. Jay Howard Geller, "Representing Jewry in East Germany, 1945–1953: Between Advocacy and Accommodation," *Leo Baeck Institute Yearbook* 47 (2002): 214.

Bibliography

Archives

Archiv der Akademie der Künste, Berlin.
Bundesarchiv Berlin.
Centrum Judaicum Archive.
Landesarchiv Berlin.
Sächsisches Staatsarchiv Chemnitz.
Sächsisches Staatsarchiv Dresden.

Newspapers

"Jüdische Bürger erzwangen in Westberlin eine Gedenkfeier für die Opfer der Kristallnacht." *Neues Deutschland*, November 11, 1953, 8.
"Klage und Ausweg. Matinee zum 30. Jahrestag der 'Kristallnacht.'" *Neues Deutschland*, November 11, 1968, 3.
"Mahnung und Warnung. Zum 25. Jahrestag der Kristallnacht—Aufruf an die Juden der Welt und alle Menschen guten Willens." *Neue Zeit*, November 5, 1963, 4.
Neues Deutschland, November 10, 1967, 2.
Schumann, Heinz. "Die 'Kristallnacht' von 1938." *Neues Deutschland*, November 11, 1947, 2.
Stettiner, Alice. "Zehn Jahre nach der 'Kristallnacht.'" *Deutscher Pressedienst*, November 11, 1948.
"'Unsere Heimat ist hier in der DDR.' Gedenkkundgebung zum 25. Jahrestag der Kristallnacht in Dresden." *Neue Zeit*, November 13, 1963, 2.

Secondary Sources

Arndt, Günter, and Christfried Berger. *"Als die Synagogen brannten . . .": Kristallnacht und Kirche. 40 Jahre Kristallnacht, 9 November 1938*. Magdeburg: Evangelisches Konsistorium, 1978.
Bodemann, Y. Michal. *Gedächtnistheater. Die jüdische Gemeinschaft und ihre deutsche Erfindung*. Hamburg: Rotbuch-Verlag, 1996.
Bredel, Willi. *Die Enkel*. Berlin (East): Aufbau-Verlag, 1953.
Brockmann, Stephen. *The Writers' State. Constructing East German Literature, 1945–1959*. Rochester: Camden House, 2015.
Classen, Christoph. *Faschismus und Antifaschismus. Die nationalsozialistische Vergangenheit im ostdeutschen Hörfunk (1945–1953)*. Cologne / Vienna / Weimar: Böhlau, 2004.

Danyel, Jürgen. "Die SED und die 'kleinen PG's.' Zur politischen Integration der ehemaligen NSDAP-Mitglieder in der SBZ/DDR." In *Helden, Täter und Verräter. Studien zum DDR-Antifaschismus*, edited by Annette Leo and Peter Reif-Spirek, 177–96. Berlin: Metropol, 1999.

Endlich, Stefanie. "'Der verlorene Transport.' Gedenken an die Toten in Tröbitz zum 70. Jahrestag der Befreiung." *Gedenkstättenrundbrief*, no. 178 (2015): 18–25.

Fache, Thomas. "DDR-Antifaschismus und das Gedenken an die Novemberpogrome 1938. Eine Lokalstudie." *Medaon* 2 (2008): 1–23.

Frei, Norbert. *1945 und wir. Das Dritte Reich im Bewusstsein der Deutschen*. Munich: Deutscher Taschenbuch Verlag, 2009.

———. *Adenauer's Germany and the Nazi Past: The Politics of Amnesty and Integration*. New York: Columbia University Press, 2002.

Frei, Norbert, Christina Morina, Franka Maubach, and Maik Tändler. *Zur rechten Zeit. Wider die Rückkehr des Nationalismus*. Berlin: Ullstein, 2019).

Gedenkstätten für die Opfer des Nationalsozialismus, edited by Bundeszentrale für Politische Bildung. Vol. 2. Bonn: Bundeszentrale für Politische Bildung, 2000.

Geller, Jay Howard. *Jews in Post-Holocaust Germany, 1945–1953*. Cambridge: Cambridge University Press, 2005.

———. "Representing Jewry in East Germany, 1945–1953: Between Advocacy and Accommodation." *Leo Baeck Institute Yearbook* 47 (2002): 195–214.

Genin, Salomea. "Erinnerungen einer Jüdin in der DDR." *Horch und Guck* 12 (1994): 44–51.

Goeseke, Gudrun. "Geschichte der Jüdischen Gemeinde zu Halle nach 1945." In *300 Jahre Juden in Halle. Leben, Leistung, Leiden, Lohn*, edited by Jüdische Gemeinde Halle, 275–86. Halle: Mitteldt. Verlag, 1992.

Goldenbogen, Nora. "Jüdisches Leben in Sachsen 1945 bis 1989." In *Juden in Sachsen*, edited by Gunda Ulbricht and Olaf Glöckner, 176–209. Leipzig: Edition Leipzig, 2013.

Grill, Tobias. "Die Reichskristallnacht als DDR-Geschichtspolitik." In *Die Novemberpogrome 1938. Versuch einer Bilanz*, edited by Andreas Nachama, 105–16. Berlin: Stiftung Topographie des Terrors, 2009.

Groehler, Olaf. "Antifaschismus und jüdische Problematik in der SBZ und der frühen DDR." In *Die SED-Politik, der Antifaschismus und die Juden in der SBZ und der frühen DDR*, edited by Olaf Groehler and Mario Keßler, 5–31. Berlin: Gesellschaftswissenschaftliches Forum, 1995.

———. "Die Diskussion um die Judenverfolgung in SBZ und DDR (1947–1953)." In *Arbeiterbewegung und Antisemitismus. Entwicklungslinien im 20. Jahrhundert*, edited by Mario Keßler, 79–86. Bonn: Pahl-Rugenstein-Verlag Nachf., 1993.

———. "Erinnerungen an die 'Reichskristallnacht' in der SBZ und DDR." In *Pogromnacht und Holocaust. Frankfurt, Weimar, Buchenwald. Die schwierige Erinnerung an die Stationen der Vernichtung*, edited by Thomas Hofmann, Hanno Loewy, and Harry Stein, 172–97. Vienna / Cologne / Weimar: Böhlau, 1994.

Hartewig, Karin. *Zurückgekehrt. Die Geschichte der jüdischen Kommunisten in der DDR.* Vienna / Cologne / Weimar: Böhlau, 2000.

Herf, Jeffrey. *Divided Memory: The Nazi Past in the Two Germanys.* Cambridge: Cambridge University Press, 1997.

Illichmann, Jutta. *Die DDR und die Juden. Die deutschlandpolitische Instrumentalisierung von Juden und Judentum durch die Partei- und Staatsführung der SBZ/DDR von 1945 bis 1990.* Frankfurt am Main: Peter Lang, 1997.

Kleinschmidt, Karl. "Kristallnacht und Kirche." *Glaube und Gewissen* 9, no. 11 (1963): 205–06.

Klemperer, Victor. "24 May 1950." In *The Diaries of Victor Klemperer 1945–59*, edited by Martin Chalmers, 317. London: Phoenix, 2003.

Kühling, Gerd. *Erinnerung an nationalsozialistische Verbrechen in Berlin. Verfolgte des Dritten Reiches und geschichtspolitisches Engagement im Kalten Krieg 1945–1979.* Berlin: Metropol, 2016.

———. "Frühes Gedenken am ehemaligen Deportationsbahnhof Berlin-Grunewald. Ein Fund aus dem Bildarchiv." *Mitgliederrundbrief Aktives Museum* 74 (2016): 18–22.

Kulka, Otto Dov, and Eberhard Jäckel. *The Jews in the Secret Nazi Reports on Popular Opinion in Germany, 1933–1945.* New Haven: Yale University Press, 2010.

Legerer, Anton. *Tatort: Versöhnung. Über die Aktion Sühnezeichen, Friedensdienste in der BRD sowie in der DDR und Gedenkdienste in Österreich.* Leipzig: Evangelische Verlagsanstalt, 2011.

Leide, Henry. *NS-Verbrecher und Staatssicherheit. Die geheime Vergangenheitspolitik der DDR.* Göttingen: Vandenhoeck & Ruprecht, 2005.

Lemke, Michael. "Kampagnen gegen Bonn. Die Systemkrise der DDR und die Westpropaganda der SED 1960–1963." *Vierteljahrshefte für Zeitgeschichte* 41, no. 2 (1993): 153–74.

Lindwer, Willy. *The Last Seven Months of Anne Frank.* New York: Anchor Books, 1992.

Meining, Stefan. *Kommunistische Judenpolitik. Die DDR, die Juden und Israel.* Hamburg: Lit, 2002.

Monteath, Peter. "A Day to Remember: East Germany's Day of Remembrance for the Victims of Fascism." *German History* 26, no. 2 (2008): 195–218.

Niven, Bill. "Remembering Nazi Anti-Semitism in the GDR." In *Memorialization in Germany since 1945*, edited by Bill Niven and Chloe Paver, 205–13. Basingstoke / New York: Palgrave Macmillan, 2010.

Ostmeyer, Irena. *Zwischen Schuld und Sühne. Evangelische Kirche und Juden in SBZ und DDR 1945–1990.* Berlin: Inst. Kirche und Judentum, 2002.

Pätzold, Kurt. "Der Novemberpogrom 1938. Die Täter—Die Opfer—Die Mehrheit der Deutschen." *Archivmitteilungen* 38, no. 5 (1988): 145–48.

Pätzold, Kurt, and Irene Runge. *Pogromnacht 1938.* Berlin (East): Dietz, 1988.

Peitsch, Helmut. "Antifaschistisches Verständnis der eigenen jüdischen Herkunft in Texten von DDR-SchriftstellerInnen." In *Das Kulturerbe deutschsprachiger Juden.*

Eine Spurensuche in den Ursprungs-, Transit- und Emigrationsländern, edited by Elke-Vera Kotowski, 117–42. Berlin: de Gruyter Oldenbourg, 2015.

Schmid, Harald. *Antifaschismus und Judenverfolgung. Die "Reichskristallnacht" als politischer Gedenktag in der DDR*. Göttingen: V&R Unipress, 2004.

———. *Erinnern an den "Tag der Schuld." Das Novemberpogrom von 1938 in der deutschen Geschichtspolitik*. Hamburg: Ergebnisse, 2001.

Shneer, David. "Eberhard Rebling, Lin Jaldati, and Yiddish Music in East Germany 1949–1962." In *Dislocated Memories: Jews, Music, and Postwar German Culture*, edited by Tina Frühauf and Lily E. Hirsch, 161–86. New York: Oxford University Press, 2014.

———. "Yiddish Music and East German Antifascism: Lin Jaldati, Post-Holocaust Jewish Culture and the Cold War." *Leo Baeck Institute Year Book* 60 (2015): 207–34.

Stach, Stephan. "Dissidentes Gedenken. Der Umgang Oppositioneller mit Holocaustgedenktagen in der Volksrepublik Polen und der DDR." In *Gegengeschichte. Zweiter Weltkrieg und Holocaust im ostmitteleuropäischen Dissens*, edited by Peter Hallama and Stephan Stach, 207–36. Leipzig: Leipziger Universitäts Verlag, 2015.

Timm, Angelika. "Der 9. November 1938 in der politischen Kultur der DDR." In *Der Umgang mit dem Holocaust. Europa—USA—Israel*, edited by Rolf Steininger, 246–62. Vienna / Cologne / Weimar: Böhlau, 1994.

———. *Hammer, Zirkel, Davidstern: Das gestörte Verhältnis der DDR zu Zionismus und Staat Israel*. Bonn: Bouvier, 1997.

Unser Appell. Halbmonatsschrift der Vereinigung der Verfolgten des Naziregimes, no. 5 (1947): 6.

Verein Aktives Museum, ed. *1945. Jetzt wohin? Exil und Rückkehr*. Berlin: Verein Aktives Museum Faschismus und Widerstand in Berlin, 1995.

Walther, Alexander. "Anti-Fascism Without Jews? Aspects of Commemorating the Shoah in the GDR's Post-Perpetrator Society." In *The Afterlife of the Shoah in Central Eastern European Cultures: Concepts, Problems, and the Aesthetic of Postcatastrophic Narration*, edited by Anja Tippner, Anna Artwińska, and Katarzyna Adamczak. Forthcoming.

———. "Distrusting the Parks: Heinz Knobloch's Journalism and the Shoah Memory in the GDR." In *Growing out of Antifascism's Shadow: Holocaust Memory in Socialist Eastern Europe since the 1950s*, edited by Kata Bohus, Peter Hallama, and Stephan Stach. Forthcoming.

———. "Keine Erinnerung, nirgends? Die Shoah und die DDR," Deutschland-Archiv, July 15, 2019, http://www.bpb.de/293937.

Wolbring, Barbara. "Nationales Stigma und persönliche Schuld. Die Debatte über Kollektivschuld in der Nachkriegszeit." *Historische Zeitschrift* 289, no. 2 (2009): 325–64.

Wolffsohn, Michael. *Die Deutschland-Akte. Juden und Deutsche in Ost und West. Tatsachen und Legenden*. 3rd ed. München: Ed. Ferenczy bei Bruckmann, 1997.

CHAPTER 13

"Kristallnacht in Tel Aviv": Nazi Associations in the Contemporary Israeli Socio-Political Debate

by Liat Steir-Livny

The Holocaust has always been a central trauma in Israel's national consciousness. The memory has not faded over the years; on the contrary, it has been the focus of increasing public discourse in recent decades. Together with the heightened awareness has come increased politicization. Both right- and left-wing public figures have used the specter of Nazism and the memory of the Holocaust in varied and sometimes contradictory ways in order to boost their agendas. The theme of Kristallnacht has surfaced within left wing discourse as a means of expressing criticism towards socio-political acts in contemporary Israel.

The chapter focuses on a violent demonstration against illegal African immigrants orchestrated by right-wing politicians and activists, which took place in South Tel Aviv on May 23, 2012. The demonstration was immediately branded "Kristallnacht in Tel Aviv" by members of the left political spectrum. The chapter analyses the appearance of this term on social media in microblogging (tweets, posts), blogs, memes and video-sharing platforms (such as YouTube).[1]

Research shows that social media platforms enable private citizens and opposition groups to take active roles in grassroots campaigns.[2] The chapter uses this research in order to introduce three main claims: 1) In Israel, a society drenched in Holocaust awareness, Kristallnacht references are used as a sociopolitical tool; 2) as a result, the historical event has been trivialized and has been turned into a series of symbols, myths, and associations; 3) Kristallnacht-related satire and black humor present similar ideas to those heard in serious debates.

POLITICIZATION OF THE HOLOCAUST IN ISRAEL

Israel encompasses a unique sphere of Holocaust awareness. Studies have shown that Holocaust memory has a very powerful presence in Israel, with a multi-generational impact. For Israeli Jews, the Holocaust is a cross-generational defining characteristic. Surveys reveal that, since the 1940s, the Jewish-Israeli population has assimilated the Holocaust as a central event, and young Jewish-Israelis consider the Holocaust to be the historical event that has had the greatest impact on them, even more than the founding of the State.[3] Research shows that Israeli media, education, culture, and public discourse all frame the Holocaust as a current, ongoing local trauma, rather than an event that ended decades ago in another place.[4]

In Israel, Nazi and Holocaust associations are a prominent socio-political tool used by politicians, journalists and educators. For many years, the political use of Holocaust rhetoric was particularly associated with the Arab-Jewish dispute. From the late 1940s until the late 1970s, under left-wing governments, a distinct parallel between Arabs and Nazis was discernible in Israeli culture. The necessity of warding off surrounding Arab armies was represented in terms of preventing an imminent "second Holocaust," and Arab leaders were described as Nazi successors.[5]

In the political upheaval of 1977, the right-wing Likud party came to power for the first time and, with the exception of a few short intervals, has been in power ever since. As right-wing attitudes spread throughout the Israeli public and the left lost its governing clout, it instead found expression through the country's intellectual, artistic, literary, and academic life.[6] Culture became the mouthpiece of the disappointed political left, which voiced its unhappiness over Israel's situation. During those decades, the political right continued to recycle the Nazi-Arab equation in speeches, interviews, etc., and also began comparing their left-wing foes to Nazis, while the left abandoned its former use of the Nazi-Arab equation. Parts of it began to highlight a reverse equation in which both national traumas (the Holocaust and the *Nakba* [lit.: disaster;

it is the Arabs' definition of their 1948 downfall]) were likened to each other. Parts of the left and especially the radical left represent Israelis in general, IDF soldiers who serve in the occupied territories and members of the right in particular, as Nazis.[7] The term "Israeli Kristallnacht" grew out of this trend.

REFUGEES FROM AFRICA IN ISRAEL

Since the year 2000, when Africans began entering Israel through the border with Egypt in growing numbers, particularly from Sudan and Eritrea, the subject of refugees and asylum seekers has created controversy and stormy debates. Most of the immigrants entered between 2007–12, before a wall was built between Israel and Egypt, and currently, in 2019, around 37,000 Africans reside in Israel, whose inhabitants number is almost nine million Israelis.[8] The debate concerning the Africans is foremost manifested in semantics. According to the left-wing narrative, the vast majority are refugees and asylum seekers who should be absorbed, while according to the right, the vast majority are infiltrators, illegal immigrants and seekers of employment who must be deported. These, however, are popular perceptions, which differ from the legal definitions.[9]

Since the Africans' arrival, right-wing governments have engaged in numerous social and judicial struggles that have not yet yielded a clear policy defining "infiltrators" and "asylum seekers,"[10] and have tried to facilitate a policy of mass deportation. This culminated in an announcement on April 2, 2018, in which Prime Minister Binyamin Netanyahu reported that the state of Israel had reached an agreement with the UN whereby sixteen thousand asylum seekers would be transferred to Canada, Italy, and Germany. Another sixteen thousand were supposed to be absorbed in Israel and sent to various *kibbutzim*, *moshavim* (a type of cooperative agricultural communities) and other areas. Several hours later, Netanyahu cancelled the plan because of pressure from right-wing political parties and right-wing public debate.[11]

From the very beginning, the vast majority of Africans were bussed to poverty-stricken neighborhoods in South Tel Aviv, where they joined Jewish residents from the lowest deciles of society who were already dealing with severe societal and economic struggles. NGOs familiar with the neighborhoods noted, over time, a rise in alcoholism, domestic violence, and increasing numbers of women turning to prostitution within these communities of Africans.[12]

Statistics published by the Israel police in 2018 noted four times as many sexual assaults and three times as much violence by Africans than in general Israeli society.[13] Some of the southern neighborhoods' original residents began trying to evict the newcomers from their neighborhoods. Right-wing politicians (as for example Danny Danon, Miri Regev, and Michael Ben Ari), who backed deportation of the Africans, often supported the protests, using them as a tool to highlight their agenda, while members of the left, who rejected deportation, worked against these attempts by writing articles, publicizing their opinions in social media, and trying to help the newcomers in the southern neighborhoods by establishing various NGOs.

THE MAY 23, 2012 DEMONSTRATION AND THE "KRISTALLNACHT" REFERENCES

The term "Israeli Kristallnacht" first appeared in April 2012, after Molotov cocktails were thrown at the homes of Sudanese and Eritreans and at a kindergarten in South Tel Aviv, in order to frighten the Africans and force them to leave.[14] But a month later, after a demonstration organized by Michael Ben Ari, a Knesset member from the National Union party, along with far-right activists Itamar Ben-Gvir and Baruch Marzel, it became an idiom. The approximately one thousand attendees at the protest demonstrated against allowing Africans to live, work, and stay in Israel—especially in South Tel Aviv. Politicians from the right, such as Danon, Regev, and Ben Ari, inflamed the raging crowd from the stage, shouting slogans against the Africans and calling for their deportation. One of the harshest phrases, which was later mentioned repeatedly in the Israeli media was voiced by Regev, who shouted that the Sudanese were "a cancer in our body" and that the left was to blame for the wretched state of the South Tel-Aviv neighborhoods. During the demonstration, African bystanders were attacked by some of the demonstrators; some were injured (blood stains were found on the road), windows of African shops were shattered, and some looting of shops took place. After the violent outbreak, several people were arrested and later released.[15]

Researchers who analyze representations of Holocaust commemoration within the virtual space, especially user-generated online platforms, and user-generated content (UGC) use the term "vernacular memory." This type of memory, as opposed to official memory, stems from everyday life, "the street," the "public space,"[16] and is compiled from "psychological, social, linguistic, and political processes that keep the past alive without necessarily intending to do so." It is a non-hierarchical, popular, informal, unplanned and sometimes subversive memory.[17] Studies have emphasized its role as a "milieu for social action and as loci of oppositional collective memory."[18] In the last few decades, user-generated content became an important part of the vernacular memory, which is "manifested more immediately after an event rather than through a retroactive commemorative perspective." Scholars examine the way "individuals negotiate, reconstruct, and share their versions of a collective memory in a given context" in online vernacular web-based commemoration.[19] The vernacular memory adds another layer of representations, associations, and meanings to collective memory. In addition, research shows that social media platforms have become powerful sites for documenting, challenging, and protesting against episodes of brutality[20] and that communicative spaces can create political and social awareness and encourage activism.[21]

This analysis of UGC shows how in this demonstration, like many other cases in contemporary Israel not related to the Holocaust, the Holocaust and Nazi themes were used as an important interpretive framework.[22] In a society steeped in Holocaust awareness, this is one of the first associations used to interpret a situation and create a critical response.

In the hours and days following the demonstration, members of the left used social media platforms to post comparisons between this demonstration and Kristallnacht, as a means of protesting against the right wing, and against this event in particular. Their claim was that Jews—led by racism, hate, fear, and a desire to keep their space "clean" and infiltrator-free—had behaved like Nazis, using verbal and physical violence against a helpless minority. Using this loaded term also signaled that this was just the beginning; a preview of much worse attacks in the future.

YNET News, the English version of the highly popular Israeli Hebrew news site *YNET*, wrote on May 26 that, "World news sites call Tel Aviv rally against influx of African migrants 'race riot' and 'Israeli Kristallnacht,'"[23] thus implying that the term was created outside of Israel. But a review of Israeli posts, tweets, blogs, and videos on YouTube in Hebrew shows that the term was first used by left-wing Jewish-Israelis, and only afterwards did it begin to appear on news sites outside of Israel.

Immediately after the demonstration, Jewish-Israeli social media was filled with posts using the terms "Israeli Kristallnacht," "Kristallnacht in Tel-Aviv," "Kristallnacht 2012," and "Kristallnacht 23.5.2012" (all used the Hebrew term "*Leil Habdolach*": the direct translation of "Kristallnacht"). For example, Aviv Maimon tweeted: "Kristallnacht Israel 2012 . . . Hitler must be giggling somewhere."[24] Hamutal Ronen felt that "The next step is ghettoizing strangers," and advised Israelis with foreign passports to "use [them] and emigrate from Israel for [sic] a better place."[25] Others uploaded links to videos from the demonstration, adding the title "Kristallnacht 23.5.2012, South Tel Aviv." Some posted in English, as well as in Hebrew, in order for the critique to be widened beyond an internal Hebrew discussion in Israel. For example: "Night of attacks against African Refugees, Tel-Aviv, Israel, 23.12.2012," tweeted Martin Kiel in English, and added the Hebrew hashtag[26] "*Leil habdolah* 2012." The Israeli activist Rotem Ilan, who founded the NGO "Israeli Children" and who fights against the deportation of the children of foreign workers, posted a long description of what she experienced during the demonstration, which she referred to as "Israeli Kristallnacht," blaming not the demonstrators themselves, but the government for incitement, racism, and neglect.[27] *The News Room*, which is an independent Israeli YouTube news channel, published an item about the demonstration titled "Tel Aviv Kristallnacht."

The term, however, did not appear in mainstream newspapers reports. The daily *Haaretz*, which is well known for its leftist stance, was the only newspaper which used the term in three different opinion columns. The first was in the column of Itamar Hendelman Smith, titled "Kristallnacht—2012 Version: look at us and remember them." The writer claimed that, as much as he dislikes comparisons of Israelis to Nazis, there are incidents which demand it:

> Less than 74 years after Kristallnacht—a well-organized pogrom of Nazi party members in the Jews of Germany, the Israelis received their own Kristallnacht. You don't really have to be a historian in order to make the necessary connection between the violent incidents in South Tel Aviv (and other towns in Israel) and the event which symbolizes the step up in Nazi brutality against the Jewish population.

According to Hendelman Smith, the comparison was inevitable. He claimed that in Nazi Germany, the Nazi establishment wanted to create the illusion that Kristallnacht was a spontaneous outburst of the masses. So, too, in Israel, Hendelman Smith wrote, the government wanted to create the illusion that it was a grassroots outburst, while in fact the right-wing officials were to blame.[28]

The *Globes* financial section of *Haaretz* featured a piece by writer Eyal Meged titled "Kristallnacht." More than a year later, the term appeared for the third time in an article about the well-known writer Yoram Kaniuk's legacy, where he was quoted as having said "The Israeli Kristallnacht . . . strengthen the feeling that Israel has changed. All those who want a stern-faced and right-wing *halachic* state will feel revived."[29] Israel's Channel Two website, in its coverage of the stormy debates surrounding the demonstration, also referred to the term. The item, which was aired on television, featured a debate between Danon from the right (who was one of the officials who spoke on stage during the demonstration), and left-wing Meretz party leader Zehava Gal-on. The website also included comments by Israelis who decided, after the demonstration, to press charges against Knesset members Danon, Ben-Ari, and Regev for incitement. Even though Kristallnacht was not mentioned within the report, the headline on Channel Two's website proclaimed: "Police Pressing Charges against Danon and Regev: Israeli Kristallnacht."[30]

Members of the right responded to the criticism and use of the expression in various ways. For instance, an anonymous group that was assisting residents of South Tel Aviv in their campaign to deport the Africans (and probably took part in the demonstration) proudly posted YouTube videos from the demonstration showing the violence, under the heading "The Neighborhood's Rage." The introduction stated:

> The Rage of South Tel Aviv: After a wave of rapes, murders, attacks and harassment from the African infiltrators, the rage of the neighborhood broke out. On May 23, 2012, the residents of the neighborhoods went out to the streets, and this is the outcome.

Knesset member Danon, who, from the stage at the demonstration, called upon the government to deport the infiltrators, posted a picture from the demonstration with the caption "Israel is at war."[31] Others spoke out against the expression "Kristallnacht," claiming that there can be no comparison between the two events, and that those who attempt to do so are hypocritical liars.[32] For example, the journalist Saul Rosenfeld wrote that

> Ignorance, malice and hypocrisy stand behind the lame, despicable and refuted comparison of the violent demonstration in Tel Aviv to the murder of hundreds of Jews, the deportation of tens of thousands to concentration camps, and the burning of synagogues.

He claimed that he supported deportation, but opposed hate speech, such as the remarks of Regev, and objected to violence and incitement against the Africans. He expressed his repugnance that "some of our 'chosen and spokesmen'" chose to use this comparison. He added, ironically, that members of the left objected when the right used Holocaust associations, but they made the same associations when it suited their agenda.³³ Others rejected violence but also opposed the comparison between Kristallnacht and the demonstration, claiming that it was disproportionate, an incitement against the inhabitants of the South Tel Aviv neighborhoods and a part of the "inability of the riotous left" to understand that a real problem existed in South Tel Aviv. On June 23, 2012, a protest for social justice took place in Tel-Aviv, organized mainly by the left. During this demonstration, the windows of a bank were shattered. "When a window in the Shapira neighborhood was broken, the left called it 'Kristallnacht.' How will these hypocrites describe the violence of this demonstration?" tweeted a surfer.³⁴

As a response to those who opposed the comparison, left-wing journalist Uri Misgav published a post that was shared many times in which he supposedly tried to explain why the Kristallnacht reference was wrong, but actually, strengthened it:

> I do not understand the absurd comparisons. Go learn some history. There [in Germany] it was done to find a scapegoat because of the economic collapse and mass unemployment. Here it was done to find a scapegoat only because of the economic slowdown and the intolerable social gaps. There it was done with the encouragement of the authorities. Here only the Interior Minister and several MKs from the coalition arrived to agitate the crowd. There they were called parasites and germ spreaders, here they only call them cancer and Aids distributors [. . .] There they punished those who employed Jews and prohibited Jews from integrating into the labor market, here they only passed the Prohibition of Employment Law [. . .] There they marked Jewish businesses and shattered shop windows, here, well, mmm, never mind. There it happened in Nuremberg and Munich, here in Tel Aviv and Arad. There it was against Jews, here it is by the Jews and this is all that matters.³⁵

FROM "KRISTALLNACHT" TO "POGROM"

In their research on Kristallnacht terminology, Ulrich Baumann and Francois Guesnet claim that there has been a recent shift in terminology from the use of "Kristallnacht" to "pogrom" in Germany to describe the events of November 9–10, 1938. According to them there is a major difference between the two terms: "Kristallnacht" is state sponsored violence, while "pogrom" is a group sponsored expression of hate.[36] Baumann and Guesnet claim, that the term "pogrom" emerged in an Eastern European context in order to describe anti-Jewish violence that took place there. In Russia, it appeared to describe incidences of mass anti-Jewish violence in 1881–82. The term broadened beyond Russia at the beginning of the twentieth century. It was used to describe a one-sided and non-governmental form of violence used against a group as a whole. According to research, authorities did not order or authorize pogroms, but the empathy expressed by officers, ministers, and monarchs in the wake of the violence encouraged a significant shift in the perception of anti-Jewish violence around 1900, as Baumann and Guesnet explain.

In the Israeli culture public discourse, "Kristallnacht" is a term commonly used. The term "pogrom" is also known in Israel, but usually in reference to smaller-scale attacks against Jews, not necessarily committed by Nazis and much less commonly used to describe the events of November 9–10, 1938. The Israelis, in their use of the term "pogrom" to describe the demonstration unknowingly echoed what researchers have seen as the key elements in a pogrom: perceived upward shift in the position of a minority or marginal group, perceived weakness and passivity of state authorities in regard to "the problem" the minority poses, and ideological reinforcement of stereotypes and prejudice legitimizing violent confrontation from the majority.

The term "pogrom" appeared in several Israeli posts, tweets, and interviews surrounding the demonstration, either with or without the addition of "Israeli Kristallnacht." For example, "This is how a pogrom looks like," tweeted activist Igaal Shtaim, who shared a link to a "demonstration against the pogrom against the refugees," and added the hashtag "Kristallnacht 2012."[37] An article by Dr. Tali Kritzman-Amir, a senior lecturer who specializes in international law, immigration, refugees and asylum seekers began, "Last night a pogrom took place on the streets of Tel Aviv."[38] "This is not Kristallnacht, it is more like a Ukraine pogrom" tweeted the surfer Ouriel Daskal: "Many uneducated people with lots of hatred and violence. In order for it to be Kristallnacht we need more organization."[39] Writer Eyal Meged used both "Kristallnacht" and "pogrom," claiming that those responsible "cannot refer to themselves as

Jews."[40] In an interview on Channel Two, Meretz head Gal-on called it "a pogrom which is a result of harsh incitement of those who created a blood libel and later danced on the blood: Prime Minister Binyamin Netanyahu, Danny Danon, Miri Regev, Eli Ishay [. . .]" and added that it reminded her of things "I don't want to talk about."[41] Knesset member Yair Lapid, who headed the centrist party Yesh Atid wrote a post that showed that the use of the word "pogrom" in relation to the demonstration was not only part of a leftist narrative. On his Facebook page he wrote:

> I support the arrest and deportation of infiltrators, and building the fence (between Israel and Egypt l.s.l) and I think that human rights' organizations should first and foremost think about the human rights of the Jewish-Israelis in south Tel Aviv. But when I see a pogrom in Israel, cultivated by loud agitators such as Knesset members Danon, Ben Ari and Regev I wonder, where do they get off calling themselves Jews? Regev, Danon and Ben-Ari, together with the group who hit infiltrators on the streets of Tel Aviv do not understand what Jewish morality is, Jewish collective memory, or what Jewish existence means.[42]

Three years later, during a demonstration in front of the Israeli president's house, neighborhood activists from South Tel Aviv published an open letter to the president claiming that their plight had not been addressed. In the letter, they mentioned that their justified protests were called a "pogrom" and "Kristallnacht" while this demonstration was, in fact, according to them, a legitimate fight for their rights.[43]

EQUATING ISRAELIS AND NAZIS—BEYOND KRISTALLNACHT

Some of the writers broadened the comparisons between demonstrators and Nazis, widening the discussion to include aspects of racism in Israeli society and going beyond Kristallnacht in an effort to create associations to Nazism in general. Dr. Kritzman-Amir wrote: "'They' were attacked violently. The windows of 'their' businesses were smashed. Cars were stopped on the streets to make sure 'they' are not driving them. Racist calls were heard to deport 'them' [. . .]. 'them' is us." And she added, it resembles racist attacks "suffered by the Jews in the 1930s and 1940.[44] By claiming it reminded her of the 1930s and 1940s, she created not only an analogy with Kristallnacht, but referred to the Holocaust.

Writer Meged wrote in *Globes* that although there were criminals among the Africans there were also criminals among the Jews who arrived in West Europe from eastern Europe after the pogroms. He drew similarities between them and the Africans, claiming that both groups learned how to survive, sometimes using shady methods, and both had to deal with racism. Acknowledging the problematic aspects of the Africans in South Tel Aviv, he also referred to the demonstration as "Kristallnacht," and described the demonstrators as "Judeo-Nazis," a notoriously controversial expression coined by Yeshayahu Leibowitz. The well-known intellectual and philosopher claimed in the 1980s that Israel holding on to the occupied territories would create a Nazi-like mentality within Israel.[45] Meged latched onto this comparison between the Jews in Israel and Nazis as he stated that "one answer to the African problem" would be to let the new immigrants work "in jobs that our supreme race doesn't see fit to engage with."[46]

In a very long post, a blogger and African immigrant activist who referred to himself as "Ishiton" ("newspaper man"), decried the principle of the Holocaust's uniqueness, claiming that precisely because of their past, Jewish-Israelis must compare their attitude towards Africans to the Nazi treatment of the Jews. According to him, this comparison was necessary in order to prevent not only the demonstrators, but all of Jewish-Israeli society, from slipping down a moral slope. He claimed that the speeches of Knesset members and other elements in Israeli discourse against the Africans reproduced the tone, words, and visuals found in Nazi Germany. The blogger provided many examples, via a table comparing what he felt were the similarities between Israeli speeches and visual elements and Nazi speeches and visuals. He also divided the Nazi/Israeli narrative into themes such as epidemics, germs, lack of hygiene, crime, violence and terror; the need for an educational system "clean of Jews/Africans," phrases such as "purity of the race," terms such as "deportation" and the idea of Africans/Jews being presented as a "demographic problem." He drew comparisons between the demonstrations, and claimed that de-humanization and racism was present in the posters and narratives both in the Nazi past and Israeli present. Moreover, he showed how contemporary right wing "hate speeches" were aimed at the left wing and at human rights organizations in the same way that Hitler and the Nazi regime addressed political opponents. The post ended with a table of visuals from Kristallnacht and the Tel Aviv demonstration, highlighting the resemblance in the attacks on businesses, broken glass, and the cleaning the next day.

"ISRAELI KRISTALLNACHT" OUTSIDE ISRAEL

The Israeli term quickly turned global. Surfers posted, tweeted, and wrote about the demonstration in English and other languages (including German), using the heading "Israeli Kristallnacht" (John Nada[47]) and adding photos and harsh critiques of Israel (Norm LittleJohn, "Israeli Kristallnacht"[48]). Some examples include: "The Israeli version of Kristallnacht, last night in Tel Aviv, is obviously disturbing if not entirely surprising" (Yaniv Oren[49]); "In a sick twist of irony, Zionists relive Kristallnacht, only now they are the aggressors. Tel Aviv 23.5.2012, Israel" (Daviv Babaiy); "Israeli Kristallnacht: Africans attacked, immigrant-owned business smashed in Tel Aviv" #shame on you (Jones Zafo[50]); "The riots in Tel Aviv spurred on by Israeli politics reminded me of Kristallnacht" (Christhesaboeuor#FBPE[51]); Surfers used the hashtags #Kristallnacht and #Tel Aviv Kristallnacht in their tweets (for example: Doorn, Bombadil Brin, Sara, Tsipi[52]). These posts appeared not only in social media but also on popular news sites outside of Israel. The website *Russia Today* referred to the events as the "Israeli Kristallnacht." The US-based *Christian Science Monitor* stressed the fact that Israel once was a nation of refugees. "In an ironic twist, Israel's most tolerant city erupted in violent riots against African migrants last night, eliciting comparisons with 'pogrom' attacks on European Jewish communities in the 19th and 20th centuries."[53]

Some added the hashtag "Zionism" to their castigating "Kristallnacht" tweets (for example: Michael Lee[54]). The hashtags "apartheid" and "racist" appeared in other tweets as well (for example, Ashley Fataar).[55] It is impossible to know if these surfers were anti-Zionist or antisemitic and simply jumped on the terminology in order to spread their ideology. There were other cases in which blogs that openly declared their anti-Zionism and antisemitism used these terms as well. The antisemitic website "The Ugly Truth," which declares that it is "intelligent antisemitism for thinking Gentiles," gave a description of the demonstration accompanied by cartoons of scissors cutting the star of David as a takeoff of the well-known "Uncle Sam" poster. Instead of "Uncle Sam wants you," it said, "I'm Israel's bitch and so are you." The expression "Israeli Kristallnacht" appeared in the comments to the blog, which described the demonstration. The blog "Jews sans frontiers: The Anti-Zionist blog—browsing the media," which supports, among other things, boycotts of Israel, on May 24, 2012 featured the headline: "Kristallnacht 2.0 courtesy of start up nation." The blog called the demonstrators "pogromists" and explained:

> Yesterday, South Tel-Aviv was the scene of a Kristallnacht. A series of marches and protests against Sudanese refugees culminated in a mob storming shops associated with Africans and attacking a car with Africans in the street. Although the perpetrators are from the slums of South Tel-Aviv, as is always the case, the racism came from up high.[56]

One should add that when the demonstration was discussed on social media in Hebrew (turning it to an internal discussion for Hebrew speakers only), it was clear to the writers and the readers that the expression "Israeli Kristallnacht" did not mean that all Israelis were involved. Within Israel it was totally clear that a certain group orchestrated it and took a part in it. When this term spread internationally, the designation "Israeli" received a completely altered and much more general meaning. For example, in one blog titled "Israeli Kristallnacht" the writer claimed the demonstrators were "thousands of Israelis."[57] Another blog elaborated on the comparisons between Kristallnacht and the demonstration in Israel, and addressed it as if all of Israel took part in the demonstration, claiming "75 years ago, the world turned its face away from Jewish refugees from Germany [. . .] Today Israel thinks that refugees are 'cancer' and 'plague.'"[58] In another article, the writer explained that these riots were carried out by some on the right wing and members of the "hard-right." He immediately added however, "While a small number of people carried out the violence, they represented the views of many Israelis."[59]

The vast majority of comparisons to Kristallnacht in Israeli social media and abroad completely ignored the fact that not every hate crime is an act of Nazism and not every violent demonstration is a Kristallnacht. The fact that Kristallnacht was executed in a completely different context; that the number of destroyed private and public properties was far higher (see Wolf Gruner's chapter in this volume); that people were murdered, and tens of thousands were deported to concentration camps during and immediately following the attacks were absent from the comparisons. Instead, a combination of racism, hatred towards the "other" and the shattered glass took over.

The coining of the term in Israel was part of a much wider struggle of the left against deportation, in which they invoke Holocaust associations. The main claim is: how can the representatives of the Jewish people, who were tossed from country to country, deport other refugees? Within this struggle some Holocaust survivors also voiced their protest, claiming that after what they had gone through, they could not agree to the deportation of other people. For example, on January 23, 2018, an article appeared on the front page of

Yediot Aharonot, one of the most prominent newspapers in Israel. A photo located on the right upper part of the front page featured Holocaust survivors and Africans holding hands. The headline, in large letters, proclaimed: "Holocaust Survivors: we will hide refugees in our homes." The subtitle described how, upon hearing that several El-Al pilots said that they would refuse to fly asylum seekers back to Africa against their will,[60] Holocaust survivors joined the protest claiming, "this is our human obligation. Have we learned nothing from the Holocaust?"

SATIRICAL RESPONSES TO THE DEMONSTRATION

For many years, Israeli culture recoiled from dealing with the Holocaust from a humoristic perspective. The perception was that a comedic approach to the Holocaust might threaten the sanctity of its memory, evoke feelings of disrespect towards the subject, and insult survivors. Official agents of Holocaust memory (for example: the educational system, canonical ceremonies, museums) continue to follow this approach, but in the 1990s, a new and unsanctioned path of memory began taking shape in tandem. Texts that combine the Holocaust with humor, satire, and parody are a major aspect of this new and controversial commemorative trend.[61]

Since the 1990s, members of the left have used various aspects of Holocaust humor as a socio-political strategy meant to criticize the right wing's policies towards Holocaust commemoration and other socio-political subjects.[62] Research indicates that humor (including black humor) has important social functions: it serves as a type of social cohesion, which helps members of the political opposition feel encouraged as part of a larger group. Laughter causes reciprocal reinforcement between members of the group when the individual laughs along with the group, it signals agreement with the group's state of mind and manner of thought.[63] Humor promotes group cohesion, relieves stress, and vents frustration within the group. It boosts the group's morale and strengthens the bonds between its members, helps obtain consensus within the group, and minimizes the distance between its members. In addition, aggressive humor which mocks others emphasizes the superiority of the group using it.[64] The political and social Holocaust satire and parody used by the left-wing gives the marginalized left a sense of power, and is used to critique, vent frustration, and also to create social cohesion.

The use of satire by the left in its battle against the right-wing's attitudes towards the Africans was evident on TV and in social media even before the demonstration and continued afterwards. For example, In March 2010, the right-wing Knesset member Yaakov Katz circulated a memorandum calling for African asylum seekers who had entered Israel through Egypt to be sent to live in a "distant city" that they would build themselves through "workfare."[65] Soon after, the satirical Israeli TV show *It's a Wonderful Country* spoofed Katz's plan. The actor Tal Friedman, in a homage to the film *Inglorious Basterds* (Quentin Tarantino, USA, 2009) depicted Katz as the Nazi officer from the film, Col. Hans Landa, who hunted down Jews in occupied France. Katz/Landa is shown going from house to house, pulling out asylum-seekers and foreign workers. Several of Friedman's lines were taken directly from the film. The skit thus used the Holocaust to make its point that the historically victimized had become the victimizers. In December 2013, following the refusal of African asylum-seekers to be sent to the Holot detention facility, a formal document was published in which the illegal immigrants were not mentioned by name, but rather given numbers. Many respondents compared these numbers to those tattooed by the Nazis on the arms of Jewish prisoners in Auschwitz. A photograph uploaded to *It's a Wonderful Country*'s Facebook page purported to show former Minister of the Interior Gideon Sa'ar preparing to tattoo an anonymous refugee. The photograph caused an uproar and received mixed responses. Some viewers were utterly appalled, while others expressed support. Due to the commotion, the image was removed a day later from the program's Facebook page.

Satirical responses also appeared intensively after the May 2012 demonstration. The left-wing produced and circulated memes[66] and caricatures using satire and black humor. These memes, published in Israeli social media, highlighted the resemblance between the demonstration and Kristallnacht and presented the right-wing demonstrators and Knesset members who took part in it as Nazis.

Studies on internet memes suggest that they represent more than just a fun pastime or simple joke, and should be taken seriously, since they shape and reflect general social mindsets and may play a role in politics. Memes offer a new kind of civic participation—one in which citizens are able to express political opinions and participate in important debates. Scholars claim that memes can be used as a persuasive tactic, based on the understanding that information stemming from peers, such as friends or family, can be more persuasive than information generated by political elites.[67] "Kristallnacht in Tel-Aviv" memes were a tactic used by the left to voice their feelings about the violent demonstration alongside the serious critique.

Political Memetic Photos

Meme-based political discourse often begins with a single "memetic photo" that relates to political actors and controversies.[68] One of the most famous pictures from the demonstration was that of a woman wearing a tank-top on which was hand-written "Death to the Sudanese." She is seen standing in the foreground of the frame, talking on the phone, while in the background, other demonstrators smile and clap.[69] This photo spread like wildfire, and was immediately turned into a meme. In one instance, Amir Schiby posted on Facebook the photo, adding a speech bubble that contained the words: "You promised me tons of 'crystal' (a play on words referring both to Kristallnacht and to cocaine), but in the end I only got redbull" (an energy drink).[70] Another example was a caption to the photo in the spirit of the "My friends went to . . . and all I got was this lousy T-shirt" catchphrase, which now read "My friends went to a pogrom and all I got was this lousy T-shirt." Racheli Rottner posted on Facebook the photo of the woman speaking into the phone, and glued Hitler's picture next to her, as if she was calling him. They both seem happy with the conversation and the caption says "No, you hang up," to hint at a romantic relationship between them.[71]

Wider Comparisons to Murderous Individuals and to Racism

The parallels to Kristallnacht or to Nazism were not the only parallels that appeared. The "death to the Sudanese" meme appeared alongside other captions meant to equate the female demonstrator with other murderous and/or racist figures. In one, the notorious sadistic murderer King Joffrey from the popular TV series *Games of Thrones* appeared alongside the protester with the caption saying "did you get the T shirt I sent you?" as the woman answered "thank you, it fits just fine." In another photo, posted by Eli Levin, with the caption "I do not compare, I only show that one can compare," the woman was in the foreground, with a picture of the Ku Klux Klan superimposed on the background, waiting for her to join the group. Another surfer altered the picture with a caption reading "how can you recognize me? I am the one in the picture that every sane person will distribute, in shock, tomorrow morning."[72] Caricaturist and illustrator Mysh Rozanov published a caricature titled "Kristallnacht," in which Knesset member Regev was seen approaching a group of Ku Klux Klan members. The group turns to her, saying "Thanks for coming to complete our *minyan*, Miri'leh." These examples, which appeared alongside the specific references to Kristallnacht, show how the historical uniqueness of Kristallnacht was flattened—it became a symbol; a trope of racist hatred, like other symbols of racism, sadism, and hate.

The satiric "Israeli Kristallnacht" memes, like other, more serious responses by the left, were part of a broader struggle against the deportations which found expression in caricatures and memes before the demonstration and continued after it. For example, Roznov used the iconic photo taken by Nazis during the Warsaw ghetto revolt in April–May 1943 of the Jewish child with raised hands, surrounded by other terrified Jews, and doctored their skin color and features so they resembled Africans. The caption read, "I'm (standing) with the refugees." In another photo he split the frame into two parts, with the left featuring a picture of Anne Frank and her family, and the right showing a family of African refugees, sketched in the same pose and with similar features. Another of his caricatures, titled "A Problem of Self-Image," featured a large, muscular man covered with tattoos saying such things as "death to the Sudanese," "a good Arab is a dead Arab," "Russians, go back to Russia," "Ethiopians, return to Ethiopia," etc. The thug is looking in a mirror, but the image he sees is not his own, but the image of the same child from the Warsaw ghetto with raised hands, the yellow star of David displayed on his coat. Roznov felt that, more than seventy years after WWII, Israelis still see themselves as helpless victims who do not understand how strong and violent they have become, and that the trauma that haunts them causes them to act violently against anyone who seems to pose a threat.[73]

"A Problem of Self-image" (by Michael [Mysh] Rozanov, Israel, 2012).

CONCLUSIONS

In conclusion, Israel represents a unique sphere of traumatic awareness in which Nazism and the Holocaust have been politicized since the establishment of the State.

The "Israeli Kristallnacht" responses on social media to the Tel-Aviv demonstration against the Africans reflect the way in which the Israeli left wing politicizes the Holocaust to meet its agenda. However, as noted, it is but one example out of many, in which the right and left in Israel politicize the Holocaust for their causes. The "Israeli Kristallnacht" responses are part of a technological change that has transferred power to the individual, who thus becomes directly involved in the circulation of political content. Internet surfers stop being passive observers of the political game and take an active part in it. The circulation of Nazi associations and critical responses is increasingly driven by audiences who share, comment, critique, reframe, and remix the content. This grassroots revolution (serious and satirical narrative alike) on the one hand, increases Kristallnacht commemoration within Israeli society, but on the other hand, completely deflates it by dissociating it from the background, facts, and characteristics of the November 9–10, 1938 events. It turns Kristallnacht into a simplistic and shallow metaphor of shattered glass and violence towards the other; a symbol and a trope mixed with other signifiers of murderous racism, which ultimately deprives it of its profound historical context and meaning.

Notes

1. All social media references are to be found in the end of the article under "Bibliography/Social Media."
2. Michele Knobel and Colin Lankshear, eds., *A New Literacies Sampler* (New York: Peter Lang, 2007), 1–24; Limor Shifman, *Memes in Digital Culture* (Cambridge, MA: MIT Press, 2013), 119–50; Lara C. Stache, "Advocacy and Political Potential at the Convergence of Hashtag Activism and Commerce," *Feminist Media Studies* 15, no. 1 (2015): 162–64.
3. Alon Gan, *From Sovereignty to Victimhood: An Analysis of the Victimization Discourse in Israel* (Jerusalem: The Israel Democracy Institute, 2014), 28–35 [Hebr.]; Dina Porat, *The Smoke-Scented Coffee: The Encounter of the Yishuv and Israeli Society with the Holocaust and its Survivors* (Tel Aviv: Yad Vashem and Am Oved, 2011), 357–78 [Hebr.]; Tova Benski and Ruth Katz, "Women's Peace Activism and the Holocaust: Reversing the Hegemonic Holocaust Discourse in Israel," in *The Holocaust as Active Memory: The Past in the Present*, ed. Marie L. Seeberg, Irene Levin, and Claudia Lenz (London: Routledge, 2016), 93.
4. Oren Meyers, Motti Neiger, and Eyal Zandberg, *Communicating Awe: Media Memory and Holocaust Commemoration*, Palgrave Macmillan Memory Studies (Basingstoke: Palgrave Macmillan, 2014).
5. Ella Shohat, *Israeli Cinema: East/West and the Politics of Representation* (Ra'anana: The Open University, 2005), 68–122 [Hebr.]; Liat Steir-Livny, "The Link between the Holocaust and the Israeli-Arab Conflict in Israeli Culture, 1950s–1970s," in *Reconstructing Jewish Identity in Pre- and Post-Holocaust Literature and Culture*, ed. Lucina Aleksandrowicz-Pedich and Malgorzata Pakier (Frankfurt am Main: Peter Lang—Internationaler Verlag der Wissenschaften, 2012), 157–68.
6. Nurith Gertz, *Motion Fiction: Israeli Fiction in Films* (Tel-Aviv: The Open University Press, 1993), 175–288 [Hebr.]; Shohat, *Israeli Cinema*, 234–66.
7. Steir-Livny, Liat. *Is It O.K to Laugh about It? Holocaust Humour, Satire and Parody in Israel Culture* (London: Vallentine Mitchell Press, 2009) 114–32.
8. "Statistics Foreigners in Israel," *Population and Immigration Authority*, April 2018 [Hebr.], https://www.gov.il/BlobFolder/reports/foreign_workers_stats_0118/he/%D7%A8%D7%91%D7%A2%D7%95%D7%9F%201.pdf.
9. "Statistics Foreigners in Israel"; Levi Uriel, "Searching for a Policy," *Davar Rishon*, June 20, 2017 [Hebr.], https://www.davar1.co.il/72906/.
10. Tali Kritzman-Amir, ed., *Where Levinsky Meets Asmara: Social and Legal Aspects of Israeli Asylum Policy* (Tel Aviv: Hakibutz Hameuhad, 2015) [Hebr.].
11. Moran Azulay and Amir Alon, "Natanyahu Folded: Pauses the Application of the Infiltrators' Agreement," *YNET*, April 3, 2018 [Hebr.], https://www.ynet.co.il/articles/0,7340,L-5217730,00.html.
12. Vered Lee, "The Murder of the Child in Southern Tel-Aviv: An Evidence of the

Fraction of the Eritrean Community," *Haaretz*, November 27, 2018 [Hebr.], https://www.haaretz.co.il/blogs/veredlee/BLOG-1.6696477.

13. Amir Alon, "Expose: The Crime Statistics of the Foreigners from Africa," *YNET*, December 14, 2018 [Hebr.], https://www.ynet.co.il/articles/0,7340,L-5426603,00.html.

14. For example, Gabi Nitzan, Facebook, April 27, 2012 [Hebr.], https://www.facebook.com/search/str/%D7%9C%D7%99%D7%9C+%D7%94%D7%91%D7%93%D7%95%D7%9C%D7%97+%D7%91%D7%AA%D7%9C-%D7%90%D7%91%D7%99%D7%91/keywords_search?epa=SEARCH_BOX.

15. "Pressing Charges at the Police against Danon and Regev: Israeli Kristallnacht," *Mako*, May 24, 2012 [Hebr.], https://www.mako.co.il/news-military/politics/Article- 4d51b5743fe7731018.htm.

16. Paul Stangl, "The Vernacular and the Monumental: Memory and Landscape in Post-war Berlin," *GeoJournal* 73 (November 2008): 246.

17. Aya Yadlin-Segal, "'It Happened Before and It Will Happen Again': Online User Comments as a Noncommemorative Site of Holocaust Remembrance," *Jewish Film and New Media* 5, no. 1 (2017): 30–31.

18. Stangl, "The Vernacular and the Monumental," 246.

19. Yadlin-Segal, "'It Happened Before,'" 30–31.

20. Yarimar Bonilla and Jonathan Rosa, "#Ferguson: Digital Protest, Hashtag Ethnography, and the Racial Politics of Social Media in the United States," *American Ethnologist* 42, no. 1 (2015): 4–17.

21. W. Lance Bennett and Amoshaun Toft, "Identity, Technology, and Narratives: Transnational Activism and Social Networks," in *Routledge Handbook of Internet Politics* (London: Routledge, 2009), 246–60; Dhiraj Murthy, *Twitter: Social Communication in the Twitter Age* (Cambridge: Polity Press, 2013), 92–114.

22. Yadlin-Segal, "'It Happened Before,'" 24–47.

23. Roi Kais, "Anti-migrant Rally Stirs Global Media Storm," *YNET* News, *World News*, May 26, 2012, https://www.ynetnews.com/articles/0,7340,L-4234354,00.html.

24. Aviv Maimon, Twitter, May 25, 2012.

25. Gil, Twitter, June 24, 2012.

26. Martin Kiel, Twitter, May 24, 2012. On the importance of hashtags which create a filing system from which information can be drawn and spotlight additional meanings that are to be found in the user generated content see Bonilla and Rosa, "#Ferguson," 4–17; Stache, "Advocacy," 162–64.

27. Rotem Ilan, "A Night Without Any Hope," *Saloona*, May 24, 2012 [Hebr.], http://saloona.co.il/blog/%D7%9C%D7%99%D7%9C%D7%94-%D7%91%D7%9C%D7%99-%D7%AA%D7%A7%D7%95%D7%95%D7%94/.

28. Itamar Hendelman Smith, "Kristhallnacht 2012 Version: Look at Us and Remember Them," *Haaretz*, May 30, 2012 [Hebr.], https://www.haaretz.co.il/gallery/nightlife/1.3277352.

29. *Haaretz* Editorial, "Kaniuk's Legacy," *Haaretz*, January 10, 2013, https://www.haaretz.com/opinion/editorial-author-yoram-kaniuk-s-legacy-1.5276669.
30. "Pressing charges."
31. Vika Keires, "Incidents in Shapira Neighborhood: The Web against Miri Regev," *YNET*, May 24, 2012 [Hebr.], https://www.ynet.co.il/articles/0,7340,L-4233811,00.html.
32. Maafiyahu, May 24, 2012 [Hebr.], https://mafyahu.wordpress.com/2012/05/24/%D7%94%D7%90%D7%9C%D7%99%D7%9E%D7%95%D7%AA-%D7%A0%D7%92%D7%93-%D7%94%D7%9E%D7%A1%D7%A A%D7%A0%D7%A0%D7%99%D7%9D-%D7%91%D7%93%D7%A8%-D7%95%D7%9D-%D7%AA%D7%9C-%D7%90%D7%91%D7%99%D7%91-%D7%95%D7%9E%D7%94/.
33. Saul Rozenfeld, "This Is Not Kristallnacht," *YNET*, May 28, 2012 [Hebr.], https://www.ynet.co.il/articles/0,7340,L-4234751,00.html.
34. Gil, Twitter, June 24, 2012.
35. Laila Odinayev, "Laugh or Cry? The Demonstrator Against the Infiltrators Flirts with Hitler," *Mako*, May 24, 2012 [Hebr.], https://www.mako.co.il/nexter-internet/Article-3a9ed9f076e7731006.htm.
36. See chapter by Ulrich Baumann and François Guesnet in this volume.
37. Igaal Shtaim, Facebook, May 24, 2012.
38. Tali Kritzman-Amir, "'Them' are 'Us,'" *Haoketz*, May 25, 2012 [Hebr.], http://www.haokets.org/2012/05/24/%D7%94%D7%9D-%D7%96%D7%94-%D7%90%D7%A0%D7%97%D7%A0%D7%95/.
39. Ouriel Daskal, Twitter, May 23, 2012.
40. Eyal Meged, "A Wild and Inflamed Herd," *Globes*, May 30, 2012 [Hebr.], https://www.globes.co.il/news/article.aspx?did=1000752751.
41. "Pressing Charges."
42. Yair Lapid, Facebook, May 24, 2012 [Hebr.], https://www.facebook.com/YairLapid/posts/373971535994537.
43. "An Open Letter to President Rivlin: The Inhabitants of South Tel Aviv Await You," *South-tlv*, June 22, 2015 [Hebr.], http://www.south-tlv.co.il/article15596.
44. Kritzman-Amir, "'Them' are 'Us.'"
45. "Prof. Leibowitz: There Are Judeo-Nazis. Israel Represents the Darkness of a State Body," YouTube, January 8, 2014 [Hebr.], https://www.youtube.com/watch?v=zM2fXTkjU2E.
46. Meged, "A Wild and Inflamed Herd."
47. John Nada, Twitter, May 23, 2012.
48. Norm LittleJohn, Twitter, June 18, 2012.
49. Yaniv Oren, Twitter, May 24, 2012.
50. Jones Zafo, Twitter, May 24, 2012.
51. Christhesaboeuor#FBPE, Twitter, May 29, 2012.

52. Doorn, Twitter, May 23, 2012; Bombadil Brin, Twitter, May 30, 2012; Sara, Twitter, May 24, 2012; Tsipi, Twitter, May 23, 2012.
53. Kais, "Anti-migrant Rally."
54. Michael Lee, Twitter, May 23, 2012.
55. Ashley Fataar, Twitter, May 25, 2012.
56. Jews sans frontieres: The Anti-Zionist blog of Mark Elf—browsing the media, http://jewssansfrontieres.blogspot.com/2012/05/kristallnacht-20-courtesy-of-start-up.html.
57. Alex de Large, The PHORA, http://www.thephora.net/forum/showthread.php?t=81765.
58. 2ndlook, May 24, 2012, https://2ndlook.wordpress.com/2012/05/24/israels-refugee-problem/.
59. Joshua Holland, "Why the U.S. Media Barely Covered Brutal Right-Wing Race Riots in Tel Aviv," *ALTERNET*, June 17, 2012, https://www.alternet.org/story/155866/why_the_u.s._media_barely_covered_brutal_right-wing_race_riots_in_tel_aviv.
60. Itay Blumental and Alon Amir, "Pilots in El-Al: We Won't Fly Asylum Seekers to a Third Country," *YNET*, January 22, 2018 [Hebr.], https://www.ynet.co.il/articles/0,7340,L-5074564,00.html.
61. Eyal Zandberg, "Critical Laughter: Humor, Popular Culture and Israeli Holocaust Commemoration," *Media, Culture & Society* 28, no. 4 (2006): 561–79; idem, "'Ketchup Is the Auschwitz of Tomatoes': Humor and the Collective Memory of Traumatic Events," *Communication, Culture & Critique* (2014): 1–16; Steir-Livny, *Is It Ok?*
62. Steir-Livny, *Is It Ok?* 114–32.
63. Arie Sover, *The Pathway to Human Laughter* (Jerusalem: Carmel, 2009), 23–25, 55–57 [Hebr.].
64. Avner Ziv, *Personality and Sense of Humor* (Tel Aviv: Papyrus, 1996) [Hebr.].
65. Arik Bender, "Ketzale's Solution for Asylum Seekers: A Work Camp," *NRG*, March 23, 2010 [Hebr.], https://www.makorrishon.co.il/nrg/online/1/ART2/085/436.html.
66. I use Limor Shifman's definition of meme: Meme: a) a group of digital items sharing common characteristics of content, form, and/or stance, which b) were created with awareness of each other, and c) were circulated, imitated, and/or transformed via the Internet by many users." See Shifman, *Memes*, 41.
67. Knobel and Lankshear, *A New Literacies Sampler*, 1–24; Limor Shifman, "An Anatomy of a YouTube Meme," *New Media and Society* 14, no. 2 (2012): 187–203.
68. Shifman, *Memes*, 138–40.
69. This photo was taken by third generation Holocaust survivor photographer Tomer Neuberg, who put in an album of pictures from the demonstration he titled "Breakdown." See Sarit Parkol, "Tomer Neuberg Who Took the 'Death to the Sudanees Picture': I Didn't Know It Will Influence," *Megaphone*, May 25, 2012 [Hebr.], http://megafon-news.co.il/asys/archives/51189.

70. Amir Schiby, Facebook [Hebr.], https://www.facebook.com/photo.php?fbid=10150837063524372&set=a.10150471870259372&type=1&theater.
71. Racheli Rottner, Facebook, May 24, 2012, https://www.facebook.com/photo.php?fbid=10150896715044140&set=a.117523159139&type=1&theater.
72. Keires, "Incidents."
73. "Meet Mish Roznov," *All Lies*, no date [Hebr.], https://www.alllies.org/blog/archives/19190#.XM6wWo4zY2w.

Bibliography

Social Media

2ndlook. May 24, 2012. https://2ndlook.wordpress.com/2012/05/24/israels-refugee-problem/.

Alex de Large. The PHORA. http://www.thephora.net/forum/showthread.php?t=81765.

Amir Schiby. Facebook [Hebrew]. https://www.facebook.com/photo.php?fbid=10150837063524372&set=a.10150471870259372&type=1&theater.

Ashley Fataar. Twitter, May 25, 2012.

Aviv Maimon. Twitter, May 25, 2012.

BlackLabor. Facebook, April 27, 2012 [Hebrew]. https://www.facebook.com/pg/j14live/photos/?tab=album&album_id=432794593415131&tn=-UC-R.

Bombadil Brin. Twitter, May 30, 2012.

Christhesaboeuor#FBPE. Twitter, May 29, 2012.

David Babiy. Twitter, May 24, 2012.

Doorn. Twitter, May 23, 2012.

Gabi Nitzan. Facebook, April 27, 2012 [Hebrew]. https://www.facebook.com/search/str/%D7%9C%D7%99%D7%9C+%D7%94%D7%91%D7%93%D7%95%D7%9C%D7%97+%D7%91%D7%AA%D7%9C-%D7%90%D7%91%D7%99%D7%91/keywords_search?epa=SEARCH_BOX.

Gil. Twitter, June 24, 2012.

Hamutal Ronen. Twitter, May 24, 2012.

Igaal Shtaim. Facebook, May 24, 2012.

"Israeli Kristallnacht: Africans Attacked in Tel Aviv Anti-migrant Demo (PHOTOS)." RT Question More, May 24, 2012. https://www.rt.com/news/israel-anti-migrant-demo-061/.

Jews sans frontieres: The Anti-Zionist blog of Mark El–browsing the media. http://jews-sansfrontieres.blogspot.com/2012/05/kristallnacht-20-courtesy-of-start-up.html.

John Nada. Twitter, May 23, 2012.

Jones Zafo. Twitter, May 24, 2012.

Maafiyahu. May 24, 2012 [Hebrew]. https://mafyahu.wordpress.com/2012/05/24/%D7%94%D7%90%D7%9C%D7%99%D7%9E%D7%95%D7%AA-%D7%A0%D7%92%D7%93-%D7%94%D7%9E%D7%A1%D7%AA%D7%A0%D7%A0%D7%99%D7%9D-%D7%91%D7%93%D7%A8%D7%95%D7%9D-%D7%AA%D7%9C-%D7%90%D7%91%D7%99%D7%91-%D7%95%D7%9E%D7%94/.

Martin Kiel. Twitter, May 24, 2012.

Michael Lee. Twitter, May 23, 2012.

Norm LittleJohn. Twitter, June 18, 2012.

Ouriel Daskal. Twitter, May 23, 2012.

Racheli Rottner. Facebook, May 24, 2012. https://www.facebook.com/photo.php?fbid=10150896715044140&set=a.117523159139&type=1&theater.
Sara. Twitter, May 24, 2012.
Tsipi. Twitter, May 23, 2012.
"Violent Tel Aviv Demo against African Migrants." *The Ugly Truth*. https://theuglytruth.wordpress.com/2012/05/24/violent-tel-aviv-demo-against-african-migrants/. Site suspended.
Yair Lapid. Facebook, May 24, 2012 [Hebrew]. https://www.facebook.com/YairLapid/posts/373971535994537.
Yaniv Oren. Twitter, May 24, 2012.
Yoav Gross. Twitter, May 24, 2012.

Media

Alon, Amir. "Expose: The Crime Statistics of the Foreigners from Africa." *YNET*, December 14, 2018 [Hebrew]. https://www.ynet.co.il/articles/0,7340,L-5426603,00.html.
"An Open Letter to President Rivlin: The Inhabitants of South Tel Aviv Await You." *South-tlv*, June 22, 2015 [Hebrew]. http://www.south-tlv.co.il/article15596.
Azulay, Moran, and Alon, Amir. "Natanyahu Folded: Pauses the Application of the Infiltrators' Agreement," *YNET*, April 3, 2018 [Hebrew]. https://www.ynet.co.il/articles/0,7340,L-5217730,00.html.
Bender, Arik. "Ketzale's Solution for Asylum Seekers: A Work Camp." *NRG*, March 23, 2010 [Hebrew]. https://www.makorrishon.co.il/nrg/online/1/ART2/085/436.html.
Blumental, Itay, and Alon Amir. "Pilots in El-Al: We Won't Fly Asylum Seekers to a Third Country." *YNET*, January 22, 2018 [Hebrew]. https://www.ynet.co.il/articles/0,7340,L-5074564,00.html.
Haaretz Editorial. "Kaniuk's Legacy." *Haaretz*, January 10, 2013. https://www.haaretz.com/opinion/editorial-author-yoram-kaniuk-s-legacy-1.5276669.
Hendelman Smith, Itamar. "Kristhallnacht 2012 Version: Look at Us and Remember Them." *Haaretz*, May 30, 2012 [Hebrew]. https://www.haaretz.co.il/gallery/night-life/1.3277352.
Holland, Joshua. "Why the U.S. Media Barely Covered Brutal Right-Wing Race Riots in Tel Aviv." *ALTERNET*, June 17, 2012. https://www.alternet.org/story/155866/why_the_u.s._media_barely_covered_brutal_right-wing_race_riots_in_tel_aviv.
Ilan, Rotem. "A Night Without Any Hope." *Saloona*, May 24, 2012 [Hebrew]. http://saloona.co.il/blog/%D7%9C%D7%99%D7%9C%D7%94-%D7%91%D7%9C%D7%99-%D7%AA%D7%A7%D7%95%D7%95%D7%94/.
"It Is Forbidden Not to Compare." *Eishton*, May 31, 2012 [Hebrew]. https://eishton.wordpress.com/tag/%D7%9C%D7%99%D7%9C-%D7%94%D7%91%D7%93%D7%95%D7%9C%D7%97.
Kais, Roi. "Anti-migrant Rally Stirs Global Media Storm." *YNET* News, *World News*,

May 26, 2012. https://www.ynetnews.com/articles/0,7340,L-4234354,00.html.

Keires, Vika. "Incidents in Shapira Neighborhood: The Web against Miri Regev." *YNET*, May 24, 2012 [Hebrew]. https://www.ynet.co.il/articles/0,7340,L-4233811,00.html.

Kritzman-Amir, Tali. "'Them' are 'Us.'" *Haoketz*, May 25, 2012 [Hebrew]. http://www.haokets.org/2012/05/24/%D7%94%D7%9D-%D7%96%D7%94-%D7%90%D7%A0%D7%97%D7%A0%D7%95/.

Lee, Vered. "The Murder of the Child in Southern Tel-Aviv: An Evidence of the Fraction of the Eritrean Community." *Haaretz*, November 27, 2018 [Hebrew]. https://www.haaretz.co.il/blogs/veredlee/BLOG-1.6696477.

"Meet Mish Roznov." *All Lies*, no date [Hebrew]. https://www.alllies.org/blog/archives/19190#.XM6wWo4zY2w.

Meged, Eyal. "A Wild and Inflamed Herd." *Globes*, May 30, 2012 [Hebrew]. https://www.globes.co.il/news/article.aspx?did=1000752751.

"The Neighborhoods' rage." YouTube, May 23, 2012. https://www.youtube.com/watch?v=9KiahzVgSCE&t=225s.

Odinayev, Laila. "Laugh or Cry? The Demonstrator Against the Infiltrators Flirts with Hitler." *Mako*, May 24, 2012 [Hebrew]. https://www.mako.co.il/nexter-internet/Article-3a9ed9f076e7731006.htm.

Parkol, Sarit. "Tomer Neuberg Who Took the 'Death to the Sudanees Picture': I Didn't Know It Will Influence." *Megaphone*, May 25, 2012 [Hebrew]. http://megafon- news.co.il/asys/archives/51189.

"Pressing Charges at the Police against Danon and Regev: Israeli Kristallnacht." *Mako*, May 24, 2012 [Hebrew]. https://www.mako.co.il/news-military/politics/Article-4d51b5743fe7731018.htm.

"Prof. Leibowitz: There Are Judeo-Nazis. Israel Represents the Darkness of a State Body." YouTube, January 8, 2014 [Hebrew]. https://www.youtube.com/watch?v=zM2fXTkjU2E.

Rozenfeld, Saul. "This Is Not Kristallnacht." *YNET*, May 28, 2012 [Hebrew]. https://www.ynet.co.il/articles/0,7340,L-4234751,00.html.

"Statistics Foreigners in Israel." *Population and Immigration Authority*, April 2018 [Hebrew]. https://www.gov.il/BlobFolder/reports/foreign_workers_stats_0118/he/%D7%A8%D 7%91%D7%A2%D7%95%D7%9F%201.pdf.

"Tel Avivi Kristallnacht." YouTube, June 4, 2012 [Hebrew].

Uriel, Levi. "Searching for a Policy." *Davar Rishon*, June 20, 2017 [Hebrew]. https://www.davar1.co.il/72906/.

Secondary Sources

Bar-Tal, Danial. *Living with Conflict.* Jerusalem: Carmel, 2007 [Hebrew].

Baumann, Ulrich, and François Guesnet. "Kristallnacht—Pogrom—State Terror: A Terminological Reflection." In *New Perspectives on Kristallnacht: After 80 Years, the Nazi Program in Global Comparison,* edited by Wolf Gruner. *Casden Annual* 17 (2019), 1–24.

Bennett, W. Lance, and Amoshaun Toft. "Identity, Technology, and Narratives: Transnational Activism and Social Networks." In *Routledge Handbook of Internet Politics,* 246–60. London: Routledge, 2009.

Benski, Tova and Ruth Katz. "Women's Peace Activism and the Holocaust: Reversing the Hegemonic Holocaust Discourse in Israel." In *The Holocaust as Active Memory: The Past in the Present,* edited by Marie L. Seeberg, Irene Levin, and Claudia Lenz, 93–112. London: Routledge, 2016.

Bonilla, Yarimar, and Jonathan Rosa. "#Ferguson: Digital Protest, Hashtag Ethnography, and the Racial Politics of Social Media in the United States." *American Ethnologist* 42, no. 1 (2015): 4–17.

Gan, Alon. *From Sovereignty to Victimhood: An Analysis of the Victimization Discourse in Israel.* Jerusalem: The Israel Democracy Institute, 2014 [Hebrew].

Gertz, Nurith. *Motion Fiction: Israeli Fiction in Films.* Tel-Aviv: The Open University Press, 1993 [Hebrew].

Gruner, Wolf. "'Worse Than Vandals.' The Mass Destruction of Jewish Homes and Jewish Responses during the 1938 Pogrom." In *New Perspectives on Kristallnacht: After 80 Years, the Nazi Program in Global Comparison,* edited by Wolf Gruner. *Casden Annual* 17 (2019), 25–50.

Knobel, Michele, and Colin Lankshear, eds. *A New Literacies Sampler.* New York: Peter Lang, 2007.

Kritzman-Amir, Tali, ed. *Where Levinsky Meets Asmara: Social and Legal Aspects of Israeli Asylum Policy.* Tel Aviv: Hakibutz Hameuhad, 2015 [Hebrew].

Meyers, Oren, Motti Neiger, and Eyal Zandberg. *Communicating Awe: Media Memory and Holocaust Commemoration.* Palgrave Macmillan Memory Studies. Basingstoke: Palgrave Macmillan, 2014.

Murthy, Dhiraj. *Twitter: Social Communication in the Twitter Age.* Cambridge: Polity Press, 2013.

Porat, Dina. *The Smoke-Scented Coffee: The Encounter of the Yishuv and Israeli Society with the Holocaust and Its Survivors.* Tel Aviv: Yad Vashem and Am Oved, 2011 [Hebrew].

Schmidt, Jan-Hinrik. "Twitter and the Rise of Personal Publics." In *Twitter and Society,* edited by Katrin Weller, Axel Bruns, Jean Burgess, Merja Mahrt and Cornelius Puschmann, 3–14. New York: Peter Lang, 2014.

Shifman, Limor. "An Anatomy of a YouTube Meme." *New Media and Society* 14, no. 2 (2012): 187–203.

Shifman, Limor. *Memes in Digital Culture*. Cambridge, MA: MIT Press, 2013.

Shohat, Ella. *Israeli Cinema: East/West and the Politics of Representation*. Ra'anana: The Open University, 2007 [Hebrew].

Sover, Arie. *The Pathway to Human Laughter*. Jerusalem: Carmel, 2009 [Hebrew].

Stache, Lara C. "Advocacy and Political Potential at the Convergence of Hashtag Activism and Commerce." *Feminist Media Studies* 15, no. 1 (2015): 162–164.

Stangl, Paul, "The Vernacular and the Monumental: Memory and Landscape in Postwar Berlin." *GeoJournal* 73 (November 2008): 245–53.

Steir-Livny, Liat. *Is It O.K to Laugh about It? Holocaust Humour, Satire and Parody in Israel Culture*. London: Vallentine Mitchell Press, 2009.

———. "The Link between the Holocaust and the Israeli-Arab Conflict in Israeli Culture, 1950s–1970s." In *Reconstructing Jewish Identity in Pre- and Post-Holocaust Literature and Culture*, edited by Lucina Aleksandrowicz-Pedich and Malgorzata Pakier, 157–68. Frankfurt am Main: Peter Lang—Internationaler Verlag der Wissenschaften, 2012.

Yadlin-Segal, Aya. "'It Happened Before and It Will Happen Again': Online User Comments as a Noncommemorative Site of Holocaust Remembrance." *Jewish Film and New Media* 5, no. 1 (2017): 24–47.

Zandberg, Eyal. "Critical Laughter: Humor, Popular Culture and Israeli Holocaust Commemoration." *Media, Culture & Society* 28, no. 4 (2006): 561–79.

———. "'Ketchup Is the Auschwitz of Tomatoes': Humor and the Collective Memory of Traumatic Events." *Communication, Culture & Critique* (2014): 1–16.

Ziv, Avner. *Personality and Sense of Humor*. Tel Aviv: Papyrus, 1996 [Hebrew].

CHAPTER 14

The Kristallnacht Paradigm in Narratives by Survivors of the Rwandan and Rohingya Genocides

by Nathalie Ségeral

Dori Laub, in his seminal essay dealing with what he calls "the imperative to tell" in *Trauma: Explorations in Memory*,[1] writes that: "The survivors did not only need to survive so that they could tell their stories; they also needed to tell their stories in order to survive."[2] Words and telling are central to the literary production of Rwandan genocide survivor Scholastique Mukasonga, insofar as she uses her written testimonies and autobiographical texts as symbolic shrouds for her parents, brothers, and sisters whose bodies she was never able to recover. Therefore, the words she chooses to use when referring to what happened to the Tutsis from 1959 to 1994 and the long lineage of racialization of identity are always the result of a careful thought process, placing added emphasis on the Holocaust paradigm as her preferred rhetorical choice.[3] The same goes for Habiburahman, a survivor of the persecution of the Burmese Rohingyas and currently a refugee in Australia, who recently published the first testimony of the on-going genocide, co-authored with French journalist Sophie Ansel and titled *D'abord ils ont effacé notre nom: Un Rohingya parle* (First They Erased Our Names: A Rohingya Speaks).[4] References to the Holocaust and, more precisely, to Kristallnacht, abound throughout the narrative, serving as a paradigm with a dual function: to render visible an invisible minority history and to express events for which a specific vocabulary does not yet exist.

According to several French and English dictionaries, "pogrom" is a Russian word meaning "to wreak havoc, to destroy violently" and was first used to designate an organized attack by one ethnic group against another. The first use of the word "pogrom" seems to have occurred in 1821 in Odessa, to label an anti-Jewish riot.[5] The word is, thus, highly connoted as pertaining to Jewish history.[6] From this perspective, it is significant that both Mukasonga and Habiburahman use the actual term "pogrom," when referring to the waves of massacres perpetrated by the Hutu against the Tutsi from the late 1950s to the culmination of violence during the 1994 genocide and to the persecution of the Burmese Rohingyas. Between April and July 1994, about 800,000 Rwandan Tutis, an ethnic minority, were killed by the Hutus; the genocide was the climax of ethnical violence and recurring massacres that had started in 1959, in the wake of the "social revolution" that led to the independence of Rwanda from Belgium, to the creation of the First Republic, and to the massive departure of Tutsis to Burundi, as they started to feel threatened without the protection of the Belgian colonizers. On the other hand, several contemporary French Jewish writers, such as Hélène Cixous and Cécile Wajsbrot, do not use the term "pogrom" at all and, instead, choose to refer to Kristallnacht and subsequent pogroms with periphrases and metaphors.[7] Therefore, this paper will highlight the ways in which the Kristallnacht paradigm remains extremely relevant to the transnational inscription of "minority" genocides into global history, as the ultimate warning sign and tipping point of genocidal violence, while having become paradoxically erased in contemporary Jewish writers' narratives, as though concealed by what followed and too anchored in Jewish history.

Scholastique Mukasonga was born in 1956 in Rwanda. When she was three years old, her family was deported, or "displaced" as the official discourse had it, to Nyamata, a polluted Tutsi refugee-cum-concentration camp in Rwanda's no-man's land, in which living conditions were extremely harsh. However, thanks to her parents' emphasis on education as a means to a better life, Scholastique was able to enter a prestigious catholic high school in Butare despite the drastic quotas imposed on Tutsis by the Hutu majority. She was then admitted to a social worker training school, which she eventually had to leave in 1973 when she fled Rwanda with her older brother to find refuge in Burundi. She settled in France in 1992, only two years before the genocide in which thirty-seven of her relatives were killed.

In 2018, the United Nations General Assembly released a statement designating April 7 as the "International Day of Reflection on the 1994 Genocide against the Tutsi in Rwanda." Let us briefly review the chronology of the genocide as it affected Mukasonga's family. On April 6, 1994, Hutu President Habyarimana's plane was shot down. On April 7, a curfew was issued in Nyamata, where Mukasonga's family lived, as well as in the rest of Rwanda, marking the beginning of the genocide. On April 11, the Kayumba assault (Kayumba being the forest where most Nyamata Tutsis had gone into hiding) was perpetrated. The families of surviving Tutsis sought shelter inside the Nyamata church, as missionaries had promised they would find protection in the church. Nevertheless, on April 14, they were all murdered inside the church. The number of casualties was estimated to be between five and six thousand. The day before the massacre, army men from the UNAMIR (the United Nations Assistance Mission for Rwanda) force had come to evacuate the white nuns and missionaries. Out of the sixty thousand Tutsis recorded in a January 1994 census in Nyamata, only 5,348 survivors remain.[8]

Mukasonga's autobiographical and fictional texts aim at giving a voice to those who, like her, have survived the historical violence that intended to silence them, and to the million whose voices were erased forever—especially the Tutsi women, who were specifically targeted and usually killed first. A similar concern serves as the basis for Habiburahman's story, made even more poignant as the genocide is on-going in a global context of general indifference. Habiburahman (who prefers not to use his last name, for fear of reprisal toward his relatives who have all remained in Myanmar/Burma) was born in 1979. His story is a succession of persecution, violence, torture, and struggle for survival, from his early childhood to his escape from Myanmar under the most extreme circumstances in 1994 to his arrival in Darwin, Australia, in 2013, via Laos, Thailand, Cambodia, Malaysia, and the Christmas islands, undergoing human trafficking and severe discrimination along the way.[9]

Building on Michael Rothberg's concept of multidirectional memory[10] and on Judith Butler's notion of the scale of "grievability,"[11] I will show the various parallels that Mukasonga and Habiburahman drew between the Rwandan genocide of the Tutsis, the Burmese mass violence against the Rohingyas, and the Nazi genocide of the Jews, creating bridges between different historical catastrophes in order to re-appropriate their own histories. I will highlight the Kristallnacht metaphor as enabling the inscription of "minority" genocides within a global context. Through literature, both Mukasonga and Habiburahman are able to sublimate the oppressors' rhetoric of violence into a rhetoric of survival, as their narratives become performative: they bear witness to traumatic events and grant visibility to minority suffering and stories that are usually invisible on the global map of power and history. For Mukasonga, words pertaining to the Nazi genocide of the European Jews become the means to re-embodying and re-appropriating her body—since the female body was specifically targeted by Hutus for its reproductive capabilities. Thus, Mukasonga's writing, which is almost entirely centered on issues of motherhood and on the female body, can be read as a writing of the body, allowing for a cathartic move beyond victimhood through the body, to counter the perpetrators' dehumanizing rhetoric. For Habiburahman, the Kristallnacht rhetoric, coupled with that of the Holocaust in general and of the Apartheid, serves as the cultural translation of an on-going historical catastrophe that does not yet have its own narrative.

PRESENTATION OF THE PRIMARY SOURCES

Inyenzi ou les cafards (The Cockroaches), published in 2006, is Mukasonga's first book. It is a testimony of the violence, discrimination, and gradual dehumanization of the Tutsi that led to the 1994 genocide. One of the specificities of *Inyenzi* is that the narrative emphasizes the long-standing genocidal attempts against the Tutsi. Mukasonga is intent on showing the world and her readers that the Hutus had been trying to exterminate the Tutsis for many decades and that the 1994 genocide was only the culmination of the on-going dehumanizing rhetoric and politics of discrimination. For her, the "inner exile" ("exil intérieur")[12] that she experienced as a child, even before her country became independent, was the first step in the genocide that revealed itself to the world in 1994. She describes a usual scene of her early childhood in terms highly reminiscent of the Hitler Youths during the first years of the Third Reich:

> Chaque jour, vers le milieu de la matinée, les jeunesses du parti unique défilaient au pas de course, le gourdin ou la massue sur l'épaule. Ils chantaient à tue-tête et leurs chansons semblaient nous être adressées: elles faisaient l'éloge de Kayibanda, l'émancipateur des Hutu; elles célébraient le peuple à jamais majoritaire, les seuls Rwandais, les authentiques, les autochtones: les Hutu.

(Every day, towards mid-morning, the youth from the sole party would march at fast pace, carrying clubs or cudgels on their shoulders. They would sing very loud and their songs seemed directed to us: they praised Kayibanda, the Hutu's emancipator; they celebrated the forever majority people, the only Rwandans, the authentic ones, the natives: the Hutu).[13]

In *La femme aux pieds nus* (The Bare-Footed Woman) (2008), Mukasonga pays tribute to her mother Stefania, whose body she was not able to cover with a shroud, as a dutiful daughter is supposed to do in the Rwandan tradition, otherwise she would be plagued with misfortune for the rest of her life. While *Inyenzi* highlights the dehumanizing words used by Hutu propaganda to discriminate against Tutsis, *La femme aux pieds nus* shifts toward the colonizers' roles in validating violence and discrimination.

The third text included here is a novel, *Notre-Dame du Nil* (Our Lady of the Nile), published in 2012. It is Mukasonga's first fictional narrative. It takes place in an elitist girls' high school, very similar to the one attended by the author in Butare, where young women are supposed to be sheltered from the temptations and dangers of the outside world. However, the microcosm of the boarding school, with its Hutu majority resulting from the ethnical apartheid system, reproduces and exacerbates the discrimination of 1970s Rwandan society, culminating in ethnic violence that foreshadows the genocide and echoes a central episode in Mukasonga's own life story, when she was chased by Hutu classmates armed with machetes.[14]

Habiburahman's *First They Erased Our Names* is a chronological first-person narrative chronicling the narrator's childhood and early adulthood in the face of escalating violence, round-ups, and massacres perpetuated by the Myanmar military dictatorship in their endeavor to "buddhify" the country ("Un désir de 'bouddhiser' le pays").[15] Before the September 18, 1988 coup, the Muslim Rohingya minority was already the target of severe discrimination and episodic massacres, even though the genocide had not been officially incorporated into the nation's political program. Despite the Rohingyas having been the target of ethnic violence for several decades, it was only in August 2018, following the mass exodus of 700,000 Rohingya people, that the United Nations' Fact-Finding Commission officially called the situation in Myanmar a genocide.[16] The report of the Independent International Fact-Finding Mission on Myanmar identified "murder, rape, torture, sexual slavery, persecution, and enslavement" among the crimes committed there. A former UN Special Representative for Children and Armed Conflicts reported that "the scale, brutality, and systematic nature of rape and violence indicate that they are part of a deliberate strategy to intimidate, terrorize, or punish the civilian population. They're used as a tactic of war that we found include rape, gang rape, sexual slavery, forced nudity and mutilations."[17] And yet, sexual violence was only very briefly alluded to by Habiburahman, at the beginning of his story, as his narrative is intent on showing that what was happening in Myanmar was not war but genocide.

TRANSLATING THE RHETORIC OF DEHUMANIZATION THROUGH THE HOLOCAUST PARADIGM IN MUKASONGA'S WRITINGS

Throughout her narratives, Mukasonga recurrently highlights the ethnic apartheid system that had been in place in Rwanda long before the actual genocide, drawing many parallels with the gradual segregation and exclusion from public life suffered by the European Jews in the years leading up to the Holocaust. For instance, when discussing the competitive examination required for entering high school, she writes that "il y avait encore moins de places pour les Tutsi puisque, selon les quotas ethniques mis en place par le régime hutu, ceux-ci n'avaient droit qu'à 10% dans la liste des admis" (There were even fewer spots for the Tutsis since, following the ethnical quotas implemented by the Hutu regime, only 10% of the selected students were allowed to be Tutsi).[18] Mukasonga describes how, in the wake of the 1959 and 1960 massacres, most Tutsis felt their lives were on hold, expecting the worst to hit at any time. In *Inyenzi*, she emphasizes the dehumanizing words instrumentalized by the Hutus, whereby *inyenzi*, the Kinyarwanda word for "cockroaches," was used to designate the Tutsi, much like the European Jews were dehumanized as "rats" or "pests."[19] The same rhetoric can be found in Habiburahman's narrative, where the Muslim Rohingyas are referred to as animals or "evil ogres."[20] Further parallels are drawn with the fate of European Jews, with remarks such as: "Chaque élève était muni d'une fiche signalétique sur laquelle était indiquée la prétendue ethnie, une marque au fer rouge" (Every single student had to carry an identity card on which their so-called ethnicity was mentioned, branded like a scarlet letter).[21]

While, in *Inyenzi*, Mukasonga emphasizes exclusively the propaganda carried out by the Hutu against the Tutsi, in *La femme aux pieds nus* (The

Bare-footed Woman), written as a tribute to her mother, and in her two subsequent novels (*Coeur tambour* and *Notre-Dame du Nil*), she also highlights the ways in which the colonizers' narratives were instrumental in foreshadowing the genocide, and hints at some of the dehumanizing effects of white people's words, with the accounts of the origin of the violence against the Tutsi varying among the different master discourses presented in her texts. Throughout her narratives, Mukasonga repeatedly points out that most white people living in pre-genocide Rwanda, including the teachers in the lycée Notre-Dame-de-Cîteaux which she attended, did not object to the apartheid system implemented by the Hutu Power majority. "Les professeurs paraissaient adhérer pleinement au système en place. La plupart étaient des Belges (. . .). Il fallait en tout cas se méfier des professeurs" (Teachers seemed to fully adhere to the system. Most of them were Belgians. One always had to beware of teachers).[22]

Furthermore, it is worth noting that in her novel Mukasonga denounces the irony of some of the colonizers' contradictory discourses, likening the Tutsi to both black Jews and to "Aryans,"[23] thereby setting them apart from the Rwandan population and contributing to their discrimination. While her autobiographical narratives tend to focus on the violence perpetrated by the Hutus, *Notre-Dame du Nil* denounces white settlers' ambivalent rhetoric and behavior, putting Tutsis on a pedestal and choosing myth over truth, thereby objectifying and dehumanizing the Tutsis. Père Herménégilde, the chaplain at the girls' boarding school, embodies the ambivalence of the narratives imposed by white people on the Tutsi, through long lectures to the female students about the similarities between the Tutsi and the Jews as chosen people, distorted through the lens of his own anti-Semitism, and accusing the Tutsis of entertaining the secret plot of conquering the world.[24]

While this parallel between the Jews and the Tutsis is pervasive in all of Mukasonga's texts, it is particularly central to *Inyenzi*, in which she relies heavily on Holocaust vocabulary to describe the Hutu genocide against the Tutsi. In *Inyenzi*, the genocide and the events leading to it are exclusively described through the lens of the semantic field of the Holocaust, with words such as "ghetto, ration, pogroms, réfugiés, déplacés, camp, déporté, épuration ethnique, solution finale . . ." (ghetto, ration, pogroms, refugees, displaced persons, camps, deportation, ethnical cleansing, final solution . . .). The following sentence is particularly striking, as she resorts to a specific Kristallnacht imagery: "Les premiers pogromes contre les Tutsi éclatèrent à la Toussaint 1959. L'engrenage du génocide s'était mis en marche. Il ne s'arrêterait plus. Jusqu'à la solution finale, il ne s'arrêterait plus" (The first pogroms against the

Tutsi occurred on November 1st, 1959. The genocide machinery had started. Nothing would now stop it. Until the Final Solution, it was never to stop again).[25] The use of the phrase "Final Solution" is of course controversial because of its specific political and semantic anchoring in the Nazi death policies. However, this concern with applying the rhetoric of the Holocaust to the Rwanda situation and with using the Holocaust as a paradigm in her earlier works can also be read as an attempt at bridging the global gap between "grievable and ungrievable lives."[26] As Butler argues, "an ungrievable life is one that cannot be mourned because it has never lived, that is, it has never counted as a life at all."[27] This echoes Rothberg's notion of multidirectional memory that denounces the limitation of the map of memory to the map of power. Thus, Mukasonga, who lived in France for almost twenty years, was aware that to elicit an affect-based response from her readers, who are presupposed to be mostly white French people since she writes in French, she needs to conjure up the specter of the Holocaust.

Mukasonga's depiction of the 1992 violence/massacre in Bugesera also relies heavily on Kristallnacht references. During the night of March 4, 1992, the minority Hutu population in the Rwandan town of Bugesera started massacring the Tutsis, burning down houses, looting shops and homes,[28] in a tragic echo of Kristallnacht, foreshadowing the "official" beginning of the genocide two years later:

> Déjà en mars 1992, on avait procédé au Bugesera à une répétition générale: les maisons avaient brûlé, les Tutsi avaient été jetés dans les latrines. (. . .) Les Tutsi de Nyamata attendaient l'holocauste. . . . La mort d'Habyarimana allait servir de déclencheur à ce qu'à Nyamata nous tenions pour inéluctable et qu'on allait désigner d'un mot que j'ignorais encore: le génocide. En kinyarwanda, on dirait *gutsembatsemba*, un verbe qui signifie à peu près éradiquer et qu'on employait jusque là à propos des chiens enragés ou des bêtes nuisibles . . . Mais comment aurais-je pu imaginer l'horreur absolue dans laquelle allait être plongé le Rwanda: un peuple tout entier se livrant aux pires des crimes sur les vieillards, les femmes, les enfants, les bébés, avec une cruauté, une férocité si inhumaines qu'elles laissent aujourd'hui les assassins sans remords.

> (Already, back in March 1992, a dress rehearsal had occurred in Bugesera: houses had been burnt down, Tutsis had been thrown into latrines. The Nyamata Tutsi were expecting the holocaust . . . Habyarimana's death was to be a trigger for what we held, in Nyamata,

as inescapable and what would later be referred to by a word I was still ignorant of: genocide. In Kinyarwanda, we would use the word *gutsembatsemba*, a verb meaning, roughly, to eradicate and that was until then used solely for rabid dogs or pests . . . But how could I ever have imagined the sheer horror which Rwanda was about to enter: an entire people committing the worst crimes against the elderly, against women, against children, against babies, with such inhuman cruelty and ferocity that they leave the perpetrators without any remorse as of today).[29]

Mukasonga's borrowing of the terminology associated with the Nazi genocide of European Jews constitutes an instance of productive "multidirectional memory" as described by Michael Rothberg in *Multidirectional Memory: Remembering the Holocaust in the Age of Decolonization*.[30] The bridges and transnational and transhistorical echoes created between the two events serve as productive comparative tools enabling Mukasonga to re-inscribe her own experience into a global historical narrative, thereby making her story heard by Western ears. The imagery itself is highly reminiscent of Holocaust scenes, as Hutu bystanders and perpetrators spit on the departing Tutsi, chased away by the rising violence: "Les gens criaient: 'Voilà les Tutsi qui s'en vont' et ils crachaient vers nous en brandissant des machettes" (People would scream: "Here are the Tutsis going away" and they would spit on us while holding high their machettes).[31]

Ultimately, Mukasonga, who struggles to find adequate words to describe what happened beyond words, explains the genocide as follows: "Ils ne pillaient pas, ils voulaient simplement détruire, effacer toutes traces, nous anéantir" (They were not interested in looting, all they wanted was to simply destroy, erase all traces, annihilate us),[32] which is, once again, reminiscent of the Shoah vocabulary (the plans included expropriation of property). Towards its end, the narrative climaxes in merging of both genocides, thereby highlighting the tragic ways in which history repeats itself transnationally: "Un rescapé, je ne sais si c'est de la Shoah ou du génocide des Tutsi, a dit que les survivants du génocide étaient des sous-vivants" (A survivor—I can't remember if he had survived the Holocaust or the Tutsi genocide—said that genocide survivors are below life).[33] Thus, both catastrophic events become merged in the author's memory, creating a single, shared narrative of suffering and violence.

And yet, it is worth remembering that using the Holocaust as a paradigm has its limitations as far as the 1994 genocide is concerned, and can conceal its own uniqueness. In Rwanda, the Tutsis were killed by their own neighbors, whereas in Europe, the Jews were usually taken outside of their usual residences and segregated from their neighbors before being killed. Several critics have argued that the genocide in Rwanda was very much an "intimate affair," the culmination of underlying violence in the banality of everyday life, with the perpetrators using rural weapons such as machetes.[34] Homi Bhabha uses the phrase "a genocide of neighbors and neighborliness"[35] and it is striking that, in most oral and written testimonies, the perpetrators are still referred to as "neighbors" and the neighborly relation between victims and perpetrators remains central to the post-genocide discourse.

THE HOLOCAUST IMAGERY AS A CATHARTIC TOOL
In Mukasonga's texts, if the dehumanizing power of words used by the Hutu propaganda is placed on an equal footing with the objectifying words of white people's projected fantasies, the Holocaust imagery is shown as serving the performative purpose of healing and re-humanizing. Like Habiburahman, Mukasonga uses literature to reclaim her story, to give a voice to those who were killed and whose very memory the perpetrators have tried to erase, and to counter the dehumanizing effects of the genocidal rhetoric.

First, she warns her readers of the fact that words can kill you a second time. When she visited Rwanda for the first time ten years after the genocide, she encountered denial and euphemism whenever she tried to speak with her former Hutu neighbors in Nyamata in hopes of understanding what happened to her relatives: "Qui aurait le mauvais goût de parler encore des 'événements malheureux,' comme disent ceux qui nient avoir participé au génocide et refusent de prononcer le mot?" (Who would still have enough bad taste to continue speaking about "unfortunate events," as those who deny having had anything to do with the genocide and refuse to utter the word itself?).[36] The understatement "unfortunate events" calls to mind the Algerian War of Independence with France, which, for many years, was denied the recognition of a fully-fledged war by Charles de Gaulle and French history books, who simply termed it "the events." Refusing to call the 1994 "events" a genocide amounts to killing the victims a second time, since their fate is denied by public discourse.

Throughout her narratives, Mukasonga's relationship to words is rather complex, as is obvious in her discussion of excision and the fact that it was not practiced in traditional, pre-genocide Rwandan society: "J'écris des mots qu'une Rwandaise ne doit ni prononcer ni écrire. Mais, après tout, ce sont des mots français et sur eux ne pèse peut-être pas d'interdit" (I am writing words that a Rwandan woman is not allowed to utter or write. However, after all, these are French words and there is no taboo on them).[37] Writing in French, a different language from her mother tongue Kinyarwanda, seems to free her from the boundaries restraining women's behaviors in traditional Rwandan society. Not only do words serve the purpose of re-humanizing genocide victims, but they also become a cathartic tool for the author's healing process through a re-gendering of her own body specifically targeted by the perpetrators for its reproductive capabilities. Joan Ringelheim, in her essay entitled "The Split between Gender and the Holocaust," recounts the story of Pauline, a Holocaust survivor who waited until 1984 before confessing that she suffered from sexual abuse and rape while in hiding and in the camps; she felt so much shame that she never confided in anyone, not even her twin sister. Ringelheim comments that:

> some might argue that rape, abortion, sexual exploitation, and pregnancy are always potentially part of a woman's life and that the ubiquity of these experiences means that they can have no relationship to an event that has been described as unique. Others feel that discussions of sexuality desecrate the memory of the dead or the living or the Holocaust itself. (...) It is not surprising, then, that most perspectives on the Holocaust have been gender-neutral or seemed to erase gender as a category of analysis.[38]

Since the publication of Ringelheim's essay twenty years ago, this "split between genocide and gender-specific trauma" has gradually started to be bridged but remains under-explored in the field of Holocaust and genocide studies. In this respect, it is interesting to note that there is no such taboo in Mukasonga's narratives, in which depictions of the gender-specific violence towards women abound. Contrary to Holocaust narratives, which generally aim at a universalizing account of the genocide, Mukasonga's texts constantly emphasize the highly gendered experience of the Hutu genocide against the Tutsi, in which women and children were killed first in an endeavor to annihilate the entire species. Among the many instances reported by Mukasonga is Merciana's story, which occurred during the 1959 and 1960 massacres, foreshadowing the genocide:

> Ils ont pris Merciana. Ils l'ont déshabillée. Ils l'ont mise toute nue. Les femmes ont enfoui leurs enfants dans leur pagne. Les deux militaires

> ont épaulé lentement leur fusil. "Ce n'est pas le cœur qu'ils visaient," répétait maman, "ce sont les seins, seulement les seins. Ils voulaient nous dire à nous les femmes tutsi: 'Ne donnez plus la vie car c'est la mort que vous donnez en mettant au monde. Vous n'êtes plus des porteuses de vie, mais des porteuses de mort.'"
>
> (They took Merciana. They undressed her. They bared her body. Women hid their children's views in their dresses. The two soldiers slowly adjusted their guns. "They were not aiming at the heart," Mama kept saying, "but at the breasts, only at the breasts. They wanted to tell us, Tutsi women: 'Stop giving life because you are giving death whenever you give birth. You no longer carry life but you carry death'").[39]

This excerpt is particularly powerful as it underlines the de-gendering aspects of the genocide, as well as the disruption of the normal course of life by the eruption of violence, since giving birth equates a death sentence. In Lawrence Langer's essay "Gendered Suffering? Women in Holocaust Testimonies," he recounts the testimony of a Jewish woman from Warsaw whose baby boy she delivered in Auschwitz and who was subsequently taken away by a nurse and killed in order to save her life. "(I)n the chaotic scheme of values created for their victims by the Germans, a birth moment is a death moment, and a mother's ambition is to leave her life to join her murdered infant."[40] These words echo many of the instances of gendered violence reported by Mukasonga in her narratives.

However, ultimately, words can heal while their performative powers can re-gender the murdered women and symbolically give them back their life-giving capabilities. As we see in the following tribute:

> Stefania, Marie-Thérèse, Gaudenciana, Theodosia, Anasthasia, Speciosa, Leoncia, Pétronille, Priscilla et bien d'autres, c'étaient elles, les Mères bienfaisantes, les Mères bienveillantes, celles qui nourrissaient, qui protégeaient, qui conseillaient, qui consolaient, les gardiennes de la vie, celles que les tueurs ont assassinées comme pour éradiquer les sources mêmes de la vie.
>
> (Stefania, Marie-Thérèse, Gaudenciana, Theodosia, Anasthasia, Speciosa, Leoncia, Pétronille, Priscilla and countless others, they were the benefactress Mothers, the benevolent Mothers, those who provided nourishment, who protected, who gave advice, who gave comfort, the keepers of life, those that the perpetrators assassinated as if to eradicate the very springs of life).[41]

With the capitalized "M" in "Mothers," echoing the documentary *Mothers of War*,[42] many female victims are re-gendered, as well as sanctified, while being given back feminine attributes closely linked to motherhood. This is significant since Mukasonga underlines the centrality of motherhood to traditional Rwandan culture and to femininity.

Lastly, the most powerful aspects of Mukasonga's genocide memoirs are the performative aspects and cathartic powers granted to language that is placed at the center of the narrative. Thus, written words become the symbolic shroud with which she can mentally cover her mother's body, thereby working through[43] her feelings of guilt at having been absent during the genocide:

> Maman, je n'étais pas là pour recouvrir ton corps et je n'ai plus que des mots—des mots d'une langue que tu ne comprenais pas—pour accomplir ce que tu avais demandé. Et je suis seule avec mes pauvres mots et mes phrases, sur la page du cahier, tissent et retissent le linceul de ton corps absent.
>
> (Mama, I was not there to cover your body and all I have left are words—words in a language that you did not even understand—to fulfill your final request. And I am alone with my pathetic words, and, on the pages of this notebook, my sentences weave over and over the shroud for your missing body).[44]

HABIBURAHMAN'S STRATEGIC USE OF THE HOLOCAUST PARADIGM AGAINST THE UNITED NATIONS' MINIMIZING DISCOURSE

Habiburahman's concern in resorting to a Nazi imagery is slightly different from Mukasonga's. Besides the lack of a specific vocabulary for a genocide that has been unfolding for decades while the world turned a blind eye, the narrative also voices a recurring fear echoed in the narratives of Holocaust victims: "qui raconte ces massacres? L'histoire des Rohingyas ne s'écrit pas" (Who talks about these massacres? Nobody writes the Rohingyas' history).[45] In inscribing his people's history and the genocide into the global map of suffering, Habiburahman focuses on parallels with Kristallnacht, especially as he managed to flee Myanmar before the culmination of ethnic violence. Therefore, his narrative is mostly centered on the gradual discrimination and roundups that led up to the actual genocide, making the comparison with Kristallnacht even more relevant.

The narrative opens with an explicit parallel: "Combien de pogroms avant qu'on soit tous anéantis?" (How many more pogroms before we are all annihilated?).[46] The words "pogroms," "round-ups," "ghettos," "deportation," "concentrationary cities," and "concentrationary universe" saturate the description of the daily violence and massacres undergone by the Muslim Rohingyas. Habiburahman even uses the word "revenants"[47] which, in French, is closely tied to the Holocaust and bears the double meaning of ghosts and those who returned from the death camps, who referred to themselves as "specters" having lost the ability to enjoy life.[48]

However, towards the end of the narrative, a shift occurs, switching the central metaphor from the Holocaust paradigm to one of apartheid. Since Habiburahman's testimony is co-authored by French journalist Sophie Ansel, it is of course difficult to know which narrative choices are Habiburahman's and which ones are Ansel's. Thus, we can't be certain whether Ansel projects her own Western cultural framework onto the Rohingyas' stories, hoping to make it more appealing to a Western (French) audience. The narrative mentions Habiburahman's segregated life "in the Arakanese apartheid" ("l'apartheid arakanais"—and the word "Apartheid" is subsequently repeated at least ten times, including in the title of a chapter called "1997: Déjouer l'apartheid" (Evading the Apartheid),[49] which opens with a description of the South African Apartheid presented as paralleling the situation in the Northern Rakhine State:

> En Afrique, il existe un pays où les Blancs sont séparés des Noirs. (. . .) En Arakan du Nord, il existe un système similaire, sans nom, la ségrégation des *kalars*, officiellement non-citoyens selon la législation mise en place par le président dictateur Ne Win, allègrement poursuivie par son successeur Than Shwe. La Nasaka continue de semer la terreur dans les villes concentrationnaires qui nous enferment. Les villages colons, *natala*, poussent comme des champignons sur les terres confisquées aux Rohingyas. Il faut "birmaniser" et "bouddhiser" l'Arakan. C'est notre apartheid.
>
> (In Africa there is a country where Whites are separated from Blacks. In the Northern Rakhine State, one finds a similar system, without a name of its own, the segregation of *kalars*, who are officially non-citizens according to the law implemented by dictator president Ne Win, which his successor Than Shwe happily continued. The Nasaka continues to breed *terror*[50] in the *concentrationary*[51] cities inside of which

we are locked up. *Colonizers'* villages,⁵² *natala*, grow like mushrooms on the lands taken away from the Rohingyas. The Rakhine State must be "burmified" and "buddhified." It is our apartheid).⁵³

This excerpt highlights the collusion of several well-known historical catastrophes to the Western audience, such as the Holocaust, colonization, and the South African Apartheid. This narrative technique conveys the underlying message that the Rohingya genocide can only be told through a combination of the darkest episodes of Western twentieth-century history in order to finally be heard and to elicit the reader's awareness and empathy. Nevertheless, the shift to an apartheid paradigm raises several issues, as it can be argued that it downgrades the genocide into a mere segregation situation, which would, in the end, reproduce the United Nations' euphemistic rhetoric denounced by Habiburahman.

First They Erased Our Names details the long list of ethnic cleansing operations conducted by the military government from 1959 to 1991. All these operations ironically bear poetic names, such as *Pyi Thaya* (Beautiful Immaculate Nation),⁵⁴ conducted under dictator Than Shwe, followed by "or pur" (pure gold) (1959) or More Purity (*Myat Mon*) from 1967 to 1971, all intending to ensure the continued domination of the majority "issus des races pures" (from pure races).⁵⁵ The *mise en abyme* of the narrator's grandmother's story in 1984, who comes to seek shelter in Habiburahman's parents' home after her village has been destroyed, is solely told in a semantic field that, without context, could as well pertain to a Holocaust survivor's story, with the words "ghetto," "parasite," "torture," "disappearances," "people who resisted were shot," "hell," and concluding with "des centaines de Rohingyas sont morts. Des milliers ont été détenus. Peut-être plus. Qui sait? Qui s'en souciera jamais? Qui documentera la réalité de ces horreurs?" (hundreds of Rohingyas have died. Thousands have been thrown in jail. Maybe more. Who knows? Who will ever care? Who will document the reality of such horrors?).⁵⁶ Habiburahman's borrowing of the Holocaust imagery, most notably of the Kristallnacht paradigm, not only serves the purpose of granting more visibility to the Rohingyas' fate, but also warns the world of the impending disaster, as the pogroms set the stage for the new Holocaust of the twenty-first century unfolding in front of our eyes.

CONCLUSION

Thus, we have seen that for Mukasonga, a survivor of the genocide against the Tutsi, and for Habiburahman, a Rohingya survivor who fled Myanmar, saturating their genocide narratives with words and imagery borrowed from the Holocaust, with explicit echoes of Kristallnacht, was a means towards (re)inscribing their stories into a global context and giving more visibility to what happened in the Rwanda—a tragedy often silenced in Western historical discourses that implicitly establish a "scale of grievability," [57] and drawing the world's attention to the on-going persecution of the Rohingyas after decades of silence. In Habiburahman's case, the Kristallnacht paradigm also serves the purpose of creating a sense of urgency, as the historical catastrophe described by the author is still unfolding. *First They Erased Our Names* is a testimony endowed with a dual function: that of giving a voice to the countless voiceless Rohingyas who have been killed or persecuted for decades, and that of warning the world against the repetition of history, i.e., a new genocide on the same scale as the Holocaust.

Let us close this overview with a citation by Mukasonga that sheds further light on her reasons for using a Holocaust vocabulary: "Dans l'humiliation, la peur de chaque jour, dans l'attente de ce qui allait venir et que nous ne savions pas nommer: le génocide. Et je suis la seule à en détenir la mémoire. C'est pour cela que j'écris ces lignes." ([We lived] through humiliation, the everyday fear, the expectation of what was to come and for which we did not have a word: genocide. And I am the only one to remember. That is the reason why I am writing these lines).[58]

In the *Jewish Journal of Los Angeles*, Stephen Smith, executive director of the University of Southern California's Shoah Foundation, declared in the wake of the Pittsburg Tree of Life Synagogue shooting, in November 2018:

> There is legal precedent following the Rwandan genocide, as determined by the International Criminal Tribunal for Rwanda established by the United Nations Security Council. Ferdinand Nahimana is serving time for running a radio station that incited hatred; Simon Bikindi is serving time for writing songs of hatred. Yes, a musician was given a life sentence by an international tribunal for song writing. The only conclusion: *words can and did kill.*[59]

In Mukasonga's genocide narratives, if the Hutu power movement's rhetoric aimed at gradually dehumanizing the Tutsi in order to pave the way for annihilation, the cathartic function of words is also highlighted. Namely, the narratives themselves are endowed with a triple performative function: that of healing, of paying tribute to the victims, and of giving a voice to those whose voices the perpetrators tried to erase from history. The author-narrator suffers from survivor's guilt and can only be a witness in absentia, since she had already left the Rwanda when the genocide happened. In this perspective, I argue that her genocide testimony operates a reversal, whereby the very words she first calls upon to corroborate her own memories—"je veux me prouver qu'ils ont bien existé" (I want to prove to myself that they actually existed)[60]—do ultimately rehumanize and heal. Mukasonga uses words to grant existence to those whose voices have been silenced from history. In this instance, the Kristallnacht paradigm enables the survivor to reclaim agency and move beyond victimhood, by re-inscribing her own history into a transnational narrative, and, in Habiburahman's case, by warning the world against the repetition of history. In both instances, the Kristallnacht paradigm is depicted as highly relevant to today's "minority" histories and as the lasting symbol of a turning point in genocidal violence.

Notes

1. Dori Laub, "The Imperative to Tell," in *Trauma: Explorations in Memory*, edited by Cathy Caruth (Baltimore: The Johns Hopkins University Press, 1995), 61–75.
2. Ibid., 63.
3. Scholastique Mukasonga, *Inyenzi ou les cafards* (Paris: Gallimard, 2006); and idem, *La femme aux pieds nus* (Coll. Folio. Paris: Gallimard, 2008).
4. Habiburahman, with Sophie Ansel, *D'abord, ils ont effacé notre nom: Un Rohingya parle* (Lyon: La Martinière, 2018).
5. CNTRL: Centre National die Ressources Textuelles et Lexicales, https://www.cnrtl.fr/definition/pogrom.
6. See chapter by Ulrich Baumann and François Guesnet in this volume.
7. Hélène Cixous and Cécile Wajsbrot, *Une autobiographie allemande* (Paris: Bourgois, 2016). Also, Hélène Cixous's most recent autobiographical novel, titled *1938, nuits* (1938, nights) (Paris: Galilée, 2019), is devoted to Kristallnacht in an attempt for the author to understand why her maternal family chose to stay in Osnabrück, Germany, after the pogrom, and were subsequently all deported and murdered during the Holocaust. However, it is striking that «Kristallnacht» (Cixous, *1938, nuits*, 81 and 98—in German in the French text) is only named twice in the 146-page narrative and is otherwise referred to as «la-nuit-qui-ne-sait-pas qu'elle est pavée de verre brisé» (Cixous, *1938, nuits*, 27) (the-night-that-does-not-know that it is paved with broken glasses), «la nuit du tournant de la mémoire sur ses gonds» (Cixous, *1938, nuits*, 29) (the night when memory turned around), and «le 9 Novembre» (November 9) (Cixous, *1938, nuits*, 44, 70). It is as though the trauma of Kristallnacht had such a lasting effect on the 80-year-old author's genealogy that she cannot assimilate the event into the French language and, as the narrative unfolds, it is subsequently called «l'an de Kristall» (Cixous, *1938, nuits*, 77) (the Kristall year) with the German spelling and «la nuit de Kristall» (Cixous, *1938, nuits*, 104) (the Kristall night), again with the German spelling.
8. See Mukasonga, *Inyenzi ou les cafards*, on Genocdie Archive of Rwanda, http://www.genocidearchiverwanda.org.rw/index.php/Nyamata_Memorial, and Hélène Dumas and Rémi Korman, "Espaces de la mémoire du génocide des Tutsis au Rwanda. Mémoriaux et lieux de mémoire" (Memorial Spaces for the Tutsi Genocide in Rwanda), *Afrique contemporaine* 238, no. 2 (2011): 11–17, DOI: 10.3917/afco.238.0011, https://www.cairn.info/revue-afrique-contemporaine-2011-2-page-11.htm.
9. Habiburahman, *D'abord*, 8–9, 231–34.
10. Michael Rothberg, *Multidirectional Memory: Remembering the Holocaust in the Age of Decolonization* (Stanford, CA: Stanford University Press, 2009).
11. Judith Butler, *Frames of War: When Is Life Grievable?* (New York City: Verso, 2009).
12. Mukasonga, *Inyenzi*, 30.

13. Ibid., 83.
14. See Mukasonga, *Inyenzi*, her autobiographical narrative, for a detailed account of this specific episode.
15. Habiburahman, *D'abord*, 51.
16. "Myanmar Military Leaders Must Face Genocide Charges—UN Report," *UN News*, August 27, 2018, accessed July 7, 2019, https://news.un.org/en/story/2018/08/1017802; and Tracey Shelton, "Myanmar's Military 'Unleashes Campaign of Violence' in Rakhine State, Amnesty International Warns," *ABC News*, May 28, 2019, accessed July 7, 2009, https://www.abc.net.au/news/2019-05-29/new-report-details-war-crimes-and-abuses-in-myanmars-rakhine/11157920?fbclid=IwAR2vxVKcv3l2vS9FFoM1_PRLd5FXy93MlUNvgH43pKf6S0M-Y-L_MrmOu7U.
17. "Myanmar Military Leaders."
18. Mukasonga, *Inyenzi*, 87.
19. Ibid., 4, 10, 12, 27, 38, 40.
20. Habiburahman, *D'abord*, 12.
21. Mukasonga, *Inyenzi*, 93.
22. Ibid., 97.
23. Scholastique Mukasonga, *Notre-Dame du Nil* (Paris: Gallimard, 2012), 73–74, 112–13.
24. Ibid., 112–13.
25. Mukasonga, *Inyenzi*, 19.
26. Butler, *Frames of War*, 9.
27. Ibid., 5.
28. "Declaration sur les massacres enc ours de la population de la region du Bugesera," accessed July 7, 2019, https://francegenocidetutsi.org/bugesera-1992.pdf.
29. Mukasonga, *Inyenzi*, 139–40.
30. Rothberg, *Multidirectional Memory*.
31. Mukasonga, *Inyenzi*, 24.
32. Ibid., 20.
33. Ibid., 145.
34. Robert Lyons and Scott Straus, *Intimate Enemy: Images and Voices of the Rwandan Genocide* (London: Zone Books, 2006).
35. Homi Bhabha, "A Memory of Neighbors: On History and the Afterlife," keynote address, "Recognition, Reparation, Reconciliation" conference, Stellenbosch University, South Africa, December 6, 2018.
36. Ibid., *Inyenzi*, 22.
37. Mukasonga, *La femme aux pieds nus*, 153.
38. Joan Ringelheim, "The Split between Gender and the Holocaust," in *Women in the Holocaust*, ed. Dalia Ofer and Lenore J. Weitzman (New Haven: Yale University Press, 1998), 344–45.
39. Mukasonga, *La femme aux pieds nus*, 28–29.
40. Lawrence Langer, "Gendered Suffering? Women in Holocaust Testimonies," in

Women in the Holocaust, ed. Dalia Ofer and Lenore Weitzman (New Haven and London: Yale University Press, 1998), 357.

41. Mukasonga, *La femme aux pieds nus*, 148.
42. Maria Rinaldo, *Mothers of War* (Columbia, MO: Documentary Group, 2009).
43. The notion of "working through" was coined by Holocaust scholar and psychoanalyst Dominick LaCapra to describe the survivors' healing process after the Holocaust trauma. See, for instance, Dominick LaCapra, *Writing History, Writing Trauma* (Baltimore: Johns Hopkins University Press, 2014).
44. Mukasonga, *La femme aux pieds nus*, 13.
45. Habiburahman, *D'abord*, 83.
46. Ibid., 16–17.
47. Ibid., 65.
48. See, for instance, several French Holocaust survivors' testimonies: Charlotte Delbo, *Auschwitz et après* (Paris: Minuit, 1970) and Madeleine Aylmer-Roubenne, *J'ai donné la vie dans un camp de la mort* (Paris: Lattès, 1997).
49. Habiburahman, *D'abord*, 129.
50. My emphasis.
51. My emphasis.
52. My emphasis.
53. "Arakan du Nord"—Habiburahman, *D'abord*, 129.
54. Ibid., 77.
55. Ibid., 79.
56. Ibid., 19.
57. Butler, *Frames of War*.
58. Mukasonga, *Inyenzi*, 58.
59. My emphasis. Stephen Smith, "Words That Kill: The Genocidal Nature of Anti-Semitism," *The Jewish Journal of Los Angeles* (November 2–8, 2018): 14.
60. Mukasonga, *Inyenzi*, 12.

Bibliography

Aylmer-Roubenne, Madeleine. *J'ai donné la vie dans un camp de la mort*. Paris: Lattès, 1997.

Baer, Elizabeth, and Myrna Goldenberg, eds. *Experience and Expression: Women, the Nazis, and the Holocaust*. Detroit: Wayne State University Press, 2003.

Bhabha, Homi. *The Location of Culture*. London and New York: Routledge, 1994.

———. "A Memory of Neighbors: On History and the Afterlife." Keynote address, "Recognition, Reparation, Reconciliation" conference. Stellenbosch University, South Africa. December 6, 2018.

Butler, Judith. *Frames of War: When is Life Grievable?* New York City: Verso, 2009.

Caruth, Cathy. *Unclaimed Experience: Trauma, Narrative, and History*. Baltimore: Johns Hopkins University Press, 1996.

Cixous, Hélène, and Cécile Wajsbrot. *Une autobiographie allemande*. Paris: Bourgois, 2016.

"Declaration sur les massacres enc ours de la population de la region du Bugesera." Accessed July 7, 2019. https://francegenocidetutsi.org/bugesera-1992.pdf.

Delbo, Charlotte. *Auschwitz et après I, II, III*. Paris: Minuit, 1970.

Dumas, Hélène, and Rémi Korman. "Espaces de la mémoire du génocide des Tutsis au Rwanda. Mémoriaux et lieux de mémoire" (Memorial Spaces for the Tutsi Genocide in Rwanda). *Afrique contemporaine* 238, no. 2 (2011): 11–17. DOI: 10.3917/afco.238.0011. https://www.cairn.info/revue-afrique-contemporaine-2011-2-page-11.htm.

Habiburahman, with Sophie Ansel. *D'abord, ils ont effacé notre nom: Un Rohingya parle*. Lyon: La Martinière, 2018.

Herman, Judith. *Trauma and Recovery: The Aftermath of Violence, from Domestic Abuse to Political Terror*. New York: Basic Books, 2015 (1992).

LaCapra, Dominick. *Writing History, Writing Trauma*. Baltimore, MD: Johns Hopkins University Press, 2014.

Langer, Lawrence. "Gendered Suffering? Women in Holocaust Testimonies." In *Women in the Holocaust*, edited by Dalia Ofer and Lenore Weitzman, 351–63. New Haven and London: Yale University Press, 1998.

Laub, Dori. "The Imperative to Tell." In *Trauma: Explorations in Memory*, edited by Cathy Caruth, 61–75. Baltimore: The Johns Hopkins University Press, 1995.

Lyons, Robert, and Scott Straus. *Intimate Enemy: Images and Voices of the Rwandan Genocide*. London: Zone Books, 2006.

Mukasonga, Scholastique. *La femme aux pieds nus*. Coll. Folio. Paris: Gallimard, 2008.

———. *Inyenzi ou les cafards*. Paris: Gallimard, 2006.

———. *Notre-Dame du Nil*. Paris: Gallimard, 2012.

"Myanmar Military Leaders Must Face Genocide Charges—UN Report." *UN News*, August 27, 2018. Accessed July 7, 2019. https://news.un.org/en/story/2018/08/1017802.

Ofer, Dalia, and Lenore J. Weitzman, eds. *Women in the Holocaust*. New Haven and London: Yale University Press, 1998.

Rinaldo, Maria. *Mothers of War*. Columbia, MO: Documentary Group, 2009.

Joan Ringelheim, "The Split between Gender and the Holocaust." In *Women in the Holocaust*, edited by Dalia Ofer and Lenore J. Weitzman, 344–45. New Haven: Yale University Press, 1998.

Rittner, Carol, and John K. Roth, eds. *Women and the Holocaust: Different Voices*. New York: Paragon House, 1993.

Rothberg, Michael. *Multidirectional Memory: Remembering the Holocaust in the Age of Decolonization*. Stanford, CA: Stanford University Press, 2009.

Shelton, Tracey. "Myanmar's Military 'Unleashes Campaign of Violence' in Rakhine State, Amnesty International Warns." *ABC News*, May 28, 2019. Accessed July 7, 2009. https://www.abc.net.au/news/2019-05-29/new-report-details-war-crimes-and-abuses-in-myanmars-rakhine/11157920?fbclid=IwAR2vxVKcv3l2vS9FFoM1_PRLd5FXy93MlUNvgH43pKf6S0M-Y-L_MrmOu7U.

Smith, Stephen. "Words That Kill: The Genocidal Nature of Anti-Semitism." *The Jewish Journal of Los Angeles*, November 2–8 (2018): 14.

CHAPTER 15

The Long Shadow of the "Kristallnacht" on the "Gujarat Pogrom" in India? A Comparative Analysis

by Baijayanti Roy

"Gujarat Pogrom" refers to three days (February 28–March 1, 2002) of intense violence—mostly perpetrated by members of the majority Hindu community against the minority Muslims—in the Indian federal state of Gujarat.

Hindu-Muslim clashes, usually referred to as communal riots, are not uncommon in India. But the violence in Gujarat was not a riot; it was a premeditated, carefully orchestrated mob attack on Muslims, instigated by right wing Hindu nationalist groups with the aim of ethnic cleansing. The state government, under the Hindu nationalist Bharatiya Janata Party (BJP), stands accused of being complicit in starting the bloodshed and condoning the perpetrators. The episode resulted in the death of between one thousand and two thousand people, mostly Muslims.[1] Around 150,000 people, also overwhelmingly Muslim, were rendered homeless.[2] Residences, business establishments and places of worship of Muslims were systematically desecrated and destroyed.

This episode has been compared in general to anti-Jewish pogroms in Central and Eastern Europe in the last several centuries, and in particular with the pogroms that took place in the villages of Jedwabne and Radzilow in Poland in 1941, during the German occupation, when Catholic Polish residents of these places murdered half of the local Jewish population (estimated at over 1,600 people).[3] This chapter contends that the "Gujarat Pogrom" has more parallels with the November Pogrom or "Kristallnacht" of 1938. These commonalities are not simply co-incidental, though the two events are separated by space and time.

In order to establish this point, the article will first provide a comparative context of the two cases and then discuss following aspects: 1) the dynamics of the episodes, particularly the fascism-inspired logic that manifested itself in both cases, 2) the distinctive traits, and 3) some of the effects of these two different yet not dissimilar events.

CONTEXTS

Hindu nationalist ideology projects India as an exclusively Hindu nation, because Hindus form the largest religious group in India and also because Hinduism is indigenous to India. By the same rationale, religious minorities like Muslims and Christians are regarded as alien to India since Islam and Christianity had originated outside the country. Other minorities like Sikhs, Jains and Buddhists are tolerated since these religions had originated in India.[4]

This brand of political Hinduism, usually referred to as *Hindutva* (literally Hindu-ness) developed in the 1920s and 1930s. It remained aloof from the secular anti-colonial movement conducted by the Indian National Congress under Gandhi's leadership. Hindu nationalism is a kind of cultural or ethnic nationalism, which focussed more on the essence of being Indian, than with the imperative to end colonial rule. Hindu nationalism propagated the motto of Hindi, Hindu, Hindustan, denoting a nation based on one language and one religion, resembling the model of the nineteenth-century European nation state.[5]

Proponents of *Hindutva* in the 1930s openly admired aspects of European fascism and Nazism. Vinayak D. Savarkar, the leading exponent of *Hindutva*, blamed the Jews of Germany for failing to assimilate, allegedly like the Muslims of India.[6] M. S. Golwalkar, another Hindu nationalist leader, wrote in "We or Our Nationhood Defined" (1939) that persecution of minorities by the Nazis was a good lesson for the Hindus to learn and profit from.[7] Though Hindu nationalists have subsequently distanced themselves from these references to the Nazis, the latter's racial-religious worldview has become entrenched in their political ideology.[8] Hindu nationalists propagate an Indian version of Blood and Soil theory, in which glorification of Vedic Aryans (who they claim were indigenous to India), caste system and notions of purity play a significant role. Whereas for the Nazis "purity of blood" was central to the construction of "race," Hindu nationalists associate "purity" of the Hindu "jati" (nation or race) with certain Hindu upper caste cultural mores like vegetarian dietary habits with an attendant abhorrence of meat eating, which is associated with Muslims.

Demonization of the Muslims in India predates the rise of Hindu nationalism. British colonizers, pursuing a divide and rule policy, encouraged tensions between the two communities using stereotypes, for example about oppressive Muslim rulers and victimized Hindu subjects in medieval India.[9] Partition of the Indian subcontinent into Hindu-majority India and Muslim-majority Pakistan in 1947 was accompanied by brutal Hindu-Muslim clashes, which has left unhealed scars in the collective psyche of both communities.[10]

After India's independence, many Hindus, including those among the political elite, continued to perceive the Muslims as the "Other" who threatened Indian society "from within." The victim of such prejudices has been the Muslim community in India whose chances of socio-economic and political progress have suffered through institutional neglect.[11] Hindu nationalist politics, espoused by the political party, Jan Sangh and its successor the Bharatiya Janata Party (BJP) used anti-Muslim prejudices to garner Hindu votes. The ultimate aim of Hindu nationalist politics is to destroy the pluralist multi-faith fabric of India and replace it with a Hindu theocracy.[12]

Animosity towards minorities as "the enemy within" remains alive in societies that feel an urge to avenge past indignities, be it colonial subjugation, as in India, or military defeat, as in Germany after the First World War. The November Pogrom in Germany was the culmination of systematic persecution of Jews from 1933 onwards, accompanied by rabid anti-Semitic propaganda. Though most of the half-million Jews of Germany had lived in the country for generations and considered themselves to be fully integrated citizens, they were often considered to be "the other" by many, a prejudice that the Nazis could exploit. The relative prosperity of the Jews gave rise to the envious view that the Jewish minority enjoyed powers and influence that were disproportionate to its actual size.[13]

Jews were singled out by the Nazi propaganda machine as "the enemy within" and blamed for Germany's defeat in the First World War. Though many Jews took part in the "Great War," and twelve thousand Jews were killed in action, Jews were branded as "disloyal shirkers" after the war.[14] The Jews were also made into scapegoats for Germany's economic difficulties after the First World War. Their position as minority rendered the Jews particularly vulnerable to oppression by the state. The purges of the administration undertaken by the Nazi government (through the Law for the restoration of the professional civil service of 1933 and the Nuremberg Race Laws of 1935, for example) led to progressive marginalisation of the Jewish community.[15]

The carnage in Gujarat, like the November Pogrom of 1938, represented a high point in the systematic discrimination against the Muslims that intensified with the Hindu nationalist BJP's coming to power in the state in 1995. The BJP has since then become entrenched in Gujarat. Its political ideology has infiltrated deep into the state's administrative and police systems, not unlike the process of "violent socialization" of the police force in the Third Reich.[16] While Muslim police officers have hardly been able to rise to important executive positions in Gujarat, a large number of Hindu nationalists and their sympathizers have been recruited among the Home Guards, a kind of municipal police.[17]

Though Gujarat is the home state of Gandhi who stood for Hindu-Muslim harmony, his philosophy did not strike deep roots here. Socio-economic and political spheres in Gujarat are controlled by a large community of upper caste Hindu and Jain traders. Commercial alliances are often formed on the basis of caste and religious ties. This nexus of religion, caste and commerce is particularly susceptible to Hindu nationalist politics with its upper-caste and pro-business agenda.[18]

The unfettered capitalist policies of the state government, along with the decline of the Gandhian ideals of social justice and tolerance, have resulted in widening the communal chasm. The marginalized workers belonging to Hindu lower castes, with low-paid, precarious jobs or no jobs at all have increasingly turned to Hindu religious politics since it gives them a sense of solidarity and a vent for their frustrations.[19] Moreover, some Muslims in Gujarat are prosperous traders, making them objects of envy, much like the Jews of Germany.[20]

The process of communal polarization in Gujarat has escalated due to the increasing segregation of the communities and a corresponding marginalization and ghettoization of Muslims in cities. It started after a riot that took place in Ahmedabad in 1985 and has accelerated after Hindu nationalists came to power.[21]

DYNAMICS

Incidents that sparked the carnage in both cases provided pretexts for the ruling parties. In both instances, ruling dispensations could present themselves not as aggressors but as protectors of the majority community against alleged threats from the minorities. In Nazi Germany, such a national community or *Volksgemeinschaft* was perceived to be a kind of racial kinship among the so-called Aryans. In order to maintain the racial purity of this "Aryan" *Volksgemeinschaft*, the Semites who supposedly represented an "impure" racial type, needed to be "cleansed" from its body politic.[22] In Gujarat, the pogrom of 2002 represented a concerted effort by the Hindu nationalists to establish a *shuddha* (pure) Gujarat. For achieving this Hindu utopia, it was necessary to "sacrifice" elements which were perceived to be "polluting" and incompatible with a "pure" Hindu community.[23]

The shooting of the German diplomat Ernst vom Rath in Paris by the seventeen-year-old Polish Jew Hershel Grynszpan on the morning of November 7, 1938 served the same function as the burning of a train coach containing Hindu nationalist political cadres at the station of Godhra, a town in Gujarat, on February 27, 2002, allegedly by a Muslim mob (it was most probably an accident). Fifty-seven people, mostly Hindus, were burnt alive in the train.[24]

In both cases, politicians in power aggravated the situations, making them conducive to pogroms. As news of the attempt on Ernst vom Rath's life reached Germany on the evening of November 7, anti-Semitic violence broke out in the region of Kurhessen. Violence began in the town of Kassel, where the synagogue was set on fire. Heinemann, the Jewish café, as well as the local Jewish school, Jewish community centres and shops were vandalised. Jewish residents were hounded out of their houses and abused.[25]

Similar atrocities spread to different areas of Hessen overnight and continued throughout November 8 and 9. These pogrom-like attacks were instigated mostly by regional NSDAP leaders and actively aided by members of various organs of the Nazi party, like the SA, NSKK and HJ. They also attracted perpetrators who were not part of the Nazi organisations. In most cases, the police either did not intervene or did so half-heartedly, even where the regional governor ordered them to.[26] In the afternoon of November 9, news of the death of Ernst vom Rath reached the Nazi ruling coterie which had gathered in Munich for the annual commemoration of Hitler's putsch attempt in 1923. Goebbels asked the "Führer" what was to be done in the present volatile situation. Hitler decided that the police was to be withdrawn so that the "spontaneous demonstrations" could continue and the Jews could feel the rage of the people. Hitler himself was careful not to let his name be directly associated with the pogrom. It was Goebbels who communicated this decision to the party officials at the evening gathering who later instructed their subordinates accordingly.[27] The nation-wide co-ordinated pogrom began.

Fast forward to Gujarat, February 27, 2002: although the administrative officer of Godhra, Jayanti Ravi, gave a public statement that the Godhra train burning was an accident, chief minister Narendra Modi (now the prime minister of India) gave an emotional address on television, calling it a pre-planned attack. The BJP, which was in power in the centre at the time, also issued statements corroborating Modi and hinting that the Pakistan's intelligence service (ISI) was responsible for the incident though no investigations had been completed at the time.[28]

That very evening Modi organised the bringing of the charred bodies of the victims of the train burning in a motorcade to Ahmedabad, Gujarat's largest city. The arrival was broadcast on television. On the next day, images of the bodies wrapped in white sheets appeared in newspapers. The same night, violence broke out in parts of the cities of Ahmedabad and Vadodara, which the police did nothing to abate—a parallel to the anti-Jewish violence that broke out in Kurhessen on November 7.

On February 28 Modi publicly claimed that Godhra incident was not a communal incident caused by long-standing hostility between two communities but a "one-sided collective violent act of terrorism from one community."[29] Attaching the label of terrorism to the Godhra incident implied a connection with Islamic terrorists whom many Hindus associate with Pakistan. Modi's insinuation thus implied that the loyalty of Indian Muslims lay with Pakistan. Though baseless, this equation played to the insecurities of many Hindus and Jains. This development of events in Gujarat is evocative of the German political propaganda on the eve of the November Pogrom, which insisted that the attack on vom Rath was the outcome of an international Jewish conspiracy. In this way, the incident was rendered a global significance that justified taking retaliatory action against Jews residing in Germany.

The co-ordinated pogrom in Gujarat started after VHP (Vishwa Hindu Parishad), a Hindu organisation allied to the BJP, called for a total shutdown of Ahmedabad on February 28 in protest against the alleged Godhra attack. The BJP government supported this demand. On that day, a large mob mostly comprising men wearing the Hindu nationalist "uniform"—khaki pants and saffron headbands—went on a rampage against Muslim lives and properties, which they identified on the basis of voter registration lists and tax records—

documents which could only have been accessed through connivance with the state administration.[30] The attackers were seen to receive regular instructions on cellular phones and they kept reporting back.[31] The role of these perfectly disciplined and co-ordinated squads in Gujarat is similar to that of the *Stoßtruppen* (assault detachments) of the SA men who were orchestrating most of the violence during the November Pogrom.

In Gujarat, the police were either absent from the scenes of carnage or were mute spectators.[32] Sometimes, the police arrived too late. Occasionally, they aided the perpetrators by firing at the victims. "We have no orders to save you," was a common refrain of the police to Muslims looking for protection.[33] Of the 184 people who died in police firing in Gujarat, 104 were Muslims.[34] Gujarat police also arrested mostly Muslims, though nowhere in the range of the thirty thousand Jews incarcerated during the November Pogrom.[35]

The pattern of complicity and inaction of the Police during the Gujarat riots is not unprecedented in India. It was manifest, for example in the anti-Sikh pogrom of 1984 which cost around 2,700 lives.[36] Anti-Sikh violence was allegedly unleashed by the ruling Congress party after the then prime minister of India Indira Gandhi was murdered by her Sikh bodyguards. This behavioural pattern is due to an inherent anti-minority bias as well as to the practice of police taking orders from politicians in power rather than from their own superiors.[37] This attitude appears to be common to the police which swore allegiance to the dictator of Nazi Germany in 1933 and which swears its loyalty not to any individual but to the secular and democratic constitution of India.

Two residential areas with relatively large Muslim population, Gulbarga Society and Naroda Patiya in Ahmedabad were hit particularly hard. Gulbarga Society is a middle- to lower-middle class residential compound at the periphery of Ahmedabad. A prominent Muslim resident of Gulbarga Society was Ehsan Jaffry, an ex-member of parliament from the Indian National Congress party, a vocal critic of Hindutva politics and Narendra Modi. On February 28, Jaffrey asked for a personal assurance of safety from the police commissioner who responded by demonstratively visiting Gulbarga Society. However, soon after the Police Commissioner's departure, a mob attacked the compound. Despite making frantic calls to the chief minister and top police officials, no help was sent to Jaffrey, who, along with many other residents of the compound was brutally burnt to death.[38]

The other residential area receiving the brunt of Hindu nationalist rage was Naroda Patiya, which, unlike Gulbarg Society, is a very poor residential area, divided into Hindu and Muslim sections. The pogrom here took the form of neighbours murdering neighbours in the name of saving Hindu religion. Muslim shops were looted and the local mosque was set on fire.[39]

There were spectator crowds who occasionally participated in looting, not unlike similar instances during the November Pogrom, for example in Berlin.[40] In Naroda Patiya, eyewitness accounts claimed that spectators who did not participate in the pogrom were admonished by VHP leaders and compelled to participate.[41] Similar happenings were recorded during the November Pogrom, when members of the Nazi party and the SA who hesitated to join the assault detachments were subjected to pressure and exhorted to "behave in the National Socialist way."[42]

By the evening of February 28, violence spread to Gandhinagar, the capital of Gujarat, and other towns. The district administration of Gujarat remained aloof as the bloodbath reached remote rural areas on March 1.[43] The November Pogrom likewise spread to different cities and provinces during the night of November 9–10. The imprisonment of Jewish men (also in some cases women) also began on the same night and continued for the next few days.[44]

During the November Pogrom, a few policemen and firefighters intervened to stem the worst excesses. Lieutenant Otto Bellgardt and his superior Wilhelm Krützfeld actually prevented the burning of Oranienburger Straße-Synagogue in Berlin.[45] Instances of police officers acting with professional integrity occurred in some places during the Gujarat carnage as well. Surat, a town which had experienced considerable communal violence in 1992, remained peaceful in 2002 due to the efforts of the local police commissioner, V. K. Gupta.[46]

However, a distinctive feature of the "Gujarat pogrom" was that the few police officers of Gujarat who tried to maintain professional integrity had to face the wrath of the ruling authorities. Rahul Sharma, the Superintendent of Police at Bhavanagar district, who saved four hundred Muslim children from the onslaught of a violent mob and arrested trouble-making Hindu activists, was chided by Gardhan Zadafia, the Home minister of Gujarat and transferred subsequently to a series of less challenging posts.[47] Such "political transfers" have a tradition in India. They are meant to demoralize those who dare to stand up to the political authorities. Sanjiv Bhatt, an officer belonging to the elite Indian Police Service (IPS), had testified against Modi, claiming that he had been present at a meeting on February 27 in which the chief minister allegedly told top police officials to let Hindus vent out their anger against the Muslims. Sanjiv Bhatt has been recently arrested on dubious charges and sentenced for life.[48]

What makes the "Gujarat Pogrom" particularly evocative of "Kristallnacht" is the purported role of the politicians. Whether Narendra Modi instructed the police not to stand in the way of Hindu backlash to the Godhra incident remains disputed, but his public legitimization of the pogrom as a spontaneous reaction of the Hindus to the criminal act that happened at Godhra, is on record.[49] It is an eerie reminder of Goebbels ascribing the "Kristallnacht" events to the "healthy instincts of German people."[50]

The fifty-seven dead in the "Godhra incident" were projected as Hindu martyrs, whose tragic death was cynically and successfully used by the ruling party for political gains. "Pay your homage to the Godhra martyrs. Cast your vote," said an advertisement for the BJP in the Gujarati media on the day of the state elections in December 2002.[51] It is notable that Ernst vom Rath was given a state funeral on November 17 in the presence of Hitler himself. Vom Rath thus became, as Rafael Gross has claimed, a new and apparently very welcome martyr to the cause of National Socialism.[52]

How much did the "ordinary people" know about the pogroms and to what extent did they participate in them? The November pogrom was carried on in full public view and the media reported about the incidents.[53] According to Eberhard Jäckel, the pogrom soon aroused misgivings due to the damages inflicted on the properties of the Jews. Also, destruction of synagogues gave rise to moral condemnations.[54] Herman Graml also claims that only a minority of ordinary Germans followed the lead of the Nazi functionaries while the majority not only disapproved but also gave vent to their disgust.[55]

Rafael Gross maintains that about ten percent of the German people took active part in the November pogrom, while most were indifferent to the fate of their Jewish co-citizens. Barring a few exceptions, the perpetrators faced no opposition from the populace. Many spectators, particularly in Berlin, were initially reluctant to participate in the pogrom but eventually gave way to their greed.[56]

Wolfgang Benz, however, claims that there was an alarming degree of participation of the "ordinary Germans," particularly younger people and children, who gleefully robbed Jewish sweet shops and toy shops. Benz emphasizes that Goebbels' appeal to the baser instincts of the people was manifestly successful.[57] Recent research by Wolf Gruner on Berlin shows that while many citizens participated in vandalizing and looting Jewish shops, a number of others "reacted with critique, protest, and even resistance" to the anti-Semitic violence and mayhem, for which they were subjected to punitive measures by the police and the Gestapo.[58]

Evidently, the response of the "ordinary Germans" to the November Pogrom was complex and variegated. In case of the "Gujarat Pogrom," the blurring of boundaries between state, political movement and people, which is a characteristic of fascist mobilizations everywhere, was more noticeable. Not only was the anti-Muslim violence orchestrated with the complicity of the state administrative machinery, there was, as Parvis Ghassem-Fachandi pointed out, a *Gleichschaltung* (co-ordination) of a comparatively large number of "ordinary" Gujaratis in whose name the violence was perpetrated.[59]

The number and percentage of ordinary people participating in the events under discussion might remain controversial, but it is clear that the everyday codes of law-abiding bourgeois conduct remained wilfully suspended. However, occasional instances of solidarity and acts of human kindness could be found in both instances. In Ahmedabad, for example, a slum inhabited by both Hindus and Muslims successfully resisted calls for communal violence.[60] There were also moments in Berlin during the November Pogrom when non-Jewish citizens prevented the organized mob from looting.[61]

The part played by the media in inciting hatred among majority communities shows surprising parallels in both cases. The story of the attack on vom Rath dominated the front pages of German newspapers, particularly of the Nazi mouthpieces, *Völkischer Beobachter* and *Der Angriff*, which spewed venom against the Jews. The *Völkischer Beobachter* wrote on November 8, 1938, that it is clear that the German people would draw consequences from this deed, adding that it is an impossible situation that within "our borders" a hundred thousand Jews dominate the shopping areas . . . while their racial compatriots outside the border call for war against Germany and shoot down German diplomats.[62]

After the Godhra incident, popular Gujarati language newspapers like *Sandesh* and *Gujarat Samachar* carried unfounded write-ups in inflammatory anti-Muslim language. These vernacular newspapers published unconfirmed reports about the abduction and rape, presumably by Muslim men, of two young women who were missing from the burning train at Godhra. Subsequently, these newspapers published macabre and untrue descriptions of the mutilated bodies of the two missing women having been found.[63] The incident turned out to be completely baseless, but these reports incited Hindu righteous rage and calls for retaliation.

However, one must note that in Nazi Germany, all official public information was orchestrated through the Goebbelsian propaganda machinery. Therefore mainstream representation of "Kristallnacht" could hardly be expected to be objective, let alone critical. In the case of "Gujarat Pogrom," there were fearless critical voices raised by local English language newspapers like *Gujarat Today*, non-Gujarati vernacular media as well as by national media.[64] These critical reports prompted the BJP led central government to claim that the media was presenting an exaggerated account of the situation in the state.[65]

In both cases, violence was not only justified by the perpetrators on the spurious ground of supposed victimization of the majority community through an inimical minority community, violence against minorities was projected as a patriotic duty.

Another trait common to both episodes was the targeting of religious establishments of the minorities. Just as more than two thousand synagogues were systematically burnt down during the "Kristallnacht," in Gujarat, 527 mosques, madrasas, cemeteries and *dargah* (small roadside shrines of Muslims) were destroyed. Hindu religious symbols like images of the monkey god Hanuman were often placed at the ruins.[66]

Destruction of the sites held sacred to the "enemy" has occurred since ancient times. It is primarily a demonstration of power and contempt for the adversary. Destruction of synagogues in 1938 represented the state sanctioned termination of Jewish socio-cultural existence in Germany. But the November Pogrom was not the first instance of destruction of synagogues in Germany. About sixty seven synagogues had already been destroyed by the Nazis since 1933.[67] What was novel in "Kristallnacht" was the nation-wide, systematic and ritualistic nature of it. It could be said, following Martin Gilbert, that the November Pogrom seemed to fulfil Martin Luther's exhortation from 1543, that the synagogues of the Jews "should be set on fire."[68] Luther's statements about Jews and Judaism were successfully used by a number of influential theologians and pastors to reinforce both Christian anti-Judaism and cultural anti-Semitism in the Third Reich.[69] There was thus a feeling, among certain circles, of historic and religious righteousness about vandalising synagogues.

Burning of mosques during the Gujarat pogrom also had, apart from a display of power, disrespect and the symbolic elimination of Muslims, a so-called historical dimension: revenge. Colonial history writing as well as postcolonial popular narratives have portrayed the demolition of Hindu temples by Muslim rulers (e.g., Sultan Mahmud of Ghazni's destruction of the Somnatha temple in Gujarat in 1026) as events creating a perpetual trauma in Hindu memorial consciousness. Such popular perceptions continue, even though historians have pointed out that motives for such destructions were varied and complex and not necessarily due to a simple binary of animosity between

Hindus and Muslims. In India, politics plays a significant role in communalization of history. As Romila Thapar has pointed out, in the case of the Somnatha temple, the supposed memorial trauma of the Hindus was "constructed" through a British debate in the House of Commons in 1843 and adopted later by colonial as well as Indian historians and politicians to serve a variety of purposes.[70]

Hindu nationalism, particularly from the 1980s on, has made this purported "historical trauma" and calls for revenge significant political instruments to mobilize Hindu sentiments (and votes). The emotional and symbolic urge to redress a "historical wrong" was manifested in the destruction of a sixteenth-century mosque, built during the reign of the Mughal emperor Babur at Ayodhya in the federal state of Uttar Pradesh, by a Hindu nationalist mob on December 6, 1992. The mosque supposedly stood at the site of a temple marking the birthplace of the Hindu divinity, Ram. Historians, however, deny the existence of any such temple.[71] In Gujarat, this communalized history has been disseminated in various ways, including school text books which also, till recently, glorified Hitler.[72]

Pogroms are often marked by sadistic conduct and sexual perversion. "Kristallnacht" saw unprecedented levels of sadistic behaviour against Jews which resulted in around a hundred murders, and several hundred deaths in concentration camps and suicides.[73] The Nazi regime was successful for a long time in concealing the number of deaths from public knowledge. In fact, as Goebbels received the news of the murder of a Polish Jew in the night of November 10, he and other Nazi leaders became alarmed since a foreigner had become the victim of the pogrom which now seemed to get out of hand. On the morning of November 10, Rudolf Hess ordered all the *Gauleiter* to "stop setting fire to the Jewish shops and suchlike" though considerations of possible damages to "Aryan" properties neighbouring the Jewish ones probably played a more significant role in ending the pogrom.[74]

The "Gujarat Pogrom" was marked by targeted killings of Muslim men, women and children and at least in one macabre instance, a foetus which was ripped out of the belly of a pregnant woman and thrown into the fire.[75] What the Jewish community in Germany faced during the November Pogrom was a monstrous amount of hate and spite, with which the Nazi regime and a part of the German society declared open war on the so-called "internal enemies." With this declaration of war, a barrier was crossed: systematic and public humiliations of the Jews began. Jewish neighbours, colleagues and co-citizens were depersonalized and stigmatized as "Jews."[76]

A similar case of depersonalisation of Muslims, a phenomenon that Martha Nussbaum described as the "collapse of moral imagination" was evident during the "Gujarat Pogrom" where "it had become possible to view Muslims not as full human beings but as mere objects that should be moved out of the way or worse still as occasions for the gratification of a lust for power and revenge."[77] In both cases, the neighbours or acquaintances were turned into impersonal stereotypes. It was evident to the world after the November Pogrom that Germany was no longer a *Reichsstaat*, a nation governed by the rule of law.[78] Similarly, law and order broke down in Gujarat though India is a democracy committed to the rule of law.[79]

The role of sexual violence in both instances is different. During the "Kristallnacht," though there were instances of molestation and rape of Jewish women, these were either not widespread or not widely reported, since they carried the stigma of *Rassenschande* or racial disgrace for "Aryans" who had sexual relationships with Jews. Offenses relating to violation of Nazi racial laws were judged more severely than other crimes. Four Storm Troopers were charged with "sullying the honour of the movement" through "racial defilement" (but not for sexual offence) by the Supreme Nazi Court after the pogrom. All four were expelled from the Nazi party.[80]

Widespread sexual violence including brutal gang rapes, sadistic tortures and murder of Muslim women was a singular feature of the "Gujarat Pogrom." The sexual offenses were pre-planned and extensive, but it is impossible to give a fair estimate of the number of victims since the data on violence against women have been both under-reported and not systematically collected.[81]

Muslims are often stereotyped as sexual predators in India. Their supposed carnal instincts are associated with their meat-eating practices. During the Gujarat riots, raping Muslim women was justified as a way of getting even with the "sexual aggression" of Muslim men, which, according to Hindu nationalists, was manifest in alleged abductions and rapes of Hindu women over centuries and which continues to threaten Hindu women. Patriarchal Hindu society regards women, or rather women's bodies as symbols of a community's honour. According to this norm, abduction or rape of a woman by an "outsider" besmirches the honour of the entire community. Both the purported past sexual offenses and possible future ones could be avenged/prevented through similar offences done to Muslim women.[82]

The sadistic treatment and killing of a large number of Muslim children is also a distinguishing feature of the Gujarat pogrom, though the number of children who perished during the carnage remains difficult, if not impossible, to ascertain. Tanika Sarkar claims that the targeting of children was due to an unfounded but widespread fear of "unchecked breeding" of Muslims who are imagined to be more fertile than the Hindus. Anxiety about an imminent outnumbering of Hindus by Muslims, also due to polygamy permitted under Muslim personal law in India, has been reflected in the mutilation and destruction of reproductive parts of Muslim women, their foetuses as well as their progeny.[83]

EFFECTS

In both the cases, pogroms were successfully used by the ruling dispensations to accrue political advantage. The November pogrom allowed the Nazi leadership to consolidate the so-called *Volksgemeinschaft* by further marginalizing the Jews. In Gujarat, Modi won the state elections soon after the pogrom by portraying himself as a protector of Hindus against "Muslim/*jehadi* terror."

In both instances, victimisation of minority communities outlasted the pogroms. Nazi Germany already achieved what it could to terminate Jewish economic and social existence in the Reich through laws and ordinances. "Kristallnacht" provided an excuse to further deprive Jews of a chance to survive. On November 10, 1938, Hitler decided to completely "Aryanize" German economy and society.[84] Two days later, Göring gave concrete shape to this decision at a meeting, where he directed every ministry to bring all Jewish firms under the control of the state. Jews were prohibited from using public space and public facilities, and as the height of irony, ordered to pay one billion Reichsmark for the damages that occurred during the "Kristallnacht." These measures were dictated as much by anti-Semitic hatred as by lure of financial profits.[85]

Lack of compassion for the victims, let alone remorse, particularly from those in power was another trait that the "Gujarat Pogrom" has in common with the "Kristallnacht." Modi, who did not offer a word of sympathy for the victims, launched a "Gaurav Jatra," or honour procession, in Gujarat soon after the riots, implying that the pogrom has actually upheld the honour of the Hindus.[86]

In Gujarat, the social and economic boycott of minorities occurred through extra-legal means. The state and central government (also BJP at the time) did not provide adequate aid to refugee camps consisting mainly of Muslim survivors of the pogrom. The representatives of "civil society" in Gujarat—NGOs, Gandhian activities and other philanthropists, famed for providing efficient aid, were notably absent. Camps for Muslim victims were run almost exclusively by Muslim organisations.[87] The Indian National Congress, which claims to be secular and which was in power in many local bodies in Gujarat, did not extend any help to the victims due to the risk of displeasing Hindu voters.[88]

The Gujarat state administration tried to close down refugee camps in April–May 2002, which were repeatedly raided by the police on the pretext that they were sheltering terrorists. [89] Modi publicly asked why aid should be provided to camps which were breeding grounds (for Muslims). Compensation for the refugees was insubstantial and the government gave them no assurance of safety if they went back.[90] The more than 100,000 people who were rendered homeless in the aftermath of the carnage, lived in 121 camps across Gujarat at the end of March and beginning of April, 2002.[91]

Officially, the number of refugees in camps was around 87,000 in April 2002, 66,000 of them being in Ahmedabad. After three months, the government registered the "return home" of 73,500 refugees (52,000 in Ahmedabad), in order to prove that things were back to normal and state level elections could be held. The volatile situation after the riot and the general difficulty of estimating population movement makes it is impossible to arrive at a fixed number of the displaced.[92]

Instances of land grab, where temples and roads have been constructed over Muslim houses, also made return difficult for the refugees, particularly because the police refused to note that temples had been established at the sites of residences.[93] In cities, many Muslim businesses were edged out since the fearful owners had to move to "Muslim" localities which were less favourable for their trade. Many Muslims had to sell their residences, incur losses and move into "ghettos"—pre-existing or new.[94] The forced migrations of Muslims were mostly internal as Muslim families tried to get safety in numbers by moving to familiar, nearby places with larger concentrations of members of their religious community.[95] A number of villages began to put up notices of being "Muslim free." [96] This is indeed a terrifying echo of places being *Judenrein* (cleansed of Jews) in Nazi Germany.

Within days of the riot, reports appeared in the local press about decisions of independent professionals like lawyers and doctors as well as traders, to boycott Muslim clients. Services of thousands of Muslim employees in the private sector were terminated without adequate notice.[97] Within months of the pogrom, squalid refugee camps began to give way to clusters of grimy single room tenements, referred euphemistically as "colonies," which were actually

Muslim ghettos. The state government refused to acknowledge many of these ghettos, which are denied basic facilities like electricity and water. The primary challenge facing the residents of these "colonies" is the collapse of their livelihoods due to the socio-economic boycott which persists informally. [98]

Most of those indicted in the Gujarat pogrom, including Narendra Modi, have managed to evade legal consequences, while victims of the riots continue to wait for justice. Though the accusations of complicity by the occupants of highest political offices of Gujarat during the riots reached India's Supreme Court, it exonerated the high ranking politicians due to an entrenched inhibition to take the evidence to its logical conclusion. This failure reveals the shortcomings of Indian legal culture.[99] State-level cases indicting the politically powerful were closed soon. In some cases, names of accused disappeared from charge sheets. There were instances of the police filing "rioting cases" against members of the minority community who were admitted into hospitals due to injuries.[100]

Relative impunity of perpetrators and inadequate justice for victims also marked the November Pogrom trials, not only in Nazi Germany but also in the judicial process of 1947–49. In the Third Reich, the Reich Ministry of Justice instructed against prosecuting those charged with criminal acts like plundering.[101] In the decades after 1945, about seven thousand people were indicted in the West German courts for "Kristallnacht"-related crimes. Only a small percentage of perpetrators were ever put on trial and even fewer actually sentenced due to various reasons, including lack of proof.[102]

CONCLUSION

"Kristallnacht" was a prelude to genocide; it signified the beginning of a new, ominous phase of *Judenpolitik* (politics exclusively concerning the Jews). The "Gujarat Pogrom" is an indicator of the predicament of minorities struggling to survive in an ambience of xenophobia and bigotry, fostered by a brand of majoritarian politics that strives to form an organic, primordial national community based on one religion by eliminating all forms of diversity. In this respect, it echoes the "Kristallnacht," which was the first concerted step taken by the Nazis towards physically marginalising and excluding those considered to be incompatible with the "pure" national community that it aimed to establish.

Both the events were culminations of phases of long standing antiminority prejudice which permeated state institutions and large sections of the majority community. Underlying this bias was the fascism-induced ideal of the nation as one unadulterated, uniform community sharing analogous norms. In both cases, violence, perpetrated by political interest groups as well as citizens, was not only sanctioned but also projected by politically motivated groups as essential for defending the supposedly primeval national community against those who did not subscribe to the majoritarian norms. This divergent group was construed as the internal enemy who formed the "anti-nation."

In both instances, the state openly relinquished its neutrality, not only during but afterwards in not offering adequate remedies or justice. However, unlike the totalitarian dictatorship of Hitler which, by 1938, had limited scope for open protest against majoritarian violence, Gujarat, being a part of a pluralist federal democracy, could not completely deny a space for civil society groups and media to dissent and also to demand justice. Whereas most of the critical reports on the "Kristallnacht" came from the international observers who happened to be present at the time, representatives of the media and civil society from Gujarat and other parts of India reported courageously on the carnage and condemned it, underscoring the spirit, however weak, of Indian democracy.

The "Gujarat pogrom" offered a horrifying glimpse of what happens if majoritarian and sectarian powers manage to completely destroy India's commitment to diversity and secularism. The present political climate of India indicates that such a future cannot be ruled out, despite the voices of protest that continue to be raised within and outside Gujarat. In Gujarat the nongovernmental organisation, Citizens for Justice and Peace continues to fight for justice for the victims of the riots.[103] Outside Gujarat, a number of journalists, activists, writers and academics, albeit representing a rather small circle of elite, largely urban, left-liberal minority across the country, are expressing their concerns against majoritarian nationalism and struggling to keep the idea of a pluralist and tolerant India alive.[104] These voices, however marginalised, distinguish democratic India from the Nazi dictatorship, at least for now.

This comparative study reveals that fascist politics of polarisation and ethnic nationalism from the 1930s can actually be successfully implemented in contemporary democratic political systems. This could be done by denying the concept of universal humanity and calling for establishing a "pure" homogenous community on the basis of religion/ethnicity, from which "others" are ruthlessly purged with tacit or active connivance of the state. The comparison offers a disturbing warning for those concerned with the maintenance of liberal, democratic and humanitarian orders, in India and the world.

Notes

1. Different accounts of the episode provide different statistics of the dead, ranging from one thousand to two thousand. The Indian government told the parliament that there were 790 Muslims and 254 Hindus killed, 2500 injured and 223 reported missing. "Gujarat Riot Death Toll Revealed," *BBC News*, May 11, 2005, http://news.bbc.co.uk/2/hi/south_asia/4536199.stm. According to Martha Nussbaum, more than two thousand Muslims were killed: Martha Nussbaum, *The Clash Within: Democracy, Religious Violence and India's Future* (Cambridge: The Belknap Press of Harvard University Press, 2007), 21. Siddharth Varadarajan also claims that the unofficial death toll is two thousand: Siddharth Varadarajan, "Chronicle of a Tragedy Foretold," in *Gujarat: The Making of a Tragedy*, ed. Siddharth Varadarajan (New Delhi: Penguin Books India, 2002), 9.
2. Parvis Ghassem-Fachandi, *Pogrom in Gujarat: Hindu Nationalism and Anti-Muslim Violence in India* (Princeton: Princeton University Press, 2012), 1.
3. Ibid., 259.
4. Chetan Bhatt, *Hindu Nationalism: Origins, Ideologies and Modern Myths* (Oxford: Berg, 2001), 98.
5. Christophe Jaffrelot, *Hindu Nationalism, A Reader* (Princeton: Princeton University Press, 2007), xi.
6. Nicholas F. Gier, *Origins of Religious Violence: An Asian Perspective* (Lexington, MA: Lexington Books, 2014), 56. Also, Marzia Casolari, "Hindutva's Foreign Tie-up in the 1930s. Archival Evidence," *Economic and Political Weekly* 34, no. 4 (January 22, 2000): 218–28.
7. Shamsul Islam, *Golwalkar's We or Our Nationhood Defined: A Critique with the Full Text of the Book* (New Delhi: Pharos Media, 2006), 204.
8. Varadarajan, "Chronicle," 18.
9. Thomas Trautmann, *Aryans and British India* (New Delhi: Yoda Press, 2004), 66–67.
10. Among the plethora of books on India's Partition, mention may be made of the following: Urvashi Butalia, *The Other Side of Silence: Voices from the Partition of India* (Durham, NC: Duke University Press, 1998); Yasmin Khan, *The Great Partition: The Making of India and Pakistan* (New Haven: Yale University Press, 2008).
11. Christophe Jaffrelot, *Religion, Caste and Politics in India* (London: Hurst & Company, 2011), 177.
12. Ibid., 376.
13. Martin Gilbert, *Kristallnacht: Prelude to Destruction* (New York: HarperPress, 2006), 119.
14. Ullrich, Völker, "'Drückeberger': Die Judenzählung im Ersten Weltkrieg," in *Antisemitismus: Vorurteile und Mythen*, ed. Julius H. Schoeps and Joachim Schlör (München: Piper, 1995), 210–17.

15. Gilbert, *Kristallnacht*, 120.
16. Wolf Gruner, "Indifference? Participation and Protest as Individual Responses to the Persecution of the Jews as Revealed in Berlin Police Logs and Trial Records, 1933–45," in *The Germans and the Holocaust: Popular Responses to the Persecution and Murder of the Jews*, ed. Alan Steinweis and Susanna Schrafstetter (New York: Berghahn, 2016), 74.
17. Jaffrelot, *Religion, Caste and Politics in India*, 386.
18. Dionne Bunsha, *Scarred: Experiments with Violence in Gujarat* (New Delhi: Penguin Random House, 2006), 238.
19. Ibid., 240, 242.
20. Nussbaum, *The Clash Within*, 24.
21. Bunsha, *Scarred*, 241.
22. On *Volksgemeinschaft*: Frank Bajohr and Michael Wildt, eds., *Volksgemeinschaft: Neue Forschungen zur Gesellschaft des Nationalsozialismus* (Frankfurt am Main: Fischer Taschenbuch Verlag, 2009); Markus Brunner et al., eds., *Volksgemeinschaft, Täterschaft und Anti-Semitismus: Beiträge zur Psychoanalytischen Sozialpsychologie des Nationalsozialismus und seiner Nachwirkungen* (Giessen: Psychosozial-Verlag, 2011).
23. Ghassem-Fachandi, *Pogrom in Gujarat*, 271–72.
24. Nussbaum, *The Clash Between*, 17–19.
25. Wolf-Arno Kropat, *"Reichskristallnacht." Der Judenpogrom vom 7. bis 10. November 1938—Urheber, Täter, Hintergründe* (Wiesbaden: Kommission für die Geschichte der Juden in Hessen, 1997), 56.
26. Ibid., 59, 67.
27. Rafael Gross, *November 1938: Katastrophe vor der Katastrophe* (Munich: C. H. Beck, 2013), 45–46.
28. Ghassem-Fachandi, *Pogrom in Gujarat*, 59.
29. Ibid.
30. Jaffrelot, *Religion, Caste and Politics in India*, 379.
31. Bunsha, *Scarred*, 23.
32. Ghassem-Fachandi, *Pogrom in Gujarat*, 39–41.
33. Jaffrelot, *Religion, Caste and Politics in India*, 280.
34. Bunsha, *Scarred*, 52.
35. Gross, *November 1938*, 57.
36. Manoj Mitta, *The Fiction of Fact-finding: Modi and Godhra* (New York: HarperCollins, 2014), 194.
37. Bunsha, *Scarred*, 53.
38. Ghassem-Fachandi, *Pogrom in Gujarat*, 101–03.
39. Ibid., 114–15.
40. Gruner, "Indifference?" 68–69.
41. Ghassem-Fachandi, *Pogrom in Gujarat*, 117.

42. Hermann Graml, *Reichskristallnacht: Antisemitismus und Judenverfolgung im Dritten Reich* (Munich: Deutscher Taschenbuch Verlag 1988), 15.
43. Jaffrelot, *Religion, Caste and Politics in India*, 379–80.
44. Gross, *November 1938*, 44.
45. Regina Scheer, "Im Revier 16" (In precinct No. 16), in *Die Hackeschen Höfe. Geschichte und Geschichten einer Lebenswelt in der Mitte Berlins*, ed. Gesellschaft Hackesche Höfe e.V. (Berlin: Argon, 1993), 74–79.
46. Bunsha, *Scarred*, 53.
47. Mitta, *The Fiction of Fact-finding*, 83.
48. "Former Gujarat Cop Sanjiv Bhatt Arrested in 22-year-old Case," *Hindustan Times*, September 5, 2018, accessed February 1, 2019, https://www.hindustantimes.com/india-news/former-gujarat-ips-sanjiv-bhatt-detained-in-22-year-old-case/story-F4eqFIMglfxFjLVsHfouxH.html; "Former IPS Officer Sanjiv Bhatt Sentenced to Life in 30-year Old Custodial Death Case," *The Economic Times*, June 20, 2019, accessed July 25, 2019, https://economictimes.indiatimes.com/news/politics-and-nation/former-ips-officer-sanjeev-bhatt-sentenced-to-life-in-30-year-old-custodial-death-case/articleshow/69871053.cms.
49. Varadarajan, *Chronicle of a Tragedy Foretold*, 22.
50. Bunsha, *Scarred*, 31; Gilbert, *Kristallnacht*, 142.
51. Bunsha, *Scarred*, 11.
52. Gross, *November 1938*, 20–21.
53. Eberhard Jäckel, "Die November Pogrom und die Deutschen," in *Die Novemberpogrom 1938: Versuch einer Bilanz*, edited by Claudia Steur (Berlin: Stiftung Topographie des Terrors. 2009), 66.
54. Ibid., 68.
55. Graml, *Reichskristallnacht*, 35.
56. Gross, *November 1938*, 11, 42, 55.
57. Wolfgang Benz, *Gewalt im November 1938: Die "Reichskristallnacht": Initial zum Holocaust* (Bonn / Berlin: Bundeszentrale für Politische Bildung / Metropol Verlag, 2018), 8, 98.
58. Gruner, "Indifference?" 67–68.
59. Ghassem-Fachandi, *Pogrom in Gujarat*, 9–10.
60. Sanjay Pandey, "An Oasis of Peace in Communally Charged Gujarat," chap. 10 "Apart—Yet a Part: Ghettoization, Trauma—and Some Rays of Hope," in Varadarajan, ed., *Gujarat*, 349.
61. Gruner, "Indifference?" 68.
62. Graml, *Reichskristallnacht*, 13.
63. Ghassem-Fachandi, *Pogrom in Gujarat*, 75, 78.
64. Nussbaum, *The Clash Within*, 47; Siddharth Varadarajan and Rajdeep Sardesai, "The Truth Hurts: Gujarat and the Role of the Media," in Varadarajan, ed., *Gujarat*, 271–304. An example of a critical report: Harsh Mander, "Cry, the Beloved Country:

Reflections on the Gujarat Massacres by an IAS Officer," *Outlook Magazine* (March 19, 2002), http://www.outlook!ndia.com.
65. Varadarajan and Sardesai, "The Truth Hurts," 271.
66. Jaffrelot, *Religion, Caste and Politics*, 389.
67. Marc Grellert, *Immaterielle Zeugnisse. Synagoguen in Deutschland. Potentiale digitaler Technologien für das Erinnern zerstörter Architektur* (Bielefeld: transcript Verlag, 2007), 82.
68. Gilbert, *Kristallnacht: Prelude to Destruction*, 16.
69. Christopher J. Probst, *Demonizing the Jews: Luther and the Protestant Church in Nazi Germany* (Bloomington: Indiana University Press in association with the Holocaust memorial Museum, 2012).
70. Romila Thapar, "Perspectives of the History of Somnatha," Umashankar Joshi Memorial Lecture, December 29, 2012, accessed February 19, 2019, http://www.umashankarjoshi.in/works/SomanathaLectureEngilish.pdf.
71. Sarvepalli Gopal et al., "The Political Abuse of History: Babri Msjid-Ramajanmabhoomi Dispute," *Social Scientist* 18, nos. 1–2 (January–February, 1990): 76–81. Accessed February 20, 2019.
72. Bunsha, *Scarred*, 266–69.
73. Alan Steinweis, *Kristallnacht 1938* (Cambridge: Belknap Press of Harvard University Press. 2009).
74. Gross, *November 1938*, 62.
75. Bunsha, *Scarred*, 37. Mandar, "Cry, the Beloved Country."
76. Gross, *November 1938*, 56.
77. Nussbaum, *The Clash Within*, 48.
78. Benz, *Gewalt im November 1938*, 185.
79. Nussbaum, *The Clash Within*, 44.
80. Steinweis, *Kristallnacht 1938*, 117–18.
81. Barkha Dutt, "'Nothing New?': Women As Victims," in Varadarajan, ed., *Gujarat*, 220.
82. Tanika Sarkar, "Semiotics of Terror: Muslim Women and Children in Hindu Rashtra," *EPW* 37, no. 28 (July 13, 2002): 2874.
83. Ibid., 2875–76.
84. Benz, *Gewalt im November 1938*, 188–89.
85. Gross, *November 1938*, 70–71.
86. Mitta, *The Fiction of Fact-finding*, 218.
87. Ibid., 46.
88. Harsh Mander, *Fear and Forgiveness: The Aftermath of Massacre* (New Delhi: Penguin Books, 2009), 46.
89. Bunsha, *Scarred*, 82–83.
90. Ibid., 85–86.
91. Sanjeevini Badigar Lokhande, *Communal Violence, Forced Migration and the State. Gujarat since 2002* (Cambridge: Cambridge University Press, 2015), 88.

92. Ibid.
93. Bunsha, *Scarred*, 85–86.
94. Ibid., 259–60.
95. Lokhande, *Communal Violence*, 88.
96. Mander, *Fear and Forgiveness*, 7. Bunsha, *Scarred*, 88.
97. Mander, *Fear and Forgiveness*, 6.
98. Ibid., 68–69.
99. Ibid., 247.
100. Bunsha, *Scarred*, 153–54.
101. Gruner, "Indifference?" 69.
102. Steinweis, *Kristallnacht 1938*, 150–51.
103. This organisation was started on April 1, 2002, by journalist activists Teesta Setalvad and her husband Javed Anand, along with others such as Father Cedric Prakash (a catholic priest), Anil Dharker (a journalist), Alyque Padamsee, Javed Akhtar, Vijay Tendulkar and Rahul Bose (all film and theatre personalities) specifically to address the injustices committed during the Gujarat riots.
104. Among prominent Indian journalists who protested against the Gujarat riots and continue to protest the *Hindutva* agenda, mention may be made of Rana Aiyub, writer of *Gujarat Files: Anatomy of a Cover-up* (Self-published, 2016), and Siddharth Varadarajan, editor of the online news portal, The Wire. Prominent academics who continue to write and speak up against Hindu nationalist majoritarianism include the historians Romila Thapar (Professor Emerita, Jawaharlal Nehru University, New Delhi), Irfan Habib (Professor Emeritus, Aligarh Muslim University), and economist Prabhat Patnaik (Professor Emeritus, Jawaharlal Nehru University, New Delhi).

Bibliography

Aiyub, Rana. *Gujarat Files: Anatomy of a Cover-up.* Self-published, 2016.

Bajohr, Frank, and Michael Wildt, eds. *Volksgemeinschaft: Neue Forschungen zur Gesellschaft des Nationalsozialismus.* Frankfurt am Main: Fischer Taschenbuch Verlag, 2009.

Benz, Wolfgang. *Gewalt im November 1938: Die "Reichskristallnacht": Initial zum Holocaust.* Bonn / Berlin: Bundeszentrale für Politische Bildung / Metropol Verlag, 2018.

Bhatt, Chetan. *Hindu Nationalism: Origins, Ideologies and Modern Myths.* Oxford: Berg, 2001.

Brunner, Markus, et al., eds. *Volksgemeinschaft, Täterschaft und Anti-Semitismus: Beiträge zur Psychoanalytischen Sozialpsychologie des Nationalsozialismus und seiner Nachwirkungen.* Giessen: Psychosozial-Verlag, 2011.

Bunsha, Dionne. *Scarred: Experiments with Violence in Gujarat.* New Delhi: Penguin Books India, 2006.

Butalia, Urvashi. *The Other Side of Silence: Voices from the Partition of India.* Durham, NC: Duke University Press, 1998.

Casolari, Marzia. "Hindutva's Foreign Tie-up in the 1930s. Archival Evidence." *Economic and Political Weekly* 34, no. 4 (January 22, 2000): 218–28.

Dutt, Barkha. "'Nothing new?': Women As Victims." In *Gujarat: The Making of a Tragedy*, edited by Siddharth Varadarajan, 214–45. New Delhi: Peguin Books, 2002.

"Former Gujarat Cop Sanjiv Bhatt Arrested in 22-year-old Case." *Hindustan Times*, September 5, 2018. Accessed February 1, 2019. https://www.hindustantimes.com/india-news/former-gujarat-ips-sanjiv-bhatt-detained-in-22-year-old-case/story-F4eqFIMglfxFjLVsHfouxH.html.

"Former IPS Officer Sanjiv Bhatt Sentenced to Life in 30-year Old Custodial Death Case." *The Economic Times*, June 20, 2019. Accessed July 25, 2019. https://economictimes.indiatimes.com/news/politics-and-nation/former-ips-officer-sanjeev-bhatt-sentenced-to-life-in-30-year-old-custodial-death-case/articleshow/69871053.cms.

Ghassem-Fachandi, Parvis. *Pogrom in Gujarat: Hindu Nationalism and Anti-Muslim Violence in India.* Princeton: Princeton University Press, 2012.

Gier, Nicholas F. *Origins of Religious Violence: An Asian Perspective.* Lexington, MA: Lexington Books, 2014.

Gilbert, Martin. *Kristallnacht: Prelude to Destruction.* London: HarperPress, 2006.

Gopal, Sarvepalli, et al. "The Political Abuse of History: Babri Msjid-Ramajanmabhoomi Dispute." *Social Scientist* 18, nos. 1–2 (January–February, 1990): 76–81. Accessed February 20, 2019.

Graml, Hermann. *Reichskristallnacht: Antisemitismus und Judenverfolgung im Dritten Reich.* Munich: Deutscher Taschenbuch Verlag, 1988.

Grellert, Marc. *Immaterielle Zeugnisse. Synagogen in Deutschland. Potentiale digitaler Technologien für das Erinnern zerstörter Architektur.* Bielefeld: transcript Verlag, 2007.

Gross, Rafael. *November 1938: Katastrophe vor der Katastrophe*. Munich: C. H. Beck, 2013.

Gruner, Wolf. "Indifference? Participation and Protest as Individual Responses to the Persecution of the Jews as Revealed in Berlin Police Logs and Trial Records, 1933–45." In *The Germans and the Holocaust: Popular Responses to the Persecution and Murder of the Jews*, edited by Alan Steinweis and Susanna Schrafstetter, 59–83. New York: Berghahn, 2016.

"Gujarat Riot Death Toll Revealed." *BBC News*, May 11, 2005. http://news.bbc.co.uk/2/hi/south_asia/4536199.stm.

Islam, Shamsul. *Golwalkar's We or Our Nationhood Defined: A Critique with the Full Text of the Book*. New Delhi: Pharos Media, 2006.

Jäckel, Eberhard. "Die November Pogrom und die Deutschen." In *Die Novemberpogrom 1938: Versuch einer Bilanz*, edited by Claudia Steur, 66–73. Berlin: Stiftung Topographie des Terrors. 2009.

Jaffrelot, Christophe. *Hindu Nationalism, A Reader*. Princeton: Princeton University Press, 2007.

———. *Religion, Caste and Politics in India*. London: Hurst & Company, 2011.

Khan, Yasmin. *The Great Partition: The Making of India and Pakistan*. New Haven: Yale University Press, 2008.

Kropat, Wolf-Arno. *"Reichskristallnacht." Der Judenpogrom vom 7. bis 10. November 1938—Urheber, Täter, Hintergründe*. Wiesbaden: Kommission für die Geschichte der Juden in Hessen, 1997.

Lokhande, Sanjeevini Badigar. *Communal Violence, Forced Migration and the State: Gujarat since 2002*. Cambridge: Cambridge University Press, 2015.

Mander, Harsh. "Cry, the Beloved Country: Reflections on the Gujarat Massacres by an IAS Officer." *Outlook Magazine* (March 19, 2002). http://www.outlook!ndia.com.

———. *Fear and Forgiveness: The Aftermath of Massacre*. New Delhi: Penguin Books, 2009.

Mitta, Manoj. *The Fiction of Fact-finding: Modi and Godhra*. New York: HarperCollins, 2014.

Nussbaum, Martha. *The Clash Within: Democracy, Religious Violence and India's Future*. Cambridge: The Belknap Press of Harvard University Press, 2007.

Pandey, Sanjay. "An Oasis of Peace in Communally Charged Gujarat." Chap. 10, "Apart—Yet a Part: Ghettoization, Trauma—and Some Rays of Hope." In *Gujarat: The Making of a Tragedy*, edited by Siddharth Varadarajan, 331–55. New Delhi: Penguin Books, 2002.

Probst, Christopher, J. *Demonizing the Jews: Luther and the Protestant Church in Nazi Germany*. Bloomington: Indiana University Press in association with the Holocaust Memorial Museum, 2012.

Sarkar, Tanika. "Semiotics of Terror: Muslim Women and Children in Hindu Rashtra." *EPW* 37, no. 28 (July 13, 2002): 2872–76.

Scheer, Regina. "Im Revier 16" (In precinct No. 16). In *Die Hackeschen Höfe. Geschichte und Geschichten einer Lebenswelt in der Mitte Berlins*, edited by Gesellschaft Hackesche Höfe e.V., 74–79. Berlin: Argon, 1993.

Steinweis, Alan E. *Kristallnacht 1938*. Cambridge: Harvard University Press, 2009.

Thapar, Romila. "Perspectives of the History of Somnatha." Umashankar Joshi Memorial Lecture, December 29, 2012. http://www.umashankarjoshi.in/works/SomanathaLectureEngilish.pdf.

Trautmann, Thomas. *Aryans and British India*. New Delhi: Yoda Press, 2004.

Varadarajan, Siddharth. "Chronicle of a Tragedy Foretold." In *Gujarat: The Making of a Tragedy*, edited by Siddharth Varadarajan, 3–41. New Delhi: Penguin Books India, 2002.

Varadarajan, Siddharth, and Rajdeep Sardesai. "The Truth Hurts: Gujarat and the Role of the Media." In *Gujarat: The Making of a Tragedy*, edited by Siddharth Varadarajan, 271–304. New Delhi: Penguin Books India, 2002.

Völker, Ullrich. "'Drückeberger': Die Judenzählung im Ersten Weltkrieg." In *Antisemitismus: Vorurteile und Mythen*, edited by Julius H. Schoeps and Joachim Schlör, 210–17. Munich: Piper, 1995.

About the Contributors

LISA ANSELL is Associate Director of the Casden Institute for the Study of the Jewish Role in American Life at the University of Southern California. She received her BA in French and Near East Studies from UCLA and her MA in Middle East Studies from Harvard University. She was the Chair of the World Language Department of New Community Jewish High School for five years before coming to USC in August, 2007. She currently teaches Hebrew language courses at the Hebrew Union College-Jewish Institute of Religion. She also serves as the USC ambassador for academic partnerships in Israel.

ULRICH BAUMANN is a historian who serves as Deputy Director of the Foundation Memorial to the Murdered Jews of Europe. His dissertation, *Zerstörte Nachbarschaften* (Destroyed Neighbourhoods), on Christians and Jews in South German rural and small-town communities, was published in 2000 (Dölling & Galitz). From 1999 to 2003 he was a research assistant for the Conference on Jewish material Claims against Germany, from 2002–2005 was one of the curators of the permanent exhibition at the Information Centre at the Memorial to the Murdered Jews of Europe, and subsequently curator, co-curator or advisor of several other exhibitions, such as "'Was damals Recht war'—Soldaten und Zivilisten vor Gerichten der Wehrmacht" (Victims of Nazi Military Justice), "Fire! Anti-Jewish Terror in November 1938," "Facing Justice—Adolf Eichmann on Trial," "Mass Shootings. The Holocaust from the Baltic to the Black Sea 1941–1944," and "Kristallnacht"—Anti-Jewish Terror 1938. Events and Remembering." Aside from the foundation's work, he is pursuing a publication project on a gender history of female entrepreneurs and business owners in Berlin between 1900 and 1961.

HASIA DINER is is the Paul and Sylvia Steinberg Professor of American Jewish History at New York University. She is the author of *In the Almost Promised Land: American Jews and Blacks, 1915–1935* (The Johns Hopkins University Press, 1977, reissued, 1995); *Erin's Daughters in American: Irish Immigrant Women in the Nineteenth Century* (The Johns Hopkins University Press, 1984), and *A Time for Gathering: The Second Migration, 1820–1880*, the second volume in the Johns Hopkins University Press series, "The Jewish People in America" (1992). *Lower East Side Memories: The Jewish Place in America* was published in 2000 by Princeton University Press and *Hungering for America: Italian, Irish, and Jewish Foodways in the Age of Migration* (2002), published by Harvard University Press, which was a nominee for the James Beard Award, in the category of Writing About Food. Basic Books released her history of American Jewish women, *Her Works Praise Her*, in 2002, which Professor Diner co-authored with Beryl Leif Benderly. The University of California Press released *The Jews of the United States: 1654–2000* in 2005. *We Remember with Reverence and Love: American Jews and the Myth of Silence after the Holocaust, 1945–1962* (New York University Press, 2009) received the National Jewish Book Award in American Jewish studies in 2010 as well as the Saul Veiner Prize for the outstanding book in American Jewish history. She recently published two books with Yale University Press, *Roads Taken: The Great Jewish Migration and the Peddlers Who Led the Way* and *Julius Rosenwald: Repairing the World*.

NORMAN DOMEIER is Assistant Professor of Modern European History at the University of Stuttgart, Germany. He studied History, Political Science and Media and Communication in Göttingen, Cambridge and at the European University Institute in Florence, Italy. The English edition of his PhD thesis, "The Eulenburg Affair: A Cultural History of Politics in the German Empire," was published by Camden House in 2015. His second book project—the focus of his current work—looks at the relationship between foreign journalists and the Third Reich. In February 2017 he discovered the secret deal between the Associated Press (AP) and Nazi Germany during the war years 1942–1945. First research results are available at (English version under "Translation"): http://www.zeithistorische-forschungen.de/2-2017/id=5484.

MARY FULBROOK, FBA, is Professor of German History at University College London (UCL). A graduate of Cambridge and Harvard, she is the author or editor of numerous books, including: *Reckonings: Legacies of Nazi Persecution and the Quest for Justice* (Oxford University Press, 2018—winner of the Wolfson History Prize); *A Small Town near Auschwitz: Ordinary Nazis and the Holocaust* (Oxford University Press, 2012—winner of the Fraenkel Prize); *Dissonant Lives: Generations and Violence through the German Dictatorships* (Oxford University Press, 2011); *The People's State: East German Society from Hitler to Honecker* (Yale University Press, 2005); and *Anatomy of a Dictatorship: Inside the GDR, 1949–89* (Oxford University Press, 1995), as well as general overviews of German history. She is currently directing an AHRC-funded collaborative research project on "Compromised Identities? Reflections on Perpetration and Complicity under Nazism" (2018–21). Among other professional commitments, Mary Fulbrook serves on the Academic Advisory Board of the Foundation for the former Nazi Concentration Camps at Buchenwald and Mittelbau-Dora. She has previously served as Executive Dean of the UCL Faculty of Social and Historical Sciences; Chair of the Modern History Section of the British Academy; Chair of the German History Society; and she was Founding Joint Editor of *German History*.

GERSHON GREENBERG is Visiting Professor in the Department of Jewish Thought at the Hebrew University of Jerusalem in the areas of religious thought through the Holocaust and the history of Jewish thought in America; and Professor in the Department of Philosophy and Religion at American University, Washington, DC, in the fields of religious ethics, and religion and violence. His published research on the Holocaust draws from newly discovered Ultra-Orthodox, Hasidic, Musar, Kabbalistic and religious nationalist sources. It also concerns the intersections between Orthodox Jewish and Catholic theology in the face of catastrophe. Published research in American Jewish thought focuses on Hebrew and Yiddish sources. In 2020 he will serve as Visiting Scholar of Holocaust Jewish thought in the Melton Centre for Jewish Education at the Hebrew University.

WOLF GRUNER is Shapell-Guerin Chair in Jewish Studies, Professor of History and Founding Director of the USC Shoah Foundation Center for Advanced Genocide Research at the University of Southern California. He is the author of eleven books, among them, *Jewish Forced Labor under the Nazis: Economic Needs and Nazi Racial Aims* (paperback, Cambridge University Press, 2008), *Parias de la Patria. El mito de la liberación de los indígenas en la República de Bolivia 1825–1890* (Plural Editores, 2015), and the coedited book *The Greater German Reich and the Jews: Nazi Persecution Policies in the Annexed Territories 1935–1945* (with Jörg Osterloh; Berghahn Books, 2015). His most recent study is *The Holocaust in Bohemia and Moravia: Czech Initiatives, German Policies, Jewish Responses* (Berghahn Books, 2019). Its original German version (2016) received the Sybil Halpern Milton Memorial Book Prize of the German Studies Association 2017 for the best book in Holocaust Studies in 2015–16 and was a finalist for the Yad Vashem International Book prize for Holocaust Research 2017.

FRANÇOIS GUESNET is Reader in Modern Jewish History in the Department of Hebrew and Jewish Studies at University College London. He specializes in the early modern and nineteenth century history of Eastern European, and more specifically, Polish Jews. He held research and teaching fellowships at the Hebrew University Jerusalem, the University of Pennsylvania (Philadelphia), the University of Oxford, the Jagiellonian University in Kraków, and Dartmouth College. His book publications include *Polnische Juden im 19. Jahrhundert: Lebensbedingungen, Rechtsnormen und Organisation im Wandel* (Böhlau, 1998), and (with Gwenyth Jones) *Antisemitism in an Era of Transition: The Case of Post-Communist Eastern Central Europe* (Peter Lang, 2014). Together with Glenn Dynner he published *Warsaw. The Jewish Metropolis. Studies in Honor of the 70th Birthday of Professor Antony Polonsky* (Brill, 2015). He is co-chair of the Editorial Board of *Polin. Studies in Polish Jewry*.

ANNE-CHRISTIN KLOTZ is currently a Claims Conference Saul Kagan Fellow in Advanced Shoah Studies and is finishing her PhD on individual and collective reactions of Polish-Jewish journalists, who were working for the Yiddish press in Warsaw on the beginning persecution of Jews in Nazi Germany during the 1930s. She received her BA in History and Jewish Studies and her MA in Eastern European Studies from Freie Universität Berlin. Among others, she worked as a volunteer at the memorial site Stutthof in Poland and as a junior research fellow in the sixteen-volume document collection project *The Persecution and Extermination of the European Jews by Nazi Germany, 1933–1945*. Between 2015 and 2018 she was a research assistant at the Selma Stern Centre for Jewish Studies Berlin-Brandenburg. Her latest article was published in the yearbook of the Selma Stern Centre ("Reiseberichte vom Rand des Abgrunds—Der polnisch-jüdische Schriftsteller Leib Malakh unterwegs im Berlin des Jahres 1936," in *Shoah: Ereignis und Erinnerung*, edited by Alina Bothe, Monika Schärtl and Stefanie Schüler-Springorum [Hentrich & Hentrich, 2019], 31–46).

JEFFREY KOERBER is assistant professor of history at Chapman University. His research focuses on the relationships between place and historical actors during the Holocaust. He holds bachelor's and master's degrees in architecture from the University of Illinois at Urbana-Champaign and earned a doctorate in Holocaust history from Clark University. His forthcoming monograph Borderland Generation: Soviet and Polish Jews under Hitler (Syracuse University Press) analyzes the prewar and wartime experiences of young adult Jews raised under distinct political and social systems.

STEVEN J. ROSS is Professor of History at the University of Southern California, and the Myron and Marian Director of the Casden Institute for the Study of the Jewish Role in American Life. His most recent book, *Hitler in Los Angeles: How Jews Foiled Nazi Plots Against Hollywood and America* (Bloomsbury Press, 2017) was named a Finalist for the Pulitzer Prize in History for 2018 has been on the Los Angeles Times Bestseller List for twenty weeks. His previous book, *Hollywood Left and Right: How Movie Stars Shaped American Politics* (Oxford University, 2013), received the Academy of Motion Picture Arts and Sciences' Film Scholars Award. *Working-Class Hollywood: Silent Film and the Shaping of Class in America* (Princeton University, 1998), received the Theater Library Association Book Award for 1999. Ross' Op-Ed pieces have appeared in the *Los Angeles Times, Wall Street Journal, Washington Post, Time, International Herald-Tribune, Hollywood Reporter, HuffingtonPost, Daily Beast*, and *Politico*.

BAIJAYANTI ROY studied Indian and European history in India. She received her PhD from Goethe University, Frankfurt am Main. Her dissertation has been published as a monograph titled *The Making of a Gentleman Nazi: Albert Speer`s Politics of History in the Federal Republic of Germany* (Peter Lang, 2016). She is currently working as a post-doctoral researcher in the DFG Project, Indology in National Socialist Germany, at the Goethe University. Her research interests include Nazi Germany, German Indology and Hindu nationalism. She regularly gives lectures and publishes articles on the aforementioned subjects.

About the Contributors 363

NATHALIE SÉGERAL is an assistant professor of French and translation studies at the University of Hawaii at Mānoa (PhD, UCLA, 2012). Her research and teaching revolve around memory, trauma, and women's studies, the Holocaust, the Rwandan genocide, and the French-speaking South Pacific. Her most recent publications include a French translation of David Chappell's *Le Réveil kanak: la montée du nationalism en Nouvelle-Calédonie* (The Kanak Awakening) (New Caledonia University Press, 2017), "(Re-)Inscribing the South Pacific in the Francophone World: (Non-)Motherhood, Gendered Violence, and Infanticide in Three Oceanian Women Writers" (*Contemporary French and Francophone Studies*, 2018), and "(Re)Claiming Motherhood during and after the Holocaust in Chava Rosenfarb's Little Red Bird and Valentine Goby's Kinderzimmer" (*Studies on the Holocaust*, forthcoming fall 2019). In 2018, she was a fellow at The Olga Lengyel Institute Summer Seminar on Holocaust Education in New York City and a fellow at the University of London's Summer Institute on the Holocaust and Jewish Civilization.

STEPHANIE SEUL is a Lecturer in Media and Communication History at Deutsche Presseforschung, University of Bremen. She studied History at Ludwig Maximilians University in Munich and holds an MPhil from the University of Cambridge and a PhD from the European University Institute in Florence. Her research focuses on British propaganda during the Second World War, on the German and international press in the era of the two World Wars, and on media representations of anti-Semitism and the Holocaust. Her writing has appeared in numerous edited volumes and journals, including the *Leo Baeck Institute Year Book*, *Jewish Historical Studies*, *Politics, Religion & Ideology*, and *Journal of Modern Italian Studies*. With Nelson Ribeiro she co-edited a special issue of *Media History* (vol. 21, no. 4 [2015]) on the BBC's foreign-language services during the Second World War.

LIAT STEIR-LIVNY is a Senior Lecturer in the Department of Cultural Studies, Creation and Production at Sapir College, and a tutor and course coordinator for the Cultural Studies MA program and the Department of Literature, Language, and the Arts at the Open University of Israel. Her research focuses on the changing commemoration of the Holocaust in Israel from the 1940s until the present. She has authored numerous articles and five books. She is the winner of the 2019 Young Scholar Award given jointly by the Association for Israel Studies (AIS) and the Israel Institute.

MAXIMILIAN STRNAD received his PhD in Contemporary History from the Ludwig-Maximilians University (LMU) in Munich, Germany. He is a historian at the Munich City Archive. His recent publications focus on the persecution of intermarried Jews in Nazi-Germany. In addition to a series of articles and book chapters, he is the author of *Zwischenstation "Judensiedlung." Verfolgung und Deportation der jüdischen Münchner 1941–1945* (Oldenbourg Verlag, 2011) and *Flachs für das Reich. Das jüdische*

Zwangsarbeitslager "Flachsröste" bei München (Volk Verlag, 2013). He also co-edited (with Michael Brenner) *Der Holocaust in der deutschsprachigen Geschichtswissenschaft* (Wallstein Verlag, 2012).

ALEXANDER WALTHER is a PhD candidate at Friedrich Schiller University of Jena, Germany. He studied history and English in a teacher's training course at the University of Jena, receiving his First State Examination (equivalent to MEd) in 2014. His research interests include Holocaust studies and memory, German and Yugoslavian history and cultures of memory. His dissertation project investigates the multi-faceted forms of commemoration practices and representations of the Shoah in the GDR.

The USC Casden Institute for the Study of the Jewish Role in American Life

The American Jewish community has played a vital role in shaping the politics, culture, commerce and multiethnic character of Southern California and the American West. Beginning in the mid-nineteenth century, when entrepreneurs like Isaias Hellman, Levi Strauss and Adolph Sutro first ventured out West, American Jews became a major force in the establishment and development of the budding Western territories. Since 1970, the number of Jews in the West has more than tripled. This dramatic demographic shift has made California—specifically, Los Angeles—home to the second largest Jewish population in the United States. Paralleling this shifting pattern of migration, Jewish voices in the West are today among the most prominent anywhere in the United States. Largely migrating from Eastern Europe, the Middle East and the East Coast of the United States, Jews have invigorated the West, where they exert a considerable presence in every sector of the economy—most notably in the media and the arts. With the emergence of Los Angeles as a world capital in entertainment and communications, the Jewish perspective and experience in the region are being amplified further. From artists and activists to scholars and professionals, Jews are significantly influencing the shape of things to come in the West and across the United States. In recognition of these important demographic and societal changes, in 1998 the University of Southern California established a scholarly institute dedicated to studying contemporary Jewish life in America with special emphasis on the western United States. The Casden Institute explores issues related to the interface between the Jewish community and the broader, multifaceted cultures that form the nation—issues of relationship as much as of Jewishness itself. It is also enhancing the educational experience for students at USC and elsewhere by exposing them to the problems—and promise—of life in Los Angeles' ethnically, socially, culturally and economically diverse community. Scholars, students and community leaders examine the ongoing contributions of American Jews in the arts, business, media, literature, education, politics, law and social relations, as well as the relationships between Jewish Americans and other groups, including African Americans,

Latinos, Asian Americans and Arab Americans. The Casden Institute's scholarly orientation and contemporary focus, combined with its location on the West Coast, set it apart from—and makes it an important complement to—the many excellent Jewish Studies programs across the nation that center on Judaism from an historical or religious perspective.

For more information about the USC Casden Institute,
visit www.usc.edu/casdeninstitute, e-mail casden@usc.edu,
or call (213) 740-3405.

www.ingramcontent.com/pod-product-compliance
Lightning Source LLC
LaVergne TN
LVHW010252260326
834688LV00044B/1251